Israeli Prisoner of War Policies

Israeli Prisoner of War Policies

From the 1949 Armistice to the 2006 Kidnappings

Alexander Bligh

LEXINGTON BOOKS
Lanham • Boulder • New York • London

Published by Lexington Books
An imprint of The Rowman & Littlefield Publishing Group, Inc.
4501 Forbes Boulevard, Suite 200, Lanham, Maryland 20706
www.rowman.com

Unit A, Whitacre Mews, 26-34 Stannary Street, London SE11 4AB

British Library Cataloguing in Publication Information Available

Library of Congress Cataloging-in-Publication Data

Names: Bligh, Alexander, 1949- author.
Title: Israeli prisoner of war policies : from the 1949 armistice to the 2006 kidnappings / Alexander Bligh.
Description: Lanham, Maryland : Lexington Books, 2017. | Includes bibliographical references and index.
Identifiers: LCCN 2016052860 (print) | LCCN 2016056123 (ebook) | ISBN 9780739194713 (cloth : alk. paper) | ISBN 9780739194720 (electronic)
Subjects: LCSH: Prisoners of war—Israel.
Classification: LCC KMK1473 .B55 2017 (print) | LCC KMK1473 (ebook) | DDC 343.5694/015113—dc23
LC record available at https://lccn.loc.gov/2016052860

∞™ The paper used in this publication meets the minimum requirements of American National Standard for Information Sciences Permanence of Paper for Printed Library Materials, ANSI/NISO Z39.48-1992.

Printed in the United States of America

To the former POWs—those awake at night

Contents

Preface

This book has two starting points. One has to do with my service as a junior Israeli Defense Forces officer who experienced the falling of two of his colleagues into enemy hands on another front during the 1973 War. The second was my sabbatical at the Department of Political Science, University of Notre Dame, Indiana, where my superiors were generous enough to provide me with the necessary technical assistance and excellent conditions for conducting a thorough search for primary sources and launching this project. Originally, I was thinking of a comparative study of both Israel and the United States through the prism of their respective prisoner of war (POW) policies. It was only when I realized that not much had been written on the topic, especially on the Israeli side, that I decided to concentrate on the Israeli angle. I hope that the interest generated by the current study will allow me one day to analyze the American dimension of this military yet clearly humanitarian issue.

The sight of seized enemy soldiers always captures news media attention, when two or more actors are entangled in an open military showdown. A picture of an enemy soldier taken prisoner, and better yet scores of them, is universally seen as a humiliation to the party sending these troops to the battlefield.[1] Whereas taking POWs is an indication of strength and deterrence in the battlefield, the conditions leading to their release are the result of the asymmetry in diplomatic power between the winning and losing warring parties, or at times, as in the Israeli case, the gap between military might and diplomatic weakness. Consequently, the issue of POWs and their military and diplomatic significance represent at least two levels of actors' behavior: what the criteria should be for taking POWs during times of military confrontation—as opposed to disarming them and sending them off—and what the mechanism employed and the prices paid in order to secure their release should be. These issues have enormous effects on national morale and the self-confidence of the fighting soldier in times of war and post-conflict. Another subject closely tied in with these two layers is the intelligence value of POWs and the degree of exposure of these POWs once they are released back to their respective countries and are able to assist their army in damage control and in rebuilding systems that are different from those compromised by the POWs. All of these policy considerations are permanently clouded by the strong pressure from the POWs' families and the news media to "get the boys back at any price," Israel being a democratic society with free speech.

All of the considerations mentioned above and many more make any study of POW-related issues complicated and highly sensitive. Questions arising from any such study would include, but would not be limited to, military tactics and strategy, ad hoc and long-range diplomatic considerations, a possible price scale for any exchange, and above all moral and humanitarian concerns. This intricacy of issues has been serving as a barrier to any comprehensive academic study of the political dimension of the topic as opposed to the psychological effects of captivity. Any search in political science/international relations databases would lead to the conclusion that the issue of POWs is indeed terra incognita. Therefore this writer intends to contribute to this field by analyzing one dimension of the issue—namely the evolving Israeli policy guidelines regarding its own troops captured by the enemy (regular or irregular) during the course of the Arab-Israeli armed conflict since the conclusion of the 1948–1949 war through the armistice agreements of January–July 1949. This book also offers suggested readings on contemporary decisions and their long-range influence on the shaping of Israeli policies for years to come.

One of the results of any military confrontation is the presence of prisoners of war on each side of the warring parties. Typically, each side loses a number of POWs, whereas it also holds a number of enemy troops. Usually conflicts are concluded by an international instrument that includes clauses relating to the exchange of POWs. However, with the exception of full and comprehensive treaties, which are rare at the conclusion of a conflict, no other form of agreement would exclude the possibility of further troops being taken prisoners of war. Consequently, any understanding short of full peace might be used as a precedent for future cases of POW exchange. Those precedents are not only significant in the humanitarian context, but may also establish part of a possible future peace process. Even though the status of captured people is central to any discussion, a clear definition of their status, whether captured through an armed conflict or terrorist attack, has never been fully studied. The only internationally recognized definition is to be found in the Geneva Convention, but the change in the nature of the modern war has rendered that definition somewhat obsolete.

As noted, only a handful of articles have been published relating to these issues. A further partial explanation of that could be that a clear-cut set of definitions might tie the hands of involved governments and, moreover, dictate an asymmetrical attitude toward terrorists: democratic governments would follow internationally accepted standards, whereas terror organizations would maintain their total disrespect for the same standards. However, the human tragedies involved and the changes in the positions of several countries on the issue of exchanging prisoners make it an acute issue at the present time. In order to understand the methodology and decision-making process surrounding prisoner exchange, the issue of terminology must be dealt with first. The current study uses the accepted definitions as the background for analyzing their current deficiencies with the growing presence of asymmetrical players.

Two methodological hurdles must be mentioned at this early stage: most national archives consulted for the purpose of this book have a thirty-year rule, meaning that most, but not all, documents would be made available to the public thirty years after their creation. Israeli military- and security-related documentation is made available after fifty years. However, still classified documents can be released at times under the U.S. Freedom of Information Act or its equivalent among other nations. Yet no document that has not reached the thirty-year mark is accessible, with some minor exceptions. Consequently, the discussion of the period from 1949 to 1984 is almost fully covered by intra-office and international correspondence. The last words of this book covering the period since 1985 are mostly supported by nongovernmental materials and press reports. That watershed line coincides with a change in the nature of the security challenges facing Israel: from a third-generation kind of warfare, usually characterized by regular armies and big formations fighting each other on behalf of nation-states, Israel became entangled in an almost exclusively fourth-generation kind of warfare—that is, in the period studied here, the kind that involves larger segments of the civilian population and facing substate actors consisting mainly of Palestinian organizations.[2] That means that in the context of this book considering that a subnational actor is not a party to any international instrument, the role of mediating international organizations faded away and the role of individuals became more significant. Watching the kidnapping policies of the Islamic State in Iraq and Syria (ISIS) might also suggests that even the time of state subnational mediation might soon be over, considering that most people falling into their hands have been executed. Anyway, even without the documents embargo covering this period, it is close to impossible to persuade private negotiators to surrender their private archives—because none of them has done so for the benefit of mankind alone and opening their documents today might reveal some hidden angles of that voluntary activity.

This research project seeks to suggest a broader definition of individuals taken by hostiles in areas of combat who must be released (to replace the narrower definitions of POW/MIA present in contemporary humanitarian law), which would include hostages, civilians of any profession found in an area of conflict (for example, diplomats, reporters etc.), and any other person taken by a hostile player due to his or her national affiliation—rather than exclusively battlefield combatants of nation-states. By investigating the history of POW/MIA issues in Israel, this study concludes by offering a couple of models, one relating to nation-states and one for subnational actors, which partially responds to this need for updating these definitions and protections according to the changing nature of contemporary warfare and to projections regarding the nature of future warfare.

The study also elaborates on the following main issues: Has a POW policy, or at least guidelines, emerged as a result of the military campaigns Israel has been involved in? Is it valid today with the emergence of subnational adversaries in addition to national ones? What are the elements necessary for making decisions today and how will their assembly into a baseline model improve decision making and research? This study not only suggests a new approach to definitions, but also divides the Israeli political history of POW/MIA issues into distinct eras leading to a clear definition of the necessary methodology to be used by Israel on this issue.

NOTES

1. Even without any pictures, the Egyptian radio broadcasts reported during the 1956 Sinai fighting capture the "hundreds of Israeli soldiers" in a show of psychological warfare. Cairo in Hebrew, November 2, 1956, 0625, in IDFA/535/2004/321, IDF General Staff/Directorate of Intelligence, Arab broadcasts summary no. 10 [Nov. 1, 1956 (*sic*)].

2. Timothy J. Junio, "Military History and Fourth Generation Warfare," *Journal of Strategic Studies* 32, no. 2 (2009): 243–69; Gregory A Thiele, "Fourth-Generation Warfare," *Marine Corps Gazette* 97, no. 6 (2013): 53–54; N. Lehaci, "The Decision-Making Process—From First Generation Warfare to the Post-Cold War Revolution in Military Affairs," *Strategic Impact* 54 (2015): 106–12.

Acknowledgments

This study could not have been carried out without the support both morally and materially of several bodies. The most outstanding among these are the University of Notre Dame, Indiana, and two of its former chairs of the Political Science Department, Michael Zuckert and Michael Desch, and Ariel University, which has supplied me with the best conditions in which to pursue this study. The staffs at the Israel National Archives, Israeli Defense Forces Archives, and the United States National Archives, College Park, Maryland, were a pleasure to work with and assisted me a great deal in my unending applications under the Freedom of Information rights. Special thanks are due to Ms. Ifat Glinik Arnon of the Israeli Defense Forces and Defense Establishment Archives, who was extremely patient with my long succession of hard queries.

A large number of private citizens who have touched upon the POW issue from one angle or another enthusiastically granted me access to their private papers or oral memoirs. I will not mention most of them by name per their request.

Special thanks to Dr. Ravit Gur-Lindenberg, who made her private collections, collected for her PhD dissertation, available to me. I also had a group of highly gifted research assistants who have catered to every request of mine and helped me out with most of the technical details. They included Kathryn M. Hughes, class of 2010, Notre Dame University, Omer Dostri, Reut Doron, Mor Jamal, Tamar Cohen, and Tomer Kerpak—most of whom are now in their postgraduate stage. A word of thanks as well to my students both at Notre Dame and Ariel who, while taking my seminars on the topic, challenged me constantly and also referred me at times to sources that I had missed.

A special thanks goes to my devoted and amazing style editor, Ms. Erica Levin, with whom I have worked for a long time, always enjoying her finesse and attitude.

On a personal note, my thanks and apologies to my wife, children, and my grandkids who waited impatiently to have me to themselves once again.

One last word: this book is warmly dedicated to the former Israeli POWs whose experiences are the subject matter of this volume. No words can describe what even the smallest amount they were willing to share meant to me.

List of Abbreviations

AIPAC	American Israel Public Affairs Committee
BGA	Ben Gurion Archives (available online)
DFLP	Democratic Front for the Liberation of Palestine
Geneva	In ISA references: The mission of Israel to the United Nations in Geneva, Switzerland
ICRC	The International Red Cross Committee
IDFA	Israeli Defense Forces and Defense Establishment Archives
ISA	Israel State Archives
ISMAC	Israel Syria Mixed Armistice Committee
Jerusalem	In ISA references: Ministry of Foreign Affairs, Jerusalem
MAC	Mixed Armistice Committee
MFA	[Israel] Ministry of Foreign Affairs
NCO	Noncommissioned officer
New York	The permanent delegation to the United Nations
PFLP	Popular Front for the Liberation of Palestine
Quai D'Orsay	[France] Ministry of Foreign Affairs
[UK]NA	[United Kingdom] National Archives, formerly PRO
UNEF	UN Emergency Force
UNGA	UN General Assembly
UNHCR	UN High Commissioner for Refugees
UNRWA	UN Relief and Works Agency
UNSC	UN Security Council
UNTSO	UN Truce Supervision Organization
USNA	UN National Archives
USRC	U.S. Red Cross
Washington	The embassy whenever foreign countries are involved; U.S. diplomats—State Department

Part I

The Legal, Intelligence, and Policy Sources of the Israeli Policies

ONE

The Internationally Agreed Upon Standards for Recognizing POWs/MIAs and the Israeli Working Definitions

Like many other terms, the term *prisoner of war* has undergone many practical changes; only a few of them have been formally and internationally recognized to date. In broad brush strokes, this is the much used term describing uniformed personnel falling into the hands of enemy military forces. However, even during the third- and fourth- generation theaters of activities, many people, military as well as civilian, who have never fallen under this definition have been treated by their respective governments as deserving not only their attention, but at times even limitless efforts to reunite them with their loved ones in their respective countries, invoking the international treaties dealing with POW status. In the Israeli context, the accumulated experience of the 1950s and 1960s demonstrates a rather wide working definition, adopted de facto by all Israeli governments since 1948: any Israeli and any Jew, who might even hold a foreign citizenship as his or her sole citizenship or as an additional citizenship (for instance, the 2011 kidnapped soldier who holds Israeli and French citizenship), who found him- or herself in enemy hands, whether abducted, left behind, deserted, or willingly surrendered to his or her captors or due to any other reason—among them espionage—is entitled to the protection of the Israeli authorities, who would do their utmost to bring him or her back. That working definition never changed, even with the transformation into more irregular fighting within the fourth generation.

The agreed upon international law foundation for the treatment of POWs is based on legal history dating back to the late nineteenth century.

The 1899 Hague II convention ("Regulations Respecting the Laws and Customs of War on Land") was probably the first modern instrument to govern the issue of prisoners of war. The 1907 Hague Second International Peace Conference adopted almost an identical document, "The 1907 Laws of War: Laws and Customs of War on Land" (Hague IV).[1]

Another text, "The 1929[2] Convention Intended to Draw the Lessons of World War One," was replaced by "The Convention (III) Relative to the Treatment of Prisoners of War," signed in Geneva on August 12, 1949. Israel joined the Geneva Convention in December 1950 and ratified the document in January 1952.[3] The Convention was modified in 1977, easing the conditions to be met by combatants of subnational players in order to be recognized as POWs.[4] Israel had never ratified the new instrument because in its view that might give the terrorist organizations reason to claim POW status should one of theirs be apprehended. This Geneva Convention, along with the 1977 updates concluding the lessons of Vietnam, is today the international instrument that is supposed to govern the status of POWs in all conflicts around the globe and that is binding on all its signatories.[5] The Israeli Supreme Court adopted in effect this view of the documents excluding the new additions.[6] How well Israel is following the binding international instruments it recognized and adopted will be discussed in the pertinent chapters. Strictly on formal grounds, a prisoner of war according to the Israeli view can only be defined as a combatant taken prisoner in a conflict between definitive nation-states or powers, according to the Geneva Convention (III). In the official language of the Convention:

> Art 4. A. Prisoners of war, in the sense of the present Convention, are persons belonging to one of the following categories, who have fallen into the power of the enemy:
> (1) Members of the armed forces of a Party to the conflict, as well as members of militias or volunteer corps forming part of such armed forces.
> (2) Members of other militias and members of other volunteer corps, including those of organized resistance movements, belonging to a Party to the conflict and operating in or outside their own territory, even if this territory is occupied, provided that such militias or volunteer corps, including such organized resistance movements, fulfill the following conditions:
> (a) that of being commanded by a person responsible for his subordinates;
> (b) that of having a fixed distinctive sign recognizable at a distance;
> (c) that of carrying arms openly;
> (d) that of conducting their operations in accordance with the laws and customs of war.
> (3) Members of regular armed forces who profess allegiance to a government or an authority not recognized by the Detaining Power.

(4) Persons who accompany the armed forces without actually being members thereof, such as civilian members of military aircraft crews, war correspondents, supply contractors, members of labour units or of services responsible for the welfare of the armed forces, provided that they have received authorization, from the armed forces which they accompany, who shall provide them for that purpose with an identity card similar to the annexed model.
(5) Members of crews, including masters, pilots and apprentices, of the merchant marine and the crews of civil aircraft of the Parties to the conflict, who do not benefit by more favourable treatment under any other provisions of international law.
(6) Inhabitants of a non-occupied territory, who on the approach of the enemy spontaneously take up arms to resist the invading forces, without having had time to form themselves into regular armed units, provided they carry arms openly and respect the laws and customs of war.
B. The following shall likewise be treated as prisoners of war under the present Convention:
(1) Persons belonging, or having belonged, to the armed forces of the occupied country, if the occupying Power considers it necessary by reason of such allegiance to intern them, even though it has originally liberated them while hostilities were going on outside the territory it occupies, in particular where such persons have made an unsuccessful attempt to rejoin the armed forces to which they belong and which are engaged in combat, or where they fail to comply with a summons made to them with a view to internment.
(2) The persons belonging to one of the categories enumerated in the present Article, who have been received by neutral or non-belligerent Powers on their territory and whom these Powers are required to intern under international law, without prejudice to any more favourable treatment which these Powers may choose to give and with the exception of Articles 8, 10, 15, 30, fifth paragraph, 58–67, 92, 126 and, where diplomatic relations exist between the Parties to the conflict and the neutral or non-belligerent Power concerned, those Articles concerning the Protecting Power. Where such diplomatic relations exist, the Parties to a conflict on whom these persons depend shall be allowed to perform towards them the functions of a Protecting Power as provided in the present Convention, without prejudice to the functions which these Parties normally exercise in conformity with diplomatic and consular usage and treaties.
C. This Article shall in no way affect the status of medical personnel and chaplains as provided for in Article 33 of the present Convention.
Art 5. The present Convention shall apply to the persons referred to in Article 4 from the time they fall into the power of the enemy and until their final release and repatriation.Should any doubt arise as to whether persons, having committed a belligerent act and having fallen into the hands of the enemy, belong to any of the categories enumerated in Article 4, such persons shall enjoy the protection of the present Convention until such time as their status has been determined by a competent tribunal.[7]

The definitions used in the original text obviously do not address the issues arising from the continued disregard of state and nonstate actors for this international instrument. Perhaps the most significant missing part of the Convention is the lack of any penalties for countries violating the Convention. Until the 1967 War, Israeli officials voiced behind closed doors their interest in the creation of an international body to supervise the implementation of the Convention that may penalize the guilty parties. The ICRC filled that function but had always been an advising or mediating party rather than a disciplining party. However, with the change in Israel's standing among the nations in the wake of the 1967 War and the growing suspicion and even enmity at times toward international organizations, the lack of sanctions became for Israel an asset rather than a liability. That status of the ICRC has been especially pertinent in attempts to deal with subnational actors, obviously not signatories to the Convention. The ICRC introduced the hostage element to their routine work in the 1960s.

As of 1975, in the wake of the 1973 War and as part of an attempt to create some typology of friendly "held people [by the enemy]," the IDF defined the populations that become subject to the treatment of the State of Israel not necessarily as formal POWs but clearly as individuals that Israel would do its utmost to recover.[8] It also created some connection between well-defined groups of people that can be exchanged for each other through the ICRC. The IDF classification has four categories:

1. Friendly POWs and enemy POWs, excluding deserters.
2. Israeli citizens [of all persuasions, living in Israel or in the territories] who:
    a. Were captured by hostiles in Israel or within the territories.
    b. Were captured overseas.
    c. Crossed the border/ceasefire line of their own free will.
3. [Arabs] living in the territories who:
    a. Were captured by hostiles in Israel or within the territories.
    b. Were captured overseas.
    c. Who crossed the border/ceasefire line out of their own free will.
4. Citizens of enemy countries, who:
    a. Were captured within Israel/the territories.
    b. Were captured across the border and overseas, including terrorists, infiltrators, trespassers, fishermen, among others.

All categories include bodies of people belonging to these groups. One group, to be discussed later, fully falls within the jurisdiction of the Foreign Ministry: Jews living in or citizens of Arab countries. All other Jews, for example, citizens of friendly countries, are not included in the document, but it is evident from the historical precedents that they are also the subject of Israeli efforts to release them, usually through the Prime Minister's Office. Noticeably, a de facto POW that for many reasons is not recognized as such has come to be known by a new term: *hostage*. A hostage would be anyone captured by an asymmetrical force with the intention of holding him or her captive and possibly using him or her as leverage for bargaining to gain a more advantageous position. The most inclusive term that can be used to describe individual actors would be *combatants*. *Soldier* would only be applied to the fighters of a recognized nation state, not to nonstate actors, and only personnel in the recognized uniform of the nation-state would be eligible for this nomenclature.

The Israeli position on the formal status of POWs is crystal clear: Both Israelis as POWs in enemy hands and foreign POWs in Israeli hands are entitled to the same status. Both populations deserve the same rights and are bound by the Geneva Convention. The IDF standing orders ("General Staff orders") are very particular as to what's right and what's wrong wherever POWs are concerned. The orders speak of the right to get medical attention, be served by a chaplain, and above all to keep the prisoner alive. The Israeli code has been going through, very much like the Geneva Convention, modifications and changes intended to respond to lacunas exposed during Israeli operations, battles, and wars.[9] It is of interest to note here that the IDF marked these orders "unclassified" and published them on the Internet.

For much of history, when similar status actors fought one other, the policy governing the exchange of POWs remained largely constant, with the norms agreed upon by the warring states and formalized in treaties such as the Geneva Convention. However, the evolving nature of warfare today, in which the lines between combatant and noncombatant, POW and hostage, and war and peace have been blurred, has called the applicability of past norms of POW policy into question. Even the basic questions of who can be exchanged, as well as when and where they can be freed, have become difficult to answer.

The taking of POWs during times of active conflict is governed by the Third Geneva Convention. Although the entire Convention covers the treatment of POWs, four articles stand out. First, Article 122 asserts that a warring state must identify without delay all prisoners held within its custody—something that no Arab party has done in real time and that Israel has done in most cases. Three more articles add important caveats: Article 117 forbids repatriated prisoners from returning to active military service, and Article 119 allows for an exception to Article 118 ("Prisoners of War shall be released and repatriated without delay after the cessation of active hostilities"): "[POWs] against whom criminal proceedings for an indictable offence are pending may be detained until the end of such proceedings, and, if necessary, until the completion of the punishment. The same shall apply to Prisoners of War already convicted for an indictable offence."[10]

These articles will prove important in assembling the Israeli arguments following the taking of Israel's own as POWs or hostages. On the whole, the body of law governing the exchange of POWs codified in the Geneva Convention seems to view POWs as passive, neutral observers that warring states are obliged to care for and who cannot be exploited for strategic gain, a view that conflicts directly with the worldwide working perception of POWs today as potential sources of intelligence and potential "bargaining chips" in order to gain political, diplomatic, and human advantages.[11] Moreover, almost as soon as these norms were codified in the Geneva Convention, they began to splinter as warring states violated them.[12]

The Korean War provided the earliest cases. For example, secret telegrams between Joseph Stalin, Mao Zedong, Zhou Enlai, and Kim Il Sung reveal that China had wanted to hold 20 percent of all U.S. POWs indefinitely. Perhaps an even more striking example comes from the case of the 800 to 1,200 U.S. POWs sent to the Soviet Union by China and North Korea. These prisoners were never repatriated to the United States and the United States never pressed for their release, even though the Eisenhower administration was aware of their continued captivity.[13] These violations of the Geneva Convention and its spirit continued during the Vietnam War. True, the official line of the U.S. government has always been that all 591 U.S. POWs publicly declared by the North Vietnamese government were repatriated in 1973 in accordance with Article 8 of the Paris Peace Accords.[14] However, evidence that has emerged since that time suggests that possibly hundreds of U.S. POWs remained in captivity even after the U.S. withdrawal in 1973. One of the most compelling pieces of evidence comes from a secret document recovered from the archives of the Soviet Communist Party Central Committee in Russia that detailed a briefing by North Vietnamese general Tran Van Quang to the Hanoi Politburo on September 12, 1972. In the briefing, Quang informed the politburo that North Vietnam at that time held 1,205 U.S. POWs captured in South Vietnam, North Vietnam, Cambodia, and Laos.[15] This is more than twice the 591 POWs publicly declared by North Vietnam one year later in 1973. Even more perplexing is the evidence that the U.S. government had reason to suspect that the North Vietnamese list of POWs was incomplete. In 1992 an investigation by the Senate Select Committee on POW/MIA Affairs concluded: "There are the Americans known or thought possibly to have been alive in captivity who did not come back; we cannot dismiss the chance that some of these known prisoners remained captive past Operation Homecoming."[16] At hearings before the committee, Roger E. Shields, Deputy Assistant Secretary for International Economic and POW/MIA Affairs from 1971 to 1977, admitted that "the Defense Department was aware of 'a list' of military personnel believed to be POWs that were not returned during Operation Homecoming."[17] Also, former Secretary of Defense Melvin Laird stated that letters sent by U.S. POWs to their families between 1960 and 1972 "suggested to US analysts that as many as 474 or 478 POWs . . . had never been included in Hanoi's lists."[18]

Considering the obvious gap in size between Israel and the United States, since its inception in 1948 Israel has witnessed many military confrontations with its neighbors and has lost a number of POWs and MIAs. These POWs were entitled to the defensive shield of the Geneva Convention. However, the changes in the nature of the Middle Eastern conflict involving Israel and its neighbors allowed the Convention to serve only as a vague background for the sporadic, usually indirect Israeli-Arab negotiations on the release of POWs. At times this humanitarian issue became a bone of contention even in the international arena, especially after the 1973 War. The Israeli legal system has had to deal with the basic issue of definitions due to the constant insistence of terrorist organizations that their captured members be granted POW status. Even though the issue has been lingering since the capture of the first al-Fatḥ terrorist in 1965, no clear legal look into the issue was taken until the beginning of the twenty-first century. It had been discussed in the courts beforehand, but the expanding legal activism of the Israeli Supreme Court under Chief Justice Aharon Barak (presided: 1995–2006) led to a more thorough look into it during his tenure and those of his successors. Briefly, he changed the role of the judicial branch from a sidelines interpreter of the law into a full policy setter, declaring the policy of taking hostages/prisoners for the purpose of a future exchange illegal. This issue will be discussed in the following chapter; however, suffice it to say here that since the 1980s most, if not all, POW exchange deals have been petitioned to the Supreme Court, almost imposing on it its new active role.

Perhaps the most pressing legal issue was the status of the people to be exchanged. On the one hand Israel demanded the release of innocent civilians and uniformed persons clearly falling under the definition of POWs. On the other hand, the subnational organizations demanded the release of de facto members of substate organizations, that is, those not entitled to enjoy POW status. Each and every exchange was intended by the subnational actors to elicit recognition of their de facto POW status while not acknowledging the Geneva Convention and its stipulations, yet using the state dimension of the POW definition in order to present themselves as legal combatants of a recognized country. Toward the 1990s even the ICRC bowed to that approach and dealt with the Lebanon-based Hizbullah people according to the international organization's well-established historical norms. That was obviously not to the liking of Israel, nor of the United States For the latter, the solution to a similar situation was the detention center in Guantanamo, Cuba, where the incarcerated people were not entitled to privileges under U.S. law. Israel has also adopted the term *illegal combatants* and established on Lebanese soil a "detainees' camp."[19] However, Israel moved some of the suspected terrorists to Israeli territory and had no alternative after the 2000 withdrawal but to bring them into Israeli sovereign territory, raising the issue of their legal status. That issue—of their exact legal status—has not been fully clarified to this day and will probably be raised again in the Israeli Supreme Court once political and military conditions necessitate that.[20] One example of the problematic nature of any attempt to define their status is found in one of the leading interpretative opinions in this regard:

> By universal agreement and practice, the law of war draws a distinction between the armed forces and the peaceful populations of belligerent nations and also between those who are lawful and unlawful combatants. Lawful combatants are subject to capture and detention as prisoners of war by opposing military forces. Unlawful combatants are likewise subject to capture and detention, but in addition they are subject to trial and punishment by military tribunals for acts which render their belligerency unlawful.[21]

The difficulty in finding an agreed upon definition is due, as stated above, to some extent or perhaps largely to the inability to clearly distinguish between terrorists and freedom fighters. It is of interest to note that the people committing extreme acts of violence in San Bernardino, California, Paris, London, and Madrid are not usually placed by the international media in the same basket as the killers of Israeli civilians in Tel Aviv and Jerusalem. It is that international mood, on top of many substantial issues, that has put successive Israeli cabinets in limbo as long as POW exchanges are on the agenda. In the same vein, it is obvious that Hizbullah in the post-2000 Israeli evacuation of southern Lebanon is still building its own legitimacy for kidnappings of Israelis on the long obsolete principle of resisting occupation.

For the purposes of this book, the term *exchange process* includes the decision-making process from the instant a combatant is taken prisoner until the moment he or she or his or her remains are released. A distinction must also be made between a captive taken during the regular operations of a military legal force and some legally uniformed personnel abducted from his or her home country during noncrossing domestic operations. Indeed, the planned abduction scenario is displayed much more often since the change from third- to fourth-generation warfare in the Middle East. The following chapters will provide ample cases of Israel's adversaries ignoring the POW-related international norms. Yet being a member of all pertinent international bodies supplied Israel with at least the context to appeal to international bodies, led by the UN Security Council and by the ICRC, and to demand justice for its own. In most cases it had no effect on the holding powers but did give Israel some moral encouragement in its release efforts. Furthermore, state actors like Egypt and Jordan tried at least to keep the appearance of adhering to the rules of just war; from time to time, when it suited their interests, they did indeed prove to be following the rules to some degree when POW issues were on the table (see especially in the chapters dealing with the 1960s).

With the change in the character of the Arab-Israeli conflict from one comprehensive encounter into a series of local conflicts, the peace treaties with Egypt (1979) and Jordan (1994), and with the emergence of significant subnational players, the old policies gradually—dating back to the early conflict-related plane hijackings in the late 1960s—disappeared. However, the Israeli leadership's nightmare has for years been the specter of one unified Arab front containing Arab armies and operating under one unified command. In spite of the change in the nature of war in the contemporary Middle East, along with the disintegration of several Arab countries, the possibility of forming coalitions for the purpose of fighting Israel still exists. Actually, while this book is being written, the coalition of Syria-Iran-Hizbullah is stronger than ever. Under these circumstances, a lacuna within the Geneva Convention may not only complicate any negotiations, but might also enable the parties to the coalitions to shift responsibility from one to another for so many years as to make the whereabouts of an MIA unknown. That did happen with the missing Israeli navigator who disappeared over Lebanon in 1986, never to be found nor returned. It is Article 12 of the Convention that provides in passing a semi-legal way of ignoring in a sense the letter, but not the spirit, of the Convention, and of getting away with an MIA for many years, maybe even indefinitely. The issue is with the wording of the article: "Prisoners of War are in the hands of the enemy Power, but not of the individuals or military units who have captured them. Irrespective of the individual responsibilities that may exist, the Detaining Power is responsible for the treatment given them."[22] According to this language it is unclear which is the "detaining power," but it is evident that it is not necessarily identical to the capturing party when a fighting coalition is formed. Consequently, each party to a coalition, usually formal but also informal, can claim with a degree of impunity that it no longer has the captive and that this person has been moved to the "detaining power." It is rather strange that this loophole has not been corrected despite the length of time since it was revealed by the U.K. Foreign Office in 1953 in the Korean War context.[23]

During times of war, and obviously in the aftermath of battles and campaigns, Israel sets up, whenever the number justifies it, POW camps. Located away from the front lines, it follows the Geneva Convention rules, and enemy POWs have access if necessary to Israeli civilian and military hospitals. As far as prison for non-POWs is concerned, Israel has two ways of detaining people: under a court verdict for a person convicted of any security-related offense or under administrative detention, which is intended to prevent an individual from committing a security-related felony.

As far as prisoners and detainees are concerned, Israel is adhering to the Geneva Convention and to two additional international instruments:[24] the International Covenant on Civil and Political Rights[25] and the Convention against Torture and Other Cruel, Inhuman or Degrading Treatment or Punishment.[26] The Israeli Prisons Commission is also bound by its own standing orders: Prisons' Orders (new edition), 1971, and Prisons' Regulations, 1978.[27] None of that covers the interrogation period, during which time the detainees fall under the jurisdiction of the military code of behavior and its set of rules, as explained elsewhere in this book. With the 2011 abduction of the Israeli corporal, the rights of the prisoners to education were revoked, never to be returned to them. At that time in 2011, 323 security-related prisoners were studying for academic degrees within the Israeli Open University system.[28]

Since the creation of the State of Israel, the IDF has been in charge of the efforts to release Israeli MIAs and POWs. It used to operate either with their counter numbers within the Mixed Armistice committees with Egypt, Syria, and Jordan. At times when the committees were not operating due to other Israeli or Arab considerations, the best avenue used to be the ICRC. After all, all the neighboring countries are signatories to the Geneva Convention. In cases of one of the parties boycotting direct military contact, the Foreign Ministry through its worldwide representatives acted among foreign governments and international organizations. Many times the initial Israeli task was to try and locate the missing Israeli; however, it was only with the large number of MIAs in the 1973 War that Israel decided to set up a military body to take care of locating the missing.[29] This function exists to this day, mainly dealing with locating the 173 IDF MIAs since the 1948 War.[30]

With the exception of the Israeli judicial branch, no other branch has ever discussed in detail the official and agreed upon interpretation of the international POW-related documents. The working definitions analyzed above have been developed almost spontaneously throughout the military and diplomatic challenges since 1948. Several attempts in the 1990s and 2000s by members of the Israeli legislature have been rejected so as not to tie the hands of the decision makers in future cases. However, the emerging working definitions allow the cabinet enough to work with, in spite of the limits put on them by the Supreme Court. These definitions are flexible as they also allow future negotiators with substate actors to trade all classes of prisoners for all classes from the other side. For this reason, the judicial limits are no major hurdle; actually all deals, whoever they involve—Israelis, foreigners, Jews, Muslims, Christians, or Druze—can be put together in the same POW basket. It is clear that each person belonging to these categories, with the exception of deserters, is entitled under the generations-long Israeli tradition to the shield of the Israeli government.

NOTES

1. Laws of War: Laws and Customs of War on Land (Hague II); July 29, 1899, http://avalon.law.yale.edu/19th_century/hague02.asp; Convention (IV) Respecting the Laws and Customs of War on Land and Its Annex: Regulations Concerning the Laws and Customs of War on Land. The Hague, 18 October 1907. https://www.icrc.org/ihl/INTRO/195; Hague IV — Laws and Customs of War on Land: 18 October 1907, http://avalon.law.yale.edu/20th_century/hague04.asp.

2. Convention Between the United States of America and Other Powers, Relating to Prisoners of War; July 27, 1929, http://avalon.law.yale.edu/20th_century/geneva02.asp.

3. http://www.justice.gov.il/Units/TergomOmanotBimLeumi/Pages/Odot.aspx.

4. Protocol Additional to the Geneva Conventions of 12 August 1949, and Relating to the Protection of Victims of International Armed Conflicts (Protocol I), 8 June 1977. https://www.icrc.org/ihl/INTRO/470.

5. Geneva Convention (III) Relative to the Treatment of Prisoners of War; August 12, 1949, http://avalon.law.yale.edu/20th_century/geneva03.asp; Convention (III) Relative to the Treatment of Prisoners of War. Geneva, 12 August 1949, https://www.icrc.org/applic/ihl/ihl.nsf/7c4d08d9b287a42141256739003e636b/6fef854a3517b75ac125641e004a9e68.

6. Supreme Court decision, case 2967/00, http://www.nevo.co.il.mgs-ariel.macam.ac.il/psika_word/elyon/0002967.pdf#xml=http://www.nevo.co.il/Handlers/Highlighter/PdfHighlighter.ashx?index=4&type=Main.

7. http://www.icrc.org/ihl.nsf/7c4d08d9b287a42141256739003e63bb/6fef854a3517b75ac125641e004a9e68.

8. IDFA/57/2014/13, Virtual collection file, January 1, 1966–December 31, 1976.

9. IDFA/46/1955/488, General Staff orders draft for comments, October 5, 1953; current edition: General Staff orders, chapter 38, https://drive.google.com/folderview?id=0B4lNqBSBfg_dTVlWQkxYeWNoUEU&usp=drive_web&urp=https://he.wikipedia.org/wiki/%25D7%25A4%25D7%25A7%25D7%2595%25D&pli=1&ddrp=1&tid=0B4lNqBSBfg_dOEVERmQzcU9LaWc .

10. http://www.icrc.org/ihl.nsf/7c4d08d9b287a42141256739003e63bb/6fef854a3517b75ac125641e004a9e68.

11. Walton K. Richardson, "Prisoners of War as Instruments of Foreign Policy," in *The Use of Force, Human Rights, and General International Legal Issues*, ed. Richard B. Lillich and John N. Moore, *International Law Studies* 62 (1980): 325–42.

12. On the history of the Convention and the need to restructure it, see Renée de Nevers, "The Geneva Conventions and New Wars," *Political Science Quarterly*, 121, no. 3 (2006): 369–95.

13. Melinda Liu, "Counting the Ghosts," *Newsweek*, October 5, 1992: 49.

14. R. Sammon, "No Proof that Prisoners Remain in Southeast Asia, Panel Finds," *Congressional Quarterly Weekly Report* 51, no. 3 (1993): 138.

15. "Hanoi's Smoking Gun," *National Review* 45, no. 10 (May 24, 1993): 18.

16. [U.S.] 103rd Congress, 1st session, Senate report 103–1, POW/MIAs Report of the Select Committee on POW/MIA affairs, United States Senate, January 13, 1993, http://fas.org/irp/congress/1993_rpt/pow-exec.html.

17. R. A. Melcher, "Pentagon Knew Soldiers Held After War, Panel Says," *Congressional Quarterly Weekly Report* 50, no. 26 (1992): 1896. Later contradicting information

was published: Sammon, "No Proof that Prisoners Remain in Southeast Asia, Panel Finds."

18. Liu, "Counting the Ghosts," 48.

19. This chapter and book deal only with the definitions relevant to the Israeli policy. For a detailed study, see Ingrid Detter, "The Law of War and Illegal Combatants," *George Washington Law Review* 75 (2011): 1049–104; Knut Dörmann, "The Legal Situation of 'Unlawful/Unprivileged Combatants," *International Review of the Red Cross* 849 (2003): 45–74.

20. Oded Mudrik, "Hahzakat 'muva'im' be-ma'azar minhali ke"klafe mikuh" [Hebrew: "Detaining 'Abducted' in Administrative Arrest as 'Bargaining Chips'"], *Mishpat ve-Zava* [Justice and Military] 16, no. 813 (2003): 833–34; Adam Roberts, "Role of Law in the 'War on Terror': A Tragic Clash," *Proceedings of the Annual Meeting (American Society of International Law)* 97 (2003): 18–23.

21. Detter, "The Law of War and Illegal Combatants," 1063.

22. https://www.icrc.org/applic/ihl/ihl.nsf/Article.xsp?action=openDocument&documentId=24B808D9F30473BEC12563CD0051AB63.

23. [UK] NA/FO/371/158, from Washington to London, February 26, 1953.

24. Orly Lotan, *Prisoners' Rights in International Law and Criticism of the Imprisonment Conditions in Israeli Jails* [Hebrew] (Jerusalem: Knesset Research and Information Center, 2006); Yaniv Ronen, *Asirim Bithonim be batei kele be Israel* [Hebrew: Security-Related Prisoners in Israeli Jails] (Jerusalem: Knesset Research and Information Center, 2009); Yaniv Ronen, *Ma'amarim Academim be nose Asirim Bithonim be batei kele be Israel* [Hebrew: Academic Studies of Security-Related Prisoners] (Jerusalem: Knesset Research and Information Center, 2013).

25. Adopted and opened for signature, ratification, and accession by General Assembly resolution 2200A (XXI) of 16 December 1966, entry into force 23 March 1976, in accordance with Article 49, http://www.ohchr.org/en/professionalinterest/pages/ccpr.aspx.

26. Adopted and opened for signature, ratification, and accession by General Assembly resolution 39/46 of 10 December 1984, entry into force 26 June 1987, in accordance with article 27 (1).

27. http://www.nevo.co.il/law_html/Law01/056_002.htm; http://www.nevo.co.il.mgs-ariel.macam.ac.il/HanhayotSearchResults.aspx; http://www.nevo.co.il.mgs-ariel.macam.ac.il/HanhayotSearchResults.aspx, 03.02.00, 2007.

28. Ronen, *Ma'amarim Academim be nose Asirim Bithonim be batei kele be Israel*, 4.

29. IDFA/47/2003/81, Locating MIAs Center, Standing orders, January 1, 1973–January 1, 2000.

30. http://www.aka-idf.idf.il/Eitan/main/.

TWO

The Intelligence Dimension of Taking and Losing POWs

No military is too eager to share its tactics regarding the intelligence developed from enemy POWs and returned friendly POWs. All throughout Israel's independence it has had to grapple with enemy regular soldiers and irregular combatants. From the intelligence point of view, there is no major difference between the two. They are all human beings uprooted abruptly from their familiar surroundings and impatient to be reunited with their comrades and family as soon as possible. Perhaps the first hours or days in a POW camp or prison are the most difficult because they have to get used to unfamiliar surroundings and new daily routines, usually under unsympathetic eyes. This is also the time when the intelligence in their minds is fresh and relevant for action. The combination of the confusion and the intelligence with an expert interrogator may produce valuable information for the capturing party and inflict the most damage on the army or military force from which the person was captured. However, it is clear that the units in charge of extracting intelligence from enemy soldiers and those in charge of recovering lost information from friendly returned POWs need different sets of qualifications. The former should be fluent in the language of the captured, their customs and habits, and have all available personal information; the latter need to recruit the help of psychologists, social workers, and other personnel specializing in reintegrating the freed POWs into their own environment, the one that they were uprooted from.

Capturing an enemy fighter holds many advantages, immediate and long term—immediate in using his or her workable intelligence and long term if he or she might become a bargaining tool for the release of friendly fighters or political figures. However, the capturing party must first decide who assigns a POW value on the tactical level and later at the POW camp and based on that assess the prisoner's value.

In many cases when a foot soldier is involved, it is much wiser to equip him or her with water and food rations and to let him or her return to his or her comrades in arms. The lower the rank the better when it comes to just feeding and releasing. The propaganda value outweighs any intelligence benefit, to say nothing of the need to care for him or her for long months in Israeli POW camps. In the context of the evolving nature of warfare today, effective POW policy must take a broad spectrum of political, strategic, moral, and ethical issues into account above and beyond the tactical battlefield considerations.

Even though taking prisoners has been practiced since the earliest wars known to mankind, two rudimentary issues should still be raised: Is it necessary at all to take prisoners for pure intelligence purposes. Is it worthwhile to maintain POW camps or jails and feed the prisoners in terms of the expected quid pro quo in the eventual exchange after the conclusion of hostilities or at a given juncture as an exchange opportunity? The former issue is more of a tactical decision many times made by officers in the heat of the battle. The latter has to do with policy makers and the larger consideration that is whether the process of making decisions based on the principles of POW/prisoner exchange is a rational process with tactical or strategic goals in mind, and if the process can differ between each actor engaged in the conflict. A differentiation among enemy POWs might obviously be the result of such deliberation.

The perceived importance of intelligence gathering in warfare, of which POW interrogation acts as one element, represents nothing new. In fact, it is as old as warfare itself. In his classic Chinese treatise *The Art of War*, Sun Tzu remarks at several points on the value of reliable intelligence as a tool for gaining tactical and strategic advantage. For example, he asserts that "all warfare is based on deception,"[1] and thus a skilled commander must both seek to deceive his enemy and avoid being deceived by gaining as much knowledge about his enemy as possible. Released POWs in the heat of battle can carry back false impressions of the capturing enemy, and captured friendly POWs can exaggerate the significance of false information. For Sun Tzu, knowledge represents a key to victory:

> Therefore, determine the enemy's plans and you will know which strategy will be successful and which will not. Agitate him and ascertain the pattern of his movements. Determine his dispositions and so ascertain the field of battle. Probe him and learn where his strength is abundant and where deficient.[2]

These lessons from *The Art of War* illustrate the theoretical basis for the modern perception of the value of intelligence in warfare. Yet it is obvious that POWs act as just one of a variety of potential intelligence sources, along with infiltration by intelligence operatives, interception of communications, the use of spy satellites, etc. Additionally, the rise of asymmetric warfare today has caused the perceived intelligence value of POWs, along with human intelligence (HUMINT) in general, to increase. This is due in large part to the nature of the opponents now faced by all countries confronting violent extremist groups. As Clauswitz stated, "The weaker the forces that are at the disposal of the supreme commander, the more appealing the use of cunning becomes."[3] In other words, substate actors such as insurgent groups and terrorist organizations today have taken Sun Tzu's aforementioned wisdom to heart and seek to nullify the conventional military strength of state actors through the use of strategies and tactics of deception. As a result, modern theory concerning asymmetric warfare argues that military might alone cannot defeat a hidden, amorphous adversary who avoids decisive battle in favor of quick strikes and ambushes. Rather, reliable intelligence becomes all the more important for seeing through such an enemy's deception. Yet not all forms of intelligence gathering are effective against an enemy engaging in asymmetric warfare. High-tech sources of intelligence such as signals intelligence (SIGINT), once the mainstay of intelligence gathering during the Cold War, have proven far less effective against substate groups:

> To avoid interception of communications traffic, the terrorist will, on the one hand, make use of sophisticated devices that encrypt communications and, on the other, communicate via such low-tech and non-interceptable means as "runners" carrying messages in their heads or on bits of paper. By actually being "backward," the terrorist can subvert technology.[4]

The historic growth of the perceived value of POWs as a source of intelligence from classic military thinking to its role as a primary source of human intelligence in asymmetric warfare theory today occurred gradually. Notably, the Geneva Convention, which represents the definitive body of international law governing the treatment of POWs, does not acknowledge them as a potential source of intelligence. In fact, it seems to prohibit states from using POWs as such. Article 17 only requires a POW to supply his name, rank, and unit identification number upon capture and asserts that "no physical nor mental torture, nor any other form of coercion, may be inflicted on prisoners of war to secure from them information of any kind whatever."[5] Also, Article 118, discussed elsewhere in the book, states that POWs "shall be released and repatriated without delay after the cessation of active hostilities,"[6] thus implicitly prohibiting the indefinite detention of POWs for intelligence purposes. Both of these articles make it clear that a warring state may neither hold POWs in secret nor indefinitely.

Thus the POW cases from the Korean and Vietnam Wars began to degrade the strict, formalized rules governing the exchange of POWs codified in the Geneva Convention. Built on the theoretical and historical base discussed above, the perceived intelligence value of POWs plays a major role in the formation of POW policy today. The continued interrogation of detainees by the United States in Afghanistan, Iraq, and Guantanamo Bay is widely known, and *Human Intelligence Collector Operations*, the U.S. military's principle manual on HUMINT, devotes large sections to detailing the techniques used "to question a captured or detained person to obtain reliable information to satisfy intelligence requirements."[7] In addition, the U.S. government is in the process of creating the High-Value Detainee Interrogation Group to "bring together the most effective and experienced interrogators and support personnel from across the intelligence community, the Department of Defense (DOD), and law enforcement" for the purpose of "gathering intelligence to prevent terrorist attacks and otherwise to protect national security."[8] However, although the perception of POWs as a valuable source of intelligence has grown in popularity, it remains a matter of debate whether or not this perception has proven correct. In other words, does the potential intelligence value of POWs translate into actual intelligence value? Answering this question will be vital for any state formulating its POW policy, for a false assessment of POW intelligence value could lead to the sacrifice of a true advantage or the pursuit of a false one, both of which could lead to disaster in war.

True, many involved in the intelligence community have championed POWs as an invaluable source of intelligence. Former Central Intelligence Agency (CIA) director and attorney general Michael Hayden asserted, "As of 2006, fully half of the government's knowledge about the structure and activities of al-Qa'idah came from those [POW] interrogations."[9] Similarly, former CIA director George Tenet stated in 2007, "I know this program has saved lives. I know we've disrupted plots. I know this program alone is worth more than [what] the [Federal Bureau of Investigation (FBI)], the [CIA], and the National Security Agency put together have been able to tell us."[10] These supporters cite prominent examples of success allegedly achieved thanks to intelligence obtained from POWs. For example, they claim that information gained from the interrogation of POWs led to the capture of Khalid Shaikh Mohammed, the suspected mastermind behind the 9/11 attacks, and of Hambali, head of al-Qa'ida's Southeast Asian affiliate Jemaah Islamiyah. They further assert that the capture of these two individuals based on POW-supplied intelligence prevented a planned "second wave" jet airliner attack against the Library Tower in Los Angeles, California.

Several considerations lay at the heart of making a decision on a POW policy; in most cases, capturing an enemy soldier is indeed advisable for a variety of reasons. Perhaps the most significant such reason today, within the fourth generation of warfare, is the difficulty for intelligence services to infiltrate close-knit organizations, which are based on following orthodox customs with a twist unique to a given organization or based on clearly noticed primordial affiliations. Under these circumstances, the best alternative to implanting an agent in a place is a deep background interrogation concentrating on the smallest everyday details after exhausting the immediate military intelligence. Obviously, given the right ways of conducting the interview, there is always the possibility of "doubling" the individual and persuading him or her to serve his or her new master. However, the lower in rank, the less access and intelligence could be gained from a POW/prisoner.

Human intelligence derived from a captive can also be instrumental in comprehending the opponent's approach through using a variety of techniques to understand the goals, objectives, requested intelligence, and interests of the enemy. Moreover, with the change from regular to irregular enemy, traditional intelligence gathering might not be effective in fighting an asymmetrical war, for the following two most common reasons: areas with no reception and no apparent enemy. Most of the activities of fourth-generation combatants are carried out by small groups and through high compartmentalization.

In the politics-related realm, states may illegally hold POWs if they believe this will give them some political, diplomatic, and/or strategic advantage vis-à-vis their opponent. This appears to be the main reason behind the Chinese proposal to hold 20 percent of all U.S. POWs during the Korean War, whom they hoped to use as diplomatic leverage against the United States.[11] This reason also seemed to motivate the decision by Vietnam and Laos to continue illegally holding U.S. POWs, as Quang stated in his briefing that they "could be used to blackmail the 'stubborn' Nixon Administration and extort US economic reparations."[12] Of course, if the North Vietnamese government did intend to use POWs to pressure the United States, why they never did remains an open question. One possibility is that after the unexpected fall of Saigon in 1975, they no longer felt it necessary to play this card. Likewise, states may decide against demanding that POWs be returned if they feel such a demand carries too high a political, diplomatic, and/or strategic cost. In the case of the Korean War POWs, the United States felt the political costs of a confrontation with China and the Soviet Union outweighed the chance that the Soviet Union would return the POWs. As retired army colonel Phillip Corso, who reported on the matter to President Dwight Eisenhower, stated, "The fear of general war [with the Soviet Union and China] tied our hands."[13] Political concerns also appear to have persuaded the United States not to press the North Vietnamese government on the issue of missing POWs. Strong domestic opposition to the war, culminating in the passage of congressional legislation in 1973 prohibiting further U.S. military action in Vietnam, convinced the United States that it could not afford to jeopardize the success of the Paris Peace Accords and the U.S. withdrawal over the POW issue. As former secretary of state Henry Kissinger warned, if the United States had continued the war because of the possible continued imprisonment of POWs by North Vietnam, "American society would have blown apart."[14] Also, as previously noted, many POWs were captured while on secret missions that violated Cambodian and Laotian sovereignty, the public acknowledgment of which would have proved politically embarrassing to the United States, both domestically and internationally.

Consequently, the technological advantage of states like the United States proves ineffective without reliable HUMINT gathered on the ground to guide it.[15] That in spite of the nature of the enemy that has offered even less potential HUMINT sources than the previous generation. For example, the decentralized, cell-based structure of terrorist organizations makes high-level infiltration by intelligence operatives extremely difficult. As a result, current asymmetric warfare theory views POWs as one of the only viable sources of vital intelligence, thus elevating the perceived importance of their intelligence value beyond that seen in classic military theory. Yet despite these assertions, many also doubt the value of intelligence gained from POWs. For instance, Lieutenant Colonel Anthony Christino, who had regular access to intelligence obtained through interrogation at Guantanamo prior to his retirement, said that the administration's claims about the value of this intelligence were "wildly exaggerated" and that information gained from POW interrogation had proven "inherently unreliable."[16] Critics argue that under interrogation, particularly coercive interrogation, POWs are just as likely to provide false information they think the interrogator wants to hear as true information. Several cases seem to support this concern. Three former Guantanamo detainees released in 2004, for example, all falsely confessed after repeated interrogations to appearing in a video with Osama bin Laden. When asked why, one of the detainees explained, "I was desperate for [the interrogation] to end and therefore eventually I just gave in and [falsely] admitted to being in the video."[17] Also, several instances of detainees making false accusations against other detainees have occurred. In one of the most extreme cases, information provided by a detainee at Guantanamo that stated he had seen sixty fellow detainees at a terrorist training camp in Afghanistan proved completely false—none of those sixty individuals were even in Afghanistan at the time the detainee claimed he saw them. In an even more high-profile case, Ibn al-Shay al-Libi, a Libyan detainee who, while under interrogation by the Egyptian security services, provided the principle intelligence linking Saddam Hussein's regime to al-Qa'ida prior to the invasion of Iraq in 2003. However, he later admitted he had fabricated his story because he thought it would bring an end to his "harsh treatment." Even Senator John McCain's experience as a POW during the Vietnam War provides another example. According to Senator McCain, when coerced to give up the names of other members of his flight squadron, he instead provided the names of the offensive line of the Green Bay Packers, "knowing that providing false information was sufficient to suspend the abuse." Critics assert that such cases illustrate the difficulty in separating valuable POW-supplied intelligence from fabrications, a problem they say at best wastes significant time and effort and at worst can lead to major strategic miscalculations.[18]

Unfortunately, it has proven difficult to determine which of these two competing assessments most closely resembles the truth. Much of the potentially definitive evidence remains classified, and both the proponents and the skeptics of the intelligence value of POWs have their own political "axe to grind," making a truly objective assessment hard to come by. Furthermore, as noted above, both sides of the debate rely heavily on "anecdotal evidence adduced ad hoc."[19] According to his testimony before the Senate Select Committee on Intelligence on September 25, 2007, former DOD senior intelligence officer Colonel Steven Kleinman stated that although he had personally participated in interrogations of POWs that had generated valuable intelligence during his career, "I submit that I have not seen—and I believe I can say that I've studied the issue at length—any definitive studies that would prove that coercive methods are at all useful in consistently producing valid intelligence information."[20] This lack of any kind of scientific analysis of the validity of intelligence obtained through interrogation of POWs combined with the aforementioned secrecy regarding potential evidence and the suspected lack of objectivity on both sides of the issue provide substantial roadblocks to the formation of informed policy concerning the intelligence value of POWs.

Intelligence developed through battlefield prisoners would usually relate to the immediate theater of operations and has timely military/tactical value.[21] Yet POWs have always had an added value in terms of the larger spheres of interest of the intelligence community: from rumors and gossip heard among the troops to visits of dignitaries, arrivals of new war material and foreign experts, and finally documents of all kinds from innocent family correspondence to parts of operationally significant documents. Intelligence developed from prisoners may many times serve as a legal currency between friendly intelligence services. Actually, the working assumption of many, if not all, Western intelligence services has been that Soviet experts were among the interrogators of Western POWs at any given time since World War II.[22] The higher the rank, the deeper the study of the POW should be, aimed at doubling him or her once he or she is returned home. One of the best ways of extracting the available intelligence is by dividing the prisoners by rank and interrogating them individually. Understandably, the higher the rank, the better potential intelligence might be available. Consequently, at the arrival of enemy POWs to their temporary quarters right upon capture, they should not only be housed by rank, but the lower ranks should instead be given war rations and released. In the ever present race between intelligence value and economic conditions during active conflict time, the latter should prevail. Israel has never followed that rule, with a few exceptions—see below, especially in the context of the 1967 and 1973 Wars—inflicting upon itself some extra expenses with no tangible results to upset that loss.

The party that captures prisoners must think of the advantages of their position before deciding whether to enter into negotiations or to avoid them. The value of a prisoner must be evaluated and determined in the face of these strategic and tactical advantages and possible disadvantages. In a rational decision-making process, only when the most advantages are attainable in combination with the fewest possible disadvantages would a trade be reasonable. It follows therefore that the most valuable prisoners are not just those of highest rank, but those that are available at an opportune time. Also the value assigned to certain individuals will vary between organizations that are analyzed. During a state of asymmetrical warfare, such as the Israeli and Palestinian conflict, it appears that more value is assigned to the combatants of the larger power, regardless of their established military rank. Although this may seem paradoxical at first, it is a result of the greater affinity felt between the power, its fighters, and the general population. For example, because of Israel's moral obligation to preserve the life and safety of its citizens and to protect IDF soldiers and members of the security forces who act on behalf of the state and fall into enemy hands, "The principle of returning POWS, MIAs, kidnapped and fallen IDF personnel has been sacrosanct since the IDF's inception in 1948."[23] A unit in the General Staff Personnel Directorate, the Unit for IDF Soldiers Missing in Action, was created following the 1973 Yom Kippur War in order to locate MIAs from all of Israel's wars and military operations. The unit makes use of overt and covert approaches of action in its attempts to obtain information and is in contact with international governmental and nongovernmental organizations to obtain information regarding MIAs and POWs. A special civilian negotiating team employed by the Prime Minister's Office works with the unit in order to obtain information and negotiate eventual releases. On the operational level, the Ministry of Foreign Affairs emphasizes that the IDF does not spare any effort to free hostages.

The potential for obtaining valuable intelligence from POWs represents one major factor in a decision to take a large number of prisoners. Although classical military theory has long accepted information obtained from POWs as an essential element of HUMINT in warfare, the perception of its value grew steadily during the second half of the twentieth century, culminating in its rise to intelligence primacy in today's asymmetric warfare environment. However, despite this perception of importance, the actual intelligence value of POWs remains a matter of debate. The evolution of the perceived intelligence value of POWs is due to three fundamentals: the theoretical basis for this perceived value in both classical military thinking and modern concepts of asymmetric warfare along with the role of HUMINT; the historical growth in importance of the perceived intelligence value of POWs from the Geneva Convention through the Korean and Vietnam Wars; and third, the role of this perceived value in warfare today and, in light of the increased focus on POWs as a primary source of intelligence, the capturing power should address the question of the actual vs. potential intelligence value of POWs.

The strategic advantages of taking prisoners are important because they have long-term consequences and are very important in any stage of asymmetrical warfare. The act of capturing combatants and their unknown fate is possibly more damaging to the enemy party's morale than the killing of their soldiers would be. This has a long-term psychological impact, which could make future operations easier to complete due to the enemy's fear of capture. In addition, by capturing opposing combatants, there is the potential for a much larger amount of media attention. In asymmetrical warfare, the smaller state can use this media attention to influence world opinion and seek assistance from sympathetic countries. In the final stages of a conflict, prisoners add a strategic advantage because they can be used as bargaining tools to regain friendly combatants, sympathetic political figures detained by the enemy, or even as tools to gain a better settlement in the final peace negotiations. Although these are advantages for the capturing party regardless of the type of conflict involved, they are particularly relevant in the case of a smaller group fighting a greater power through a violent strategy of asymmetrical warfare. These strategic advantages, especially through the increase in media attention, grant a smaller power an amount of legitimacy not easily attained from other sources.

Not all of the advantages gained by the capturing state are purely strategic; some are more tactical in nature. The primary and immediate advantage of having a hostage in order to escape from a difficult situation is a major tactical advantage to an outnumbered combatant. In addition, if a captive has pertinent information or can be traded for pertinent information that may impact the captors' operations or policy, it is an immediate tactical gain. Although the psychological impact of capturing a soldier can be a long-term strategic advantage, it has tactical implications as well. Seeing either a combatant or a combatant's body taken during a firefight would immediately shock the remaining participants in a skirmish, possibly impairing their ability to continue the fight. The tactical advantages of taking a prisoner captive seem to be more salient to the larger power than to the smaller group when considering asymmetrical warfare. Although each side can potentially gain similar advantages from capturing a combatant, the strategic information possibly gained from the captive would be more easily disseminated by the organized forces of the larger power. Tactical information gained would be instant awareness of enemy troops, armament, and type in the immediate area. As most nation-states use a standard of military equipment and patrol type, much of the immediate advantage would be negated through the predictability with which a nation-state wages war. Although there are several tactical advantages, especially for the larger power involved in asymmetrical warfare, the tactical disadvantages may well outweigh the gains. It is much more difficult to care for and transport a prisoner, which could result in losing the hostage altogether if the enemy manages to attack during such a process. Also, although the long-term psychological impact may well be disheartening, in the immediate aftermath of a person being captured, his or her parent organization may gain a boost of morale aimed at regaining the lost comrade. The smaller guerilla forces would not be able to easily compensate for the care and transportation of a prisoner in the immediate period during and just after a capture. Once again we see that in tactical terms it is more advantageous for the larger, more organized nation-state to capture combatants in order to discover any immediate information about the current conflict. The larger power would also be able to protect the prisoner for an extended period of time, enough time to easily transport him or her to a secondary location in order to begin taking strategic advantage of the situation. In some cases, the bodies of dead combatants have been taken by the opposing actor; in these cases, similar disadvantages due to the difficulty of transportation as well as care for the remains would still be applicable to either of the participants, but is again more easily overcome by the nation-state or larger power due to its higher degree of mobilization and greater access to the appropriate resources.

Although it seems that there are only tactical advantages to taking prisoners for the capturing power, at times it may be argued otherwise. Of immediate concern is always the securing, transport, and holding of the captive; an interruption at any point would create vulnerability due to the extra concern given to the captive. With the advent of the modern media, any size group can now reach a worldwide audience with relatively minimal effort. Although the strategic advantages of additional media coverage have already been discussed, the media is a particularly double-sided issue. Taking a prisoner almost always brings more attention to a particular conflict. Although there is a possibility of a gathering support for those who captured the enemy combatant, it is also very likely that nations or other groups will lend support—financial, political, or military—to the effort to regain the captured soldier. As we have seen in previous cases, especially in the relationship between the United States and Israel, this is not an uncommon nor unexpected outcome. This long-term disadvantage could have political and economic implications after the end of the conflict even if the forces that captured the soldier are the eventual victors. The media could also influence the resident population of a region, pushing a more hostile attitude, which would damage the long-term recruitment and control the guerilla movement would otherwise enjoy in an area or region.

In addition, although it would be against the Geneva Convention to leave a subdued combatant on the battlefield, it is not in the nation-state's best interest to hold large numbers of prisoners for extended periods of time, so it may also not be advantageous to take prisoners at every opportunity. Holding large numbers of enemy fighters captive does harm the asymmetrical organization's operational capability; however, it also allows large groups of insurgents to gather and trade ideas in a protected environment. Because of this surplus of prisoners and the disadvantages associated with grouping them together, a nation-state must consider very carefully when deciding whether or not to take a prisoner. A specific mission to capture prisoners would only be advantageous if they could guarantee a very high-level combatant would be captured with a relatively low risk of discovery. The asymmetrical power, on the other hand, should take advantage of the irrational affinity between the larger power and its soldiers and capture as many soldiers as possible. In order to gain additional notice and maximize the utility of their hostages, the asymmetrical power should also occasionally take a civilian hostage. In this way they will be able to increase the identification between soldiers and the rest of a nation-state's population and thereby increase each hostage's value.

That unique feature associated with the intelligence collecting from POWs is atypical of most intelligence services. Their most common functions are much more standard and involve basic intelligence, such as accurate order of battle, officers' names, positions, and ranks, and less tangible intelligence, like morale, resilience, loyalty to the regime, and how rumors are spread within the rank and file. How is this information developed? Because the most worrying element of collecting intelligence is that the crucial piece would fall through the cracks, priority has to be given to the right categorization of the enemy POWs. The higher in rank the better. Moreover, it is not always a military man who holds the keys to the next move. Consequently, each intelligence service has to distinguish between certain categories of captured enemy personnel. That means that questioning of potential bearers of information has to be divided between civilians and military men. The civilians are further divided into suspected enemy agents, legal and illegal refugees, and people crossing borders between hostile countries for whatever reason—usually with the exception of bona fide international organizations. On the military side, the most common phenomenon in wartime is obviously uniformed personnel—that is, in order of position and rank: air crew and special forces, naval forces, especially submarines and infantry. Once the interrogation is over, the captured personnel are moved to POW camps and are seldom called for further questioning.[24]

Undoubtedly, POW and enemy prisoners, whatever the legal definition, may prove to be a one-time opportunity to corroborate existing information and to call intelligence attention to hitherto unknown fields. However, that depends solely on the abilities of the interrogator and the legal limits of his or her investigation. On this, all Western powers do suffer from a deficiency when it comes to fourth-generation intelligence collection. The almost total inability to implant human sources among subnational/terror organizations is discussed elsewhere in the book. Suffice it to say at this point that fully mastering the necessary languages is an imperative, but certainly not sufficient. Moreover, each interrogation compromises to some, hopefully minimum, extent the interrogator's information. The interrogator must at all times impress upon the prisoner that nothing of what he or she says is indeed new, and in this way lure him or her into telling more. If the interrogator is not familiar with his or her subject matter, he or she will not know how to extract the right information and he or she may mistakenly compromise his or her own information.[25] On top of all these tactics, each imprisoning party would tend to benefit from employing psychological warfare on the prisoners so that even if the prisoners are not to be doubled, they would be positively positioned in regard to the capturing party.[26] However, no free world country allows unlimited investigating tactics. They are all bound by clear-cut codes that prohibit certain approaches to POWs.[27] Consequently, it is reasonable to assume that as part of friendly fighters' preparation for imprisonment through specialized training, they are taught about potential enemy tactics, but do not necessarily ever experience them first-hand. Obviously most, if not all, armies prepare their respective members for such contingencies.[28] That, along with guidelines for POWs and other enemy captives, constitutes the "tool box" of every intelligence service—for attempting to develop intelligence from hostiles or trying to recover from returned captives the amount of damage they had inflicted on their respective armies.[29] Clearly, both kinds of prisoners level complaints against their interrogators. Perhaps the most noted of these came from the returned Israeli 1973 POWs, who were put in an appropriated hotel, largely isolated from the world, and according to their accounts questioned in rather unpleasant ways, to say the least.

Deciding on the capturing or releasing of prisoners in the heat of the battle is usually a tactical decision, even if the high command would like it to be otherwise. However, the return of POWs is always within the realm of the political highest echelons. Decisions regarding who, when, and where to return POWs can have either a positive or negative impact on both sides of a conflict; consequently states must take contextual factors into account in order to determine their POW policy on a case-by-case basis. However, the precedent set during the Korean and Vietnam Wars has greatly complicated the issue, making it difficult to ignore international standards and to allow states to determine their own policies on the exchange of POWs within the context of their own national interest. With the evolution of warfare blurring the lines between war and peace and combatant and noncombatant, policy makers today feel unsure how to apply even the most basic laws governing POW exchange in the Geneva Convention to prisoners taken in the War on Terror. For example, with ongoing violence hovering below the level of conventional war but above the level of peace, how can one determine when hostilities have ceased and POWs should be repatriated? Also, with so many detainees hailing from states not directly involved in the conflict, where should they be repatriated to by their captors? There has even been significant debate over whether or not those captured in the War on Terror qualify as POWs. Although the Third Geneva Convention Relative to the Treatment of Prisoners of War of 1949 was created to apply to situations that involve only nation-states, the author believes that it is necessary to reevaluate the Geneva Convention when dealing with subnational actors because at the time of its inception, terrorist organizations (such as Hamas and Hizbullah in the Israeli-Palestinian/Arab context) either did not exist or did not play the large role that they do within the world today. Therefore, as this chapter lacks adequate space to fully delve into and address this complex question, it will simply assert that these detainees qualify as de facto POWs insofar as they were captured as part of a military conflict, and those not charged with crimes must eventually be released somewhere. Given this assumption, the issues facing policy makers fall into two categories: concerns about security and concern for the safety of repatriated prisoners.

Security concerns about repatriation center on the fear that prisoners released will not comply with Article 117 of the Geneva Convention, which forbids repatriated prisoners from returning to active military service, and will rejoin the conflict. For example, according to the Almagor Terror Victims Association, 854 of the 6,912 Palestinian terrorists released in confidence-building measures between 1993 and 1999 were subsequently arrested for acts of murder and terrorism (as of August 2003). In fact, 80 percent of the terrorists released committed criminal offences related to terrorism, "whether as commanders, planners, or murderers." In addition, since the year 2000, terrorists who had been released from Israeli jails have murdered 180 Israelis. The Department of Defense currently estimates that of the nearly 540 detainees released from the detention center at Guantanamo Bay, Cuba so far, "18 . . . have been confirmed as 'returning to the fight' and another 43 are suspected of having done so."[30] Although critics dispute the accuracy of this count, it seems clear that at least some former prisoners have reentered the conflict, the most high profile being Said Ali al-Shihri, a former Guantanamo detainee now believed to head al-Qa'ida operations in Yemen.[31] Receiving states like Yemen worry policy makers the most because they believe the political volatility and significant terrorist presence in such countries increases the chances that prisoners repatriated there will rejoin the conflict.[32] With Yemenis comprising the largest national group within the Guantanamo prisoner population, this represents a major concern. Although the United States in principle supports the idea of using rehabilitation, counseling, and job training to reintegrate former detainees into society and prevent their return to the conflict, disagreements over who should fund such a program, the United States or the receiving state, have so far prevented its implementation (Yemen, for example, reportedly wants $1 million per detainee).[33] Consequently, the U.S. government seems resigned to continuing its policy of holding prisoners it considers a threat indefinitely, even those it does not plan to charge with any crime. According to CIA Director Leon Panetta, "There's going to be a group of prisoners that, very frankly, are going to have to be held in detainment for a long time."[34] It is also possible that an unwillingness to disclose detainees acquired through extraordinary rendition and held in secret detention centers influenced this choice. In any case, such a decision represents a temporary measure, not a permanent policy solution.

The second main concern focuses not on threats from but threats to repatriated prisoners. Many detainees come from states with poor human rights records such as Syria, Saudi Arabia, Egypt, and China, and if returned there, they will likely face imprisonment, torture, or death. Cases of such crimes have already occurred, like that of a Libyan released from a CIA detention center in 2006 who was found dead in his cell in May 2009, having apparently succumbed to torture by his jailors.[35] There is also the case of the eighteen detainees returned to Yemen so far, all of whom were detained by the security forces, some for months, and at least one of whom was tortured while in captivity.[36] Concern about these incidents prevents the United States from returning the approximately sixty detainees at Guantanamo currently cleared for release.[37] The United States has pursued releasing prisoners to third countries as a possible solution. This idea has a historical basis, as Chapter IV, Section 1 of the Geneva Convention permits detaining states to release POWs into the care of neutral third powers, albeit for medical reasons. The United States has achieved some success in this, with Albania taking five Chinese Uyghurs, France taking one Algerian, and the United Kingdom taking one Ethiopian. Portugal has also agreed to take two Syrians, and Hungary and Ireland have likewise committed to receiving former detainees with "several other European countries . . . weighing the possibility."[38] However, these small commitments remain too few to accommodate in third countries all those prisoners awaiting release. Much like the U.S. government itself, the governments of many potential host states feel unwilling to accept the risk or the domestic political cost of publicly allowing former prisoners bearing the stigma of "terrorist" to live freely within their respective countries.[39] Consequently, as with the abovementioned security concerns, the only solution currently available seems to be continued incarceration, although again, this represents a temporary solution at best.

When the established power makes exchanges that are not equal and are actually beneficial to its enemies, it makes sense for these enemies to continue the illegal activity that is advantageous to them. The established power, such as Israel, therefore inadvertently creates a "bait situation" by keeping terrorists alive in custody, giving terrorist groups an opportunity to free their men by ransoming the established power's kidnapped prisoners. Terrorists therefore can find comfort in the fact that if they are caught and convicted, there is a good chance that they will one day be exchanged for the established power's kidnapped prisoners. These prisoner exchanges greatly damage the larger, established power's deterrence because it encourages future kidnappings and rewards imprisoned terrorists by releasing them early, allowing them to commit the same acts in the future.

A relatively new development has been the capture of enemy remains. Although this may seem a strange development from a rational perspective, it appears that the affinity felt for a nation's soldiers extends to their physical remains after their death. This affinity turns the capture of remains into a surprisingly rational process. Part of this affinity may be explained by the fact that the only way to confirm a death is to recover the remains of combat personnel. However, the value assigned to these remains is once again disproportionately high. In the Israeli-Palestinian conflict it appears that the remains of an Israeli soldier are worth almost as much as a living captive. This once again leads to an irrational exchange of prisoners, allowing the guerilla group to regain a significant number of living combatants, more than four hundred in some cases, which only strengthens their next attacks.

From a strategic and tactical standpoint, there is no reason for a larger power to engage in prisoner exchange negotiations unless there is at least equal proportion of exchange. Otherwise there is no immediate advantage to an exchange. From a strategic perspective, the only advantage to be gained is on the side of the smaller guerilla military. The incredibly disproportional value assigned by industrialized nations to their soldiers allows long-term gain to be made by the smaller force. Ultimately, for the larger power, prisoner exchanges harm its deterrence, encourage future kidnappings, endanger the lives of those who may be taken hostage by a terrorist group, and encourage additional support, recruitment, and donations to the guerilla organizations. If a rational and correctly proportional decision-making process were instituted, the strategic value of taking prisoners would decrease to a nearly negligible amount. Through the use of a rational policy when approaching the decision about whether or not to take and exchange prisoners, nearly every benefit, either tactical or strategic, is nullified for the smaller guerilla force. There were very few tactical advantages for the larger force in the first place; however, the strategic concerns remain in effect even after the rational policy toward exchange is adopted.

The political value associated with prisoners also affects their exchange value. During the modern age of media attention, it seems that the soldiers of the larger power have a higher political value in general (as stated in above section). The constraints placed on the nation-state in regard to prisoner treatment, such as the Oslo Accords of 1993 and Geneva Convention of 1949, cannot be applied to a nonstate actor. Also, the affinity the population feels for the captured soldier due to shared citizenship generates additional political pressure for the return of said soldier. This is yet another factor leading to the use of an irrational policy in determining whether or not to engage in the exchange process. The influence and interaction of the media in each case is particularly pertinent when discussing the political value placed on captured combatants or the captured remains of a combatant. If there is popular unrest, the exchange could be viewed as a tool in order to regain popularity, and the same could be true when trying to gain popularity due to an upcoming election.

The above evidence of violations of the international laws governing the exchange of POWs begs the question of why. Why would any nation continue to secretly hold POWs after the cessation of hostilities, and why would any nation ignore the fact that some of its POWs have not been repatriated? The reasons behind these actions fall within two categories: intelligence-related and politics-related. In the intelligence-related category of causes, states decide to hold POWs illegally because they feel they can gain some intelligence benefit from them. This includes not only information gained from interrogating POWs, but, as is suspected in the case of the Korean War and POWs sent to the Soviet Union, a state can use information about POWs' lives as cover stories for its own intelligence agents.[40] Similarly, a state may choose to ignore the fact that an adversary holds members of its military if acknowledging those POWs would jeopardize intelligence operations. This reason may factor into the U.S. decision to deny the existence of POWs captured during illegal missions carried out in Cambodia and Laos during the Vietnam War.

This chapter has sought to trace the evolution of policy governing the exchange of POWs from a formally codified body of international law in the Geneva Convention, through the eroding of these laws during the Korean, Vietnam, and Arab-Israeli wars, to the current complex debate over what policy to apply to prisoners taken during the ongoing war on subnational groups. The apparent malleability of these rules begs the question of whether it is possible to enforce strict international norms applying to POWs held in all conflicts or whether states must form their own POW policies based on the context of each conflict—taking possible political, diplomatic, and strategic advantages and disadvantages into account. It is high time to pose the question as to whether the Convention should be modified by introducing the idea that POWs do not exist as neutral, passive observers on the sidelines.

The great affinity between the power, its fighters, and the general population felt by belligerent powers such as Israel often leads to an irrational decision-making process rather than the rational one needed to deal with these situations. This irrational affinity vastly inflates the price a government is willing to pay for a single captive. The pattern that emerges will be studied in the last chapter of the book. The guerilla force is most often able to take advantage of this pattern to regain a disproportionately large number of fighters or other concessions in each exchange, allowing them to greatly strengthen their effort while giving a negligible exchange in return. From a point in the 1970s on, asymmetric prisoner exchanges have been taking place between Israel and subnational actors. Therefore, when choosing which targets to capture, it would seem natural that the smaller guerilla force would choose to take the best targets of opportunity involving the lowest risk of defeat, yet any prisoner of higher rank would be an added bonus. The established power, on the other hand, is forced to try and capture only the highest-ranking combatants of the guerilla force due to the apparently disproportionate value assigned to their combatants. Only then would there be an advantageous, or at least a more proportionate, exchange of prisoners.

Most if not all the accumulated lessons of U.S. interrogation techniques and consistent no compromise with terrorists policy regarding POW exchanges are universal and are probably shared with the U.S. allies, Israel included. However, the issue at hand is how much of it Israel chooses to include in its briefings to its own military and prisoner investigators along with what elements are unique to Israel. Structurally speaking, Israel has been following the Western example of two separate and different units dealing with captured enemy POWs and friendly returned POWs. The former are the responsibility of the military intelligence, whereas responsibility for the latter rests with the IDF Directorate of Manpower.

Years ago, the (British) RAF intelligence considered the establishment of a special unit based on reservists to be called to duty a while before the day on which mobilization commences or is due to commence for battle in order to prepare rescue operations beforehand. The working paradigm of the planners was that each campaign commences with heavy bombardment of certain areas. The unit's duties would be to implant dormant agents or to kidnap civilians in areas scheduled for British bombing so that when the time came and planes were shot down, there would be enough topographical intelligence and people on the ground to delay the collection of the pilots by enemy forces, so as to allow the parachuting pilots enough time to find temporary shelter.[41] Obviously, at times the local responder would have to be replaced once his identity is exposed.

As one of the 1973 War lessons, the IDF adopted a detailed procedure to be followed upon the capture of an Israeli soldier in enemy hands.[42] As future developments would prove, that method could only partially work because in that procedure Israel basically underlined the role of the ICRC, which has not always been the preferred mediator by Israel's adversaries. Nor does the document detailing the procedure specify the issue of price, which since the late 1970s would turn out to be more significant than the identity of the mediator.

Almost seventy years of accumulated Israeli experience in the field of POWs in all its aspects has taught its decision makers to try and aim high for valuable POW assets. However, with the lack of such targets at hand, Israel has tried to pursue a policy that would use the intelligence value of the prisoners and then return them—no matter how many—in exchange for one Israeli. The cost of keeping prisoners in jail, on top of enemy countries and later the organizations squeezing Israel into least prestigious solutions, have shaped Israeli policy for years. Nevertheless, those Arab positions could not prevent Israel from checking out the perceived intelligence value of POWs, based in classic military wisdom and crucial to modern theory on asymmetric warfare. Today, the potential intelligence value of POWs seems largely accepted. However, can states realize the potential advantage, and if so, how? This question remains a matter of significant debate, one which the necessity for secrecy and the influence of politics makes difficult to objectively and scientifically analyze. Yet such analysis must be made because this question is not merely academic. Failure to accurately assess the actual value of POWs as a source of intelligence could have real strategic consequences in war.

NOTES

1. Sun Tzu, "Laying Plans," in *The Art of War*, trans. Lionel Giles (Internet Classics Archive, n.d.), principle 18, http://classics.mit.edu/Tzu/artwar.1b.txt.
2. Mark R. McNeilly, *Sun Tzu and the Art of Business: Six Strategic Principles for Managers* (Oxford: Oxford University Press, 1996), 204.
3. Carl von Clausewitz, *On War*, trans. Michael Howard and Peter Pare (Princeton, NJ: Princeton University Press, 2003), 203.
4. Rod Thornton, *Asymmetric Warfare; Threat and Response in the 21st Century* (Cambridge: Polity Press, 2007), 45.
5. Geneva Convention (III), "Treatment of Prisoners of War" August 12, 1949, http://www.icrc.org/ihl.nsf/7c4d08d9b287a42141256739003e63bb/6fef854a3517b75ac125641e004a9e68.
6. Ibid.
7. Headquarters, Department of the Army, "Human Intelligence Collector Operations," Field Manual No. 2–22.3 (FM 34–52), September 6, 2006, 5–13.
8. Department of Justice, Office of Public Affairs, Special Task Force on Interrogation and Transfer Policies Issues Its Recommendations to the President, August 24, 2009, http://www.justice.gov/opa/pr/special-task-force-interrogations-and-transfer-policies-issues-its-recommendations-president.

9. Michael B. Mukasey, "The Waterboarding Trial to Bin Laden," *The Wall Street Journal*, May 6, 2011, http://www.wsj.com/articles/SB10001424052748703859304576305023876506348.

10. Charlotte Lepri, "Obama's Intelligence Policy: Meeting New Challenges," in *National Security Under the Obama Administration*, ed. Bahram M. Rajaee and Mark J. Miller (New York: Palgrave-MacMillan, 2012), 69.

11. Melinda Liu, "Counting the Ghosts," *Newsweek* 5 (October 1992): 49.

12. "Hanoi's Smoking Gun," *National Review* 45, no. 10 (1993): 18.

13. Liu, "Counting the Ghosts," 50.

14. Ibid., 49.

15. Thornton, *Asymmetric Warfare*, 162.

16. Philip Rumney, "The Effectiveness of Coercive Interrogation: Scholarly and Judicial Responses," *Crime, Law and Social Change* 44, no. 4 (December 2005): 474.

17. Ibid., 472–73.

18. Ibid., 473–74.

19. Douglas C. Lovelace Jr., "Commentary on Interrogation Methods: State of the Debate," in *Terrorism: Commentary on Security Documents: Terror-based Interrogation*, ed. Kristen E. Boon, Aziz Z. Huq, and Douglas C. Lovelace (Oxford: Oxford University Press, 2010), 382.

20. U.S. Interrogation Policy and Executive Order 13440, Hearing before the Select Committee on Intelligence of the United States Senate, One Hundred Tenth Congress, first session, September 25, 2007. 2009, 5. http://www.intelligence.senate.gov/sites/default/files/hearings/110849.pdf.

21. IDFA/535/04/521, combat intelligence (temporary [edition]), January 1, 1949–December 31, 1949, 31–34; National Security Council Intelligence Directive No. 3, Washington, January 13, 1948, Coordination of intelligence production, https://www.fas.org/irp/offdocs/nscid03.htm, clause 3; IDFA/121/535/04, Special intelligence report, including special intelligence reviews, January 1, 1956–December 31, 1956.

22. Cf. [UK] NA/AIR40/PRG/100/197, from The Foreign Office, to Air Ministry, November 3, 1953.

23. Israel Ministry of Foreign Affairs, Background on Israeli POWs and MIAs, 26 January 2004.

24. [UK] NA/WO32/0103/8753, Interrogation in the UK in war, n.d., ca. 1954/1955; correspondence in: IDFA/637/1956/56, 626/1957/29, 535/2004/481, operational conclusions and lessons, January 1, 1949–December 31, 1957.

25. Cf. IDFA/1087/2004/535, First Brigade report in concluding the Sinai campaign, n.d.

26. Cf. ISA/FM/6178/2, Egypt, foreign relations with Israel, January 2, 1957–October 31, 1957, news for the Israeli overseas representations, no. 1276, February 20, 1957.

27. Please follow the development of these concepts between CIA, KUBARK Counterintelligence Interrogation, July 1963, http://nsarchive.gwu.edu/NSAEBB/NSAEBB122/CIA%20Kubark%201–60.pdf and the Israeli instruction, only partially leaked to the public, as put together by the then retired Justice Landoi that would be later summarized for the public in two short sentences: "non-violent psychological pressure" and "moderate physical pressure." Supreme Court of Justice, 2581/91; 5100/94; 4054/95; 6536/95, The Public Committee against Torture in Israel v. The State of Israel, 1999. http://www.nevo.co.il.mgs-ariel.macam.ac.il/psika_word/elyon/9405100.pdf#xml=http://www.nevo.co.il/Handlers/Highlighter/PdfHighlighter.ashx?index=0&type=Main, and others, http://www.nevo.co.il.mgs-ariel.macam.ac.il/psika_word/elyon/9405100.pdf#xml=http://www.nevo.co.il/Handlers/Highlighter/PdfHighlighter.ashx?index=0&type=Main.

28. Cf. [UK] NA/AIR40/0103/8753, From Frank B. Berry, MD, [U.S.] Assistant Secretary of Defense, Washington, DC, to Lt. General Alexander Drummond, The War Office, London, October 21, 1958; CIA, KUBARK Counterintelligence Interrogation, July 1963, http://nsarchive.gwu.edu/NSAEBB/NSAEBB122/CIA%20Kubark%201–60.pdf.

29. IDFA/734/1965/1034, from General Staff HQ, Intelligence Directorate to Assistant Chief, Directorate of Operations, February 10, 1957; Collection file relating to the debriefing of a soldier returning from terrorists' capture on June 6, 1982; IDFA/49/2012/64. Collection file relating to the debriefing of a soldier returning from terrorists' capture on June 6, 1982.

30. Kenneth Jost, ed., "Closing Guantanamo." *CQ Researcher* 27 (February 2009): 181.

31. Ibid.

32. Letta Tayler, *No Direction Home: Returns from Guantanamo to Yemen* (New York: Human Rights Watch, 2009), 2.

33. Michael Crowley, "Prisoners Dilemma," *The New Republic* 17 (June 2009): 10.

34. Jost, "Closing Guantanamo," 183.

35. Crowley, "Prisoners Dilemma," 9.

36. Tayler, *No Direction Home*, 37.

37. Crowley, "Prisoners Dilemma," 9.

38. Nicholas Kulish, "Hungary: Deal on Guantanamo Prisoner," *The New York Times*, September 17, 2009; "Portugal: Pact on Guantanamo Prisoners," *The New York Times*, August 8, 2009: 8.

39. Crowley, "Prisoners Dilemma," 10.

40. Liu, "Counting the Ghosts," 50.

41. [UK] NA/AIR2/Air Ministry File No. A.42559/50, March 1950.

42. IDFA/57/2014/13, 13/1957/14.

THREE

Early Indications of an Emerging Policy

Strategic Defeats and Tactical Success, 1949–1955

In the summer of 1949 the guns fell formally silent. The 1948–1949 conflict over the former Mandatory Palestine was finally over with the signing of the armistice agreements between Israel and its neighbors: Egypt, February 24; Lebanon, March 24; Transjordan, April 3; and Syria, July 20. The State of Israel became a reality, while the neighboring Arab countries continued to deny its right to exist. However, all parties to the conflict—including Iraq, which refused to sign an armistice agreement with Israel—became engaged in a process of prisoner exchange that had actually begun in earnest even before the formal signing. By sheer coincidence, the old Convention relative to the Treatment of Prisoners of War, Geneva, July 27, 1929, was replaced in August 1949 by Convention Three Relative to the Treatment of Prisoners of War.

By January 1950, all prisoners of war of all warring parties returned home. However, that marked only the beginning of the next phase of the Arab-Israeli conflict: a low-intensity warfare broken at times by more intensive exchange of fire, including land, sea, and air battles. Over the years between 1950 and 1967, the POW issue became one way of fighting: all parties took POWs and kidnapped civilians and soldiers; one party, Syria, did not even admit at times to the kidnapping of Israelis, but kept them in jail for prolonged periods. The Israeli policy became almost routine: capturing enemy soldiers, preferably officers, and exchanging them for Israeli POWs. There is no indication in available contemporary documents that that policy was the result of any deliberate decision by any high authority. It appears from contemporary Israeli military documents that it was a decision made by the military hierarchy alone, perhaps even by field officers. However, many of the 1954 and 1955 Israeli operative orders included a sentence to the effect that one of the aims of the operation was the taking of enemy POWs for the purpose of exchange.[1]

In early 1950 representatives of the Allied forces were still debating the fate of the former German POWs, preferring to return them to their pre-war locations;[2] on another note, the Western powers were debating the fate of the approximately one million POWs that had "vanished" during the war inside the Soviet Union. This author knows of no minutes of any Israeli cabinet discussion relating to either of the above circumstances. Perhaps there is an explanation for that lacuna, but in retrospect, it presented the first opportunity for Israel to contribute to POW issues related to its interest in getting back its POWs/MIAs. Moreover, considering that the Arab-Israeli conflict was not resolved by the armistice agreements and fearing that more Israelis might find themselves in enemy prisons, Israel had to try to influence at least to a minor degree the emerging world position on POWs. Such steps might have served its cause in years to come. However, it is completely clear that no one at that early stage of the conflict could realize the significance of the Israeli situation for the future.

The issue of German and Japanese POWs in Soviet hands had a bearing on the concern about people made to "disappear" by their captors—which was to bother Israel for many years to come and probably up to this very day. By 1950 a number of German POWs had not yet been released and a large number of POWs were unaccounted for. The United States and Great Britain put on the agenda of the UN General Assembly a draft resolution calling for the appointment of an independent commission of inquiry mandated to investigate the whereabouts of the missing. In mid-December 1950 Israel abstained from casting its deciding vote for two main reasons: not to alienate the Soviet Union, whose leader Stalin was already conducting a harsh campaign against the Soviet Jews, and because no Israeli leader could, only five years after the conclusion of the war and the Holocaust, instruct any Israeli representative to vote for anything even remotely positive for the Germans and the Japanese. On December 14, 1950, the United Nations General Assembly, by a vote of 43 for, 5 against, and 8 abstentions, adopted a resolution expressing concern over the large number of prisoners of war that had "neither been repatriated nor otherwise accounted for."[3] The Israeli position would at least weaken its stand from a moral perspective in the years to come, while it attempted to find out the whereabouts of Israelis lost across the border.[4]

Perhaps the issue of border skirmishes was the easiest in terms of Israeli decision making because it involved in most cases low-level combat troops whose return could usually be settled through the Mixed Armistice Committees established as part and parcel of the armistice agreements. On January 13, 1950, the last Jordanian POWs from the 1948 War returned home. A short while later and because of the almost daily border skirmishes between Israel and its neighbors, a long series of border incidents led to both sides taking POWs.[5] All in all, under a variety of circumstances about 170 Israeli civilians and 36 military personnel were held for various periods of time by the countries surrounding Israel, Egypt, Jordan, and Syria until the October 1956 Operation. Concurrent with that, Israel captured about 2,800 civilians, many of whom crossed the borders for criminal and sabotage purposes, but no more than 20 soldiers qualified as POWs.[6] These numbers allude to deteriorating security conditions between Israel and its neighbors in the first half of the 1950s. That escalation in the armed dialogue eventually led to the October 1956 Sinai campaign, yet was still unnoticed as of 1950. Actually, in spite of the unmarked border between Israel and its neighbors, a significant number of infiltrations from Arab territory into Israeli areas came about from a humanitarian need to visit the families that stayed behind and did not leave for Gaza, the Hashemite Kingdom of Jordan, or Syria. Next came crossings aimed at committing criminal offenses inside Israel, such as stealing cattle and horses; the terrorists were only in third place among the infiltrators. Due to distraction by the needs to absorb a large wave of immigrants into Israel and to establish Israel's position among the nations, all border incidents were left to the military. It dealt with them in two distinct ways. First, the military chased suspects into Arab territory and stole back cattle or water pipelines belonging to citizens living in the neighboring Arab countries. Whenever enemy troops provoked Israel by opening fire, its forces responded in kind and at times initiated their own attacks.[7] The second way the military faced border clashes—those that involved taking civilian hostages or military POWs—was through asking the MAC to convene and reach an ad hoc agreement for the release of the people captured by the adversary. Clearly, the armistice borderline was not very well marked on the ground and both sides tried their best to claim sovereignty over certain important spots. Consequently, both sides sent patrols beyond what the other considered its own and each side captured the other's patrolling soldiers. Moreover, with the absence of clear borderlines, even civilians walking on foot for recreational purposes found themselves at times in hostile territory. The various Mixed Armistice Committees resolved many of those cases. On top of these cases, Israel was also engaged in looking for its approximately 950 MIAs from 1948 and did not want to alienate the other side and the respective MAC's chairmen from the UN.[8] However, as already indicated, none of these cases involved any high-ranking officer or the highest echelons of the Israeli political system. The stated position of the MAC was clear and simple: that any prisoner of war should be returned at the earliest by each party. However, that directive was not followed by any of the opposing parties.

Analyzing a large number of POW-taking incidents (1951–1956) within the context of the Israeli reprisal operations in the wake of terrorist activities reveals a clear and unmistakable picture. In most cases, the captured civilians or soldiers were exchanged through the MAC. However, the Israeli response to its own POWs being taken and not returned within a short span of time was to cross the border and act in kind—by kidnapping civilians and uniformed personnel of the other side.[9] The return from Jordan, at least, had to be approved by the higher echelons in order to deflect accountability from a military figure in the future.[10] That line of action was adopted as binding policy with the formation of the first Israeli commando unit in 1953 and the transformation of the IDF from a militia-type army into a well-organized force with clear battle doctrines.[11] Prior to that policy shift Israel used to distinguish between soldiers and civilians; even though Egypt seized two small Israeli fishing boats that were carried aboard a larger ship trying to cross the Suez Canal on November 6, 1953, Israel offered to return an Egyptian fishing boat captured on November 11. When the Egyptian authorities refused to foot the bill for storage of the Israeli ship and accommodations for its crew, in effect leaving them at the mercy of Israel, the latter decided to free the captured Egyptians and their boat without any financial demand or asking for the return of the Israeli boats.[12]

However, that was probably the last act of this kind. In October 1953 a special commando unit under a young and rising officer, Ariel Sharon, took over the IDF regular parachute unit and disseminated the idea later to be followed by the rest of the military that no hostile action would be left unanswered. In early December Moshe Dayyan, a hardliner and a protégé of Prime Minister and Defense Minister Ben Gurion, was nominated by the latter as the new chief of staff while removing his predecessor from office prematurely. Consequently, with Ben Gurion in self-imposed retirement as of December 1953, an inexperienced new Minister of Defense and a dovish prime minister—all the ingredients for a change in policy—were in place. Meanwhile, across the borders, a military figure, Adib Shishakli, became president of Syria in July 1953, only to flee his country in February 1954, leaving the scene for an all-out power struggle in Syria. About that time Nasser, the man behind the scenes in Egypt, became its official leader in November 1954. With two political systems hostile to Israel looking for national common denominators and Israel entangled in its own power struggle,[13] all positions along the confrontation lines became much less flexible than at any time before and perhaps even eager for a national unifying military test.

The changing strategic climate was reflected, *inter alia,* in the POW issue. Indeed, the 1954 collection of operational orders and planning blueprints reveal a change in the overall mood of the military.[14] Orders began to be issued aimed at taking POWs as one of the objectives of most strikes at the Egyptians, Jordanians, and Syrians. All operations were intended to put a high price tag on the small-scale warfare declared by all neighboring countries (with the exception of Lebanon) against Israel. However, with soldiers crossing the lines in reprisal activity, there is always the risk of losing soldiers and their being captured as POWs. Moreover, as of early 1954 Egypt began to launch its own operations intended to capture POWs.[15]

Even though the domestic tremors felt in Egypt and Syria were not present in Jordan until 1956, the lack of any significant barrier between the Kingdom of Jordan and Israel coupled with the activities of Nasser's sympathizers in the West Bank of the kingdom led to increased infiltration and terror activities in Israel in early 1954. Many times their perpetrators left from Egypt and found refuge later in Jordan. In the wake of one such activity, a seven-paratrooper unit crossed into Jordan in late June 1954, targeting an Arab Legion (Jordanian army) encampment south of Nablus. One wounded Israeli was left behind, with the capturing Jordanians convinced of his importance due to his advanced gear. Consequently, they did not rush to release him, sparking a series of Israeli commando raids aimed at capturing Jordanians who would serve as "bargaining chips."[16] In spite of its wide use, this practice was not deep-rooted in Israeli tactical behavior. Ben Gurion, one of the leading proponents of this policy, at the time in semi-retirement, wrote to the director general of the Ministry of Defense asking for an explanation once he heard that five Jordanian POWs were returned before the Israeli commando POW found his way home.[17] That policy did indeed eventually lead to an exchange. All of the above happened along the Jordanian front.

Along the Syrian front, Israel was at loss trying to figure out Damascus's POW policy. In the summer of 1954 Syria agreed to minor exchange deals based on a civilian for a civilian and returned an Israeli fishing boat captured earlier that year.[18] Alongside that, however, it continued to hold Israeli soldiers and civilians apprehended as far back as 1949.[19] Eight of the eleven Israelis held by the Syrians would be released in December 1963, after Israel launched a deliberate military operation that led to the capture of the family of the then "strong man" of Syria, Amin al-Hafiz. Perhaps the difference between the fate of those exchanged and those who were held in jail for prolonged periods had to do with the fact that the returned fishermen managed to inform Israel of their imminent seizure and later of the degree of intervention by foreign powers. None of those returned in the 1960s after long years in captivity were the subject of noteworthy Israeli discussions with other extra-regional powers. The captured fishing vessel became a cause célèbre right from the moment it was apprehended. Yet in spite of the tense relations with Syria, a way to reach an exchange was found.

With the Syrian POW issue deteriorating due to the apprehension of a five-man intelligence group on Syrian territory in December 1954, Israel resorted to some more radical action than kidnapping hostile soldiers. It went as far as to force a Syrian civilian plane to land in Israel, hoping that it would constitute a winning ace in bargaining with the Syrians.[20] The plane was released in order to not be seen in the international arena as a violation of international law. However, the mere fact that it was forced to land in Israel in hopes of an exchange did serve as a clear indication of the general mood of the Israeli decision makers at the time regarding effective, if not legitimate, ways to secure the release of Israeli POWs. That approach was typical of the way that the fighting troops interpreted the hostile POW policy. They believed that each of the wounded or dead had to be carried back to Israeli territory at almost any price, lest he fall into enemy hands, with a difficult process involved in securing his release.[21]

Successive Israeli governments have developed a tradition of sorts of shying away from passing binding resolutions unless driven into making such choices by pressing needs. The year 1954 did provide many opportunities for the cabinet, or at least for some ministers, to reach a critical juncture in the Israeli POW policies. Again, that was not the result of long-range strategic thinking, but rather of chaos and wrangling among the higher echelons, which led to, among other developments, the capture of Israelis by Egypt and Syria. The period preceding the 1956 Israeli-British-French operation against Egypt saw POW-related policy decisions. They were made on three distinct fronts:

1. The capture of two Israeli sabotage cells in Egypt in July 1954.
2. The September 1954 Egyptian detention of the Israeli ship *Bat Galim*, including its crew, while attempting to overcome the Egyptian ban on Israeli shipping through the Suez Canal.
3. The usual border skirmishes with combat troops falling into the hands of the other side. "Operation Cricket" in December 1954 marked a watershed line with the loss in Syrian territory of five Israeli POWs and the later suicide of one of them.

The accumulation of these episodes, all resulting from Israeli actions, raises obvious uncertainty as to the circumstances leading to each turn of events: Were any of the above sheer coincidences? Did any of them result from an aggressive premeditated policy that took into account the possibility of losing POWs? Were any of them attributable to anything else at all?

It is clear from the chronicles of Israeli history that the years 1954 and 1955 were among the most difficult in the international and regional arenas. Domestically as well as in the field of foreign relations Israel witnessed ominous signs. On January 26, 1954, the Foreign Minister of Israel, Moshe Sharett, was sworn in as the second prime minister, after the resignation of the founding father of the state, David Ben Gurion. Sharett served in this capacity until his replacement by Ben Gurion on November 3, 1955. However, this meagre chronology does not reveal the byzantine nature of relations behind the scenes as analyzed by a number of writers. Concisely put, five figures divided among three political sects (see below) influenced the security-related decision-making process in Israel at the time:

1. Ben Gurion, who lived in self-imposed semi-political exile in southern Israel (January 22, 1954–February 20, 1955 on leave from his position as Minister of Defense; January 22, 1954–November 3, 1955 on leave as prime minister), but who continued to be briefed by the top military establishment.
2. Lavon, a trade union leader with no prior security experience, Ben Gurion's replacement as the Minister of Defense (January 22, 1954), who was forced by Ben Gurion's followers to resign on February 21, 1955, leaving Prime Minister Sharett under the huge shadow cast on him by the new appointee as the Minister of Defense, Ben Gurion.
3. Moshe Sharett, the Foreign Minister of Israel and a great believer in the idealistic school in international relations, contrary to the neo-realist positions of Ben Gurion (Sharett served as the prime minister January 26, 1954–November 3, 1955; Foreign Minister May 15, 1948–June 18, 1956).
4. Lieutenant General Moshe Dayyan, the chief of staff, appointed by Ben Gurion in late December 1953 on the eve of Ben Gurion's departure, and who served until January 1958.
5. Shimon Peres, another of Ben Gurion's protégés, who served as the director general of the Ministry of Defense before and after Lavon's tenure.

Usually the public debate in Israel related to the events of 1954 would concentrate on the calamity in Egypt and the fact that the surviving members of the Israeli sabotage network were not released in the wake of Israel's 1956 Sinai campaign. However, the picture of relations among the abovementioned figures suggests much more.[22] There were three sects affecting Israeli security policy:

1. David Ben Gurion and (so-called by his contemporaries) "Ben Gurion's youngsters" (Dayyan and Peres), usually seen from the documentation as being on the "hawkish" side.
2. Moshe Sharett, a great believer in international law, and usually perceived as "dovish."
3. Pinhas Lavon, the inexperienced Minister of Defense, a "dove" turned into a "hawk" while serving.

All three mutually disagreed with each other, whereas Ben Gurion, who had his people—Dayyan and Peres—navigating the security policy equally, did not appreciate the two other sects.[23] In spite of these personal animosities, Israel had to implement a security policy, whether defensive or aggressive, which might end—as it did—in the loss of Israelis in enemy hands. Was there any connection among the three 1954 instances of Israeli losses? Not an obvious one. However, when Israeli prime minister Levi Eshkol spoke in 1964 in the context of the 1954 Egyptian debacle at the meeting of his ruling party executive committee, he used the term *a Pandora's box of catastrophes*. He clearly indicated that he did see a connection between all three incidents.[24] The occurrence of all three under one administration and the identity of the players raise two main questions: Did the figures deciding on the military operations consider at any early stage the possibility of capture by the Egyptian or the Syrian military or both and the arrangements necessary to release the people involved? Moreover, were they aware of the difference in status between Egyptian citizens secretly drafted as officers of the IDF and the sailors who were simply citizens on a political-military mission coordinated by the Israeli Ministry of Defense and the infiltration into Syria of a small, not particularly elite, military unit in full uniform that was not fully prepared for prison? On first sight, only the apprehension of the group on Syrian land deserved shelter under the wings of the Geneva Convention. Question two has to do with the attempts to release the people involved: Did Israel invest every possible effort in getting the people back? Alternatively, would it be correct to assume that at least one of the ruling sects had no particular interest in the release of the sabotage cell members?

In foreign relations, Israel had to deal with the implications of the upcoming British withdrawal from the Suez Canal area and the Western-Eastern blocs' competition for the sympathy of the Egyptian president, Nasser, who took over the presidency in late February 1954 after being the "strong man" since July 1952. Great Britain was about to evacuate the Suez Canal under a formal agreement with Egypt, leaving that strategic waterway in the hands of an archenemy of the State of Israel. At that time Israel was still under a U.S. arms embargo and dependent to a large degree on contributions collected from within the United States. The overall feeling, which grew firmer with advancing time, among the contemporary Israeli highest echelons, was that of being under siege. Looking at the 1954 Israeli position from a sixty-odd-years perspective clearly leads to the conclusion that at least some of the decision makers were desperately looking for a game breaker that would change the rules in favor of Israel. The orders to the sabotage cells in Egypt to move from planning to action in July 1954 reflected such an interest. Even though the Israeli public debate since 1954 has concentrated on the identity of the person who gave the order to launch the bungled operation, that question is no longer significant. The general impression today is that people in positions of authority at the time saw the sabotage activities as a means of perhaps persuading the Western powers not to sign an agreement with Egypt. Once that approach failed, a new tactical approach took over.

A commercial ship was sent through the Suez Canal so that its apprehension, should it occur, would expose the Egyptian denial of free shipping rights in violation of international conventions. This way, so this logic went, the powers would refrain from turning that waterway into the hands of a rogue country. Consequently, once the Egyptian-British agreement was signed on October 19, 1954[25] (after it was initially signed on July 27, 1954), both approaches failed, leaving Israel with no ammunition to encounter what was seen by its leaders as an ominous development. In September 1954 the representatives of the Israeli aggressive school, the members of the sabotage cells, were in jail, as well as the representatives of the dovish school, the civilians aboard the ship.[26] Unsurprisingly at this point, the records available today speak volumes about the benefits expected to stem from these two operations. However, there is no record available indicating a "Plan B" in case the operations failed. However, even the declassified documents available contain no reference whatsoever to such discussions.

The capture of two Israeli sabotage cells in Egypt in July 1954 led to three sets of issues that the Israeli government had to grapple with. One dealt with the status of the captured agents formally and through Israeli eyes. The second concerned the preparation, if any, for arrest. Finally, why were the agents not released in the wake of the 1956 Israeli operation and the ensuing POW exchange? Why was this exchange delayed until the aftermath of the 1967 War?

At the time of their arrest all of the members of the apprehended cells except one were Egyptian citizens. One was Tunisian born, holding French citizenship but legally residing in Egypt.[27] It is evident from many sources that at one point between the recruitment of the cells members in June and July 1951 and their activities in July 1954, they were all drafted to the Israeli Defense Forces and were granted officers' ranks.[28]

The legal proceedings in Egypt took place from late 1954 to early 1955, with some behind-the-scenes involvement of the Israeli government coordinated by the Military Intelligence Director, who had been sent to Paris by Dayyan to provide any appropriate help he could to the defendants.[29] It was an uphill battle because the Israeli predicament was obvious. Any action on behalf of the agents might have compromised the official Israeli line that all the Egyptian moves, including jail, trial, and conviction, were the actions of a new Egyptian leadership eager to validate its credentials among its people through the spread of anti-Israeli and anti-Semitic feelings.[30] Evidently, official Israel could not agree on the right attitude toward its captured agents. The founder and handler of the two cells insisted that Israel should distinguish between two groups of convicted agents: those who were jailed should remain in custody until some unspecified time, whereas the fate of the two condemned to death by hanging should be made into an official Israeli *casus belli*. While meeting with then Prime Minister Sharett, he proposed that a reserve brigade be called in and deployed along the border with Egypt so that the enemy would realize that hanging, unlike prison terms, might trigger a military confrontation.[31] Sharett listened but expressed no position and eventually, as history tells us, did not adopt that approach. Curiously enough, the detailed diary of Sharett, published in 1978, does not corroborate even the occurrence of that meeting.

The court proceedings and the verdict sparked intensive Israeli diplomatic activity but to no avail.[32] In spite of much effort by the Israeli government and assistance by foreign dignitaries, Nasser was able to mislead all interested parties within and outside the region by what he presented as possible peace moves until the hangings of two of the convicted agents and the imprisonment of the others.[33] With the superpowers probably much more interested in advancing those peace moves than in not alienating Nasser over the verdicts, it is no wonder that no meaningful U.S. or British intervention could be recorded.[34] Even the routine of exchanging enemies for Israelis did not work this time. That became evident through an incident involving a group of four high school students from the Gaza Strip who crossed by mistake into Israeli territory in early February 1954. Usually such cases were resolved by an exchange brokered by the MAC. In this case, the students were arrested by Israel before July 1954 and were not sentenced for unclear reasons, but once Israel needed some "bargaining chips," an Israeli court sentenced them to a period in jail along with other people crossing the border from Gaza. It is quite possible that the convictions for espionage were correct; however, the fact that December 1954 saw a number of such cases that were followed by a warning to Egypt through the U.S. State Department of a possible death sentence for Egyptian citizens convicted in Israel for espionage raises the obvious question of whether Israel planned to use its own proceedings to promote the idea of an exchange.[35] As Israel would later learn under different circumstances, Egypt did not care about getting its own back; quite the contrary, it gave Egypt an excuse to create some symmetry between the two protagonists—whenever their respective security situations were threatened, both sides had every right to take steps against any guilty party. This point was even reinforced by the "personal-cloaked" assessment of the Israeli Ministry of Foreign Affairs, dating back to December 30, 1954, that the Egyptians had no interest in being too tough on the defendants, with the exception of the two who would later be executed.[36] That internal and secret evaluation was not shared with any player outside of the Ministry. After all, Israel had two condemned persons to rescue and a number of imprisoned persons and no viable international help.[37]

Two members of the sabotage cells were executed in January 1955 without Israel having admitted that they had operated as Israeli agents. All efforts to rescue them and to free the imprisoned had been made under the pretense that they were Jews being persecuted simply as an expression of anti-Semitism. However, knowing the truth of the matter so well, Israel continued to try to help the prisoners, always careful not to admit its direct responsibility and involvement in their activities.

It is evident that between January 1955 and the POW exchange in the wake of the Sinai operation in November and December 1956, Israel was at loss and could not devise any way to get the agents back. However, that was not all due to the Egyptian position. With the conclusion of the Egyptian court proceedings in January 1955, the status of the persons in question was formally changed in the eyes of world opinion from possibly innocent defendants into convicted criminals. Moreover, Egypt, expecting international pressure over the upcoming political trial, had placed the prisoners in a criminal, not political, jail. That meant that according to the Egyptian version, which was adopted de facto post-trial by the international community, the prisoners were no more than Egyptian citizens acting against their own homeland. Without any Israeli admission to the contrary, which would have exposed the prisoners to even harsher charges and perhaps even more penalties, there was not much that official Israel could do.

Actually, official Jerusalem was extremely frustrated because it clearly realized that it had no viable course of action that could lead to the release. Moreover, the commander of the unit responsible for the failed activities was replaced in late 1954. His replacement, preferring not to be identified with anything occurring before his time, discharged all active personnel involved in the affair. His actions had two simultaneous consequences directly affecting the status of the imprisoned agents:

1. On the personal level of assisting the prisoners and their families, Israel lacked the means to support them financially. Even if there had been a way to secure the necessary funds, there was no way to get in touch with the agents or their families. Moreover, Israel was very careful not to use any official or semi-official channel to raise sympathy for the agents or their families, having been so harmed by exposure of its humanitarian efforts on their behalf. As if this were not enough, even though Israel did not officially and openly admit its responsibility for their actions, the bare facts were undeniable—and those facts stripped Israel of any way to approach the already unsympathetic administration in Washington, whose sites in Egypt were the intended targets of the two cells.[38] Consequently, one major potential way to obtain humanitarian assistance was permanently eliminated for Israel.
2. On the structural level, the responsibility for the fate of the prisoners was changed from intelligence to the newly formed "Committee on the Zion Prisoners in Arab Lands" (probably in September 1955).[39] The committee was in charge of finding solutions to the issue of several Israeli agents who were local or dispatched from

> Israel and apprehended in Egypt and Iraq. The Iraqi case is not covered in this book because its connection, if any, to the topic of the current study is negligible. However, the five-man committee was chaired by a senior Mossad agent and its members included one more Mossad, one from the Foreign Ministry—a leading expert on Arab affairs who would play a role in the POW exchange after the June 1967 War—one from the internal security services, and one from the IDF Directorate of Military Intelligence. In sum, the minutes of the committee do confirm the lack of stable contact with the prisoners. The six-page document does not reveal any operational planning. However, the way it was edited, probably by the chairing Mossad official, might indicate an interest in finding as much intelligence as possible concerning the agents' location, most likely with the intention of a rescue attempt.

Apparently even their exact location was unknown until the Egyptians allowed three mothers of the convicted into Israel. Consequently, in July 1956 the Mossad could inform the Foreign Ministry that the 1954 convicts were being held at the time in the Tura prison by Hilwan, south of Cairo, and that one female prisoner was incarcerated in the central Cairo prison.[40] Whatever the operational planning was, the dispersion of the people excluded any possibility of a raid. However, prior to the launching of Musketeer Operation (the tripartite British-French-Israeli attack on Egypt known by the Israelis as the Kadesh/Sinai Operation), Israeli intelligence wrongly assumed that upon commencement of operations chaos would engulf Egypt and the agents would be in grave danger.[41] Consequently, Israeli intelligence initiated an operation, based on a prior plan, aimed at releasing the Israeli agents through a commando raid on the prison in which they were wrongly supposed to be held.[42]

The Israeli Sinai campaign, from October 29, 1956, to November 7, 1956, led to the capture of about 5,500 Egyptian POWs. However, even before discussing their return to Egypt and if it should include the members of the two Israeli cells, Dayyan decided that it would be POWs for POWs and no more.[43] Not including them in the deal once again raises the issue of how the Israeli agents were prepared for falling into the custody of the Egyptian authorities, if at all, and why were they not included in the exchange.

After being chosen for the mission, most of the people involved found ways to get out of Egypt for short periods and to be trained in Israel.[44] In his single testimony years later, the case officer (the agent in charge) claimed to have instructed the agents to evade any question during the first twenty-four hours of the interrogation in order to give the others an opportunity to flee Egypt.[45] This is the only reference to the issue of preparation for such a situation in the body of documents consulted for the current study; even the book based on the memoirs of the agents involved does not mention any such preparation or any briefing beyond that.[46] The two cells became operative and were both apprehended in 1954. Is it possible that during that time, from 1951 to 1954, the agents were not briefed on the possibility that the Egyptian authorities might capture them? Moreover, the escape passports promised by Israel were never supplied, and the members of the cells did not know the details of an emergency plan, if there was one. All of that dramatically curtailed the agents' ability to leave everything behind in case they needed to and to put together a way out.[47]

The chain of mediocrity and the lack of professionalism did not stop there. In spite of a deliberate exchange process before the 1956 Israeli campaign, these agents were not included. Why were they not released at that time and during the ensuing POW exchange and what was the nature of the change responsible for their very late release after the 1967 War? Perhaps the key figure here was the chief of staff, General Dayyan.[48] He was indeed the link between the military operations of 1954 and the 1956 Sinai campaign. Prime ministers changed, as did Ministers of Defense; only Dayyan stayed on as the chief of staff. Moreover, all relevant 1954 intelligence figures had already found their way out of uniforms or out of the intelligence community. Dayyan was in a unique position to enjoy a moment of glory and bring the agents home. But that was not to be the case. From the meagre information dealing with his conduct it appears that he was not involved in a meaningful way in the exchange process. The only exception was his instruction to the military personnel of the occupied Gaza Strip to keep local dignitaries (including the brother of the Egyptian leader Abd al-Hakim Amir) for future exchanges that would include "Egyptian Jews, POWs, and the Cairo convicts" (in this order).[49] That was not the first display of almost indifferent and definitely passive behavior by Dayyan. As early as May 5, 1955, during a meeting with Ben Gurion, Dayyan suggested capturing "Egyptians" for a possible exchange.[50] This was in spite of his knowledge of the failure of that approach on that very issue a short while earlier (see the beginning of this chapter). Releasing these Israeli agents continued to stay on the Israeli agenda in the aftermath of the 1956 and 1967 military campaigns until their release in 1968. Clearly, as will be presented in the coming chapters, official Israel did not want them back home. Why? Without a clear-cut answer to that, all explanations are valid or invalid to the same degree.

In an atmosphere of a vanity competition among the Israeli leaders of 1954–1955, with the Israeli intelligence playing to the tune of all players, more Israeli prisoners were taken victim. The issue of freedom of navigation in the Red Sea Straits and the Suez Canal triggered the second episode after the falling of the two cells in Cairo and Alexandria: the September 1954 Egyptian detention of the Israeli ship *Bat Galim*, including its crew, while attempting to overcome the Egyptian ban on Israeli shipping through the Suez Canal.

In February 1954, against the background of the aforementioned imminent British-Egyptian agreement to hand over the Suez Canal to Egypt, Israel decided to focus world attention on the issue of the Egyptian ban on Israeli shipping through the straits of Eilat/Aqaba and the Suez Canal, in violation of the 1888 Constantinople Convention.[51]

As was the case with the sabotage cells turned active, here again the burden of implementing the policy was on the Military Intelligence Directorate. The crew had been picked by the Commander of the Navy from his sailors; however, all other dimensions of the plan fell within the realm of the intelligence (authorities). The contemporary documents reveal an elaborate plan, including an itemized budget and careful selection of the participants, among other steps, indicating a thorough preparation process.[52] Even though the temporary Director of Military Intelligence was one of the early planners of the operation, he relinquished all authority to the permanent director upon his return from studies overseas.[53] Between March 1954 and May 1955—that is, throughout the period of activities by the cells in Egypt, including the test ship and Operation Cricket—one hand was in charge: that of Colonel Gibli.

Assuming that the policy guidelines were imposed by political figures, still the planning, financing, and implementation were all left to the colonel. Indeed, in all three cases, and please see the Syrian segment in the following pages, the same POW-related deficiencies were exposed: no preparation for the possibility of falling into the custody of the enemy, no cover story when applicable, and no civilian supervision over the actual activity. In all three incidents, the people on the ground reported back to whomever they believed to be the legitimate representative of the appropriate command, but there is no record of the military personnel informing the civilian authorities in full and in real time of the final outcome.

On the policy level, the picture provided by the contemporary documents available today is no less complicated. It reveals a rather fierce brawl between two sects within the decision-making circles, each breaking with its own previous policy behavior with the bone of contention being the right reaction to the Egyptian naval blockade. In 1954 and until the aftermath of the 1956 operation, the Straits of Tiran leading to the Israeli port of Eilat, as well as the Jordanian port of Aqaba, were under a permanent Egyptian blockade, and the Suez Canal was tightly closed to any shipping that had to do with Israel—from any size payload to full-fledged commercial ships. However, Eilat might have been more crucial to Israel because it provided an outlet to the (then) awakening Far East. Moreover, making Eilat into a faraway settlement within Israel might have served the Egyptian interest of cutting off the southern part of Israel, the Negev desert, from the main population centers and paving the way for a takeover as a prelude to an intervention in the Hashemite

Kingdom of Jordan. The main benefit of an attempt to break the blockade along this route was that it was much less central than the Suez Canal and might have provided Israel with a small victory, while reducing the risk of Israeli sailors being taken prisoner by Egypt. Shipping through the Canal carried many more strategic risks, whereas it did not add too much to Israel's economy considering that the main Eastern countries were just recovering from World War II and were not as significant to Israel as they are today.[54] The power struggle between the two sects of decision makers in Jerusalem was expressed through the question: Which predictable failure will give Israel more legitimacy while arguing its case for free shipping before the UN? In this case the question as to whether Israeli citizens would be taken prisoner was of no significance to the powers that were. That would have been a demonstration of the Egyptian refusal to abide by international law, and any price in POWs/hostages was acceptable.[55] Along a more cynical line it can also be argued that bad treatment of the POWs/hostages might have provided the (on leave) Ben Gurion and Dayyan, a military commander eager to fight Egypt, with an even stronger casus belli.[56]

On July 15, 1954, one day after the second operation of the Israeli agents on Egyptian territory and just a couple of days before the initial signing of the Anglo-Egyptian agreement, the Minister of Defense instructed the chief of staff to "move as early as possible through the Straits of Tiran the recently purchased ship under the Israeli flag while providing aerial support to the vessel."[57] Even though no mention was made of any possibility of falling into enemy custody, the aerial cover did provide a glimpse into the concern for the life of the crew. With the members of the Cairo and Alexandria sabotage cells being seized between July 23 and the end of July along with the July 27 agreement regarding the Canal, nationalist tempers took over in Egypt. Ignoring those developments, the groundwork for a blockade breaker trip continued. Even if Egypt had any thought of turning a blind eye on a single Israeli boat crossing the Canal, and there is no indication to substantiate such a policy, it would have risked its own hard-acquired sympathetic relationship with the people. After all, concurrent with the confrontation with Israel, the Egyptian leadership had to meet the threat posed by the Muslim Brotherhood, which culminated in an assassination attempt on President Nasser in late October 1954.

Could any of this escape the observing eye of the Israeli decision makers? That is impossible to answer, and yet as of early August 1954, facing that multifaceted diplomatic and military challenge, Israel reinforced its decision to once again challenge Egypt. In late July to early August 1954, Sharett, the prime minister and Minister of Foreign Affairs, and Lavon, the Minister of Defense, were entangled in a ferocious power struggle over responsibilities. The apparent issue at stake was control over the Israeli representation to the MAC. Lavon believed that he should be in exclusive control because the MAC activity fell within the mandate of the military. The prime minister advanced the point that the MAC activity was more diplomatic than military in nature and that in any case the activities of the defense establishment had to be carried out according to the cabinet's instruction.[58] That feud was not clearly resolved until, at the earliest, deliberations took place regarding the dispatch of the test boat along the Suez Canal. Furthermore, the picture drawn from Sharett's testimony shows that, unlike dovish Sharett, Lavon became extremely activist in his security orientation. That meant that he advocated for radical steps to be taken against Israel's Arab enemies, steps that were not in line with Israel's traditional policies and definitely not to the liking of Sharett and his cabinet colleagues.[59] However, whether or not Dayyan, the chief of staff and the protégé of Ben Gurion, would adopt at least some of Lavon's ideas was not clear. After all, Dayyan was a hard-liner and his support or lack thereof could have had a significant bearing on whether Ben Gurion decided to continue his self-imposed retirement or to take back the reins of power, removing Sharett and others from their positions. In any case, Sharett's feeling of despair over his lack of influence in the shaping of Israel's security policy was even transmitted in a rather definite way to the U.S. administration.[60]

Amid these personal and intra-cabinet intrigues, a decision had to be made regarding the next move that Israel hoped would sabotage the transition from an initialed Anglo-Egyptian agreement into a binding international instrument. As early as February 1954, Sharett got the cabinet to approve the sending of Israeli-bound cargo aboard a ship flying a foreign flag through the Suez Canal and an Israeli ship through the Eilat/Aqaba Gulf.[61] Based on the facts known to the public, it was not an obvious decision: the Egyptian blockade over the Straits could not be denied, whereas the passage of goods through the Canal was allowed at times and was banned at other times. Still, in tonnage terms the goods shipped to and from Israel in 1954 was triple the number for 1953.[62] Israel could not decipher a pattern in the Egyptian behavior in the Canal—in spite of Egypt's declared policy of banning any passage of any goods and ships bound for Israel. With the final signing of the Anglo-Egyptian agreement approaching, Israel found itself in limbo. It did need a crisis in order to underline the usual Egyptian violations of the principle of free passage for all nations, Israel included, through the Canal. However, in the failed clandestine effort that led to the arrest and finally the execution of Israeli agents, one road had not been taken: diplomacy. With Sharett being a great believer in a diplomatic approach and having difficulty controlling the military, he could find only one way to prove his point: to send a test ship that would be apprehended by the Egyptians and its crew thrown into Egyptian jail—Sharett himself being supplied with the necessary backing for petitioning the UN Security Council. Sharett, while ignoring the interests of the United States and Great Britain in finalizing the bilateral agreement, wrongly believed that they would unconditionally stand for the principle of justice. After all, they had supported Israel in September 1951 with UN Security Council Resolution 95 that condemned Egypt for its violation of the principle of free passage.[63] Yet Sharett did not take into account Egypt's changing circumstances: from monarchy to republic, from a pro-Western regime to an object of courtship for Western players in the context of the Cold War, and perhaps above all, enjoying unconditional Soviet support.[64] However, Sharett's ploy was obvious to the United States, leading it to a rather noncommittal if not outright hostile policy toward Israel. Parker T. Hart, Director of the Office of Near Eastern Affairs of the State Department, was clear in his words to General Mahmoud Riad, Head of the Arab Section, Egyptian Foreign Ministry, and member of the Egyptian Delegation to the General Assembly: "I felt more inclined to believe that the Israel Government had sent the *Bat Galim* in the belief that she would be seized and with the intention of forcing the hand of the United States on a matter of principle involving Suez Canal traffic."[65]

With this assessment unknown to the Israeli decision makers, the cabinet and military consultations continued unabated—even after the capture of the Israeli sabotage cells in Egypt—with no indication in available documentation of any party making a connection between the two.[66] Unfortunately, Sharett's misconception was not the only motivation behind the *Bat Galim* affair.[67] The chief of staff wrote in his operational diary that he had discussed the matter with Ben Gurion. In this conversation between an incumbent senior official and a private citizen, they discussed ways of using the *Bat Galim* issue as a casus belli. In Dayyan's mind, the incident gave Israel the opportunity to occupy the Gaza Strip (and put an end to terrorist activities emanating from the Strip). Further, it could help Israel sink Egyptian naval vessels. The reconstructed picture of the motivations behind the incident is clear: all war-minded Israeli decision makers perceived the attempt to send *Bat Galim* through the Suez Canal as the trigger for Israeli-initiated military actions.[68]

In early August 1954 the Director of Military Intelligence notified his agent in Greece that the route of the test ship had been changed and that now it would move along the more easily discovered and public path of the Suez Canal.[69] On September 9, the Minister of Defense instructed the chief of staff that the boat, *Bat Galim*, should leave Eastern Africa for the Suez Canal on September 14.[70] However, once again the leadership rift between Dayyan, the chief of staff, a member of the unofficial Ben Gurion camp, and his traditional adversary, Lavon, the Minister of Defense, on one side, and the prime minister and Minister of Foreign Affairs, Sharett, on the other, led to a change of plan. Now the vessel had to go through the Canal and not the Straits, exposing its crew to a greater risk of falling into enemy hands.[71] Four days later, the prime minister ordered a delay in the departure of the ship in order to allow more time for diplomacy.

Actual action was not taken until September 20, 1954, concurrent with the trial proceedings of the Israeli sabotage cells, probably indicating the relentless Israeli effort to inform and underline the Egyptian violations of international instruments on the eve of the British withdrawal.

On September 28, 1954, upon the arrival of the ship to the southern entrance to the Canal, an Egyptian force stopped it and its entire crew was apprehended.[72] Apparently, the convenient timing for Israel and the inconvenient timing for Egypt on the eve of the final signing of the Anglo-Egyptian agreement were not enough. Further, the public impression created by the United States that the embargo on Israeli shipping was over was not true. Actually, the United States was furious because the Israeli move was induced by its interest in:

1. Creating complications during the final stages of the Suez base negotiations,
2. Embarrassing the US in its efforts to lead the GOE [Government of Egypt] into a more constructive position in the ME,
3. Maintaining Arab-Israel tension in an effort to compel the UN and West to force the Arabs to meet with Israel.[73]

The international players as well as some domestic players within the Israeli political system met the Israeli move with indifference and in some cases with enmity.[74] All hopes for the international community led by the United States to stand by Israel were dashed. The *Bat Galim* incident was resolved in early 1955 by the release of the cargo and crew, apparently due to Egyptian interest in avoiding any discussion of its rights in the Canal with the UN Security Council.[75] Israel released as quid pro quo the Egyptians apprehended and sentenced to prison terms in the context of the sabotage network in Egypt.[76] Apparently, similar policy was also behind the Egyptian effort to delay any discussion by the MAC claiming that many more complaints were waiting to be discussed.[77]

THE DECEMBER 1954 "OPERATION CRICKET" AS A WATERSHED LINE

The bungled "Operation Cricket" (night of December 8 and 9, 1954) could not have come at a worse time than it did. Israeli agents were awaiting the verdict in Cairo and Israeli seamen were in Egyptian hands after their failed attempt to cross the Canal. Yet a group of five Israeli soldiers was sent across the Syrian border in order to change the batteries in a monitoring device attached to a phone pole not far from a Syrian outpost on the Golan Heights.[78] As reported to the cabinet by the Minister of Defense in its January 16, 1955, meeting, the soldiers chosen were not right for the job and had been ill prepared. Judging from the context, the hidden message was that they had been ill prepared for the possibility of arrest by the Syrian military.[79] As is customary in a hierarchical system, the minister asked the chief of staff prior to the cabinet meeting for a detailed account of the incident (request: January 14). The minister addressed his colleagues on January 16. On the very next day, the 17, the chief of staff, in clear defiance of the statement by his direct superior, the minister, said in a written statement that the task had been assigned to the most highly trained military unit and approved by the legitimate military authority.[80]

Here again, the small, insignificant fact that Ben Gurion did not hold any official position did not deter him from investigating the matter. That, probably with the help of the chief of staff, Dayyan, was in clear violation of the right work procedure of any government. Ben Gurion was concerned in a way reminiscent of his prolonged reaction to the Egyptian calamity, with the issue of "who gave the orders." Once he found out from Dayyan that the authorizing officer was the IDF Director of Operations/Directorate of Operations, he turned his wrath once again upon the Minister of Defense, Lavon, rather than on the chief of staff, his protégé.[81] In this case, once again, the leadership split dramatically affected how Israel dealt with the captured troops. The pressing issue for the decision makers was the release of the captured soldiers, not ensuring a sincere and unbiased inquiry into the circumstances leading to their apprehension. Typically enough, the suicide of one of the cell members and the return of his body without the release of the rest of the group[82] diverted attention from the "who gave the orders" issue, as had been the case of the calamity in Egypt with the glorification of the soldier who committed suicide in order not to betray his country. Israel in 1954 could not investigate itself; the dead hero provided a pretext for granting him a place in the Israeli pantheon without too many questions asked. Moreover, the Syrian prosecution of the soldiers in effect eased domestic pressures in Israel and focused the attention of decision makers on that potential violation of the Geneva Convention and on ways to counter that.[83]

The old familiar modus operandi was much more convenient and indeed very much in line with customary policy. The immediate Israeli reaction to the incident was almost impulsive: Dayyan instructed the IDF Directorate of Operations to devise a series of operations aimed at seizing Syrian and Egyptian officers and soldiers and forcing both Egypt (*Bat Galim* and the agents) and Syria (Cricket Operation POWs) into a speedy exchange of POWs. As soon as December 10, a series of operational orders were presented: one to take place in Syria and two in Egypt.[84] Instead of conducting land operations, four days after the capture of the Israeli soldiers in Syria, Israel forced a Syrian civilian passenger plane to land in Israel, hoping for a speedy exchange—POWs for passengers.[85] The official military document simply stated, "creating pressure leading to the release of the team held in Syria."[86] That forced landing sparked almost a clash of titans between Lavon and Sharett. The latter, usually known for his polite and diplomatic language, did not just disapprove of the action. He depicted it as worthy of "jungle behavior." His reaction in real time and later did not leave the military any alternative but to let the plane take off without any gain for Israel or movement on the POW issue.[87] Based on the testimony of Sharett at the time, the Minister of Defense still tried to save face by reporting at the weekly cabinet meeting on December 19 that once it had been verified that the five Israeli soldiers were alive, the plane had been released. That attitude not only alienated the military, which looked upon taking "bargaining chips" as a necessary first step in getting the soldiers back, it also lowered Israeli public opinion and led to a no confidence vote at the Israeli parliament. In the wake of a stormy debate, the coalition under Sharett prevailed, but the discussion clearly manifested a growing gap between the cabinet under Sharett and the Israeli public.[88] In hindsight the prime minister commented that Israel as a state player could not afford subnational tactics in order to get its soldiers back. This definitely constituted rather significant input to the oral tradition of POW policy and undoubtedly challenged the traditional "prisoner for prisoner" strategy. However, like the Egypt tragedy, the Cricket Operation catastrophe resulted to some extent from the lack of open briefing channels between the military—basically the chief of staff, his superior, the Minister of Defense, and his own superior, the prime minister. The personal tragedy was perhaps the only reason that the "who gave the orders" issue was not raised in this case as well.

Perhaps one more lesson that can be drawn from comparing the abovementioned cases to another one on the Jordanian side is that two lines of POW policy could be defined in 1954 and perhaps until the early or mid-1960s. Whenever the issue climbed up the hierarchy, it became more complicated, sparking the interest of the highest echelons. It was also reflected in the local media, making any mutual Israeli-Arab concessions more unlikely. However, on the tactical level, a centuries-old tradition of "mine for yours" could continue unabated as long as the top politicians did not intervene. One such case involved an Israeli sergeant of an elite unit that was left behind by his fellow soldiers falling into Jordanian captivity—an episode that shaped the Israeli tactical approach to the issue of POW exchange for many years to come.[89]

The reprisal period produced a large number of incidents in which Israeli and Arab soldiers were taken as POWs by the other side. That routine of attacks and counterattacks while taking prisoners also produced a well-defined practice of reacting to prisoner taking by a raid aimed at taking hostile troops as prisoners and then implementing a mutual exchange. However, even though the small border conflagrations were definitely tactical and a far cry from the two 1954 encounters with Egypt (the sabotage cells and the ship case) or even "Operation Cricket" with Syria, the highest Israeli policy and military authorities still insisted on approving each and every border crossing for the purpose of taking hostages/POWs for exchange.[90]

Perhaps the most outstanding case in question is that of a sergeant who was left behind across Jordanian lines in a reprisal operation in late June 1954, contrary to the new standards that the IDF was trying to disseminate among its troops at that time.[91] These standards came in the wake of an Israeli operation within Jordanian sovereignty in which one trooper went unnoticed, and later his dead body was found. Since then the Israeli high command instructed that all crossing into enemy territory would return whatever the price.[92] In the 1954 case, the sergeant had given his consent to be left behind because carrying him, as badly wounded as he was and with sunset approaching, would have endangered his fellow combatants. That improvised decision on the ground ran contrary to the interests of the Israeli military. While it was trying to instill values into the soldiers, the exact opposite of those values played out on the ground. However, because diplomatic contacts with the Jordanians through the MAC failed, the IDF allowed, and actually even planned, a series of three operations inside Jordan in order to capture the necessary "bargaining chips."[93] One of the peculiarities of the evolving situation was that even Great Britain, at the time the official defender of the Hashemite Kingdom, did not oppose that Israeli policy. Perhaps it even discreetly agreed to it in spite of its basic position of not condoning such actions.[94] In late October 1954, after Israel detained five uniformed Jordanian personnel, an exchange was arranged through the MAC.[95]

That Jordanian-Israeli encounter and later the exchange illuminated an additional dimension in their mutual relations. Both countries had a clear interest in calming down the border area. In 1954 and 1955 it gradually became an arena of the Arab-Israeli conflict second only to the deteriorating conditions along the Egyptian-Israeli border, especially along the Gaza Strip confrontation line. Egyptian-operated terrorists crossed into Israel, acted against civilian and military targets, and returned to Jordan, exposing it to Israeli reprisal.[96] That emerging situation along with an aggressive Egyptian policy aimed at unseating King Hussein worried the young and inexperienced king. After long deliberations and in the wake of an Israeli proposal to renew their mutual commitment to the Geneva Convention regarding the treatment of POWs, such an agreement was finally reached and signed in mid-May 1955 by the respective representatives to the MAC.[97] Israel hoped that the agreement would lead to a more comprehensive understanding on mutual conduct along the borderline, but to no avail. Both countries had enough domestic constraints beyond the scope of this book to not proceed further, in spite of the Israeli public's interest in reaching some agreement with Jordan, to the benefit of both countries that would ensure quiet along the borderline.

Strength and deterrence might be the best motto to represent the Israeli POW policy from 1953 to 1956. Briefly, this meant that any taking of an Israeli POW would almost automatically, even though it had to be approved by the civilian decision makers, spark a chain of events that would inflict damage on the capturing player and lead to the arrest of one or more of its troops. However, this concept was effective as long as it concerned tactical conflagrations along the borderlines, but meant almost nothing once the confrontations acquired more and more of a strategic dimension.

In many aspects the early period of Israel's independence discussed in this chapter provides some glimpses into the future. Undoubtedly, the higher echelons of the Israeli political and military systems that at times in the 1950s were interwoven preferred military action to any other approach to gain the release of Israelis in hostile prisons. The best solution at that time was to undertake a direct rescue operation that would end up with the prisoners back home. Failing that, the second best solution would be to acquire enemy figures, preferably high up in the hierarchy, political or military, for the purpose of an exchange. That approach, being as effective as it was, came to be known as "bargaining chips" and would be outlawed by the Israeli judicial branch years later. Failing all that, only by unorthodox measures could an exchange be achieved. Any analysis of the first years of POWs' and other prisoners' issues cannot avoid the unpleasant conclusion that people operating for Israel, whether in disguise or in uniform, were not prepared for the possibility of being imprisoned by the enemy. That phenomenon would be observed in a series of POW-related cases until, as a result of the 1973 War, it would be corrected. Moreover, Israel has never been too keen on admitting that certain people have fallen prey to this phenomenon and consequently deserve open and full acceptance and backing by the Israeli authorities. Many of these characteristics of the Israeli POW modus operandi are still valid today. They will be studied in the following chapters.

Structurally speaking, as early as the mid-1950s Israel created a governmental body to follow all efforts to release its prisoners on a regular basis and to take an active part in the release attempts. That early beginning would undergo a series of changes in the years to come, but one clear connection still exists among all of these bodies—they have all been members of the intelligence community and therefore privy to all information, barring nothing, available to Israel. This access is a further indication of the priority given to the POW issue among the Israeli decision makers to this day.

NOTES

1. IDFA/626/1957/10, IDF Operations Directorate, Reprisal Activities, n.d., ca. 1965; 626/1957/ 11; 626/1957/13; 626/1957/29; 636/1956/7; 636/1956/12; 636/1956/13, Syria (operation *Pilegesh* [mistress]), Egypt (operation *Yitro* 1+2 [Jethro]), n.d.; 636/1956/32; 637/1956/15, IDF Operations Directorate, n.d., ca. 1955; 637/1956/17; 637/1956/18; 637/1956/

56; 675/1974/ 184, Reprisal Activities, 1950–1953 (Until the Establishment of Unit 101), n.d., ca. 1954.

2. [UK] NA/FO1032/2532, from Control Commission for Germany (British Element), to London, April 6, 1950.

3. UN General Assembly Resolution 427 (V): Measures for the Peaceful Solution of the Problem of Prisoners of War, December 14, 1950. http://www.un.org/en/ga/search/view_doc.asp?symbol=A/RES/427(V).

4. [UK] NA/FO1032/2532, from Control Commission for Germany (British Element), to London, October 7, 9, 1950. http://www.worldlii.org/int/other/UNGARsn/1950/102.pdf; Walton K. Richardson, "Prisoners of War as Instruments of Foreign Policy," in *The Use of Force, Human Rights, and General International Legal Issues*, ed. Richard B. Lillich and John N. More, *International Law Studies* 62 (1980): 328–29.

5. IDFA/1338/1979/3/2/2–180, from Israel Delegation HJK-I MAC [Hashemite Jordan Kingdom—Israel Mixed Armistice Committee), to Acting Chairman, H[shemite]J[ordan]K[ingdom]-I[srael] MAC, January 4, 1951; IDFA/1338/1980/210, IDF History Branch, *POWs—apprehension and release*, March 31, 1971.

6. IDFA/1338/1979/3/2/2–180, IDFA/626/1957/10, IDF Operations Directorate, Reprisal Activities, n.d., ca. 1965.

7. IDFA/675/1974/178, Reprisal activities, 1950–1953 (until the establishment of unit 101), n.d., ca. 1954.

8. IDFA/79/2007/37, from IDF Manpower Directorate, to all Military Regions, May 30, 1950; IDFA/79/2007/37, from IDF Manpower Directorate, to Chief of Staff, July 19, 1951.

9. IDFA/540/1955/114, Border activity, monthly report no. 8, August 14, 1953; IDFA717/1979/1338, Monthly Report from the Israeli delegation to the MAC, April 1954. Some raw data in this context: that practice was accepted as the IDF norm to the point that legacy cites of combat units mention them to this day: 202nd Israeli Paratroopers Brigade, "Operation Cigarette," 1954, http://202.org.il/Pages/tagmul/peulot/tfisatmitzrim.php; also cf. IDFA/8/1956/46, regarding the Jordanian interrogation of the Israeli POW from the June 29, 1954, Israeli raid on a Jordanian outpost.

10. Cf. [UK] NA/FO/371/111106/1033/221/54/, from Amman, to [Jordanian] Jerusalem, September 17, 1954.

11. Perhaps the first operation intended, *inter alia*, in writing for the taking of hostile POWs took place on April 2, 1954, IDFA/626/1957/10, [1956?], IDF Operations Directorate, Reprisal activities, n.d., ca. 1956.

12. *al-Ha-Mishmar, Herut*, November 8, 1953; *Ma'ariv*, November 23, 1953; IDFA/1338/1979/717, January 1954 activity summary of the Israeli delegation to the MAC, February 20, 1954.

13. Moshe Sharett, *Personal Diary*, vol. 2 (1954–1955) (Tel Aviv: Ma'ariv, 1978), 554. One must wonder how much of the border activity was carried out with the prime minister's consent or even knowledge. Sharett diary hints quite strongly at the possibility that he was not privy to at least one of those activities carried out on July 10, 1954, in Egyptian territory.

14. IDFA/637/1956/12.

15. Cf. IDFA/1338/1979/717, March 1954 activity summary of the Israeli delegation to the MAC, April 5, 1954; IDFA/1338/1979/717, April 1954 activity summary of the Israeli delegation to the MAC, May 5, 1954.

16. IDFA/8/1956/46, [n.d.], Intelligence Interrogation report, n.d.: [UK] NA/FO/371/111104/VR1091/173/, from [Jordanian] Jerusalem, to London, August 14, 1954; cf. Meir Har-Zion, *Pirkei Yoman* [Hebrew: Chapters of a Diary] (Tel Aviv: Levin-Epstein, 1968), 219–22; Gil'ad Sharon, *Sharon—The Life of a Leader* (Tel Aviv: Matar, 2011), 97–98.

17. David Ben Gurion Archive, 1954, September 5–11 Correspondence file, BG letter, September 5, 1954.

18. *Ma'ariv*, July 6, 1954; [UK] NA/FO/371/111104/VR109/174/, from Damascus, to London, August 16, 1954; *Davar*, August 16, 19, 1954; [UK] NA/FO/371/111104/VR109/179/, from Damascus, to London, August 18, 1954.

19. Yehezkel Hameiri, *Shevuei Suria: sipuram shel israelim be tzinok suri* [Hebrew: Captives in Syria: The Story of Israelis in Syrian Confinement] (Tel Aviv: Am Oved, 1965); *Davar*, December 22, 1963.

20. IDFA/637/1956/15, [1956/15], IDF Operations Directorate, n.d., ca. 1955; *Ma'ariv*, December 12–19, 1954; *Davar*, December 13–15, 1954; Sharett did not record any of his whereabouts between late November 1954 and early January 1955. Moshe Sharett, *Personal Diary*, vols. 2, 3 (1954–1955) (Tel Aviv: Ma'ariv, 1978).

21. IDFA/626/1957/10, IDF Operations Directorate, *Reprisal activities;* cf. Har-Zion, *Pirkei Yoman*, 219–22.

22. The following analysis is based on the following sources: Yechiam Weitz, "A Riddle Named Lavon", review of *Iyyunim bi-tekumat Israel,* 9 [Hebrew: Studies in Israel's Revival] (1999): 560–67; Yemimah Rosenthal and Luiz Fisher, ed., *Moshe Sharett, the Second Prime Minister; Selected Documents related to His Life Chapters (1894–1965)* (Jerusalem: Israel State Archive, 2006), 488–97.

23. Cf. David Ben Gurion Archive, Correspondence file, January 27–31, 1967, BG: letter, January 30, 1967.

24. "David Ben Gurion letter," *Davar*, October 16, 1966; David Ben Gurion Archive, Correspondence File, October 6–10, 1966, BG: letter, October 9, 1966.

25. U.S. Department of State, "Anglo-Egyptian Agreement Regarding the Suez Canal Base, Cairo, October 19, 1954," in *The Suez Canal Problem; July 26–September 22, 1956; a Documentary Publication* (Washington: Department of State Publication 6392, 1956), 22–23.

26. Cf. Yemimah and Fisher, *Moshe Sharett*, 506–14.

27. *Ha-Tzofeh*, Hebrew, Daily, January 30, 1955; Avri El-Ad with James Creech III, *Ha-Adam Ha-shlishi* [Hebrew: The Third Man] (Tel Aviv: Special edition, 1976), 173, 210.

28. El-Ad and Creech, *Ha-Adam Ha-shlishi*, 167–66, 170; a word of caution regarding this source: El-Ad was convicted of felonies connected with the collapse of the operation in late 1960. Consequently, his account should be read as an apologetic text. However, other sources confirmed more than a few details in later years. Hence the author of the current book decided to carefully use some details from this source that look relatively unstained; Haggai Eshed, *Mi natan et ha oraha; parashat Lavon* [Hebrew: Who Gave the Order; The Lavon Affair] (Jerusalem: Idanim, 1979), 31, 48. These two sources symmetrically opposed in their reading of the episode do agree on the drafting to the IDF; Private collection, Interview with Avraham Dar, the Israeli agent in charge of the operation, raw notes, December 4, 2007, 12.

29. Eshed, *Mi natan et ha oraha; parashat Lavon*, 97.

30. Cf. Mordechai Bar-On, *Shearei Azah: mediniut ha bitahon ve ha hutz shel Israel, 1955–1957* [Hebrew: The Gates of Gaza: Israel's Defense and Foreign Policy, 1955–1957] (Tel Aviv: Am Oved 1992), 127.

31. Private collection, Interview with Avraham Dar, the Israeli agent in charge of the operation, raw notes, December 4, 2007, 2–3.

32. Naomi Barzilai, ed., *Documents on the Foreign Policy of Israel, Vol. 9: 1954* (Jerusalem: Israel State Archives, 2004), doc. 310.

33. Private collection, Internal MFA memo, February 1, 1955, detailing twelve such cases; interview with Avraham Dar, the Israeli agent in charge of the operation, notes, December 4, 2007, 6. This is the current author's reading of the British MP attempts at reaching some agreement between Israel and Egypt. The U.S. Jewish leader Blaustein continued his efforts to encompass additional mutual areas between Israel and Egypt. Cf. Private collection, from Jerusalem, to Washington, "top secret," February 1, 1955; Private collection, Internal MFA memo, cloaked, urgent, April 25, 1955; one of those misled was the Israeli prime minister, Sharett, who was convinced that Nasser realized that Egypt and Israel would coexist side by side. "From the Diary of Moshe Sharett, chapter 11," *Ma'ariv*, June 21, 1974.

34. Cf. Michael B. Oren, "Escalation to Suez: The Egypt-Israel Border War, 1949–56," *Journal of Contemporary History* 24, no. 2 (April 1989): 372n43; Michael B.

Oren," Secret Egypt-Israel Peace Initiatives Prior to the Suez Campaign," *Middle Eastern Studies* 26, no. 3 (July 1990): 351–70.

35. *al ha-Mishmar*, Israel, Hebrew Daily, February 7, 1954; *Ma'ariv*, December 1, 8, 1954; *Davar*, December 9, 1954; *al ha-Mishmar*, December 9, 1954; *Ma'ariv*, December 22, 1954; *al-Ahram*, Egypt, Arabic, daily, December 22, 1954; *al ha-Mishmar*, December 23, 1954; *Davar*, December 23, 1954; Private collection, MFA memo, December 28, 1954; Private collection, IMFA cable, from Jerusalem, to Washington, January 28, 1955.

36. Private collection, memo, from The Chief Assistant to the Minister of Foreign Affairs, to Director General, MFA, Director of military intelligence, Speaker of the parliament (Knesset) committee on foreign and security affairs, n.d.

37. Barzilai, ed., *Documents on the Foreign Policy of Israel, Vol. 9: 1954*, docs. 539, 541.

38. Especially revealing in this context is a "top secret" letter from the deputy Director General of the MFA (Harman) to the Israeli policy in the Israeli Embassy, Washington, DC, Reuven Shiloah, a former head of the Israeli foreign intelligence service (the "Mossad") and a former commander of the unit responsible for the compromised network in Egypt. Private collection, "top secret" letter, September 30, 1955.

39. Private collection, minutes of the meeting of the Committee on the Zion prisoners in Arab lands, "top secret," February 24, 1956; second meeting, June 29, 1956.

40. Private collection, IMFA, from Jerusalem, to London, July 9, 1956.

41. Private collection, Interview with Avraham Dar, the Israeli agent in charge of the operation, raw notes, December 4, 2007, 6.

42. El-Ad and Creech, *Ha-Adam Ha-shlishi*, 238; Private collection, Interview with Avraham Dar, the Israeli agent in charge of the operation, raw notes, December 4, 2007, 6–7, 10.

43. Cf. Private collection, Interview with Avraham Dar, the Israeli agent in charge of the operation, raw notes, December 4, 2007, 6–7, 10.

44. Private collection, Interview with Avraham Dar, the Israeli agent in charge of the operation, raw notes, December 4, 2007, 1; El-Ad and Creech, *Ha-Adam Ha-shlishi*, 130; cf. Golan Aviezer, *Mivtzah Suzanna* [Hebrew: Operation Suzanna], as told by Marcelle Ninio, Victor Levy, Robert Dassa, and Philip Natanson (Jerusalem: Idanim, 1976), 42–60.

45. Private collection, Interview with Avraham Dar, the Israeli agent in charge of the operation, raw notes, December 4, 2007, 2.

46. Aviezer, *Mivtzah Suzanna*.

47. El-Ad and Creech, *Ha-Adam Ha shlishi*, 140, 153, 167; Eshed, *Who Gave the Order; The Lavon Affair*, 172; see testimony by a former agent, *Ma'ariv*, April 23, 1986.

48. Cf. Aviezer, *Mivtzah Suzanna*, 234–39.

49. Moshe Dayyan, *Story of My Life* (Tel Aviv: Idanim and Dvir, 1976), 323.

50. Ibid., 144

51. Full text: Constantinople Convention, October 29, 1888, http://www.suezcanal.gov.eg/sc.aspx?show=37; Moshe Sharett, *Personal Diary*, vol. 2, 369.

52. BGA/STA/File 40, Container 5, from "Yanis," to Col. Harkavi, "Comments on Operation Bat Galim"; BGA/STA/File 40, Container 5, Operational order, n.d., ca. August 10/11, 1954. Due to the extremely secret nature of the connection between the IDF and the operation, the order is hand written [no date, circa August 10/11, 1954].

53. *Davar*, March 30, 1954.

54. Cf. Alan Ray, "Another Partition of Israel?" *New Republic* 132, no. 15 (April 11, 1955): 17–18; Michael B. Oren, "The Diplomatic Struggle for the Negev, 1946–1956," *Studies in Zionism* 10, no. 2 (1989): 197–215.

55. Cf. Moshe Sharett, *Personal Diary*, vol. 2, 681.

56. BGA/STA/File 40, Container 5, The Chief of Staff Diary, December 14, 1954.

57. BGA/STA/File 40, Container 5, Minutes of the weekly meeting of the Minister of Defense and the Chief of General Staff, July 15, 1954; see also BGA/STA/File 40, Container 5, Minutes of the weekly meeting of the Minister of Defense and the Chief of Staff, July 22, 1954.

58. Moshe Sharett, *Personal Diary*, vol. 2 (1954–1955), 553–85.

59. Ibid., 561–62.
60. U.S. Department of State. "No. 900, The [U.S.] Chargé in Israel (Russell) to the Department of State," in FRUS, 1952–1954, Volume IX, Part 1, The Near and Middle East (In Two Parts), Tel Aviv, October 1, 1954. https://history.state.gov/historicaldocuments/frus1952–54v09p1/d900, Original: National Archives, 684A.85/10–154: Telegram.
61. Moshe Sharett, *Personal Diary*, vol. 2 (1954–1955), 369.
62. This assessment is based on U.S. Department of State, "No. 940, The Secretary of State to the Embassy in Egypt," in FRUS, 1952–1954, Volume IX, Part 1, The Near and Middle East (In Two Parts), Washington: December 21, 1954, https://history.state.gov/historicaldocuments/frus1952–54v09p1/d940, Original: National Archives, 984A.53/12–2154: Telegram; Appropriating Israeli bound cargo: *Davar*, January 26, 27, 1954; *al-ha-Mishmar*, February 27, 1954; *Davar*, March 14, 1954; *Ma'ariv*, August 8, 1954; Not seized: *Herut*, February 14, 1954; *Davar*, March 9, 24, 1954; *al-ha-Mishmar*, July 29, 1954; Israeli admission regarding the lack of a clear pattern of Egyptian behavior: *Davar* editorial, May 2, 1954.
63. UN Security Council, Resolution 95, September 1951, http://www.un.org/en/ga/search/view_doc.asp?symbol=S/RES/95(1951).
64. US Department of State "No. 925, The Secretary of State to the United States Mission at the United Nations," in FRUS, 1952–1954, Volume IX, Part 1, The Near and Middle East (In Two Parts), Washington: December 2, 1954, https://history.state.gov/historicaldocuments/frus1952–54v09p1/d925; Original: 674.84A/12–254: Telegram.
65. U.S. Department of State, "No. 907, Memorandum of Conversation, by the Director of the Office of Near Eastern Affairs (Hart)," in FRUS, 1952–1954, Volume IX, Part 1, The Near and Middle East (In Two Parts), Washington: October 10, 1954, https://history.state.gov/historicaldocuments/frus1952–54v09p1/d907; Original: National Archives, 674.84A/10–1054, and compare U.S. Department of State, "No. 933, The Acting Secretary of State to the Embassy in Israel," in FRUS, 1952–1954, Volume IX, Part 1, The Near and Middle East (In Two Parts), Washington: December 15, 1954, https://history.state.gov/historicaldocuments/frus1952–54v09p1/d933, Original: National Archives, 984A.53/12–1054: Telegram.
66. Moshe Sharett, *Personal Diary*, vol. 2, 565.
67. Cf. U.S. Department of State, "No. 923, The Ambassador in Israel (Lawson) to the Department of State," in FRUS, 1952–1954, Volume IX, Part 1, The Near and Middle East (In Two Parts), Tel Aviv: November 30, 1954, https://history.state.gov/historicaldocuments/frus1952–54v09p1/d923, Original: National Archives, 984A.53/11–3054: Telegram.
68. BGA/STA/File 40/Container 5, Chief of Staff's operational diary, December 14, 1954.
69. BGA/STA/File 40/Container 5, Minutes of the weekly meeting of the Minister of Defense and the Acting Chief of General Staff, July 15, 1954; BGA/STA/File 40/Container 5, Minutes of the weekly meeting of the Minister of Defense and the Chief of Staff, August 12, 1954.
70. BGA/STA/File 40, Container 5, Minutes of the weekly meeting of the Minister of Defense and the Chief of Staff, September 9, 1954; Dayyan, *Story of My Life*, 132.
71. Dayyan, *Story of My Life*, 132.
72. U.S. Department of State, "899. The [U.S.] Ambassador in Egypt (Caffery) to the Department of State, Cairo," in FRUS, 1952–1954, Volume IX, Part 1, The Near and Middle East (In Two Parts), September 28, 1954, https://history.state.gov/historicaldocuments/frus1952–54v09p1/d899, Original: National Archives, 984A.53/9–2854: Telegram; *Davar*, September 30, 1954.
73. U.S. Department of State, "No. 904, The [U.S.] Ambassador in Egypt (Caffery) to the Department of State, Cairo," in FRUS, 1952–1954, Volume IX, Part 1, The Near and Middle East (In Two Parts), October 7, 1954, https://history.state.gov/historicaldocuments/frus1952–54v09p1/d904; Original: National Archives, 984A.53/10–754: Telegram.

74. For example, *Matzpen*, Israel, weekly, Hebrew, October 5, November 24, December 22, 1954; *Herut*, Israel, daily, Hebrew [organ of the main opposition party], September 30, 1954; *Ma'ariv*, December 21, 1954; *Lemerhav*, Israel, daily, Hebrew, December 24, 1954; *Ma'ariv*, December 21, 1954; *Lemerhav*, Israel, daily, Hebrew, December 24, 1954.

75. U.S. Department of State, "899. The [U.S.] Ambassador in Egypt (Caffery) to the Department of State, Cairo," in FRUS, 1952–1954, Volume IX, Part 1, The Near and Middle East (In Two Parts), September 28, 1954, https://history.state.gov/historicaldocuments/frus1952–54v09p1/d899, Original: National Archives, 984A.53/9–2854: Telegram; *Davar*, September 30, 1954.

76. *Davar*, *al ha-Mishmar*, December 20, 1954; IDFA/636/1956/33, from [Israel] Staff officer, to the Chief of Staff and others, December 30, 1954, January 3, 1955.

77. IDFA636/1956/33, Reports from the Israeli liaison officer to MAC to the Director of Military Intelligence and the MFA, November 9, 13, 14, 30, 1954.

78. A detailed account of the operation: Private collection/Phone conversation with Meir Mozes, one of the apprehended soldiers, December 11, 2007; Judy Baumel Schwartz, "The Last Will and Testimony of Uri Ilan," *Iyunim Bi-tkumat Yisrael* [Studies in Israel's Revival] 15 (2005): 209–38.

79. BGA/Shabtai Tevet Archive [STA], File 13, Container 2, Minutes of cabinet meeting 315/23, January 16, 1955.

80. BGA/Shabtai Tevet Archive [STA], File 13, Container 2, Ben Gurion note, May 5, 1964.

81. BGA/Shabtai Tevet Archive [STA], File 13, Container 2, Ben Gurion's note, July 18, 1963, quoting a January 17, 1955, letter from Dayyan to Lavon.

82. *Maariv*, *Davar*, January 14, 1955.

83. Geneva Convention (III), Treatment of Prisoners of War, August 12, 1949. Articles 83 and 84; https://www.icrc.org/applic/ihl/ihl.nsf/INTRO/375?OpenDocument; *a l ha-Mishmar*, January 18, 1955.

84. IDFA/636/1956/13—Syria (operation *Pilegesh* [mistress]), Egypt (operation *Yitro* 1+2 [Jethro]), n.d.

85. For a more detailed study of the contemporary Israeli ethos cf. Yechiam Weitz "Discussion: Kasztner's Changing Image as a Reflection of the Public Image of the Holocaust," *Cathedra* 69 (September 1993): 138.

86. IDFA/637/1956/15, IDF Operations Directorate, Survey of actions.

87. Full text of the letter: Sharett, *Personal Diary*, vol. 2, 606–7.

88. Sharett, *Personal Diary*, vol. 3 (1955), 653; Knesset Meeting 573, January 17, 1955, 590–94, http://www.knesset.gov.il/review/data/heb/plenum/kns2_170155.pdf.

89. 202nd Israeli Paratroopers Brigade Military Decorations, Description of Event: Operation *Barukh* June 1954, April 1973, http://www.202.org.il/Pages/iturim/personal/gibli.htm; 202nd Israeli Paratroopers Brigade, Gill Operations, 1954 http://202.org.il/Pages/tagmul/peulot/gil.php.

90. Dayyan, *Story of My Life*, 132; cf. Sharon, *Sharon—The Life of a Leader*, 97–98.

91. Cf. Benny Morris, *Israel's Border Wars, 1949–1956: Arab Infiltration, Israeli Retaliation, and the Countdown to the Suez War* (Oxford: Oxford University Press 1993), 306–9.

92. Shabtai Teveth, *Moshe Dayyan: Biography* (Tel Aviv and Jerusalem: Schoken, 1971), 400–402; for the English edition, see Shabtai Teveth, *Moshe Dayyan: The Soldier, the Man, the Legend* (Boston: Houghton Mifflin Harcourt, 1973).

93. IDFA/636/1974/13, operational order, August 27, 1954; IDFA/675/1974/178, *Reprisal activities, 1950–1953 (Until the Establishment of Unit 101)* n.d., ca. 1954. Operational Order, 1954. Photocopies of some of the orders: IDFA, 890th Battalion Report to General Staff: "Operation Barukh," June 1954, http://idfarchives.bloger.co.il/118164/.

94. [UK] NA/FO371/111104/no. 207, from [Jordanian] Jerusalem, to London, August 14, 1954; [UK] NA/FO371/111106/(1033/221/54), from Amman, to London, September 17, 1954.

95. *Ha-Tzofeh*, October 31, 1954; IDFA/626/1957/10.

96. Cf. Morris, *Israel's Border Wars, 1949–1956*, 292–354.

97. On the Israeli proposal, the simultaneous negotiations on the exchange of prisoners and the actual signing, see IDFA/1338/1979/200, numerous documents, March 1–15, April 5, 1955; *Herut*, March 15, 1955; *ha-Tzofeh*, March 15, April 29, 1955; May 11, 1955; *Davar*, *Ma'ariv*, May 11, 1955.

Part II

Israel and the Arab Nation States: The Emerging POW Rules in Light of the Regional Battlefields, 1955–1967

FOUR

De Facto Policy in the Shadow of a Coming War, 1955–1956

The atmosphere in the corridors of power in Israel since the beginning of 1955 was that of looking for a way out of the Israeli predicament: the terrorist activities continued unstopped and no relief was on the way. A few moves helped to reshape the strategic standing of Israel. First, Ben Gurion, the activist, returned to his position as Minister of Defense in late February 1955, almost concurrent with a major raid on Egyptian military bases in Gaza. Second, in July the ruling party, that of Prime Minister Sharett and Ben Gurion, declined from 45 to 40 seats in the 120-strong parliament in a popular manifestation of frustration with the security situation. Last but not least, all that happened while the cabinet discussed behind heavy curtains several plans for military occupation of Egyptian positions in an attempt to stop the small warfare unofficially launched by the Nasser regime. Needless to say, with the September 1955 Egyptian-Czech arms deal a large number of the puzzle pieces were put in place for the imminent showdown.

Yet in spite of the clear escalation between Israel and its neighbors, the practice of the Egyptians, the Syrians, and the Jordanians of preplanned taking of POWs was nearing its end toward the approaching major confrontation, which eventually took place on October 29, 1956. That process could be due to the amalgamation of two main reasons: At that point, none of the Arab players wanted to provoke Israel into a major attack on an Arab country. The keg of firepower was about to explode because of the almost daily attacks on Israel, but no Arab player desired to give Israel a clear casus belli. After all, a shooting incident can always be blamed on the other side, whereas the taking of a POW is self-evident. Second, taking Israeli POWs meant taking the risk of a retaliatory action that might lead to the taking of hostages as "bargaining chips" from the

Arab side. However, even that policy had two exceptions: the Egyptians captured one soldier in September 1955 during an incident in which two of his colleagues were killed, and a while later in October 1955 two more were captured by the Egyptians.[1] The Israeli reaction, in line with past precedents, was to launch an operation intended to take Egyptian prisoners. The operation took place five days after the border incident and led to the capture of about thirty Egyptian soldiers and officers.[2] Unfortunately for all concerned, time was already running out. The final exchange of the period with Egypt before the largest operation, the Sinai/Kadesh operation, would not be conducted until January 1957 after that round of hostilities.

In keeping with experience, the Syrian regime, while struggling for its own very existence on the home front, continued its "call to the flag" approach. Concurrent with the continued confrontation with Israel, in 1954 Syria entered a period of uncertainty upon the removal of its leader, Adib Shishakli. Syria's union with Egypt would replace its domestic instability in early 1958. Against that unstable backdrop and the lack of a "strong man" to lead the nation, no one in Damascus had any interest in presenting him- or herself as a partner of Israel on the prisoners' issue.[3] The immediate outcome was not only a continued policy of kidnapping Israelis, but also limiting that issue to the border area units. Consequently, when an Israeli soldier was abducted from its territory in mid-October 1955, the details of that incident were probably not shared with Damascus. All that was unknown to Israel at the time. It only knew that the four surviving members of the Cricket group were still in jail and that one more soldier was missing. That assessment along with the tradition of forcing an exchange on the enemy led Israel to launch in late October the Se'ir Operation, which resulted in four Syrian soldiers and one officer being taken by Israel.[4] That raid gave Egypt an excellent opportunity to invoke the newly signed Egyptian-Syrian Mutual Defense Pact (October 20, 1955).[5] Only four days after the Israeli raid on Syrian territory, Egypt responded in kind, attacked an Israeli post, and took two Israeli POWs one day after arriving at their base and before they were briefed on a possible capture (see above).[6] At the end of that round of hostilities in mid-December and after one last major operation within Syrian territory,[7] Israel knew of five soldiers in Syrian hands (in the 1960s it would realize that the number was much higher—see the relevant chapter) and three in Egyptian hands. Syria admitted it had the Cricket group but denied that it had the missing soldier, whose fate is unknown to this day. Egypt, on the other hand, did not allow visits with the POWs until at least late 1955 and probably later than that.[8] Israel held at that point thirty-five Syrians and seventy-nine Egyptians.[9] However, as can be judged from the contemporary documentation, that did not lead to any coordinated effort by the two Arab actors and each continued to deal with its respective POW issues separately. Yet both countries, whether by coincidence or not, were steadfast in their unequivocal rejection of any release of the prisoners: Syria for lack of an agreed upon decision maker and Egypt because it did not want the returned POWs to lower the morale of the Egyptian army, which was facing an imminent confrontation.[10] Israel signaled several times that it would be prepared for a deal; at times Egypt responded in kind, but nothing was accomplished in part because Ben Gurion insisted on including the convicted sabotage cells in the deal.[11] Sharett preferred taking back whomever the Egyptians were willing to set free. It is not farfetched to speculate that the prolonged prison time of the three soldiers (two of them masquerading at first as "policemen" so as not to violate the limitations on the presence of military personnel in the demilitarized zones) was largely due to the difference of opinion between the two leaders.

On the international level, UN Secretary General Dag Hammarskjöld was clearly aware of the deteriorating situation in the Middle East and he enlisted Canadian general Eedson Louis Millard Burns, Chief of Staff, United Nations Truce Supervision Organization, as his emissary to try to at least pressure the weak Syrian regime to free the POWs they were holding. Beyond diffusing some tension, the secretary general was also looking for somewhat improved relations with Israel that was distasteful to both Hammarskjöld and Burns.[12] However, the Syrians, who continued their resistance to any exchange, rebuffed the first serious approaches by Burns. Their main excuse was that their soldiers in Israeli hands were clearly POWs, whereas the Israelis, who had been captured with no military markings, were simply spies.[13] The Egyptian approach was no better; in January 1956 they informed the chair of the MAC that they would allow UN personnel to interrogate the Israeli POWs.[14] The Egyptian way of thinking was clear: two of the Israelis were in violation of the 1949 armistice agreement because they were taken from the demilitarized zone, where military personnel were not permitted to be. Furthermore, they were dressed as police in order to deceive the UN observers. Consequently, even though the Egyptians presented themselves as offering a gesture of goodwill, they were in reality trying to lay a trap for the Israeli side. However, even that move was conditional on Israel not connecting in any way the fate of the soldiers to that of the people convicted earlier in an Egyptian court. Simultaneous with voicing that position, the Egyptians allowed a visit by a representative of the ICRC with the three uniformed persons they were holding, clearly indicating that such rights could not be extended to the members of the sabotage cell.[15] The same representative also visited the four soldiers incarcerated in Damascus.[16] Israel returned the humanitarian gesture—this is how the Syrian and Egyptian moves were perceived in Jerusalem—and returned with full military honors the bodies of four Egyptian soldiers killed on Israeli soil in early 1956.[17] Obviously, none of those moves was the result of a new more humanitarian approach to the issue of POWs and those killed in action. They were all trying to elicit goodwill from the members of the UN Security Council that was about to meet in mid-January to discuss the Israeli action against Syria in December 1955. Within that context, Burns began preparing a formal report to be presented to the Security Council and to serve as the platform for the discussions he was about to conduct during his visit to the region in late January. He also met with the Syrian chief of staff in Damascus and discussed inter alia a possible exchange to include four Israelis and thirty-two Syrians.[18]

The unanimous decision of the United Nations Security Council (no. 111) of January 19, 1956, somewhat changed the balance of power and the picture of interests. It harshly criticized Israel and its military policy toward the armistice agreement with its Arab neighbors. However, the silver lining that jump started the exchange process at least with the Syrians was Article 8: "[The Security Council] calls upon the parties to arrange with the Chief of Staff for an immediate exchange of all military prisoners."[19] Syria could only use that resolution emanating from the Israeli attack on its territory to try to gain more international recognition of its shaky standing domestically and globally.[20] The UNSC resolution brought the International Red Cross, which by definition was the body in charge of implementing the Geneva Convention, back to an effective role. Israel for its part was reminded in some unambiguous terms that Article 8 was not only part and parcel of the resolution, but that Burns had already instructed the chairman of the Israeli-Syrian MAC to act upon it. Why was there no parallel instruction for his counterpart on the Egyptian front? It was probably because the secretary general and the chief of staff were about to leave for a meeting with Nasser in Egypt and because the Israeli-Egyptian MAC did not function at that point due to the increased tension along the confrontation line.[21] Anyway, a process of UN and ICRC personnel shuttle diplomacy began and was in full swing between the UN resolution and the actual Syrian release on March 29, 1956.[22] The indirect Israeli-Syrian negotiations pushed Israel into an extra intelligence effort aimed at exposing all Israelis incarcerated by Syria. Consequently, the number of POWs/MIAs demanded by Israel rose from the four members of the Cricket group to sixteen.[23]

Israel at that time was still a young nation looking to develop its own national character and ethos. The suicide of Ilan only accentuated the fact that his comrades in arms behaved in a way that did not conform to the expectations of the contemporary leading Israeli decision makers. Two of the four surviving members of the team were put through the Israeli military judicial system and were convicted of several felonies. From later orders of the chief of staff in the wake of the Sinai campaign and the return of the POWs, it appears that at least until that point standing orders demanded that the chief of staff decide once a POW is returned whether he or she should be prosecuted.[24]

Egypt, on the other hand, presented a more complex picture: the arms deal was proven to be larger than first believed by Israel and the Western actors, the Arab masses began to picture Nasser as the "leader of the Arabs," and the superpower courting of the Egyptian president was translated into a diplomatic victory.[25] Against that backdrop Israel felt isolated and without a secure source of armaments to defend itself. Even France, later to become a permanent source of war materials until 1967, was not yet the solution to Israel's troubles, as would happen later in late 1956.[26] Considering the contrast in international standing between Israel and Egypt and the Egyptian realization of the importance Israel attached to the return of the POWs, Egypt played on the Israeli side repeatedly.[27] Egypt's main goal was to present itself as the one player that abided by the international rules and behaved in a rather reasonable way, unlike Israel. This issue of public image had been significantly reinforced by UNSC Resolution 111, which had already done some of the damage to Israel's image. The ICRC for its part shared the view that Egypt was much in line with international norms compared with Israel. It needed a success but could not blame its lack thereof on Egypt, the rising star of the nonaligned world that might help in the future in faraway arenas, and Israel was the clear culprit to blame.[28] Numerous meetings between Israeli, UN, and ICRC figures produced much hope on the Israeli side, but to no avail. The Egyptian interest at that point just did not justify any concessions to Israel. Even the impression created that an exchange with Egypt was imminent was dashed.[29] During that period, Israel acted on the premise of a clear separation between two groups of prisoners: the well-defined three POWs and the members of the sabotage network. Israel insisted on the early release of the former, whereas it was satisfied with some easing of the prison conditions of the latter.[30] Not long beforehand, the Israeli POWs continued their stay in an Egyptian prison only to avoid creating the impression that they deserved a different treatment by Israel. Yet that distinction was a paradigm for the Israeli decision makers in February 1956. Even if that was a logical reading of the conditions of the two groups, there was still no record available to explain that change. Without any strong evidence that anyone seriously discussed that change, it appears that it was an improvised guideline for the negotiators without any legal backing. However, whatever the Israeli line was, it became outdated with the Egyptian decision to break off the talks in February. Once again, in May the UN tried to resume contacts with both parties and get the mutual release of all POWs.[31] That effort came to its premature end after the two warring parties could not agree on the names of the Egyptians held by Israel.[32] Israel once again tried to call to the attention of the Egyptian authorities the anxiety of the Egyptian POWs who were not accustomed to the living conditions, including the food, in the Israeli POW camp.[33] However, even that almost pathetic attempt by Israel did not work; after all, the basic lack of Egyptian interest in getting back their own had never changed.

On October 29, 1956, Israel, Great Britain, and France attacked Egypt. The tripartite campaign against Egypt ended on November 5, 1956. That military campaign is not within the scope of this study. However, in spite of the large-scale fighting that led to the almost full occupation of the Sinai Peninsula by Israel, it lost only one POW. Strictly formally speaking, Israel held about 5,600 Egyptian uniformed personnel who met the Geneva Convention requirements to be recognized as POWs. At the end of the campaign, Egypt held four Israeli uniformed, three captured before the campaign and one a pilot during the campaign. However, this count does not include the failed 1954 sabotage operation prisoners. These numbers do include two Egyptian generals, one of them Fuad Dighwi, who had chaired the trial of the Israeli cell that led to the execution of two of the Jews and the imprisonment of the rest. As can be verified today, Fuad Dighwi was indeed interrogated, but he did not shed any additional light on the trial nor did he volunteer any additional intelligence, diplomatic or military, that could lead to the release of the cell members.[34]

Shortly after the armed stage of the October/November conflict ended, Cairo began its own POW campaign against Israel, claiming that the Egyptians in the Israeli camps were starved.[35] Israel, for its part, eager to get its POWs back and familiar with the hurdles encountered prior to the military campaign, suggested that The Netherlands serve as a "protecting power." The latter's "duty it is to safeguard the interests of the Parties to the conflict. For this purpose, the Protecting Powers may appoint, apart from their diplomatic or consular staff, delegates from amongst their own nationals or the nationals of other neutral Powers. The said delegates shall be subject to the approval of the Power with which they are to carry out their duties."[36] In the eyes of the Israeli foreign ministry, appointing such a power meant that Egypt would have to answer to a neutral power rather than to Israel and would consequently be put under some international pressure to return the POWs. In a sense that suggestion was also a delayed reaction to the frustration with the failure of the MAC, and essentially the UN, to secure at least the release of the three soldiers—because the convicted members of the cells had never been the topic of any significant discussion at the MAC. Moreover, even by that early stage of the existence of the State of Israel, its leaders had already concluded that international bodies, by voicing an international consensus of the Arab countries, led the nonaligned and others not to be objective where Israel was concerned. That was true regarding not only the UN and its long arm, the MAC, but of the International Red Cross. By splitting responsibilities between observing the imprisonment conditions on a regular basis (ICRC) and the negotiations leading to their release (The Netherlands), Israel hoped to avoid any hostile intervention whenever a deal was on the agenda.[37] Structurally speaking, such a change would have meant that, as the bodies mandated with POW release lacked at times any coordination, the MAC under the military General Staff and the Foreign Ministry would have to operate together through the ministry.[38] This not only improved the expediency of the process, but in a sense put an end to the struggle between diplomats and military men over the control of the MAC that had raged since 1954.

The Foreign Ministry representative to the General Staff meeting mentioned an additional issue—that of the *Magen David Adom* (Red Shield of David), which fulfilled all ICRC functions in Israel, in effect serving as the link to the international organization. That would mean that the Israeli organization, unrecognized then and now as a legitimate affiliate of the ICRC—unlike, for instance, the Red Crescent—would gain some de facto recognition of his activities and status. Egypt for its part tried to avoid even a hint of cooperation with the ICRC lest that would be internationally interpreted as some degree of recognition for the ICRC-MDA. Therefore even the Israeli attempt to launch a confidence-building gesture by returning twenty-seven badly wounded Egyptians through the ICRC was originally rejected by Egypt. The latter tried to circumvent such a move by unilaterally sending its own planes and medical staff to pick up its own. Israel along with the ICRC insisted on a plane arranged by the organizations and staffed by ICRC personnel, which was taken care of on December 3. On that narrow angle of the much larger conflict, Israel had its way, but that carried no long-range influence on future deals whatsoever.[39] The only resemblance to a diplomatic accomplishment was the public admission by the ICRC that neither Israel nor the ICRC were to be blamed for the delay in the return of the POWs. Israel was also rebuked by Egypt on the "protecting power" issue. Egypt stated, pure and simple, that it would not agree to the appointment of The Netherlands as such simply because no state by the name of Israel existed.[40] That meant going back to square one and working only with the Red Cross in spite of Israeli reservations.[41] Israel suspected the ICRC of not being objective enough and of not making sure that its staff was impartial among the warring nations.[42] All along, Israeli mistrust of international organizations, especially of the UN—the highest authority for the MAC and the body in charge of exchanges until the military campaign—reached a new peak.[43] Clearly, by early to mid-December 1956, Egypt did whatever it could in order to use international organizations, at times against the organizations' interests, in order to extract not only a propaganda victory, but also a diplomatic victory from Israel. It did so by several means:

1. It acted as though the Geneva Convention did not exist (no "protecting power," no exchange of POW details, no visits for the Israeli POWs until close to their release[44]).
2. Nasser had an open channel to the UN secretary general, who visited Cairo in mid-November. He withheld most of the contents

of his talks with the Egyptian president from the members of the UN Security Council. This way he made the Security Council a tool in the hands of Hammarskjöld and Nasser, leaving both as final authorities on the terms for concluding the armed conflict.[45]

3. On November 22, the Egyptian parliament adopted a law that was eventually put in the form of an official decree "that made all Jews not in possession of Egyptian nationality liable to immediate deportation, while those who have acquired Egyptian nationality after 1922 were to be deprived of their citizenship and deported as well."[46] The Israeli Foreign Minister estimated the number of Jews involved at 21,000.[47] Knowing very well that this was impossible even for technical reasons alone, the Egyptians' hidden message was simple: let Israel take care of them. In spite of the carefully worded message to Israel, its meaning was clear: for the first time since the end of the 1948–1949 armed conflict, a player tied in the fate of the local Jews with that of the POWs.

Nasser also made every effort possible to employ the United Nations High Commissioner for Refugees (UNHCR) to deal with the deported Jews, indicating that it was yet another outcome of the war that was atypical of the larger Arab-Israeli conflict, or as he preferred to present it: the Palestine question.[48] Had Egypt been successful it could have scored a major diplomatic victory—in distinguishing between the Arabs harmed by the 1948 War and dealt with by UNRWA (which had initially been established by the UN General Assembly in December 1949 in order to assist the "Palestine refugees") and the Jews forced to leave Egypt in 1956. The former would continue to be the sole responsibility of UNRWA and seen as the result of Israel's immoral behavior, whereas the latter would be only one group among many such groups all over the world with no specific party to blame its existence on.

At that point, about a month after the end of military operations, Israel was caught unprepared for a situation of some 5,500 to 5,600 Egyptian POWs in its hands who were difficult to feed. The chief delegate of Israel to the MAC even confided in the acting chief of staff of UNTSO that Israel was eager to return the POWs as soon as possible—no word on the expected quid pro quo.[49] That admission along with similar expressions in the Israeli media constituted a grave diplomatic mistake because it clearly lowered the price that Israel could get for the Egyptian POWs, assuming that their homeland did want them back (see below). Moreover, contemporary documents indicate that Israel was trying to limit the scope of the exchange to the one pilot captured during the fighting on top of the three already held by Egypt. The members of the sabotage cells were not mentioned in any documents open today to the public. Egypt on the other hand was trying to change the rules of the game: no more POWs for POWs.

Indeed, with one pen stroke, the term *POW exchange* changed into Egyptian POWs for the Jewish community and the four military POWs. Here, due to an Egyptian move, Israel became the recognized representative of the Jewish community, which was the bright side of the Egyptian UNHCR maneuver. On its own, this development was not new; however, an Egyptian de facto agreement to that representation was fully aligned with the Israeli interest of being the Jewish State and taking care of Jews anywhere. That linkage would play out in the years to come in many ways, including the Israeli treatment of immigration (*Aliyah*) secret emissaries to Arab countries as POWs (see later in 1958). Yet the Egyptian position could be interpreted in an opposite way: these are Egyptian, not Israeli, citizens and because Israel might lack the means or the interest to absorb them, it would refrain from doing so and consequently would not let the Egyptian POWs go home. Simply put, this is the symmetry: because you, Israel, do not want your own, we will not take in our own and will burden you with the responsibility for their needs. Israel would interpret such a move as a threat against Egypt, whereas Egypt truly did not want them back. Under these circumstances the British government, one of the parties to the Sinai campaign, considered the possibility that Hashemite Jordan or Hashemite Iraq, two allies of Britain, would serve as the country or countries to accept the POWs from Israel. This way Jordan and Iraq would bolster their position in the Arab world without any substantial input on their part.[50] That plan never materialized and yet it did contribute to the Israeli-Arab POW issue two more frames of reference: first, Israel and the Arab countries did see the rescue of Jews from hostile countries as part of any POW negotiations; and second, the British suggestion of inter-Arabization of the issue meant a change from the perception of a bilateral issue of exchanging prisoners into a multilateral one.

Within that context of all players, trying to sway any future exchange in their favor, Israel notified the ICRC of its position: "prepared to repatriate all privates from Egyptian prisoners of war [*sic*] in Israel against all Israeli privates held prisoner, Egyptian NCOs against Israeli NCOs and Egyptian officers against Israeli officers."[51] The Israeli semi-official newspaper *Davar* added, quoting "Israeli circles" (indicating sources close to the prime minister or the chief of staff), that Jews incarcerated in Egypt should become part of the deal.[52] While all pertinent players were trying to put together their modus operandi, one outside player was busy trying to gain some diplomatic benefit without even the pretense of being objective. Not even a month after the end of the British-French-Israeli coalition, the British came up with a new idea. Israel should be pressed for the return of the Egyptian prisoners without any quid pro quo just to reinforce the position of Britain in the region after its military move and consequently to exonerate the Hashemites of Jordan and Iraq from their cooperation with the British. Being the hero of the day, so that logic goes, would mean that in spite of its aggression, as depicted in Arab public opinion, Britain was the only power to press Israel for surrender. As unfair as it might look in 1956, that precedent, pure and simple, would be strongly replicated in the aftermath of the 1973 War when the Israeli POW issue would become a tool for gaining power by a leading world force.[53]

Unlike the British, the most unlikely ally of Israel at that particular moment was the ICRC. Representatives of the organization did approach the Egyptian authorities concerning the position of the Jews residing in Egypt. The main point made to Cairo was that all Jews subject to any persecution resulting from the war were entitled to the protection of the (Geneva) Convention (IV) Relative to the Protection of Civilian Persons in Time of War.[54] One of the main points conveyed to the Egyptian government was that under the accepted norms of international law only individuals could be expelled from a country, whereas any collective expulsion is impossible. Furthermore, any move involving expulsion must be coordinated with the protective power.

Israel had its own reservations regarding additional issues that it saw as being very significant: the lack of a list of its own POWs in Egyptian hands and the lack of visits by the ICRC representatives with the Israeli POWs. That was in blunt violation of the Geneva Convention, which Israel mentioned its adherence to repeatedly.[55] Nevertheless, even that Egyptian policy was not oblivious to humanitarian gestures and upon the return of the twenty-seven badly wounded Egyptians (see above), it did release to Israel the name of one captured pilot. Because it did not specify the number of Israelis in its hands, Israel could not know at that point that the pilot was the one and only Israeli POW captured in the military campaign. Israel strongly believed that he was only one of twenty, who apparently became MIAs, who were unknown to Israel at that time. That development induced the ICRC, one day after the return, to offer another round of humanitarian exchanges hoping to gain more information regarding Israel's prisoners while taking care of the badly wounded Egyptians.[56] Israel refused to make the transfer of the POW list a precondition for any additional move, fearing that Egypt might this way demand a quid pro quo for any name of an Israeli prisoner.[57] Without any tangible proposal by the ICRC for an exchange, a resemblance of negotiations by proxy developed wherein each player tried to include as many bargaining chips as would suit its own interests. The Egyptian assets were a number of prisoners unknown to Israel who fully met the stipulations of the Geneva Convention. They added thousands of Jews residing in Egypt, but would not throw into the potential give and take the members of the sabotage network. Israel, on the other hand, had thousands of POWs whom it could not feed and kept a large number of reservists on active duty just to guard them. Egypt made every effort not to distribute to its own POWs' families the letters from their loved ones and demonstrated all throughout their captivity a clear disinterest in getting them back.[58] In an article published in April 1957 the head of the Cairo Red Crescent mentioned that only sixteen letters got to their destination in Egypt during the captivity of the Egyptians. The actual number of letters sent was in the thousands.[59]

An additional group that Israel held consisted of Egyptian civilians—former civil servants who clearly did not meet the criteria for POW status or fall under the Fourth Convention because they were not Gazans. Officially, Gaza was not part of Egypt and consequently their exact status was not fully clear. That, however, was the only group that Egypt was interested in, so much so that the Israeli chief of staff ordered that Israel keep members of this group's upper echelons for a future exchange with the Jews, the POWs, and members of the network.[60] Considering that the negotiations leading to the release of people would fall into the category of a "zero sum game," it is evident that Egypt held better cards: the members of the network symbolized a clash of loyalties among the convicted because while being Egyptian citizens they worked for Israel. For Israel, they were heroes, for Egypt they were traitors; accordingly, the holding party could not afford to let them go. Second, the Jews could leave for whatever country they wished and therefore through Egyptian eyes no concession to Israel was involved. Finally, the POWs were at that time devoid of any relevant intelligence, if they had it at all at any time. Moreover, Egypt did not really need its own POWs, perhaps with the exception of the senior officers and the civil servants. It is no wonder that once negotiations began Israel had much less to offer to Egypt than the other way around. In that test of wills, the lower hand, Israel, blinked first. On December 14 the prime minister and the chief of staff decided that the Egyptian civilians along with 2,500 POWs would be returned to Egypt. The reasons conveyed to the Foreign Ministry were that Israel did not desire to have Egyptian civil servants in the Gaza Strip, probably indicating an Israeli interest in annexing Gaza to Israel, and it could not fund 2,500 POWs. Some additional 2,500 Egyptian POWs of higher ranks would continue to stay in Israeli POW camps until an agreed upon exchange should take place. Initially, that Israeli move was presented as a unilateral one and no more. After the Foreign Ministry intervention, the message to Egypt was changed so as to reflect a unilateral return of the civilians, but sending off of the POWs for Israeli ones.[61]

Exchanging possible scenarios through the ICRC did start a mechanism of indirect negotiations. Even though it is evident that tangible negotiations started only in mid-December, Israel mistook the Egyptian attempt to study its position as the beginning of give and take.[62] However, it was only once the Egyptians did understand the Israeli position that actual proposals began to be exchanged. Here again it was the impatient party, Israel, that supplied the trigger. On December 14 an Israeli diplomat confided in the ICRC personnel that Israel was missing about twenty people and that without the names of people held by Egypt it could not verify whether they were POWs or MIAs. On that occasion, Israel did share with the ICRC the details of the twenty people's mission. In hindsight, that was the icebreaker. Later on that day the ICRC got from Egypt a list of four POWs: one from the October campaign and the three captured beforehand.[63] Within forty-eight hours of that announcement, the first post-campaign visit of all four by the ICRC representative took place.[64] Concurrently, Israel dispatched to Egypt, through the services of the ICRC, a second group of wounded Egyptian POWs.[65] With the issue of the MIAs that the Egyptians were eager to capture[66] over, the basic terms of a deal were beginning to emerge—privates for privates, NCOs for NCOs, and officers for officers—the idea that had already been proposed at an earlier stage. If the issue was POWs for POWs a deal could be struck on that day.[67] Indeed, on December 11 and 13, the Israeli Minister of Defense and the chief of staff put together a formal proposal along these lines for an exchange, probably without consulting the Ministry of Foreign Affairs on its merits.[68] Yet it took the diplomats of all sides more than ten additional days of intensive meetings, with the ICRC taking the lead, to transmit the formal Israeli exchange proposal to Egypt.[69] Even that stage added to the asymmetry between the two regional actors: it was Israel not Egypt that asked for the exchange, signaling its interest, unlike that of Egypt, in the process. Perhaps part of the Egyptian reservations stemmed from the sharp contrast between the magnificent Egyptian victory as presented to the Egyptians and to the Arab world at large and the realities on the ground. The Egyptian interest was to take in the least number necessary in order to be seen in the international arena as taking care of their own and to demonstrate that the Israeli occupation would be removed shortly. The Egyptians found themselves in such dire straits and so unwilling to take back the POWs that they made it known to the ICRC representative dealing with them that there was much anger with those captured, probably reflecting the feeling that they should have not be surrendered.[70] This is perhaps in line with Soviet doctrines of not letting anyone fall into captivity. Thus the families of the civil servants in Gaza were allowed back into Egypt, whereas the men, meaning the position holders, were not. The Egyptian predicament was clear and brutal: how to return the Israeli POWs in order to be reaffirmed as a legitimate member of the international community without getting back its own. On the other hand, getting rid of the Israelis with no clear quid pro quo would obviously have stained Egypt as a collaborator with its perennial enemy. Without getting deeply into the Egyptian psyche, an Israeli diplomat remarked on December 28, "There is no stipulation in the Geneva Convention that forces a country to take back its own POWs," and later, clearly out of some misunderstanding of the way Egypt was thinking, "perhaps the idea is to create a Trojan horse."[71]

One more no less serious issue could have become a source of trouble by thwarting the Israeli efforts. This time it was the in-house wrangling between the security people led by the prime minister and the chief of staff who made the decisions and among the diplomats as well. Simultaneous with the sensitive indirect negotiations with Egypt conducted under the instructions of the decision makers, at least some diplomats, either because they were not enchanted with the policy or because they were not aware of the details, tried to formulate their own independent approach. It was based on the wrong premise that petitioning the ICRC about the large number of violations of the Geneva Convention would create bad world opinion for Egypt and might force them into an exchange.[72] How that initiative was stopped is unclear from the documentation, but it definitely saved Israel some uncalled for developments. Perhaps the only reason for the end of that side initiative was the Egyptian leak to the media around January 13 that an agreement had been reached and that within days the POWs of both countries would be exchanged. The UN spokesperson in New York confirmed those unofficial reports.[73]

The agreement to free the POWs reached in mid-January did not turn into a national celebration in Israel, a country so much preoccupied with its own (Jews and Israelis) in foreign prisons. The agreement reached did not include a word on the fate of the Jews residing in Egypt whether as citizens or aliens. The organization of immigrants from Egypt in Israel went as far as filing an official protest with the government, but as expected, to no avail.[74] Another decision was no less problematic, but could not make it into the headlines: the deal struck did not include the members of the sabotage cells. Due to the secrecy and heavy censorship imposed by the Israeli authorities, nothing on this matter reached any media within Israel or outside. Actually, none of the contemporary reports on the negotiations with the ICRC reported anything related to that issue. A document of the Ministry of Foreign Relations is clear on the issue: the Ministry and the ICRC were dealing with the deported Jews (from Egypt) along with the Israeli and Egyptian POWs.[75] It contained no word on the other people—namely the members of the cells. Their fate was probably left in the hands of the chief of staff alone.

On January 21, 1957, Israel handed over the first batch of Egyptian POWs to the commander of the United Nations Emergency Force. The commander and the Israeli chief of staff agreed on the details of the exchange, including the exact staging of the return of the Israeli POWs.[76] Indeed, a couple of days later, Egypt deposited the Israeli POWs with UNEF in preparation for their return to Israel. On January 27, the Israelis returned home concurrent with the continued return of the Egyptians.[77] They all complained of repeated abuse and torture by the Egyptians. Israel was quick to react and presented the stay of the Egyptian POWs as an acceptable experience that included hospitalization whenever necessary and tours all over the country.[78] One Egyptian officer liked life in Israel so much that he asked for political asylum and others would have loved to do so, according to the Israeli sources, but were apprehensive about the fate of their families.[79] The application of the exchange understandings reached its end on February 5, 1957.

Exchanging POWs symbolized a short negotiations intermission between two ardent enemies. Obviously it did not put an end to the enmity; neither did it establish a mechanism enabling the two parties to deal with civilians or military men who for one reason or another found themselves incarcerated by the enemy. If anything, the next topic on the bilateral agenda was again the freedom of navigation through the Suez Canal and the Straits of Tiran.[80] These matters were left vague at best after the Sinai campaign and the Israeli withdrawal. Hence the next crisis was not a matter of if, but of when. Indeed, on several occasions Israeli citizens, civilians, were used as part of the struggle over freedom of navigation, especially during Israeli attempts to cross the Suez Canal and create new realities. There is no record available suggesting that anyone in a position of influence was concerned with the fate of the potential Israeli hostages. Actually, one of the Knesset members went even further and expressed a degree of indifference to the fate of the crew of a test ship once it is apprehended by Egypt.[81]

Before the October/November 1956 campaign the de facto Israeli POW policy was rather clear to its intended audience: its adversary neighbors. Israel did manage to build a degree of deterrence regarding its POWs—not returning POWs within a certain period of time, or five to six months, was interpreted by Arab countries as casus belli. Because none of the Arab players wanted to provoke Israel into a major attack on an Arab country, an agreement was always attainable as long as Israel knew the identity of the prisoners. The Arab position was that with the exception of the known prisoners (POWs during operations, in border crossing cases, etc.) they never shared the names of Israelis in their hands. With that in mind it is clear that no formal convening of the cabinet or any other official forum to discuss POW policy was necessary. The result of the policy was that a process of mutual abduction of prisoners became the only way to get most of the POWs, known and unknown, back. However, that policy was not the result of a policy consensus among the decision makers. It was the outcome of a power struggle between strong representatives of two symmetrically contradicting policy approaches: the realists in international relations terms, led by Ben Gurion and Dayyan, and the idealists, who advocated the principle of adhering to international law first and getting the prisoners later. That dichotomy is still valid as this book is being written. The idealists also claimed that deriving goodwill from the international community would constitute the best guarantee of Israel's security, not necessarily the release of a few prisoners.

On two issues there was no argument among the top Israelis, both before and after the campaign. First, Israel did not rush to admit responsibility for the non-Geneva-defined POWs, that is, its agents apprehended in 1954. The distinction between the two types of POWs was probably one of the reasons for not freeing those captured earlier, in the wake of the military operation. Second, Israel made it publicly known how eager it was to return the POWs as soon as possible, without even a public hint as to the expected tradeoff. That was a grave mistake during the negotiations process.

Shifting from the policy level to the individual POWs reveals a rather unpleasant picture: there was no preparation on the Israeli side for imprisonment by the enemy, a shortcoming that would not be remedied until after the 1973 War.

As seen from Israel, not much changed on the Arab side in its policies from before to after the campaign. There was only an enhanced Israeli comprehension of the Egyptian and Syrian position. None of the Arab countries was interested in its own captured troops. Formally speaking, there is no stipulation in the Geneva Convention that forces a country to take back its own POWs.

The Arab POWs' exposure to life in Israel could not be tolerated by any authoritarian regime in their own countries. Moreover, with the absence of a "strong man" in Syria, negotiations became impossible. No one would take responsibility lest he or she be accused of wrongdoing or depicted as an agent of Israel. An additional characteristic of the Syrian side was lack of communications between their outposts and the main HQ. That led to the killing of POWs instead of reporting captures to Damascus.

In spite of the lack of apparent changes on the Arab side, some first indications of the imminent end of POWs for POWs could already be established. What used to be a POW exchange based on privates for privates, etc., changed into Egyptian POWs for the Jewish community and the four military POWs—in full alignment with Israel's interest in being the Jewish State and in taking care of Jews anywhere. Both Israel and the Arab countries did see the rescue of Jews from hostile countries part of any POW negotiations.

On the international level, Britain preferred that what was previously a bilateral issue—Israeli-Arab relations—become an inter-Arab, perhaps even international one.

One last lesson of the period was the almost complete violation of the Geneva Convention by Egypt and Syria: no letters allowed from Egyptian POWs to their families in Egypt, no letters from Israelis home, and no visits by the ICRC.

Within that rather pessimistic picture, Jordan stood out as respecting the Convention and trying, at times successfully, to be fair to the Israeli POWs.

NOTES

1. IDFA/626/1957/29, Initial report of the October 26 incident by Lieutenant Colonel Zeevi.

2. IDFA/626/1957/11, Egged operation operational order 16/55, October 27, 1955; cf. IDFA/637/1956/17, Egged operation.

3. General Burns, UNTSO Chief of Staff, heard that firsthand in Syria in the spring of 1955. BGA/Correspondence/March 1955, from Tekoah at the MFA, to main decision makers, April 25, 1955, same document: ISA/FM/2406/13 (closed); BGA/Correspondence/May 1955, from Ben Gurion, to Mrs. Ya'acobi (mother of a member of the Cricket operation group), May 12, 1955.

4. IDFA/637/1956/17, Se'ir operational order 14/55; IDFA/626/1957/62, Chief of Staff Office, *Issues of Armistice and Infiltration*; *Davar*, October 24, 1955.

5. "Egyptian-Syrian Mutual Defense Pact (October 20, 1955). Egyptian-Saudi Arabian Mutual Defense Pact (October 27, 1955)," *Middle East Journal* 10, no. 1 (Winter 1956): 77–79.

6. IDFA/717/1338/1979, The Israeli Delegation to the MAC May 1956 monthly report, June 8, 1956.

7. IDFA/637/1956/17, Olive Leaves operation operational order 24/55; IDFA/637/1956/18, Olive Leaves operation operational order 25/55; on the larger picture and the non-POW interests of Israel, see Mordechai Bar-On, "Olive Leaves: The Raid at the Lake of Galilee on the Night of December 12, 1955," *Iyyunim bi-tekumat Israel* [Hebrew: Studies in Israel's Revival] 9 (1999): 87–127.

8. ISA/FM/20/33/2891, from Geneva, to Jerusalem, December 12, 1955; 2903, December 18, 1955; 2910, December 23, 1955.

9. IDFA/1338/1980/210, IDF History Branch, *POWs—Apprehension and Release*, March 31, 1971; IDFA/626/1957/11, Debriefing of *Har Ga'ash* [Volcano] operation, November 2, 1955.

10. Cf. *Davar*, November 21, 1955, based on Western sources; cf. BGA/Correspondence/early June 1956, from Ben Gurion, to B. Enikster [father of one of the three Israeli POWs in Egypt], June 12, 1956.

11. BGA/Correspondence/additions/Addition 4, from Sharett, to Ben Gurion, January 18, 1955.

12. Lt. Gen. E. L. M. Burns, *Between Arab and Israeli* (London: George G. Harrap, 1962), 102–4; cf. Library and Archives Canada/RG2, Privy Council Office, Series A-5-a, Vol. 5775/Reel T-12185; International situation; contribution to United Nations Emergency International Force; Cabinet Meeting Date: 16 November 1956.

13. BGA/General chronological documentation/June 1955, Tekoah's minutes of his meeting with Burns, June 21, 1955; BGA/General chronological documentation/September 1955, from New York, to Jerusalem.

14. IDFA/717/1338/1979, The Israeli Delegation to the MAC January 1956 monthly report, January 30, 1956.

15. ISA/FM/20/33/2922, from Geneva, to Jerusalem, January 6, 1956.

16. *Davar*, January 6, 1956.

17. *Davar*, January 11, 1956.

18. *Ma'ariv, Davar, ha-Tzofeh, Herut*, January 16, 1956.

19. http://daccess-dds-ny.un.org/doc/RESOLUTION/GEN/NR0/109/45/IMG/NR010945.pdf?OpenElement.

20. Cf. Douglas Little, "Cold War and Covert Action: The United States and Syria, 1945–1958" *Middle East Journal* 44, no. 1 (Winter 1990): 51–75.

21. BGA/Correspondence/January 1956, from Burns, to Sharett, January 21, 1956.

22. *Davar*, January 25, 26, 30, 31, March 1, 26, 30, 1956; *Herut*, January 26, 29, February 1, March 29, 30, 1956; *Ma'ariv*, January 26, 30, February 21, 23, March 25, 26, 29, 30, 1956; *h a-Tzofeh*, February 23, March 26, 1956; ISA/FM/20/33, from Geneva, to Jerusalem, March 16, 1956.

23. *Ma'ariv*, February 26, 1956.

24. IDFA/1034/1965/734, from the Chief of Staff Office to the Directors of Directorates of Intelligence, Manpower, and Operations, March 4, 1957.

25. IDFA/535/2004/543, Director of the Intelligence Directorate presentation to the General Staff of IDF, February 8, 1956; IDFA/644/1956/88, IDF, General Staff, Directorate of Intelligence, "top secret" intelligence dispatch: Syria-Egypt treaty.

26. Moshe Dayyan, *Story of My Life* (Tel Aviv: Idanim and Dvir, 1976), 183–84.

27. IDFA/717/1338/1979, The Israeli Delegation to the MAC February 1956 monthly report, March [1?], 1956.

28. *h a-Tzofeh*, February 21, 1956.

29. *Ma'ariv*, February 21, 1956; *Davar*, February 21, 1956.

30. ISA/FM/20/33, from Geneva, to Jerusalem, February 26, 1956.

31. *ha-Tzofeh*, May 31, 1956.

32. Cf. IDFA/717/1338/1979, The Israeli Delegation to the MAC June–July 1956 monthly report, August 7, 1956; ISA/20/33, from Geneva, to Jerusalem, June 24, 27, August 20, 1956.

33. *Ma'ariv*, July 26, 1956

34. Most of the pertinent material is found in IDFA/1093/2004/278, 409, the General's interrogation transcripts, which are closed to the public.

35. IDFA/535/2004/321, IDF General Staff/Directorate of Intelligence, Arab broadcasts summary, Ramalla [Jordan] Radio, November 21, 1956, 0700.

36. Convention (III) Relative to the Treatment of Prisoners of War. Geneva, 12 August 1949, article 8, https://www.icrc.org/applic/ihl/ihl.nsf/7c4d08d9b287a42141256739003e636b/6fef854a3517b75ac125641e004a9e68.

37. ISA/FM/1987/18, 1956–57, from Jerusalem, to New York, November 1, 1956.

38. ISA/FM/1987/18, 1956–57, Minutes of a meeting at the General Staff, November 1, 1956.

39. This episode is covered in the following sources: ISA/FM/1987/18/1956–57, from Jerusalem, to Geneva and New York, November 15, 1956, "for the weekly digest," November 25, 1956, internal memo, "The Return of the Wounded Egyptians Affair," November 27, 1956, from Jerusalem, to Geneva, December 3, 1956, "for the weekly digest," December 4, 1956; ISA/FM/18/2, from Geneva, to Jerusalem, December 4, 1956, and the Israeli press, November 20, 1956–December 4, 1956; [UK] NA/FO371/121839/VR1551/6/857, from Tel Aviv, to FO, December 3, 1956.

40. ISA/FM/1987/18, 1956–57, from Jerusalem to IDF Headquarters, November 16, 1956; [UK] NA/FO371/121839/VR1551/3/844, from Tel Aviv, to FO, November 29, 1956.

41. ISA/FM/18/2/3420, from Geneva, to Jerusalem, December 5, 1956.

42. Same document: ISA/FM/18/2/22/57, ISA/FM/21/11, from Geneva, to Jerusalem, January 6, 1957.

43. [UK] NA/FO371/118874/JE1074/24/J/1296, from New York [UK mission], to the Foreign Office, November 20, 1956.

44. ISA/FM/18/2/3426, from Geneva, to Jerusalem, December 7, 1956.

45. LAC/RG25 [External Affairs], Vol. 6100, file 50366–40, November 24, 1956, UNEF—Canadian Contribution.

46. ISA/FM/18/2/3420, from Geneva, to Jerusalem, December 5, 1956.

47. Ibid.

48. ISA/FM/18/2/3421, from Geneva, to Jerusalem, December 6, 1956.

49. [UK] NA/FO371/121839/VR1551/1/476, from [Jordanian] Jerusalem, to FO, November 21, 1956; *Ma'ariv*, November 23, 1956, 5.

50. [UK] NA/FO371/121839/VR1551/2/832, from Tel Aviv, to FO, November 26, 1956.

51. ISA/FM/20/33/8802/33286, from Geneva, to Jerusalem, November 27, 1956.

52. *Davar*, November 29, 1956.

53. [UK] NA/FO371/121839/VR1551/4, "Egyptian Prisoners in Israel," a memo by E. M. Rose [FO], November 29, 1956.

54. https://www.icrc.org/applic/ihl/ihl.nsf/INTRO/380?OpenDocument; ISA/FM/18/2/3412, from Geneva, to Jerusalem, November 30, 1956.

55. Cf. for instance, ISA/FM/1987/18, 1956–57, from New York, to Jerusalem, December 2, 1956; [UK] NA/FO371/121839/VR1551/6/857, from Tel Aviv, to FO, December 3, 1956; *Davar*, December 5, 1956.

56. *Ma'ariv*, December 4, 1956; ISA/FM/1987/18, 1956–57, from Jerusalem, to Bern, December 5, 1956 (two messages); ISA/G/5460/10/1956–58, from Jerusalem, to Bern, December 5, 1956.

57. ISA/FM/18/2/3426, from Geneva, to Jerusalem, December 7, 1956.

58. ISA/G/5460/10/1956–58, from Jerusalem, to Bern, December 11, 1956; *ha-Tzofeh*, December 21, 1956; *Ma'ariv*, December 23, 1956; *Davar*, January 11, 1957.

59. ISA/FM/21/11/268/57, from Geneva, to Jerusalem, June 6, 1957.

60. Dayyan, *Story of My Life*, 323.

61. ISA/G/5460/10/1956–58, MFA memo, December 16, 1956.

62. ISA/FM/18/2/3469, from Geneva, to Jerusalem, December 28, 1956.

63. Israeli press, December 15, 1956.

64. *Davar, Herut, ha-Tzofeh*, December 20, 1956.

65. *Ma'ariv, Davar*, December 21, 1956.

66. ISA/FM/20/33/3472, from Geneva, to Jerusalem, December 31, 1956.

67. ISA/FM/18/2/3438, from Geneva, to Jerusalem, December 14, 1956.

68. ISA/G/5460/10/1956–58, from the IDF Directorate of Intelligence, to military addressees and the MFA, December 25, 1956; ISA/FM/21/11, from Geneva, to Jerusalem, January 2, 1957.

69. *Davar, Herut*, December 28, 1956.

70. ISA/FM/20/33/3472, from Geneva, to Jerusalem, December 31, 1956.

71. ISA/FM/18/2/3469, from Geneva, to Jerusalem, December 28, 1956.

72. Same document: ISA/FM/18/2/55/57, ISA/FM/21/11, from Geneva, to Jerusalem, January 6, 1957.

73. *Davar, Ma'ariv*, January 14, 1957; *Ma'ariv, ha-Tzofeh*, January 15, 1957.

74. *Herut*, January 15, 1957.

75. ISA/FM/1987/18, 1956–57, from Geneva, to Jerusalem, January 23, 1956.

76. IDFA/1034/1965/734, "Report on the Beginning of the Exchange," ISA/FM/1987/18, 1956–57, from Jerusalem, to Geneva, January 21, 1956; *al-Akhbar*, Daily, Egypt, January 22, 1957.

77. The Israeli press, January 28, 1957; [UK] NA/FO371/128203/VR1551/91, from Tel Aviv, to the Foreign Office, January 28, 1957.

78. For example, *Davar*, January 28, 29, 1957, *ha-Tzofeh*, January 29, 1957, *Herut*, January 29, 1957.

79. *ha-Tzofeh, Ma'ariv*, January 30, 1957.

80. For a comprehensive study of the issue, see Eitan Barak, "The Forgotten Diplomatic Battle: Israel, Egypt, and the Freedom of Navigation through the Suez Canal, 1957–1967," *Iyunim Bitkumat Israel: Studies in Zionism, the Yishuv and the State of Israel* [Hebrew] (2002): 80–131.

81. Ibid., 97.

FIVE

Israel Extends Its Own Working Interpretation of the Term POW

Prisoner Issues in the Wake of the 1956 Conflict to Late 1962

The post October–November 1956 armed conflict time period saw the emergence of new players concerning the issue of Israeli prisoners in hostile hands. Israel and Egypt kept a quiet border until the tense days of May 1967; consequently no POWs were taken from a battlefield, although prisoners were taken by and from both sides. That time span saw for the first time the need to formulate policies and tactics regarding subnational actors. The final issue on the agenda was how to convince Syria to return prisoners it never admitted it had.

With the 1956 War over and Nasser the leading figure among the Arab masses, he had no interest in another round of military confrontations with Israel. Yet he needed to keep the flame of hostility toward Israel and the "imperialist" forces burning in order to maintain his position as leader of the Arabs. Israel was no military target, only a target of an active propaganda machine. Most efforts were invested in many attempts to meddle in other Arab countries' domestic affairs. The one and only attempt at somewhat changing the post-1956 prisoners' rules had to do with taking civilian Israeli prisoners from high seas. That attempt, however much effort it required of Israel to get the fisherman back, did not in any way change the Egyptian-Israeli modus operandi. Briefly, it was an attempt to impose on Israel a return to the MAC after the 1956 campaign. It did not succeed.

On three different occasions the Egyptian authorities apprehended Israeli citizens/civilians. The first was a reporter masquerading as a crewmember on board a Danish ship carrying goods from Burma (Myanmar) to Israel (July 1957).[1] In this first instance, perhaps the false presentation of the person in question raised Egyptian suspicion. At no point did they allow him ICRC visits, and actually rebuffed all ICRC attempts to get involved in the issue. The Egyptians interrogated him while he was imprisoned, and that unprepared individual, a reporter of an opposition weekly magazine, shared his limited knowledge with his captors. Upon his return to Israel, he was convicted for that. However, the main issue in this case is not necessarily the Egyptian rejection of any ICRC visits until the reporter's release in August 1957. There is the larger question of whether the Egyptians had the right to arrest him while on board a neutral (Danish) ship crossing an open international waterway. Moreover, it is not clear at all whether forcing him into Egyptian sovereign territory might or might not be considered under international law to be pure and simple kidnapping.[2]

On September 23, 1957, not long after the return of the reporter, Egyptian warships seized an Israeli fishing boat off the coast of el-Arish in northern Sinai. Egypt accused the six crew members of being engaged in espionage against Egypt within Egyptian territorial waters.[3] Following the arrest of the boat and its crew, Egypt filed an official complaint with the MAC to that effect.[4] In November, the Egyptian authorities arrested an Israeli citizen who while studying in The Netherlands served aboard a Dutch ship crossing the Canal. They released him on January 2, 1958.[5] All three cases, the fishing boat, the reporter, and the sailor, have much in common. They all happened within a short period of time, only a few months after the final withdrawal of the Israeli forces from the Sinai, the deployment of UNEF, and the exodus of about 20,000 Jews from Egypt, most for Israel. These moves, especially the deployment of UNEF and the Jewish departure could have been used in the hands of the Saudi and Hashemite leaders to present Nasser as giving away the collective Arab interests for his own. Moreover, the Israeli withdrawal in 1957 was not followed by Egyptian redeployment of its own forces in the Sinai Peninsula, which could have been interpreted by the hostile monarchies as giving away some elements of sovereignty over Arab land. UNEF along these lines provided Egypt with an excuse not to put together another round of hostilities lest the international force be harmed, and the release of Jews clearly added to the strength of Israel. Nasser for his part had to devise a ploy that would reflect his continued commitment to the war on Israel yet would not lead to an additional wide military conflict. By 1957 the benefits stemming from the 1956 "victory" over the tripartite aggression were at their peak, and there was no reason to foolishly endanger them. These considerations greatly affected the way Egypt handled the three interconnected prisoners' crises, from the three captures to the release of all involved.

The Egyptian effort to maximize and prolong its 1956 triumph started with the careful designation of the international arena in which to present the crises, which did not interest the global system players anymore. In line with past practice, Egypt did not like to cooperate with the ICRC, and whenever it did, its cooperation was limited to visits with the prisoners and only a few humanitarian gestures. The preferred arena was the UN for a couple of reasons: the warm relations between Nasser and the secretary general and because the UN provided Egypt with an advantage over Israel due to the composition of the international body of non-aligned countries, Muslim countries, and the Soviet Block along with its satellites, all sympathetic to Egypt. The secretary general had already reached a series of understandings that actually left the decision on the conditions for removing UNEF in Nasser's hands. That was indeed proved in late May 1967 on the eve of the June war. Israel for its part continued post-1956 its refusal to deal with Egypt through the UN-sponsored MAC system. The Egyptian position did not allow the ICRC to play any meaningful mediating role lest it be interpreted by Israel and the rest of the world as an indication of a shadow of de facto recognition of Israel.[6] That point, as an Egyptian senior officer explained to the ICRC representative, meant that Egypt was not bound by any of the Geneva Conventions as long as Israel was not existent.[7]

The fact that the ICRC as well as the UN did not accept that Egyptian interpretation that did not recognize Israel in any way did not mean a thing for the Egyptian authorities.[8] The ICRC even drew the conclusion that it had to be very sensitive to the Egyptian demands and positions in order not to be curtailed in their activities within that country.[9] On the other hand, Egypt saw the MAC as a local and limited military type of arrangement that had no diplomatic meaning whatsoever. Furthermore, even before the October–November 1956 campaign Israel boycotted the MAC for what Israel perceived as lack of objectivity. This way, the Egyptian interest presented no surprise: the MAC had to be the one and only body to deal with the issue of the captured Israelis. The reasoning behind that was simple: The Armistice Agreement that created the various MACs was, from the Egyptian point of view, just a temporary military low-level agreement; the use of the MACs by military personnel on all sides underlined that. Israel, eager for any indication of recognition by Egypt and weary of what it termed the lack of objectivity by the UNTSO personnel, left that forum before the Sinai campaign. Forcing Israel back would have meant success for Egypt and failure for Israel, a typical "zero sum game." Being part of the indirect diplomatic dialogue and this time fully understanding its meaning, the Israeli diplomats approached the secretary general without asking to convene the Security Council[10]—knowing very well that any pro-Israeli resolution would always be vetoed by the Soviet Union and that the (unfriendly to Israel) U.S. administration would not support it. The secretary approached the Egyptian representative to the UN who in turn asked that Israel turn to the MAC, a stand that the secretary general did not support, realizing that it would lead to a dead end.[11] That vicious circle meant one thing: Israel did not have a partner or an honest broker that would put any effort into reaching a formula enabling the release of the captured persons. Even the Israeli hope that the Italian government would intervene, because the captain of the boat was an Italian citizen, was dashed. The Italians—pure and simple—left the issue in the hands of the Israeli authorities.[12]

Two main misconceptions catch the eye in the context of the three incidents, but most noticeably concerning the ship. First, Israel was too narrow in its interpretation of the incident. Egypt's intended audience was the Arab world. Israel was just an available and convenient tool. Consequently, the diplomatic avenue was not necessarily the preferred line of action. Perhaps, according to Israel, a combination of military pressure and diplomatic moves could bring back the sailors somewhat earlier. Second, Israel dealt too much with formalities rather than engaging in a serious behind-the-scenes discussion of the way to secure the crew's release. Much time was devoted to a rather marginal issue under the circumstances: the formal status of the people held by Egypt. Israel was not sure of the status of the boat crew either. Clearly, they were not POWs because they did not meet any of the requirements qualifying them as such. They did not meet the conditions necessary under the Fourth Convention either. Formally speaking, Israel did not know what status to claim for them. Consequently, the term chosen was *sea piracy* to describe the Egyptian move.[13] Strangely enough, or perhaps in order to justify their capture, Egypt informed the ICRC that it would not allow visits until the "judicial enquiry [is] terminated."[14] That enquiry served once again to manifest the impartiality of the Egyptian investigative organs: the Egyptian officers, assisted by UNEF personnel, could not attain conclusive evidence that the boat was indeed in Egyptian territorial waters when captured. Furthermore, during the investigation Egypt gave UNEF personnel the first opportunity to briefly meet with the boat crew.[15] That did not mean there would be routine visits, and obviously the ban on ICRC visits continued. Along with the continued rejection of any ICRC visits until November 7, it meant that Egypt did not see the fishermen as entitled to Geneva Convention protection either as military personnel or merely civilians, being, as indicated by the continued use of the MAC, violators only of the Armistice Agreement.[16]

The two Israeli misconceptions could have been resolved in a short period of time had the Israeli decision makers read carefully and understood the message that kept coming out of Egypt from mid-October on: a token quid pro quo should be given to Egypt—then everything would be over. Egypt claimed that on September 30, 1957, about one week after the capture of the Israeli vessel, Israel seized a similar Egyptian boat. The Egyptian request was amazingly simple: get us ours back and we will get yours to you. All levels of government dealing directly or indirectly with Israel affairs repeated that line. Even the Egyptian chief of general staff spoke of such an exchange while meeting with the ICRC representative (although indicating that the fishermen would be freed but that Egypt would appropriate the boat).[17] Perhaps considering the possibility that Israel did not have the boat, he offered, as if to settle the matter, an additional way of resolving the crisis. His request was that Israel shed some light on the whereabouts of an Egyptian plane lost over the Mediterranean with sixteen officers aboard on the eve of the Sinai campaign. The Egyptian chief of staff was supposed to have been on that plane but he never boarded it upon departure from Damascus.[18] Clearly, the ICRC reports conveyed to Israel create the impression that the surviving Egyptian senior officer was the person in charge of resolving the crisis. In late December, he probably concluded that Israel could not provide any pertinent response and was looking for a face-saving compromise: "If Dayyan [the Israeli chief of staff] would give me, as one officer to another, his word that Israel did not hold any Egyptian ship and that it knew nothing of the plane, I would accept it,"[19] obviously indicating a possible way out of the Egyptian and Israeli dilemma. That comment would much later on, in the aftermath of the 1967 War, inspire the formula that would enable the release of the members of the sabotage cells.

However, in spite of that high-level involvement and pressure, Israel still claimed to have never captured any such vessel and obviously never admitted any connection to the shooting down of the plane. Consideration of the Egyptian attitude to its own in the context of the October 1956 POWs would have revealed that Egypt did not care if Israel had taken over an Egyptian boat—then, after loudly condemning the Israeli piracy, would have exchanged one boat and crew for another. This way Egypt could once again have proven its steadfast opposition to the "Zionist enemy." Israel, working under the watchful eyes of its judicial branch and the media (although a far cry from their involvement in such issues from the 1980s on—see below), could not even comprehend Egypt's mindset and kept denying any knowledge of the whereabouts of the boat.[20] Great Britain, an "old hand" in Middle Eastern affairs, could not but guide Israel in the right direction, an indication so settled that even leading Israeli diplomats of the time badly missed.[21] However, he was alone because even the Swedish secretary general was at a loss concerning the Egyptian insistence on the so-called hijacking of their civilian boat.[22] However, even though the MFA could not even agree to the principle of open sea hijacking, the Israeli military personnel, realizing the futility of the situation, did plan and execute the takeover of an Egyptian fishing boat sometime in mid-November. Israel did not publicly report that move, and it did not find its way to the contemporary Israeli press. However, with that move, Israel did have the necessary "bargaining chip."[23]

The fishing boat incident underlined the Israeli feeling of isolation. At that time the Soviet Union was clearly and openly against the Israeli position, partly because of Israel's July 1950 decision to adopt the Western line regarding the Korean War. The United States had been at loggerheads with Israel since the beginning of the Eisenhower presidency, especially after the 1956 military operation, and insisted on an Israeli return to the MAC forum.[24] Relations with the United Kingdom were not close either. Even Italy, the homeland of the Captain, and France, an ally of Israel, refrained from helping at all. Israel was left in late October/early November 1957 with only two paths to explore: first, approaching national trade unions overseas, especially those dealing with fishing, and through them reaching their respective governments; and second, approaching the Federal Republic of Germany (West Germany). The first idea was based on the Israeli leadership—most of whom were members of the social democratic *Mapai* party [Hebrew: party of workers of the Land of Israel]—still believing that they had common grounds with other socialist parties. As for the second approach or German connection—the fishing boat had been bought by reparation funds paid by Germany to Israel in the wake of the Jewish Holocaust.

Unsurprisingly, the first group to voice public support for the Israeli stand was the Public Transportation Association of Stuttgart.[25] At first, Israeli decision makers probably saw such a public solidarity with Israel as merely a means for West Germany to advance its diplomatic efforts. With the passing of time, however, and the realization that Israel stood alone, it decided, as a matter of policy, to dispatch a delegation to meet with sailors' and fishermen's associations to enlist their support and to ask for public condemnation of the Egyptian move. Realizing Israel's political isolation, the guidelines for the meetings were simple: do not discuss politics; speak of the human suffering of the people and the families.[26] That approach was perhaps a "last resort" because by late October all other avenues except, obviously, for kidnapping an Egyptian vessel had been fully exhausted to no avail.

The fishing boat incident and the two similar cases involving individual sailors on foreign ships not only accentuated Israel's failure to accurately read the global diplomatic map. Indeed, they also highlighted a variable totally within the jurisdiction of any government, the Israeli government included. That variable is caring about the families and the returning prisoners' quality of life once they were united with them. Israeli authorities left those matters within the jurisdiction of the shipping company, no less, as a result of their inability to find any funding for the families. At first, the MFA tried to find a way through the law of disbursement for border area affected people (1956; in effect 1956–1982). However, no direct connection between any hostile military activities in the border area could be established for the current purpose, leaving the people and their families in limbo.[27]

Egypt never released the boat, but on January 27, 1958, it returned the crew to Israel. Israel returned to Egypt six fishermen whom it had apprehended about two months after the capture of the Israeli one. Their release did not include the boat either. Who gave the orders, when they were given, and how to capture the Egyptian fishing boat are unknown to this day because the IDF documents on this matter if they exist at all are not accessible. Nonetheless, it is clear that the Israeli move triggered the exchange process. Once communications began, the intensive efforts of the ICRC, composed of frequent visits to Egypt and constant pressure on the Egyptian authorities, were perhaps the main moving power behind the scenes.

Not too long after the fishing boat incident, another event related to Israeli citizens in hostile hands occurred. Two Israeli agents went missing in Algeria, sending the Israeli system into a frantic effort to verify that they were alive and what the quid pro quo to be paid to the capturing side would be. There are two initial stages in identifying a missing person: first, establishing that the person is indeed missing; and second, attempting to discover his or her whereabouts. Obviously, it is a painful task that does not always yield conclusive results. In this case, the *Agence France Presse*, a wire service well established within the Arab world, broke the news that two Israelis had been kidnapped in Algeria on February 19, 1958.[28] There is no indication in the sources consulted for this study as to which interested party served as the source for AFP. Israel would later find out that the two persons were abducted from their taxicab en route to southern Algeria on February 17.[29] The gap in time between the actual kidnapping and its discovery is usually crucial in such cases because the first forty-eight hours may present a better chance of recovering the kidnapped person. However, with the passing of time many forensic indications disappear. It is quite probable that under the chaotic conditions in Algeria at that time the window of opportunity for discovering any traces of the abduction was even more brief than usual. The country was at the time undergoing a bloody civil war between the Algerians represented by the Front de Libération Nationale (FLN) and the European non-Algerians, mostly French (*pieds noirs*), who were divided politically among themselves. The year 1958 saw the peak of those confrontations and the country plunging into a state of disorder. Against that background, the Jewish Agency, a nongovernmental organization in Israel that has had strong mutual relations with Algeria's central government, at times acting as its long arm, sent several *Aliyah* (immigration to Israel) emissaries to Algeria. No mission was possible at the time without at least a degree of coordination between Israel and FLN on the one hand and the French on the other hand. Because the body in charge of such foreign relations in Israel is the Mossad, the Israeli secret services, it stands to reason that the emissaries, although acting under the immigration organization the Jewish Agency, were helped by the Mossad. Moreover, the immigration activities were strongly connected by the Jewish armed underground in Algeria that had to provide the local Jews with some defense until another force could come to the rescue. That underground movement was established and maintained by the Mossad.[30] It is no coincidence that the Israeli national memorial for the intelligence community operatives includes the two emissaries in question as killed in action.

Even though it is rather difficult to trace all of the Israeli moves, several hindering factors stand out. For the first time, the adversary holding Israeli citizens was not a nation-state. The FLN was not only a subnational actor, but was also financed and equipped at times by Egypt's Nasser and indeed defined all non-Algerians as enemies. This way Israel had no real partner to negotiate with and no territory that could be defined as its own—and consequently be a potential target for either a retaliation or taking bargaining chips. Even a rescue operation was not possible due to the fact that Algeria was not an enemy country and consequently collecting intelligence on Algeria was not justified. Moreover, the elusiveness of the FLN and probably the activity of a number of Algerian groups rendered any mission an impossibility.

Second, no international organization, especially the ICRC, would negotiate at least publicly with an opposition actor. As long as the French were the sovereign there was no internationally accepted way to approach the FLN. Moreover, by the time the Israelis were kidnapped, several similar cases involving other nationalities had already occurred. The organization knew from experience that there were no negotiation partners and that the chances of finding the agents alive were slim at best.[31]

As far as the ICRC was concerned, there was an additional hurdle stemming from the rumors, probably spread by the FLN, that the Israelis had been kidnapped for ransom and that there was no political motive behind the incident.[32] That put the affair in the criminal arena rather than regarding it as a humanitarian one among hostile nations, as is the custom with the FLN. From an Israeli point of view that brought a ray of hope because Israel was willing to pay any amount of money in order to guarantee a safe return.[33] Considering the warm relations at the time between Israel and France, it was only natural that the negotiations with the FLN were conducted by the Jewish Agency even though the Foreign Ministry had to secretly give it its own stamp of approval once a deal was struck. Even though the first reports of negotiations proved wrong, there was still hope considering that the initial connection had already been made.[34] Even though there are no reports available on any negotiations between the two actors, an indirect channel through Tunisia, one of the main supply routes of the FLN at the time, was open to some extent for a while. On March 6 a message arrived from Tunisia reaffirming a previous report that the two were alive and well and that they would be released within a week in Tunisian territory.[35] That report was corroborated by an

ICRC report quoting officials at the Quai d'Orsay. However, the latter claimed that the FLN was already engaged in release negotiations with representatives of the World Jewish Congress, a non-Israeli based Jewish organization.[36] As would be discovered later the FLN did indeed use a parallel channel to deal with the emissaries issue. The choice of the WJC was deliberate: it was perhaps the Jewish organization least connected with Israel, and its leader was known to have many disagreements with successive Israeli prime ministers. Moreover, dealing with a Jewish organization meant that the Algerian rebels did not have to deal directly with Israel, an enemy of the Arab nation and an ally of France, and that they could count on the organization pursuing policy not necessarily identical to that of Israel. Having the WJC as an additional negotiator also meant that the FLN could at least try to drive a wedge between the organization and Israel and extract a higher price from Israel. Briefly stated, about a month after the disappearance of the two emissaries there seemed to be several players involved in the efforts to get them back. They included Israel, through its Geneva diplomatic mission, the Jewish Agency, and the Mossad; the ICRC through its Tunisia representative, who had had no record of success getting French hostages back; the French government, through its Foreign Ministry; and the WJC. All tried to talk to the FLN without actually being aware that the organization did not at the time enjoy full control over all its wings and groups.[37] Clearly, the main issue facing all efforts was the lack of a clear player to negotiate with.

The Algerian Red Crescent stepped right into that vacuum. It is unclear which authority that organization had. Anyway, it was associated with the FLN and was probably part of the infrastructure for an independent Algeria. In April 1958 the Algerian Red Crescent secretary general kept in touch with the ICRC representative in Tunisia, who promised the secretary general that the two Israelis who were at that time with the rebels not far from the Moroccan border were alive and well and that they would be returned at the "next appropriate opportunity."[38] In spite of the tendency of the people involved in the efforts to receive that news as a good omen, the Israeli representative, a veteran of many exchange deals in the mid-1950s, remained pessimistic. Not too long after, his report to Jerusalem was answered by a report from Jerusalem telling him rumors of the execution of the two.[39] With the news kept from the families and yet very much on the minds of the Israeli officials dealing with the issue, it came as a shock to the families that AFP published those unconfirmed reports. The MFA responded by asking the president of the WJC to approach its FLN partner in negotiations—the FLN representative in New York—and ask for proof that the two captives were alive and for letters for the families. If this were not done, so went the message, Israel would publicize "the whole thing."[40] Unfortunately, that was a hollow threat. Many civilians had been killed by that time in Algeria with no effective opposing steps taken by any international player. Furthermore, no move could at that point in time hurt the Algerian struggle for independence that was already legitimized by large segments of the French public.

Meanwhile, the rollercoaster continued with an additional round of rumors that the people were alive finding its way to the Israeli agencies in charge, the MFA, the Jewish Agency, and the Mossad. That left them all at a crossroads, struggling, without success, to find a way to develop some new sources of intelligence.[41] That did not take long; in mid-May the Israeli ambassador to the UN in Geneva informed his superiors in Jerusalem that the emissaries were not alive any more. He was not sure about the exact circumstances but the end result was brutally clear-cut.[42] All along, the FLN people continued to talk indirectly to emissaries on behalf of Israel and the ICRC claiming to work for an exchange deal.[43] In late May, even the FLN people realized that their partners in negotiations knew the facts and the FLN admitted somewhat halfheartedly that the Israelis were no longer alive.[44] By mid-July, the Israeli operatives and diplomats read the situation negatively: in spite of the lack of hard evidence, the hostages were clearly dead. Israel reached that conclusion from the accumulation of bits and pieces of reports mainly from the ICRC and French and Israeli sources, such as the discovery of a number of bodies in the assumed location where the Israelis had been last seen and the overall chaos and wave of killing of *pieds noirs* all over Algeria.[45] On August 18, the MFA distributed among its representations a brief prepared by the Jewish Agency. It summarized in three points the Israeli failed attempt to rescue the hostages: the emissaries' activities were of a peaceful nature; Israel got many commitments from the rebels that were not fulfilled; and the rebels used deceit in their negotiations with proxies working on behalf of Israel.[46] In September, the direct supervisor of the two published a eulogy for the two in a leading Israeli newspaper.[47] In the 1970s they were recognized by the Israeli government as "killed by the sovereign"—that is, people who lost their lives while on a mission of a Jewish nature. The term was first used during Roman times referring to Jews who were executed by the Romans for standing by their religion and its commandments. Since the establishment of the State of Israel the term has indicated people killed while serving Israel, usually in connection with immigration and security.[48]

With the curtain going down, two conclusions can be drawn and should be added to the emerging Israeli POW/MIA policies. First, there was no distinction between uniformed personnel and civilians as long as they were working for Israel's security in its widest interpretation, namely immigration, inter alia. Secondly, analysis of that episode today, decades after the events, reveals that the lack of a central hand dealing with the issue did not matter. The captives were probably killed shortly after their abduction. However, the picture that emerges from contemporary documentation is of several bodies working on behalf of Israel with only a limited degree of coordination among them all. That picture would change not long afterward, with Israeli authorities closing ranks in regard to the Israeli agent, Eli Cohen, who was apprehended by Syria in early 1965.[49]

While the focus in Jerusalem was on the fate of the two emissaries and the tragic conclusion of this chapter, something else happened in Israel. On July 31, 1958, the prisoners, Jews and Arabs, in a maximum-security jail rebelled, and within a short time scores of Arab convicts found their way to the (Jordanian) West Bank. Israel apprehended the leader of the rebels, who was an Egyptian intelligence agent spying on Israel under the cover of a reporter.[50] Strangely enough and in an almost unprecedented way, Egypt not only showed interest in the prisoner, but it also insisted that ICRC staff visit him. The simple explanation for that Egyptian move could be that Cairo grasped the power of presenting Israel as the player that did not adhere to international covenants. But there was probably a more implicit reason: in February 1958, Egypt and Syria announced their union under the name the United Arab Republic. That union would be abolished in a Syrian military revolution that redeclared Syria's independence in September 1961.[51] During the 1950s and 1960s Syria had the reputation of holding onto Israeli captives for long periods, at times even without admitting having them. Nasser, as the sovereign of Syria, needed some ammunition in case a prisoner crisis erupted for one reason or another, with Israel meeting the standards set by his second province, Syria. Going back to the breakout from the Israeli jail, the leader of the escape operation could well serve the Nasserite principles of presenting a new courageous Egypt that would not bow under pressure from the imperialist powers.

Almost three months after the prison break, the ICRC paid a visit to the convicted leader in response to an Egyptian request.[52] In the following months, Egypt invested in his well-being hitherto unknown amounts of time and effort, while involving the ICRC and the UN secretary general personally.[53] Additionally, the Egyptian authorities started their inquiries regarding five of their soldiers missing since the October–November 1956 operation.[54] That atypical behavior might have indicated some Egyptian interest in building a case for an exchange of prisoners: theirs for a number of Israelis—some of whom were deserters, some in poor health. The purpose behind that move was probably their concern for their agent on Israeli soil, feeling he had already served his homeland and should be united with his handlers and family. According to the Israeli newspaper *Davar*, which served at times as the outlet for security items cleared by military censorship for the purpose of psychological warfare, the agent was indeed senior. Ali Ṣabri, one of the members of President Nasser's inner circle, had called him years earlier to the flag and instructed him on his mission. He arrived in Israel under an assumed name in late September 1957 and the Israeli security authorities put him under surveillance almost right away until his arrest in early November.[55] Because Israel was convinced of his mission but did not catch him red-handed, its security officers put him under administrative detention, which by definition is intended to stop suspects from carrying out their missions. Moreover, under Israeli law, as long as a suspect is not convicted or arrested for interrogation, it is absolutely forbidden to interrogate him in any way. After his leading role in the prison break, the agent was arraigned on criminal charges stemming from that attempt. That classification gave the Israeli authorities a degree of leeway in questioning him. All of that was probably the background for the change in Egyptian POW policies.

As expected, Israel did desire to use that opening and to use it for the release of the Cairo and Alexandria cell people. Israel was also interested in the return of quite a few more people who found themselves in Egyptian hands as discussed earlier in the book. If under different circumstances Israel had failed to grasp the meaning of the Egyptian signals, this time it was the ICRC's turn to repeat that mistake. The international organization had been involved in the case insofar as the conditions of convicted Egyptian citizens (probably on humanitarian grounds) were the issue since 1957.[56] While in Cairo in late December 1958, the ICRC general delegate for the Middle East raised several issues with his hosts, including the request by the family of the Egyptian alleged spy to release him as well as the five Egyptian soldiers who supposedly had been left in Israel during the 1957 POW exchange.[57] In spite of his earlier promises to his counterpart at the Israeli Ministry of Foreign Affairs, the ICRC general delegate did not even try to visit a female member of the jailed cells in Cairo. He reported, however, that he had heard her conditions were fine and that she was even allowed to walk outside of the prison. Not only was that a strange report based on unclear sources, but it was also totally out of place considering that the Egyptians had laid the groundwork for some substantive requests by the ICRC. Instead of somewhat relieving Israeli worries regarding the imprisonment conditions of its people, the report only aggravated them. The MFA and the Prime Minister's Office insisted on open and formal ICRC visits with the prisoners.[58] Such visits did not materialize, and the probably intentional uncertainty created by the Egyptians continued. On top of Egypt's refusal to report to the ICRC any details regarding the female prisoner, they found an indirect way to persuade the Israeli authorities that any effort of any kind to try and get details might harm the female prisoner.[59] In April/May 1958, Israel passed to the ICRC letters from the prisoners' families in Egypt for delivery to Egypt.[60] There is no indication that Egypt had encouraged this, but precedents indicate that at least the ICRC believed it was possible for the letters to reach the inmates.

All of that points to a probable mood among the Israeli decision makers that release was impossible, therefore they had to continue their efforts to improve the conditions of the internees instead of working for their release. That could be done in two ways. First, considering their food needs, Israel asked the ICRC to serve as the intermediary in supplying them with food packages.[61] Second, regarding visits—the male prisoners had already been granted one visit, the female had not. In addition, the Israeli MFA[62] also asked for permission to send the internees some food and a weekly allowance of £5 each.[63] About a month later, the ICRC in Nazareth, Israel, ostensibly in a move independent of any other move regarding other prisoners, Israeli or Arab, requested that the Israeli police in charge at the time of the Israeli prisons hand some canned food and a small amount of money to the Egyptian agent. Once again, in that subtle matter Israel missed its mark by not allowing the prisoner to receive the food. The MFA did agree to that almost six months later when Israel realized its mistake, but the Prisons Authority continued to disapprove of allowing the prisoners to receive such food and money.[64] The Israelis, however, were in favor of the latter.[65]

Concurrent with the small confidence-building measures, Egypt continued its demand for the return of the Egyptians allegedly held by Israel since the 1956 campaign and the handing over of a comprehensive list of all Egyptians jailed in Israel. As far as one can tell from the ICRC report to the Israeli MFA personnel, Egypt had not unambiguously offered an exchange but had created the impression—not lost on the ICRC—that once they got the list of Egyptians in Israel a major hurdle might be removed.[66] One of the two missing Egyptians in mid-1959 was eventually found in Jordan, meaning that like others before him in the 1950s he had simply crossed Israel en route to Jordan.[67]

While Israel was mainly concerned with its own people in Egyptian jails, a new prisoners' front opened. It is hard to figure out which event sparked the interest in Israeli citizens in Syrian hands. Following the POW/civilians in enemy hands issue since 1948 shows that Israel had invested enormous intelligence efforts in successive attempts to verify the whereabouts of missing Israelis. It is quite reasonable that with the Egyptian-Syrian union, Israeli intelligence assets in Egypt, the main Israeli arena of interest, a trusted source could shed some additional light on Syrian affairs as well.[68] In the spring of 1959 Israel became aware of the fact that about twelve Israeli citizens considered missing were in Syrian hands, some for many years. One of these, an Israeli soldier walking alone outside one of the villages in northern Israel, was kidnapped by a Syrian patrol in March 1953. Israel decided to treat that case and those of the other Israelis in the Syrian jails as humanitarian, not POW cases. The reasoning was probably twofold: first, some of them were on active duty while crossing the border but none was on a military assignment; and second, by that time Israel believed that innocent citizens would be better treated and that they had better chances of release than uniformed personnel.[69] These hopes were dashed time and again and even the ICRC could not get a permit to visit the Israelis in jail.[70] From a different angle it is possible that Israel, realizing Egypt's leading role in the united foreign policy, believed that the precedents set south of the border would be followed by all parties north of the border. That was not to happen; Syria did not disclose any names or other prisoner-related details that Israel was not already aware of. That policy, in spite of the changing regimes and the civil war that would begin many years later in 2011, never changed. In any case, from September 1959 until the actual partial exchange took place in late 1963, the Syrian position was clearly attempting to forestall any meeting between anyone from the outside with the Israelis, and certainly no confirmation of any prisoner's name was transferred to Israel. Lacking any information, Israel could not even discern which of the Israelis in Syrian prisons was a POW, a deserter, or a kidnapped civilian.[71] The only clue Syria communicated through the ICRC was that Israel should approach Syria through the MAC,[72] advice that Israel could not accept considering its traditional reluctance involving any MAC activity. Concurrent with the POW issues, which were obviously marginal for the Syrians, much more fateful events occurred in Syria. In September 1961 Syria seceded from the United Arab Republic, inaugurating what came to be known among the Arab masses as the era of *infiṣal* (cessation, a pejorative in Arabic). Even before that, in April 1961, all Arab chiefs of general staff decided at their meeting to prevent by all means, military included, the diversion of the Jordan River waters within Israel. Because the closest was Syria and because it had to prove its loyalty to the "Arab cause" in spite of the obliteration of the Union, its leaders had to take upon themselves the fight against Israel. Even though Syria saw a number of coups d'état in the 1960s, all successive regimes shared that conviction. In the context of the POWs and the others held by Damascus, those changes meant nothing.

Through Israeli eyes the fishing in the Lake of Galilee, which under the 1949 Armistice Agreement and the farming within Demilitarized Zones (DMZ) defined by that agreement, was a mini casus belli. Consequently, with the continued Syrian interruption of fishing in the lake in early 1962 Israel decided to launch a military operation intended to build deterrence and remove at least for a while the Syrian threat from the sovereign territory of Israel in the lake. All the while Syria was holding Israeli citizens with no military operation for their release on its agenda. In the tension between building military deterrence and kidnapping "bargaining chips," the former was obviously taking priority in 1962. Israel launched Operation Martin (*snunit* operation) during the night of March 16/17, 1962. The operation was not a success in spite of the usual chatter in its aftermath.[73] Israel lost seven dead and two MIAs. Within five days of the operation, Israel and Syria exchanged the one Syrian

POW for the body of a dead Israeli soldier.[74] The other is considered MIA to this day. The speed of the exchange and the price paid—one body for one Syrian—clearly fell outside the Israeli-Syrian modus operandi in the POW context before and after this episode. The difference lay not only in the short time elapsed between the taking and the releasing of a POW, but also in Syria coveting their soldier who was ostensibly not an officer nor a relative of any leading Syrian figure. Israel for its part for the first time exchanged only one live enemy soldier for a body. No Israeli from among those in Syrian jails, the topic of endless contacts through third parties, especially the ICRC, was included in the deal—again atypical of Israel. Similar deals had occurred in the past but had always included living and dead soldiers on both sides. The circumstances surrounding this unique exchange strongly suggest that Israel needed the POW back in order to somewhat discourage any possible public interest in the actual IDF conduct during battle. Israel preferred, in one of the last POW cases of David Ben Gurion as prime minister and Minister of Defense, to publicly save face and not extract intelligence that the Syrian prisoner possibly possessed. It is hard to say what access the prisoner had, but considering that Syria started in the early 1960s to receive sophisticated Soviet war material, it might be safe to speculate on his connection to such new systems.

Perhaps the Israeli POW diplomatic and military behavior in the post-1956 campaign should be studied along two lines: the mistakes committed and the way Israel understood them, if at all; and second, the accumulated policy lines and the way they have added, if at all, to a coherent policy.

One mistake was the failure to acknowledge the subtle signals by the Arab parties. They did not recognize Israel in any way and consistently ignored it. However, at times they needed a particular prisoner back and signaled the terms of a future process, signals that in most cases were ignored for lack of understanding of the Arab side's gesture language. Israel also failed to connect any particular prisoner issue with the larger political, international, and regional picture as seen from the Arab capitals. That made the choice of mediators difficult to impossible for Israel. Likewise, Israel was too much concerned with the issue of giving the impression that it was yielding to the other side. However, no responsible body has ever drafted any "red lines" or fallback positions, which meant that any exchange required going through the process of reinventing them, at times with no coherent line connecting such positions to past precedents.

Yet in spite of the many inconsistencies, some policy lines did emerge after October–November 1956: the diplomatic avenue was not necessarily the preferred line of action; even the MFA, unlike during the early 1950s, realized that at times taking enemy hostages was imperative. That connects well with the impression created at that period that no return can be unilateral and that each side had to offer something as a quid pro quo. No humanitarian gestures. Another lesson, still valid today when dealing with Egypt: a commitment by an Egyptian officer is worth more than a third-party signature on a formal agreement. That was not the case with Syria, and the lesson on that front was much more pessimistic: Syria, under whatever circumstances and regime, would not share any information regarding Israeli prisoners—and without a substantial intelligence effort by Israel, no piece of information would be willingly transmitted. Along that front and far removed from the headlines, Israel created in 1962 a precedent to be repeated many times in the years ahead: exchanging one live enemy soldier for only the body of an Israeli combatant. That brings up an additional Israeli insight: it is pointless to start conveying messages to the Arab side before Israel did its utmost to verify the fate of the MIAs. Not doing the utmost means paying high prices for bodies or people whom the other side is in no position to return. One last Israeli conclusion fell within the domestic arena: the obligation to define each person falling into the hands of the enemy under whatever conditions as a "must be brought home at any price."

Finally, and on the Israeli domestic political track, the return of POWs and hostages are always a reason to celebrate in Israel. At times, especially with botched military campaigns, paying whatever price for that happy occasion may divert attention from a failing operation or political behavior, thus discouraging domestic political pressure.

NOTES

1. *Davar*, July 23, 1957; ISA/FM/18/2/398/57, from Geneva, to Jerusalem, August 2, 1957, ISA/FM/18/2/407/57, from Geneva, to Jerusalem, August 7, 1957; ISA/FM/18/2/424/57, from Geneva, to Jerusalem, August 16, 1957.
2. For some a preliminary discussion of the issue, see ISA/FM/18/2/407/57, from Geneva, to Jerusalem, August 7, 1957.
3. ISA/FM/2096/16/9–12/57, from Jerusalem, to New York, October 11, 1957; ISA/FM/2096/16/9–12/57, from Rome, to Jerusalem, October 24, 1957.
4. *Davar*, September 25, 1957; ISA/FM/2096/16/9–12/57/311, from Jerusalem, to Geneva, September 25, 1957; ISA/FM/2096/16/9–12/57/, from New York, to Jerusalem, October 2, 1957.
5. ISA/FM/2096/14/11/57–1/58/3801, from The Hague, to Jerusalem, November 6, 1957; ISA/FM/2096/14/11/57–1/58/480, from The Hague, to Jerusalem, November 6, 1957.
6. ISA/FM/2096/16/9–12/57/508/57, from Geneva, to Jerusalem, October 2, 1957, same document: ISA/FM/18/2/508/57.
7. ISA/FM/2096/16/9–12/57/508/57, from Jerusalem, to New York, October 15, 1957, and see above in the context of the October campaign POWs and the "protective power" issue.
8. ISA/FM/2096/16/9–12/57, from Geneva, to Jerusalem, October 2, 1957; ISA/FM/2096/16/9–12/57, from Jerusalem, to New York, October 3, 1957; ISA/FM/2096/16/9–12/57, from New York, to Jerusalem, October 9, 1957.
9. ISA/FM/2096/16/9–12/57, from Jerusalem, to Geneva, October 21, 1957.

10. ISA/FM/2096/16/9–12/57/682, from Jerusalem, to Washington, November 7, 1957.

11. ISA/FM/2096/16/9–12/57, from New York, to Jerusalem, October 5, 11, 1957; ISA/FM/2096/16/9–12/57, from Geneva, to Jerusalem, October 12, 1957; ISA/FM/2096/16/9–12/57/631, from Jerusalem, to Washington, October 23, 1957; ISA/FM/2096/16/9–12/57/452, from New York, to Jerusalem, November 7, 1957.

12. ISA/FM/2096/16/9–12/57, from Rome, to Jerusalem, October 7, 1957; ISA/FM/2096/16/9–12/57, from Jerusalem, to New York, October 15, 1957; ISA/FM/2096/16/9–12/57, from Rome, to Jerusalem, October 25, 1957; ISA/FM/2096/16/9–12/57, from Rome, to Jerusalem, October 30, 1957.

13. ISA/FM/2096/16/9–12/57/508/57, from Jerusalem, to New York, October 4, 1957; ISA/FM/2096/14/11/57–1/58/600, from Jerusalem, to The Hague, November 8, 1957.

14. ISA/FM/2096/16/9–12/57/316, from Jerusalem, to Geneva, October 11, 1957.

15. ISA/FM/2096/16/9–12/57/316, two messages from Jerusalem, to Rome and Geneva, October 18, 1957.

16. Cf. ISA/FM/18/2/524/57, from Geneva, to Jerusalem, October 23, 1957; ISA/FM/2096/16/9–12/57/63, from Geneva, to Jerusalem, November 7, 1957; ISA/FM/2096/16/9–12/57/6010, from Jerusalem, to several addresses at MFA and UN and U.S. representations, November 7, 1957.

17. ISA/FM/18/2/540/57, from Geneva, to Jerusalem, November 8, 1957.

18. An IDF plane shot it down as part of an attempt to sabotage the Egyptian preparations for the upcoming confrontation. IDF released those details of Operation *Tarnegol* [Rooster] in 1989 many years after all involved were dead.

19. ISA/FM/2096/16/9–12/57/616, from Jerusalem, to New York, December 24, 1957.

20. ISA/FM/2096/16/9–12/57/508/57, from New York, to Jerusalem, October 14, 15, 17, 1957; ISA/FM/2096/16/9–12/57, from London, to Jerusalem, October 24, 1957.

21. ISA/FM/2096/16/9–12/57/398, from New York, to Jerusalem, October 29, 1957.

22. ISA/FM/2096/16/9–12/57, from New York, to Jerusalem, October 29, 1957.

23. *Ma'ariv*, January 27, 1958.

24. ISA/FM/2096/16/9–12/57/416, from Washington, to Jerusalem, October 30, 1957; ISA/FM/2096/16/9–12/57/333, from Washington, to Jerusalem, October 30, 1957; ISA/FM/2096/16/9–12/57/334, from Washington, to Jerusalem, November 5, 1957.

25. ISA/FM/2096/16/9–12/57/2654, from the Israeli Reparations Mission, Köln, to Jerusalem, October 8, 1957.

26. ISA/FM/2096/16/9–12/57, Internal MFA memo addressed to the FM, October 29, 1957; ISA/FM/2096/16/9–12/57/473, from Jerusalem, to Brussels, November 4, 1957.

27. The law of disbursement for border area affected people (1956) [in effect 1956–1982], http://www.nevo.co.il.mgs-ariel.macam.ac.il/law_html/law19/BTL0225.htm; ISA/FM/2096/16/9–12/57, Internal MFA memo, November 6, 1957.

28. *Ha'aretz, Herut*, February 20; *Davar, Ma'ariv*, February 21, 1958.

29. CSA/S6/7295, Internal Jewish Agency memo, February 26, 1958.

30. Eli Duvdevani, "Letter to the Editor," *Ha'aretz*, November 26, 2007, cf. Michael M. Laskier, "The Israeli *Mossad* and Muslim-Jewish Coexistence in Colonial Algeria: The Constantine Affair of 12–13 May 1956," *Pe'amim* [Hebrew] 75 (Spring 1998): 129–43, especially 132–33.

31. ISA/FM/2096/13/67/58, from Jerusalem, to Geneva, February 20, 1958; ISA/FM/2096/13/78/58, from Geneva, to Jerusalem, February 21, 1958, same document: ISA/FM/18/2/78/57; ISA/FM/18/2/273/58, from Geneva, to Jerusalem, June 25, 1958.

32. *ha-Boker*, March 23, 1958; CSA/S6/7295, an embargoed Jewish Agency press release to the Israeli media, March 9, 1958.

33. CSA/S6/7295, Internal Jewish Agency memo, February 27, 1958, 8:45 p.m.; ISA/FM/2096/13/, from the Jewish Agency, to MFA, Jerusalem, February 28, 1958.

34. CSA/S6/7295, Internal Jewish Agency memo, March 2, 1958; CSA/S6/7295, from the Jewish Agency, to MFA, Jerusalem, March 2, 1958.

35. CSA/S6/7295, Internal Jewish Agency memo, March 6, 1958.

36. ISA/FM/2096/13/114/58, from Geneva, to Jerusalem, March 19, 1958.

37. CSA/S6/7295, Internal Jewish Agency memo, February 25, 1958; ISA/FM/2096/13/114/58, from Geneva, to Jerusalem, March 19, 1958.
38. ISA/FM/2096/13/138/58, from Geneva, to Jerusalem, April 4, 1958; CSA/S6/7295, from the Jewish Agency, to MFA, April 16, 1958.
39. ISA/FM/2096/13, from Jerusalem, to Geneva, April 27, 28, 1958.
40. ISA/FM/2096/13, from Jerusalem, to New York, May 11, 1958; ISA/FM/18/2/273/58, from Geneva, to Jerusalem, June 25, 1958.
41. Cf. *ha-Boker*, May 11, 1958; ISA/FM/2096/13, from Jerusalem, to Geneva, May 12, 1958; *la-Merhav*, May 12, 1958.
42. ISA/FM/2096/13/190/58, from Geneva, to Jerusalem, May 14, 1958.
43. ISA/FM/2096/13, from Jerusalem, to Geneva, May 18, 1958.
44. ISA/FM/2096/13/222/58, from Geneva, to Jerusalem, May 30, 1958; ISA/FM/2096/13/131, from Geneva, to Jerusalem, June 3, 1958; ISA/FM/18/2/273/58, from Geneva, to Jerusalem, June 25, 1958; ISA/FM/2096/13/305/58, from Geneva, to Jerusalem, July 15, 1958.
45. ISA/FM/2096/13/238/58, from Geneva, to Jerusalem, July 25, 1958, two versions.
46. ISA/FM/2096/13, from Jerusalem, to all representations, August 19, 1958.
47. *Ha'aretz*, September 10, 1958.
48. CSA/S6/10372, Jewish Agency internal memos, August 4, 1976, February 28, March 11, 1984.
49. Parts of this paragraph are based on a "top secret" letter from the Israeli ambassador in Paris to the MFA and the Jewish agency, CSA/S6/7257, September 3, 1958.
50. *Ma'ariv*, August 3, 1958.
51. Although the Egyptian-Syrian union existed only for three years (1958–1961), President Nasser kept the name United Arab Republic until his successor, President Sadat, changed it back to the Arab Republic of Egypt (1971).
52. ISA/FM/20/26, from Jerusalem, to Geneva, October 21, 1958; ISA/FM/20/26/485/58, from Geneva, to Jerusalem to, October 24, 1958; minutes of the interview: ISA/FM/20/26/11203–1172, from Israeli Police/Interrogations Directorate, to MFA, Jerusalem, October 28, 1958; ISA/FM/20/26, from Jerusalem, to Geneva, November 12, 1958.
53. ISA/FM/20/26, from Jerusalem, to New York, November 17, 1958.
54. ISA/FM/2096/13, from the [Egyptian] Director of Palestine affairs Department, to [the Egyptian] Ministry of War, November 21, 1958; ISA/FM/2096/13, from MFA, to IDF/Armistice Department, December 31, 1958.
55. *Davar*, August 4, 1958.
56. ISA/FM/2096/16/9–12/57/517/57, from Geneva, to Jerusalem, October 16, 1957.
57. ISA/FM/20/26, from Jerusalem, to Geneva, Report on the visit, January 1, 1959; none of the people mentioned by Egypt had stayed in an Israeli POW camp during the operation, ISA/FM/2096/13, Internal MFA memo, January 28, 1958.
58. ISA/FM/2096/13/, from MFA, to the Prime Minister's Office, March 31, 1958.
59. ISA/FM/20/26/249/59, from Geneva, to Jerusalem to, April 22, 1959, same report: ISA/FM/20/24/249/59.
60. ISA/FM/2096/13, from Jerusalem, to Geneva, May 23, 1958; ISA/FM/2096/13/236/58, from Jerusalem, to Geneva, June 6, 1958.
61. ISA/FM/20/26, from Jerusalem, to Geneva, February 11, 1959; ISA/FM/20/26/118/59, from Geneva, to Jerusalem, February 20, 1959.
62. ISA/FM/2096/13/, from MFA, to Israeli police, July 20, 1959.
63. ISA/FM/20/26, from Jerusalem, to Geneva, February 26, 1959.
64. ISA/FM/2096/13/6288/4/18, from Prisons Authority, to MFA, August 18, 1958.
65. ISA/FM/20/26, from MFA, to Israeli Police HQ, Jerusalem, March 30, 1959, same communication: ISA/FM/2096/13; ISA/FM/20/26, from MFA, to ICRC, Geneva, April 19, 1959.
66. ISA/FM/20/26/249/59, from Geneva, to Jerusalem, April 22, 1959, same report: ISA/FM/20/24/249/59.
67. ISA/FM/20/24/331/59, from Geneva, to Jerusalem, June 10, 1959.

68. Cf. ISA/FM/2096/13, from Jerusalem, to Geneva, June 3, 1959; ISA/FM/2096/13, from Jerusalem, to Geneva, June 14, 1959.

69. ISA/FM/20/26, from MFA, to the Magen David Adom [= Red Shield of David, the Israeli version of a national ICRC], Tel Aviv, May 28, 1959.

70. ISA/FM/2096/13, from Jerusalem, to Geneva, July 3, 1959; ISA/FM/2096/13/496/59, from Geneva, to Jerusalem, August 18, 1959; ISA/FM/2096/13/528/59, from Geneva, to Jerusalem, August 26, 1959.

71. ISA/FM/21/14/76/60, from Geneva, to Jerusalem, January 27, 1960.

72. ISA/FM/2096/13, from Jerusalem, to Geneva, September 6, 1959.

73. Col. M[ordechai] Gur, "Golani Operations, Tawfiq and Nuqeib," *Ma'arkhot* [Hebrew] 174–175 (April 1966): 18–23.

74. *Herut*, March 22, 1962.

SIX

New Regimes, Old Policies, and the Connection between Regime Changes and the Fate of Israeli Agents in Hostile Hands, 1963–1967

Once more, the fate of civilians became tossed about by the hands of politicians in 1963. In early March a new Ba'ath regime took over in Damascus while in mid-June David ben Gurion resigned his position as the prime minister never to return to this position. His successor, Levi Eshkol, had the image of a compromising person, perhaps a figure to take care of the country until a new stronger leader emerged. Meanwhile the retiring leader insisted on opening the case of the sabotage cell in Egypt in 1954, focusing his efforts and attention on finding the person responsible for that fiasco. Because Egypt was too preoccupied with inter-Arab politics and especially its competition with Iraq over the leadership of the Arab world and—due to the existence of UNEF as a buffer of sorts with Israel—Nasser was temporarily at least out of the conflict with Israel. The Ba'ath and Syrian commitment to fight Israel to the end became the call of the day. What a good time to challenge Israel—while its leader was weak and preoccupied with internal politics!

In mid-July 1963 the imminent showdown materialized. Syrian soldiers kidnapped a boat with six persons on board—three tourists and three Israelis.[1] The foreigners were released right away with the Israelis remaining in Syrian hands. In this case, unlike the others, these civilians were not kidnapped without leaving a trace; their whereabouts were documented and they were last seen boarding the boat. Realizing this, the Syrians were quick to admit that they held the six but refrained from allowing them access to the UNTSO/MAC personnel. Soon enough they conveyed to Israel, through the UN, their desire for an exchange: three

Syrians for the three civilians.[2] The proposed deal was obviously intended to create yet another precedent—three kidnapped civilians for three legitimate POWs, leaving out all other prisoners. At that time, the UN believed that Syria held eight Israelis and Israel held ten Syrians and that they all should be exchanged regardless of their formal legal status.[3] Israel refused to such a deal based on the differing definitions that could be attached to the prisoners. However, it realized shortly after adopting that approach that expressing approval of any exchange plan might not only bring all home, but in case the Syrian government did not consent, it would only help to expose its belligerent attitude toward Israel and the UN.[4] That Israeli position was only strengthened in the wake of the UN Security Council meeting on September 4 that was devoted to the situation along the Israeli-Syrian border and was concluded by an appeal of the Security Council president calling on both sides, inter alia, to resolve the prisoners' issue. However, no UN intervention bore any fruit. Israel found itself at a dead end.

In the absence of any other solution, Israel resorted to the old-fashioned practice, out of use for a while (probably since 1956), of capturing "bargaining chips." "Israel" in this case probably consisted of a small group including the new prime minister and Minister of Defense Levi Eshkol, who due to his weak image in military affairs had to prove himself, the Minister of Agriculture, the former chief of staff, General (ret.) Dayyan, and the contemporary chief of staff, Tzvi Tzur, a confidant of Dayyan. From later evidence it is quite reasonable to speculate that the cabinet did not take part in reaching this decision.[5] The lack of interest by Syria in its own troops captured by Israel almost deemed such an idea impractical. Israeli decision makers concluded that the only way to get the Israelis back from Syria was with unorthodox methods—namely kidnapping a Syrian or Syrians high enough in rank to be exchanged for the Israelis in Syrian hands. The implementation of that decision occurred through a naval military operation that remains mostly "top secret" to this day. From the meagre details available today emerges the following picture:[6] A private Lebanese yacht carrying the wife of a leading Syrian figure and three children left a Syrian port en route to Egypt in late October 1963. The yacht, *St. Hilarion,* kept moving outside the Israeli sovereign waters until reaching a certain agreed upon point; it crossed that line and continued for a few minutes within Israeli waters. At that time, a waiting Israeli submarine, ostensibly on a routine patrol, stopped the yacht. People who were not regular members of the submarine crew ordered the four passengers on the yacht to move to the vessel, and while shielding them from the crew escorted the passengers until the submarine arrived in Haifa port. These four were immediately moved to one of the best hotels in town and were kept incommunicado. The time-sensitive nature of accurate intelligence did not allow for much planning, especially at a time when many of the high command of the Israeli navy were on overseas assignments. Yet the Syrian civilians were apprehended without a single shot being fired.

Who were the four people? Due to the sensitive nature of the operation, the chances of a leak, and the possibility of some irrational Syrian reaction, even the senior officers who did not participate were led to believe (this is the official version to this day) that it was the family of the then Syrian Minister of Defense, Brigadier General Abdullah al-Ziadeh. The minister was not a major player on the Syrian political scene and came to his position precisely because of his nonalignment among the various struggling Syrian political cliques.[7] Actually, had his family been the target of the operation, there is little doubt that the Syrian "strong man" Amin al-Hafiz would have dismissed him from his position without any effort to release his family. The process that began right after the kidnapping, its relatively quick and successful conclusion, as well as reports by eyewitnesses to the actual incident all suggest that it was the family of Amin al-Hafiz himself. Under these circumstances an exchange and a quick one for that matter became a must for the Syrian leader. This was not an issue of intelligence, it was simply his failure to keep his family safe, which naturally did not fit well with his position of leader assigned with providing security to his people at large. In this case an issue of honor and prestige turned into a major political and diplomatic crisis. All the while, Syria was undergoing a leadership crisis that eventually led to the replacement of the prime minister. The winner in that showdown was Amin al-Hafiz, who clearly wanted his family back as soon as possible and without any publicity, let alone the sort of publicity that would indicate even the slightest degree of capitulation to Israel. This time the Israeli leaders did read the map of interests correctly. On the surface Syria and Israel continued their fruitless negotiations through the UN; however, shortly after the kidnapping, the two parties started a negotiations marathon initiated by Syria. It was conducted through the good services of the UK military attaché in Turkey who, besides reporting back to London on a need-to-know basis, maintained full secrecy as requested by Syria and Israel. Not even a fortnight after the kidnapping, Syria notified Israel without conditions on secrecy that they were proposing a prisoners exchange.[8] The Israeli military High Command instructed the responsible authorities about that time to prepare the exchange for November 16, 1963. However, in spite of the Syrian preparations for the exchange as witnessed by the prisoners, that date was not met.[9]

The actual exchange took place on December 21, 1963, a Saturday with relatively little media coverage. "The four sailors of the St. Hilarion" were also included in the exchange, according to the Israeli official statement.[10] Israel got back the three boat passengers and eight more, all of whom had spent years in Syrian jails and as noted above, whose presence there was unknown to Israel until the early 1960s. With their return it became evident to Israel that ten more Israelis were still in Syrian hands.[11] Based on the Israeli request, the ICRC agreed to try and find out about their conditions.[12] Within the Israeli inner circles the main concern in late December was the lack of Syrians in Israeli hands. Unlike Syria, Israel did not keep some wild cards for a possible rerun of a POW scenario. Consequently, the main issue facing the Israeli decision makers in late 1963 was not the need to get the Israelis back, but the lack of any new ways to force Syria into such a deal.[13] It is extremely important to note that the critical POW consultation was only one item on the agenda of the ministers. The other had to do with the nuclear reactor of Israel. This is a clear indication of the extreme significance of the Israeli perception of the prisoners' issue. On a different note it is evident from the indirect negotiations preceding the exchange that the Syrians were not sure until the last minute which of the prisoners should be reunited with their families in Israel. Regarding one of the prisoners in particular, the Syrians notified Israel repeatedly of his imminent return; however, they did not let him cross into Israel in December 1963. Once again they denied that they held him and reported that he had left for a third country. Eventually they would return him in August 1966. All indications in this case suggest that the prisoner himself had reservations about going back to Israel.[14]

Israeli approaches to the UN through UNTSO and the ICRC continued unsuccessfully until August 1966 when unexpectedly a new POW exchange deal materialized, for reasons to be discussed later. The period between the 1963 and 1966 exchanges is unique because it contributed to Israeli public opinion the first indication of a civil society activity dealing with POWs or prisoners in enemy hands. In early February 1964 the "Committee of the Parents of the Syria Prisoners" held a press conference in Tel Aviv and presented their cause to the local and foreign press.[15] It was not a routine practice back then—publicly opposing the government or even trying to press it for one policy or another was hitherto unknown. However, with the change to a more liberal government during Eshkol's term in office (1963–1969), such challenges to policy were not considered flagrant acts of opposition. Yet the semi-official newspaper *Davar* did not report the press conference, an event that probably had no impact on the decision-making process in Jerusalem. That press conference, however, heralded in a way the full-fledged intervention by families in the exchange process, which would reach two major peaks in 1973 and 1982 and on.

On the diplomatic level, it was time to "take stock": The MFA conveyed a message to UNTSO's chief of staff listing all prisoners still held by Syria after the exchange, as follows: Group One, detainees last seen alive on or shortly before the December exchange—five people; Group Two, detainees definitely located during 1963—two, both Muslim Israeli Arab citizens; Group Three, missing, whereabouts unknown—three.[16] If nothing else, the list indicated once again the lack of clear and undisputed intelligence regarding Israelis in Syrian hands—and was used in turn by Damascus to return to its policy of withholding information and actually playing all international involved parties against each other. That ritual continued one way or another until the next exchange in August 1966 and has continued until this very day. In short, Syria informed the UN bodies that they did not have any Israelis, then denied the existence of one or another Israeli. This caused Israel additional friction with Syria on top of its existing discord with UNTSO stemming from Israel's feeling that the UN and the ICRC could do more.[17]

Dealing with POW and prisoner issues between Israel and Syria has become over the years a ruthless competition over regional and international reputations and the fates of innocent bystanders who have found themselves trapped in the crossfire. The Syrian arrest of the Israeli intelligence agent Eli Cohen in late January 1965[18] was an exception. It never occupied any place in any bilateral or multilateral negotiations for two main reasons. First, the Syrian officers who invaded his Damascus apartment found him transmitting to Israel, and he had no way to deny it. Second, Cohen first arrived in Syria in late 1961 after secession and due to his connections became active in the internally torn Ba'ath ruling party of Syria. Those sects were entangled in early 1965 in an unyielding power struggle. The exposure of Eli Cohen as a spy for Israel might have become a tool in the hands of one group or another and perhaps even cause a chain reaction of executions. By condemning Cohen to death in a court without any legal representation, both factions assured themselves that their connections with Cohen would not be used against them. For the Syrian politicians his execution meant defusing a potential time bomb. It also meant that Israel would not try to launch any military operation, like those mentioned above in this book, to kidnap Syrian dignitaries. After all, it was the family of the incumbent Syrian leader who had been kidnapped on the high seas only nineteen months earlier.

Cohen's trial ended in late March 1965 with the fateful but expected death sentence. The Israeli MFA instructed all Israeli representations all over the world to prevail upon their foreign government liaisons, along with local political and spiritual leaders, to persuade the Syrians to spare the life of the Israeli agent.[19] Two French lawyers who asked to represent Eli Cohen were rejected by the Syrian authorities.[20] The gist of the Israeli appeals was simple: spare his life and Israel will disregard anything else, at least for moment. Yet Syrian domestic politics and considerations along with the feeling of national humiliation took priority and pushed aside all political advantages that Syria could extract from devising some formula with the world players. The public hanging of Cohen, as well as the continued refusal to this day to return his remains,[21] speaks volumes about the indignation the Syrian government and people felt upon the revelation that an enemy—especially an Israeli—managed to infiltrate their decision-making centers.

Cohen's execution and the cruelty of the Syrian behavior only highlighted the predicament of the Israelis still in Syrian custody. Official Israel as well as the opposition demanded a speedy return of the Israeli citizens still in Syrian hands. The Israeli decision makers probably believed that once the free world witnessed the events in Damascus it would be more attentive to the issue of the seven people in Syria. That was the figure used by the Israeli officials, probably indicating a loss of hope for the lives of the others.[22] In spite of the Israeli hopes that Syria would be concerned with its international image and would be more lenient, nothing happened. The old routine continued as though there was no tragic break in it between March and May 1965: Israel appealed to UNTSO, the Syrians stalled any talk or denied altogether that they held any Israelis, UNTSO's chief of staff traveled to Damascus, nothing resulted; more intelligence confirmed there were Israelis in Syria and so on and so forth.[23]

Syria was not the only arena of confrontation involving Israel in 1965. The summer and fall of that year saw an increase in the number of terrorist activities initiated by the Syria-sponsored al-Fatḥ organization under Yasir Arafat. Those acts were usually started in the West Bank of Jordan in spite of the Jordanian authorities' persistent efforts to avert them. Syria, which was engaged in a mini war of attrition against Israel concerning the diversion of the tributaries of the Jordan River, followed the Egyptian example of the 1950s and sent the perpetrators through Jordanian territory. This way Syria wanted to incriminate Jordan, the emerging regional silent partner of Israel, and provoke Israel into hitting Jordanian targets. Indeed, due to the secret nature of the Jordanian-Israeli understanding, Israel felt that it had to publicly take minor actions against Jordan from time to time. Yet the Israeli decision makers felt that on top of sporadically bombing the Syrian water diversion project, Israel had to supplement its air and artillery exchanges with some ground operations. With Israeli-Syrian tension reaching new heights and the possibility of a showdown growing by the day, Syria took the one and only step that was sure to stop any Israeli move. On October 7 it proposed to Israel an exchange of two Israelis for the whole alleged forty-nine Syrians in Israeli jails—some, according to Syria, since the 1948/1949 conflict. The Israeli reaction was cautiously calculated: Israel did not launch a ground operation and did not respond until December. That month was rather difficult for the Damascene leaders: domestically, the rivalries in the upper echelons of the regime intensified, pitting pro-Soviet and pro-Chinese sects against each other and Sunnis against Alawites; externally, in early December the Kremlin leadership changed and the nuances of the new regime were still a mystery to foreign observers, Syria included. Regionally, in spite of Syria's unequivocal commitment to its own water diversion project, intended to deny Israel water from the Jordan River, there was a clear united Arab front to support Syria's project. All in all, this was almost a golden opportunity for Israel to escalate its own war against Syria. Perhaps the only ace up the Syrian sleeve was the issue of prisoners. Above all, the exact date of the Israeli response speaks volumes: on December 22 the Syrian cabinet resigned in what was described at the time by foreign observers as one of the most serious crises of the Ba'ath regime. On December 24 Israel indirectly conveyed to Syria its agreement for an exchange based on the principle of one for one—in this case, meaning two for two. The Israeli signal was crystal clear: respond now or the dialogue comes to an end with dismal and unavoidable consequences to the Syrian regime.[24] What seemed to be the beginning of a dialogue turned very quickly into the old pattern of stalling.

Syrian domestic politics came once again to play a role in the prisoners' fate. An almost routine request from Jerusalem to Geneva to resume diplomatic dealings with the issue of the detainees in Syria[25] crossed with a major development in Syrian domestic politics: on February 23 the Marxist wing of the Ba'ath party, later to be known as the neo-Ba'ath, took over and brought to power the Alawite elite, supported by Druze officers. As far as Israel was concerned, the new regime was very vocal in its calls for a "national liberation struggle" against Israel, and it continued in earnest the Syrian war of attrition, using not only regular army units—mainly artillery—but also guerilla warfare by al-Fatḥ.[26] Through that prism there was not much of a change compared with past regimes. However, unlike its public image, the new regime adopted a careful approach to Israel and tried to avoid an all-out confrontation at any price as long as its alignment with Egypt and the Soviet Union was not reestablished. This was the understanding at least until August 1966: provoke Israel but offer a prisoner or two so that a confrontation can be averted. It is rather conceivable that such a motivation was behind the Syrian overtures by the ISMAC chairman on March 1 and 7 indicating their interest in an immediate exchange of one prisoner on each side.[27] The Syrians were so eager to deliver on their intentions that in the second of their two messages they went as far as to suggest a protocol identical to the one used in December 1963. The benefits for Syria were clear: not only would they calm Israel down for a while, but the new semi-Marxist regime would earn points with the United States because the United States would probably interpret their move as an indication of moderation. Moreover, the UN Middle Eastern apparatus along with the ICRC did not trust the Syrian government's policies.[28] They would see such a minor exchange as a manifestation of interest in cooperating with the international body and as a first step in helping to ease regional tensions. All in all, a good deal—although not, in Israeli eyes, the dream deal they had hoped for. Israel wanted an "all for all" deal, but that was not possible.[29]

Diplomatically, the ICRC responded favorably to the Syrian move. In addition, because the Yemeni civil war necessitated the ICRC representative's presence for a few more weeks, the timing was excellent for Syria.[30]

No one at the international organization realized that this time it was for real and that, due to its constraints, the newly installed Syrian regime did mean to go ahead. Both parties were keen in their intentions and they did not intend to wait for the ICRC. They expressed their interest in an exchange by performing an act of building mutual confidence: on March 10 Syria handed Israel a U.S. youngster who had crossed into Syria in June 1964, whereas Israel returned to Syria a young Syrian national who crossed into Israel in March 1965 with his cattle. Because neither had appeared on any list these were indeed humanitarian gestures, nothing more. However, this exchange did give some impetus to the UN/ISMAC mediating role intended to set free all people on both sides.[31] A couple of days after the exchange the Syrian delegate to the MAC responded to all queries raised by Israel to the ISMAC chairman. In sum, he did not add any new information, but the essence of his message was that indeed Syria was doing its best to deliver clear and precise answers. He even referred to the case of the Israeli MIA missing since the 1962 Israeli raid, asking for possible other names he was known by.[32] At this stage the negotiations between Israel and Syria, with the ICRC getting involved, turned into a kind of technical give and take—the circumstances under which each prisoner ended up in the custody of the other side were compared, the Syrians trying to keep some degree of equal terms for similar cases.[33] Yet in spite of the goodwill demonstrated during the indirect talks, Syria was not fully honest. For one thing, it failed to mention that one of the Israelis, a sailor who had been forced to leave a Finnish vessel upon arrival in Syria in 1951, had died in prison sometime in 1964.[34] Syria never bothered to notify Israel of his imprisonment and obviously did not inform Israel of his death, leaving Israel to act on his behalf when he was already dead. His body has never been returned to Israel. The negotiations continued parallel with the Israeli efforts to find out more on the fate of the sailor and the circumstances surrounding his death.[35]

In May Syria took one more step. A relatively low-level diplomat, the vice director general of the Foreign Ministry, conveyed to the ICRC delegate a list of requests from Israel, all sounding reasonable and very much in line with past negotiations. At the end of the meeting he said that most of the Syrian cabinet members "*sont sensible*" [French: are sensitive] to the cause of the Syrians in Israeli hands.[36] That was unprecedented; no other Syrian official ever used that expression before or since. Against this background the message from Damascus was not difficult to decipher; Syria wanted and needed a deal. Yet neither Israel nor the ICRC comprehended the hidden message.[37]

In keeping with that mood, Israel made a new move, one that was long overdue but that essentially had nothing to do with the ICRC representative's mission. On May 19, 1966, the prime minister in his capacity as the Minister of Defense issued an order to all Israeli security branches that any citizen of an enemy country crossing into Israel by land or sea (or by air, although that was not clearly stated in his order) would be arrested and that his or her fate would be decided upon by the prime minister personally.[38] That order, naturally kept secret, could not affect in any way the continued indirect dialogue on the prisoner exchange. In late June Israel gave up on its demand to receive the remains of Eli Cohen and the dead sailor.[39] The road was open except for one element: border clashes between Israel and Syria continued, which might have delayed the process. Yet the UN suggested one date for the procedure in order to set in motion the technical negotiations over that procedure rather than over the identities of those to be exchanged, which by mid-July were pretty much agreed upon.[40] In early August 1966 Israel and Syria finally consummated an exchange of four Israelis for six Syrians. None of the Israelis were in good health and there was no denying the harsh conditions of their imprisonment.[41] The 1966 exchange with Syria was the last before the 1967 War and the POW exchange that followed.

With the closing of this chapter in Israeli-Syrian POW related relations, there were still several open cases in Israeli-Egyptian relations. The relative lack of belligerency along the Israeli-Egyptian border was broken from time to time by incidental cases of Israelis crossing into Egyptian territory, usually by mistake. Simultaneously, Israel continued its surveillance and apprehension of agents/spies for enemy intelligence services. These two processes did coincide from time to time in relation to the issue of exchange of civilians. In 1966 the ongoing practice was simple: one for one, no matter the circumstances under which the detainees in question fell into the hands of the other side. In early 1966 Egypt held three Israeli civilians who crossed into the (Egyptian-held) Gaza Strip while inspecting a field of watermelons and were turned over to the Egyptian authorities by a UNEF patrol[42]; Israel held an Egyptian in his twenties who had been trained in Egypt to pose as a Jewish Israeli newcomer and sent to be drafted into the Israeli armored force and from that position to convey back intelligence. He was apprehended in December 1963. At that time Israel still had the Egyptian reporter/spy whom the Egyptian authorities did not want back. In 1966 he was already a "cold case" and no one in the Egyptian intelligence community was still interested in his fate.

Because both belligerent parties did have an interest in getting their own back and because the Israeli Egyptian MAC had not operated since 1955, the two parties talked to each other through Ralph Bunche, an American working for the UN and the architect of the 1949 Armistice Agreements between Israel and its neighbors. In early March 1966 Israel conveyed to him its reaction to the Egyptian demand that the newly apprehended spy be returned along with three people who had served their time in Israeli jails for terrorist activities—all of that for the three Israelis. Israel saw in that message only the beginning of a negotiations process and did not accept its contents. Israel, on humanitarian grounds, had been trying in vain to get the three civilians for the reporter/spy who was coming to the end of the prison term imposed by the court.[43] While Egypt was taking its time, official Israel was getting anxious about the approaching Passover feast. In Jewish tradition the holiday symbolizes freedom, as it commemorates leaving Egypt after four hundred years of slavery. It is customary in Israel to grant amnesty and release inmates from jail on that occasion. Thus the Israeli diplomats felt that they had to secure the release of the three civilians held by Egypt in order for them to get home for the holiday.[44] Such considerations did not interest the Egyptian authorities. They demanded the younger spy and voiced no interest in the reporter/spy who had topped their lists for years. By 1966 the Egyptian figures handling the reporter/spy case were already fulfilling other posts and did not want anyone to awaken dormant ghosts. For official Egypt in March 1966 it was a clear-cut offer: the younger spy or no deal.[45] Pressed by its own self-imposed deadline, the Israeli Minister of Foreign Affairs asked the Minister of Justice to recommend to the president granting amnesty for the younger spy.[46] The Israeli change of heart—that is, including the younger spy in the exchange—was welcomed by the Egyptian authorities. Israel on the other hand, for some unclear reason, asked for the exchange to be conducted in two stages: four Egyptians for the three Israelis in the first, probably public, stage, and a second round later at an unspecified time, consisting of one of the Egyptians—probably the reporter/spy and one more Egyptian—for an Israeli soldier whose whereabouts were unknown to Israel.[47] The intense negotiations along with the commitment of the UN produced an exchange on March 29, 1966. The three Israeli civilians were reunited with their families, as were the young Egyptian agent/spy and two Egyptian intelligence officers.[48] The exchange also included twelve Israeli civilians who had crossed into Egypt of their own free will.[49] All in all, in the summer of 1964 Egypt held a group of thirty-three Israeli civilians who had crossed the border hoping to use Egypt as a staging ground for a better life in a third country. Perhaps the reasons for that crossing should be studied using theories and terminology from the discipline of sociology. In this study, suffice it to say that the issue of Israeli prisoners in enemy hands has always been shrouded by mystery and heavy censorship. Ordinary citizens do not fully realize the intensive efforts, many times over years, put into releasing those people.

The ceremony at the border crossing concluded the first stage of the one and only exchange since 1957. In all other cases Israel and Egypt had returned those apprehended within their sovereign territory without negotiations and with no quid pro quo. The process analyzed here serves as an additional indication of the slowly escalating situation between Israel and its neighbors. Israeli-Syrian relations deteriorated and the Palestinian organizations were noticed more and more within Israel. That led to a number of minor strikes against the Hashemite Kingdom. Nasser's subversion against Jordan and the media attacks he launched against the Kingdom led to the Jordanian king accusing the Egyptian president of not militarily attacking Israel because of the shield UNEF supplied him. Egypt took these assertions seriously and found at least one way of distinguishing itself from the king: to break with the Jordanian POW policy of returning Israelis home soon after their capture, without demanding any quid pro quo.[50]

In the last documented correspondence related to this exchange, the reporter/spy wrote to the Israeli Prison Commissioner that he had been notified on April 27, 1966, that the Egyptian authorities would readmit him to his homeland. Consequently, he expressed to the commissioner in writing his wish to return home as soon as possible.[51] Lacking any further correspondence, it is only possible to speculate that the exchange also included an Israeli soldier whom Egypt had insisted on not returning. Both persons have since disappeared with no trace anywhere in any source accessible to this author.

With the POW issue between Israel and Egypt temporarily resolved until the June 1967 War, there was still one unresolved issue: the convicted members of the Cairo/Alexandria Israeli cells were still in jail. Two had already been released in 1961 when their time came, but the other four were in a state of limbo: official Israel did not recognize them, at least publicly, as its own, and did not include them in any substantial negotiations with the Egyptian authorities. In spite of the Israeli unwillingness to officially recognize the four people, it did encourage (1959) the leaders of the remaining Jewish community in Egypt to approach the ICRC concerning the condition of Robert Dasa.[52] The local Jewish community was careful enough to present their concern as a humanitarian one lest they be identified with the convicts. Still, the Egyptian authorities did not respond favorably. All ICRC attempts to meet with the prisoners failed. Egypt did not even agree to a visit with the female prisoner, Marcelle Ninio.[53] They were also denied the general amnesty declared in Egypt on Revolution Day on July 23, 1959.[54] Away from the limelight, Israel's Prime Minister's Office also tried in 1959 to hire an Egyptian lawyer to deal with the female prisoner case; if successful he would try to help with the sick Robert Dasa as well.[55]

With the passing of time, the issue of these people in Egyptian jails lost its priority status and became just one more issue on the agenda. It is hard to find during the period from 1957 to 1967 any clear Israeli initiative aimed at getting the prisoners back. When former UK ambassador to Iraq Sir John Monro Troutbeck suggested in early 1960, about six months before the affair was partially leaked to the Israeli media, an exchange between the Israelis and the jailed Egyptian reporter/spy in Israeli hands, not only did Israel not follow up, but there is not even a record of any serious Israeli examination of the idea. Even the job description of the

British diplomat given by the Israeli MFA in internal consultations was wrong.[56] The ICRC once again tried for over a year later to arrange visits with the Egyptian spy, hoping that might advance contacts regarding an exchange. This time, in 1961, with the approaching release of two convicts and the ICRC's assurances that the female prisoner was fairly treated, Israel deferred its decision. Contemporaneous with that, realizing the deadlock between Israel and Egypt regarding the spy exchange, the ICRC decided on its own, against the official Israeli position, to ask the Egyptian authorities for amnesty for the female prisoner.[57] Israel opposed that approach for two reasons. First, releasing only one POW ran contrary to the Israeli ethos that all POWs share the same fate, let alone the fact that messages from that prisoner indicated that she was in acceptable health.[58] Second, and perhaps much more significantly, Israel was concerned that the deal would include either a full confession or at least an admission of guilt, neither one constructive for Israeli interests. A question remained as to whether the ICRC refused to intervene on behalf of the cell members because they were not entitled to POW status. What happened that caused that change of heart? Actually, the ICRC position has been all along that it was responsible for the Jewish civilians in Egypt on humanitarian grounds under the Fourth Geneva Convention. The purpose allowed the ICRC, in its own opinion, to try to act for the release of the prisoners.[59] The failure of that effort as well did not prevent the use of the ICRC's services in future cases in which a political-diplomatic issue turned into a humanitarian problem.

However, the impossibility of getting the cell members back was not only the result of a degree of Israeli negligence. The unswerving Israeli refusal to recognize them as its agents was no less of an issue. To circumvent that problem, Israel preferred that any Egyptian lawyer hired to talk to the Egyptian authorities would formally represent the ICRC. That body, for its part, refused to do so on the grounds that none of the prisoners fell into the category of POW. Indeed, this is one of the cases in which the Israeli working definition of POW collided head on with that of the ICRC. For Israel, as mentioned elsewhere in this book, any Israeli in any hostile prison due even remotely to the Arab-Israeli conflict was a POW.[60] For the ICRC and according to their reading of the Geneva Convention, one had to fit the formal definitions of the Convention to be considered one. The Israeli prisoners in Egypt clearly did not qualify as POWs under those definitions.[61]

With the beginning of their tenth year in Egyptian prison, no comforting signs for the Israeli detainees could be seen on the horizon. What began as yet another exhausting year ahead for the prisoners eventually turned out to be a crossroads of sorts. In March 1963, Major General Meir Amit became head of Mossad, concurrent with his term as the head of the IDF Military Intelligence Directorate. He was not part of the covert Israeli activity in Egypt in the early 1950s, as he served then in the operational branch of the IDF. Hence he was able to try, as the IDF most senior intelligence officer and later as Mossad chief, to retrieve the people in Egypt without any concern about a skeleton in his closet being exposed. In one of his early decisions regarding the prisoners he restructured the effort to free them. That was the result of his acknowledgment that the "Committee on the Zion prisoners in Arab lands" (established ca. September 1955) was fading away due to its inability to get any tangible results, let alone to find a way to release the prisoners. Instead of a committee that translates into a collective excuse for helplessness, he appointed a contact man mandated with the task of getting the prisoners back or at least making their jail conditions a little more bearable.[62] The appointee's personality and biography made him the best-suited person for the job: simultaneous with that position he was the chief Mossad agent in Europe, located in Paris, and in his resume was the capture of the Nazi war criminal Adolf Eichmann in 1960.[63] This agent was replaced in early 1966 by the retiring commander of the Israeli Navy, Yohai Bin Nun, a decorated general and an organ of the Israeli establishment. However, neither of the two, in spite of the free hand granted to them by the Mossad and indirectly by the prime minister, could point to any change in the positions of the imprisoned in Egypt. That free hand was granted to them by the then prime minister Levi Eshkol, Ben Gurion's successor, who had not been involved in any direct way in the 1954 affair. Consequently, the circumstances post-June 1963 (Ben Gurion's resignation) were clearly changed in comparison with the post-1956 period, contributing to a different end to the issue after the 1967 War.

All of that was obviously not translated into action before the June 1967 War, with only minor exceptions: In 1965 Egypt allowed food packages paid for by Israel to be shipped and handed over to the female prisoner. In the wake of that agreement both Israel and the ICRC cooperated in handing them over.[64] In spite of that minor change, or even because Israel realized it needed some more dramatic actions to get the people back, its activity became somewhat more intensive. In that year and in spite of the relatively calm border between Israel and Egypt, Israel managed to collect a number of Egyptian citizens in its prisons, hoping to keep them as "bargaining chips" once the time came. On the diplomatic level, Israel under Prime Minister Eshkol never stopped its efforts to secure the release of the "Cairo prisoners," as they were nicknamed in Israeli official internal correspondence. The same was true of the international bodies that Israel tried to enlist in order to secure the release. In early 1965, as part of its ongoing effort, the Mossad prepared a list of Egyptian citizens held in Israel and conveyed it through the Israeli MFA and the ICRC to Egypt.[65] The message attached was easy to decipher: Israel was ready to pay any price requested by the Egyptians in order to get the people back. Even the idea of getting the members of the cells in exchange for the Egyptian reporter/spy was still raised from time to time.[66] However, nothing seemed to work and Israel probably did not want to risk the relative quiet along the Egyptian border by taking extraordinary steps like the naval operation that led to the release of eleven jailed Israelis.

A new approach started to take shape in 1966, an additional indication of the endless effort to try and resolve that lingering intelligence yet very much humanitarian crisis. The path tried this time was through Greece. Lacking a Greek agreement to the appointment of an Israeli ambassador to Athens, Israel had to be satisfied with a "diplomatic envoy." This Israeli representative managed to develop his own trusting relationship with a Greek shipping businessman, who in turn had his influential connection in Egypt: the newly appointed vice president (October 1965) Ali Ṣabri, a leading figure with a history of being involved in the Egyptian intelligence war on Israel. Through that system the Israeli asked the Greek to approach Ali Ṣabri regarding the fate of one of the prisoners, Victor Levi, who suffered from health problems.[67] Even though the meeting did not take place, Israel continued to try the Greek conduit, believing that the warm relations between Cairo and Athens might eventually yield some benefit for the Cairo prisoners.[68] In this case, as in others discussed here, no approach helped. The one and only topic not to be discussed by the Egyptian representatives, official as well as unofficial, was the release of this group of people.

It is evident from contemporary evidence that sometime in the mid-1960s Israel lost hope of securing the release of all convicted in this context. Under Amit, Israel adopted a piecemeal approach calling for the return of one at a time on humanitarian grounds; such was the case first with Marcelle Ninio and in early 1966 with Victor Levi. It is also evident that the practice by Israeli government officials of pushing away responsibility ended during Amit's term in office. The new spirit in attempting to free the prisoners was evident in the travels of the new person in charge of the issue, the retired senior naval officer. Soon after taking charge, he traveled to the United States, hoping to distinguish between the U.S. public's lack of desire to get involved and the actual sentiment in the corridors of power. On his way back he stopped in Paris and suggested to the Israeli ambassador that it might be possible to help the prisoners by trying to persuade the French government to intervene with Egypt. That could be done during the planned visit being prepared at that very time of the French Minister of Culture to Egypt, including a meeting with President Nasser. The Israeli envoy also suggested that the Israeli Minister of Foreign Affairs stop in Paris on her way from the United States in order to personally convince her French counterpart to grant his blessing and approval to the proposed French approach to the Egyptian president.[69] Based on his activity along with the ambassador's lobbying at the Quai d'Orsay, the French Foreign Minister sanctioned a formal French approach to Nasser on humanitarian grounds.[70] In spite of all efforts and the formal approval along the way, the issue was not discussed at the meeting because the French minister felt that it would be out of place considering the general mood of this meeting.[71]

The setback with France and the successive failures in getting the people out of jail pushed Israel into a problematic last resort tactic: approaching the U.S. president.[72] Because all attempts to involve the State Department had been of no consequence, Israel felt that it had to enlist President Johnson, a rather sympathetic commander in chief, for that mission.[73] An approach of this kind is indeed exceptional because the prisoners were originally planning to bomb U.S. targets and because a small country is very careful in asking for U.S. presidential involvement. That is generally saved for decisions of war and peace, as when caught in cross superpower fire, as would happen during the post 1967 War of Attrition. This idea only served to demonstrate that Israel would remove any obstacles in its humanitarian and foreign policy challenge of getting the prisoners back. Nonetheless, as much as the idea appealed to the prime minister and his Minister of Foreign Affairs, it was the Washington ambassador who ruled out such an intervention. He correctly pointed to the growing rift between Egypt and the United States and the accelerated rapprochement between the former and the Soviet Union.[74] He was not alone because the U.S. diplomats with whom the idea was discussed believed that such an overture to a president might have jeopardized his position, which was not particularly strong, as a trustworthy partner to Egypt. Nevertheless, the Israeli insistence on getting results this time impressed the U.S. administration, which operated from the White House, in this context, rather sympathetically toward Israel.[75] Their polite rejection of the unofficial Israeli request led the Israeli Washington ambassador to suggest an alternative. He proposed that Israel intervene, probably through AIPAC, one of the most influential bodies affecting U.S. policies, in order to try and stop U.S. surplus food delivery to Egypt as long as those people are not free. His idea was thoroughly rejected by his minister. At the core of the rejection was the paradigm that Israel cannot and should not bargain, or worse, dictate with the president of the United States. If he agrees to intervene, so this logic goes, it would be out of humanitarian motives and not because of any Israeli pressure on the United States.[76] The internal Israeli debate was naturally kept among the few who dealt with the issue. However, the endless appeals to the State Department finally worked, and the State Department agreed that during the coming routine meeting with the Egyptian ambassador he would be asked to receive a B'nai B'rith delegation to discuss the matter. That organization, as one of the leading Jewish bodies in Washington and the nation at large, took upon itself to serve as the go-between in this case.[77] That did not satisfy Israel. The feeling in Jerusalem was that twelve years in jail were too much, especially considering that even hostile players like the United States and the Soviet Union, who were engaged in a Cold

War, exchanged spies. The most famous such exchanges occurred in 1962 and 1964, long before the convicted enemy agents had served their time. For Israel as much as for Egypt, the continued stay of the four in Egyptian jails served as a constant reminder of one of the biggest failures of the State of Israel at large and its intelligence community in particular.

It is significant to emphasize once more that the thirteenth cabinet of Israel, headed by Levi Eshkol, did not include any of the figures involved directly or indirectly in the original failure in Egypt. Consequently, their activities were totally free of any personal grudges or interests. That would change about a year later with the formation of the first Israeli national unity government on the eve of the June 1967 War. That cabinet would include the 1954 chief of staff General Dayyan and would get the people back in spite of his opposition.

Looking back at the years since Prime Minister Levi Eshkol came to power reveals several lessons for future Israeli POW policies. Perhaps the most significant lesson is that exchanging prisoners became a state-level issue. The tactical exchanges so common in earlier periods gradually disappeared and each deal was the result of diplomatic and military considerations at the highest levels. Furthermore, just as a border incident can delay the implementation of a deal, so can ongoing negotiations that could restrain Israel from hitting back during times of military tension. The connection between POW issues and politics do not stop here. Arab regimes, especially Syrian, used this issue in order to guarantee timeout from the conflict with Israel, as long as they did not feel safe domestically. These commonalities among various regimes surrounding Israel notwithstanding, this was the time when Israel had to begin developing a distinct POW policy relating to any of the neighboring countries and to the early beginnings of subnational actors, especially on the Palestinian scene. For Egypt, the magic expression was "officer to officer." Once an Egyptian officer gave his word as an officer to an Israeli counterpart, it was binding and could be trusted. Syria on the other hand earned during that time its reputation as an untrustworthy enemy in regard to POWs. Sometimes no prisoners' names were given, sometimes prisoners were never handed over to Israel, and most of the time information on the prisoners was lacking. Through Israeli eyes, this was the era in which Israel realized that no Israeli prisoner in Syrian hands was immune from inhumane treatment or torture, no matter what the circumstances in which he fell into their hands. Jordan was a different matter altogether: Israel and Jordan have conducted secret negotiations since 1960; the two respective elites have maintained mutual respect and the two countries have a tacit understanding on immediate POW exchanges. Alas, that good will did not spread to Jordan's military and its people. That meant that Jordanian treatment on the ground was often unacceptable, whereas exchanges were usually speedy.

On a different level, this period saw the first instance of the president of Israel granting amnesty for a convicted citizen of an enemy country in order to enable his release, in a sense circumventing the Israeli legal system. That practice would become, in the 1980s, one of the leading points made by people opposed to the exchange deals of that time. Obviously, in the early period studied in this chapter there was only one prisoner involved, while from the 1980s on there were scores of them. An additional precedent had to do with abandoning the principle of getting all Israeli prisoners back at once. Realizing the insurmountable difficulties in pursuing such a policy, Israel gave it up regarding the Cairo/Alexandria cells' members, and later did the same in other contexts as well. That period saw not only fruitless efforts to release them, but also no effort spared for Eli Cohen before his execution and later in order to get his body back. These two cases, Cohen and the Egyptian cells, have perhaps been the most difficult in terms of retrieving those captured or saving them from hanging in Cairo (two people) and in Damascus because for both Arab countries each case was a matter of violating their national pride. None of these Arab governments assessed these cases as pure and simple issues of prisoner exchange.

NOTES

1. *Davar*, July 16, 1963.
2. *Ma'ariv*, August 5, 1963; *Davar*, August 6, 1963.
3. *Davar*, *Ma'ariv*, August 27, 1963.
4. Cf. *Ma'ariv*, September 5, 1963; *Davar*, September 11, 16, 1963; [UK] NA/FO371/170530/1081/63/, from Washington, to London, October 3, 1963.
5. Cf. ISA/A/7934/8, Ministers consultation minutes, December 31, 1963, 6:30 p.m.
6. Based on: Israeli Navy Association, Prisoner Exchange, November 30 ,1963, http://www.amutayam.org.il/?CategoryID=617&ArticleID=1543, retrieved April 21, 2015; Israeli Navy Legacy, http://www.hi-teach.com/infohub/Main.asp, retrieved February 1, 2014; Phone interview with "Israel," Chief discovery, navigation and communications officer of the submarine, July 24, 2015.
7. The Syrian domestic political scene on those days is thoroughly examined in Itamar Rabinovich, *Syria under the Ba'ath 1963–66: The Army-Party Symbiosis* (Jerusalem: Israel Universities Press, 1972), 96–108, lists of pertinent cabinets: 220–21.
8. *Ma'ariv*, November 11, 1963
9. Yehezkel Hameiri, *Shevuei Suria: sipuram shel israelim be tzinok suri* [Hebrew: Captives in Syria: The Story of Israelis in Syrian Confinement] (Tel Aviv: Am Oved, 1965), 204–5.
10. *Davar*, December 22, 1963.
11. *Davar*, December 24, 25, 1963; ISA/FM/748/15/1964–65, from MFA/Armistice Department, to Lt. Gen. Odd Bull, Chief of Staff, UNTSO, January 16, 1964, August 19, 1964, August 19, 1964; ISA/FM/748/15/1964–65, from Jerusalem, to London, May 4, 1964.
12. *Davar*, December 30, 1963.
13. ISA/A/7934/8, Ministers consultation minutes, December 31, 1963, 6:30 p.m.
14. ISA/FM/748/15/1964–65, MFA "confidential" weekly survey no. 183, January 3, 1964.
15. *Heruth*, February 5, 1964.

16. ISA/FM/748/15/1964–65, from MFA/Armistice Department, to Lt. Gen. Odd Bull, Chief of Staff, UNTSO, January 16, 1964.

17. *Herut*, April 12, 21, 28, 1964; *Davar, Herut*, April 30, 1964; ISA/FM/748/15/1964–65, from Jerusalem, to London, May 4, 1964; ISA/FM/748/15/1964–65, MFA internal memo, May 19, 1964; *Ma'ariv*, July 13, 1964.

18. http://www.elicohen.org/resources/chronology.php.htm.

19. ISA/FM/1508/6/65–70/249, from Jerusalem, to all representations, March 22, 1965; ISA/FM/1508/6/65–70/266, from Jerusalem, to all representations, March 23, 1965; ISA/FM/1508/6/65–70/134, from Jerusalem, to all representations, May 18, 1965.

20. ISA/FM/1508/6/65–70/249, from Paris, to Jerusalem, quoting *Le Monde* piece, May 10, 1965; also ISA/FM/1508/6/65–70, from [Lawyers] Jacques Mercier and Paul Arrighi, Paris, to the President of Syria, May 20, 24, 1965.

21. ISA/FM/1508/6/65–70/155, from Jerusalem, to all representations, May 20, 1965.

22. *Davar, Herut*, June 10, 1965.

23. *Davar*, June 10, 1965; ISA/FM/748/15/1964/65/488, from Jerusalem, to all representations, June 11, 1965; *Ma'ariv*, June 16, 1965; *Davar, Herut*, June 21, 1965; *Herut*, July 10, 1965; *Davar*, July 20, 1965; ISA/FM/28/1, from Jerusalem, to Geneva, September 9, 1965; ISA/FM/28/1, from Geneva, to Jerusalem, October 4, 1965; ISA/FM/28/1, from Geneva, to Jerusalem, October 26, 1965.

24. ISA/FM/748/15/1964–65, from MFA/Armistice Department, to Minister of Foreign Affairs, Prime Minister's private Office, the Chief of Staff, and major representations, December 26, 1965; Israel even recycled the message originally sent to Odd Bull: ISA/FM/748/15/1964–65, from MFA/Armistice Department, to Col. Wm. H. Marsh, Acting Chief of Staff, UNTSO, December 24, 1965, original messages: January 16, 1964, August 19, 1964; ISA/FM/27/10, from Jerusalem, to Geneva, January 13, 1966; ISA/FM/3838/3, from Geneva, to Jerusalem, January 24, 1966; ISA/FM/1392/12, from Jerusalem, to Geneva, February 1, 1966.

25. ISA/FM/3838/3/207, from Jerusalem, to Geneva, February 23, 1966.

26. Joseph Mann, "The Conflict with Israel According to Neo-Ba'ath Doctrine," *Israel Affairs* 13, no. 1 (2007): 116–30.

27. ISA/FM/1508/6/65–70, from Chairman, ISMAC, to Lt. Col. Spann, Israel Senior Delegate, ISMAC, March 1, 1966; ISA/FM/1508/6/65–70, from Syria Senior Delegate, to Chairman, ISMAC, March 7, 1966.

28. ISA/FM/3838/3, from Geneva, to Jerusalem, March 2, 1966.

29. ISA/FM/1508/6/65–70, from Israel Senior Delegate, ISMAC, to Chairman, ISMAC, March 7, 1966.

30. ISA/FM/3838/3, from Geneva, to Jerusalem, March 7, 1966.

31. ISA/FM/1508/6/65–70/86, from Jerusalem, to all representations, March 10, 1966; ISA/FM/1508/6/65–70/96, from Jerusalem, to all representations, March 11, 1966; ISA/FM/1392/12/L/50/361, from Jerusalem, to all representations, March 11, 1966; ISA/FM/1508/6/65–70, Armistice survey no. 400, March 1966.

32. ISA/FM/1508/6/65–70, from Chairman, ISMAC, in Damascus, to Israel Senior Delegate, ISMAC, March 12, 1966; ISA/FM/1508/6/65–70, from Chairman, ISMAC, in Damascus, to Israel Senior Delegate, ISMAC, March 15, 1966, repeated as ISA/FM/1508/6/65–70/122 to major representations.

33. ISA/FM/3838/3/66–67/1, from Geneva, to Jerusalem, March 14, 1966; ISA/FM/1508/6/65–70, from Chairman, ISMAC, in Damascus, to Israel Senior Delegate, ISMAC, March 15, 1966, repeated as ISA/FM/1508/6/65–70/122 to major representations; ISA/FM/1392/12/L/73/405, from Jerusalem, to London et al., March 15, 1966.

34. Cf. ISA/FM/27/10/405, from Jerusalem, to London et al., March 15, 1966; ISA/FM/27/10/32, from Geneva, to Jerusalem, March 16, 1966.

35. ISA/FM/3838/3/66–67/43, from Geneva, to Jerusalem, March 21, 1966; ISA/FM/3838/3/66–67/44, from Jerusalem, to Geneva, March 22, 1966; ISA/FM/27/10, from Geneva, to Jerusalem, April 1, 1966; ISA/FM/3838/3/66–67/2, from London, to Jerusalem, April 1, 1966; ISA/FM/1508/6/65–70, from Jerusalem, to Paris, April 10, 1966.

36. ISA/FM/27/10/35, from Geneva, to Jerusalem, May 18, 1966, based on the handwritten notes of the ICRC delegate, Andre Rochat, of May 17.
37. ISA/FM/27/10/41, from Jerusalem, to Geneva, May 19, 1966.
38. ISA/FM/3838/4/1250/Q, from the military secretary to the PM, to IDF Chief of Staff, and the Israeli Police Commissioner, May 19, 1966.
39. ISA/FM/27/10/41, from Jerusalem, to Geneva, June 26, 1966.
40. ISA/FM/27/10/76, from Jerusalem, to Geneva, July 17, 1966; ISA/FM/27/10/66, from Jerusalem, to Geneva, July 20, 1966.
41. ***Davar*, August 9, 1966.**
42. ISA/FM/1508/6/65–70/228, from Jerusalem, to all representations, March 29, 1966; ISA/FM/1392/12/L/136/518, from Jerusalem, to all representations, March 29, 1966.
43. ISA/FM/3838/3/66–67/1, from Jerusalem, to New York, March 1, 1966; ISA/FM/3838/3/66–67/174, from Jerusalem, to New York, March 20, 1966.
44. ISA/FM/3838/3/66–67/174, from Jerusalem, to New York, March 20, 1966.
45. ISA/FM/3838/3/66–67/215, from Jerusalem, to New York, March 24, 1966.
46. ISA/FM/3838/4, from Minister of Foreign Affairs, to Minister of Justice, March 27, 1966.
47. ISA/FM/3838/3/66–67/237, from Jerusalem, to New York, March 28, 1966; ISA/FM/3838/3/66–67/264, from New York, to Jerusalem, March 29, 1966.
48. *Ma'ariv*, March 29, 1966; ISA/FM/3838/3/66–67/518, from Jerusalem, to major representations, March 29, 1966
49. *Ma'ariv*, March 30, 1966.
50. Cf. USNA/RG59/DEF4 ARAB/14710/December 16, 1966, from Cairo; USNA/RG59/POL 32–1 ISR-JORDAN/3194/December 3, 1966, from Amman.
51. ISA/FM/3838/4, from Ahmad Uthman, to the Prison Commissioner, April 27, 1966.
52. ISA/FM/2096/13/482/59, from Geneva, to Jerusalem, July 14, 1959.
53. ISA/FM/2096/13, from Jerusalem, to Geneva, September 6, 1959.
54. ISA/FM/2096/13, MFA internal memo, September 17, 1959.
55. ISA/FM/2096/13/638/59, from Geneva, to Jerusalem, October 23, 1959; ISA/FM/2096/13/482/59, from MFA, to Prime Minister's Office, October 27, 1959; ISA/FM/211/12, from Geneva, to Jerusalem forwarding the ICRC letter, November 2, 1959; ISA/FM/211/12, from Paris, to Jerusalem forwarding the World Jewish Congress letter, November 5, 1959; ISA/FM/2096/13, from Paris, to Jerusalem, November 16, 1959; ISA/FM/2096/13, from Jerusalem, to Paris, November 20, 1959; ISA/FM/2096/13, from Paris, to Jerusalem, November 30, 1959; ISA/FM/2096/13, from Jerusalem, to Geneva, December 3, 1959.
56. ISA/FM/21/14/06.1, from New York, to Jerusalem, March 9, 1960.
57. ISA/FM/22/4, from Geneva, to Jerusalem, May 29, 1960; ISA/FM/22/4/861, from Jerusalem, to Geneva, May 30, 1960.
58. ISA/FM/2717/26/68–69, from Geneva, to Jerusalem, June 22, 1961.
59. ISA/FM/2717/26/68–69, from Geneva, to Jerusalem, August 10, 1961.
60. ISA/FM/2717/26/68–69, from Geneva, to Jerusalem, October 13, 1961.
61. Cf. ISA/FM/21/14/1723/52-DU/50, from Israeli General Security Services, to Jerusalem, September 26, 1960; ISA/FM/21/14/2074/52-DU/50, from Israeli General Security Services, to Jerusalem, November 18, 1960.
62. Cf. ISA/FM/21/14/336/60, from New York, to Jerusalem, May 13, 1960; ISA/FM/21/336/60, from Jerusalem, to Geneva, June 16, 1960.
63. Meir Amit, *Rosh be-Rosh* [Hebrew: Face-to-Face; Personal Look on Vast Events and Clandestine Matters]. (Tel Aviv: Hed Artzi, 1999), 249.
64. "Aharoni's Biographical Details," *The Telegraph*, internet edition, August 16, 2012, http://www.telegraph.co.uk/news/obituaries/military-obituaries/special-forces-obituaries/9481084/Zvi-Aharoni-and-Yaakov-Meidad.html.
65. ISA/FM/28/1, from Geneva, to the *Mossad* [Aharoni], January 8, 1965.
66. ISA/FM/28/1, from Geneva, to the *Mossad* [Nisiyahu], January 19, 1965.

67. ISA/FM/28/1, from Geneva, to Jerusalem, March 2, 1965.
68. ISA/FM/3838/3/66–67/183, from Athens, to Jerusalem, February 17, 1966.
69. ISA/FM/3838/3/66–67, from Athens, to Jerusalem, May 27, 1966.
70. ISA/FM/1508/6/65–70/230, from Paris, the Ambassador to Jerusalem, Minister of Foreign affairs, February 28, 1966, identical message: ISA/FM/3838/3/66–67/230; ISA/FM/1508/6/65–70/2, from Paris, to Jerusalem, March 1, 1966.
71. ISA/FM/1508/6/153, from Paris, to Jerusalem, March 15, 1966.
72. ISA/FM/1508/6/39, from Paris, to Jerusalem, April 6, 1966; ISA/FM/3838/3/66–67/39, from Paris, to Jerusalem, April 6, 1966.
73. ISA/FM/3838/3/66–67, from Jerusalem/Chief of Staff, to the Minister of Foreign Affairs to Washington/ambassador, May 9, 1966.
74. ISA/FM/3838/3/66–67/128, from Washington, to Jerusalem, May 17, 1966.
75. ISA/FM/3838/3/66–67/47, 48, from Jerusalem, to Washington, June 7, 1966.
76. ISA/FM/3838/3/66–67/23, from Jerusalem on behalf of the prime minister, to [Tananarive, probably a typo] Washington, June 9, 1966.
77. ISA/FM/3838/3/66–67/42, from Jerusalem, to Washington, July 6, 1966; ISA/FM/3838/3/66–67/100, 104, from Washington, to Jerusalem, July 15, 1966; ISA/FM/3838/3/66–67/128, 169, from Washington, to Jerusalem, July 18, 1966.

SEVEN

The 1967 War

Extending the Israeli Definition of POWs

At the end of the June 1967 War and in its aftermath Israel entered a period of euphoria. All went according to plan up to that point including the exchange of POWs. Israel even managed through a series of political moves to get back its agents incarcerated in Egypt. Basically, the exchange entailed the return of all POWs from all parties, whatever their number. The principle applied was clear-cut and very much in line with the traditional Israeli policy that all who are captured in the context of the armed conflict are to be returned and no distinction should be made among officers, regular troops, and civilians. This application of the principle resulted essentially from the defeat of the Arab armies, which led to a relatively short process of negotiations and exchange: the fifteen Israeli POWs for a little over 6,700 Egyptian, Syrian, Jordanian, and other Arab uniformed personnel and citizens. The course of negotiations and exchange began around the time the war ended and came to its successful completion with the return of the last POWs in January 1968.

The 1967 June War broke out after eighteen days of tense suspension. The Israeli government hesitated because the traditional Israeli view was that the closure by Egypt of the Straits leading to the Israeli port city of Eilat constituted a casus belli, but due to Israeli domestic political considerations a decision was delayed. One day after the outbreak of hostilities, on June 6, Israel used the good services of the ICRC to transmit to Egypt the necessary forms and the list of Israeli military ranks in line with the Geneva Convention.[1] Four days later the fighting ended. In spite of the Israeli victory and perhaps due to the decisive outcome of the war and the destruction of large sections of the Arab armies, it was not easy to uncover data regarding the Israeli POWs. As had already occurred in the past, no word on the whereabouts of the missing Israelis, presumed POWs, was conveyed to Israel.[2]

With the guns falling silent at sunset of June 10, Israel launched its POW campaign, which at least during its initial stages looked totally different from any other policy moves taken. There is no record of any cabinet resolution dealing with the issue, and even the army that was well prepared for the war and that held many meetings in May and June discussing everything from logistics to operations did not devote a minute to any aspect of POWs—either Israeli in hostile hands or Arab in Israeli hands. Consequently, the policy that emerged after the war was extemporaneous and left all elements of the issue, whether military or diplomatic, in the hands of the military.[3] The POW effort was double-pronged: verifying the situation of the POWs and MIAs while concurrently offering an immediate exchange of prisoners.

Interestingly enough, the first documented appeal in the effort to find out the identities and locations of the POWs/MIAs was made to the French. Quite a few French diplomats were not yet accustomed to the sharp turn in French foreign policy from steady support of Israel to a rather alienated position. They, in all probability with the blessings of the Minister of Foreign Affairs Maurice Couve de Murville (1907–1999; Minister: 1958–1968), were instrumental in the first stages of picking up bits and pieces of information. As early as June 12, only a couple of days after Israel launched its information-gathering campaign, Paris responded with a telling message: Damascus, that traditional bastion among French regional connections, refused to surrender any information. Cairo, on the other hand, exposed one layer of its post-June Israeli POW policy: Israelis captured in the areas lost in battle (Gaza, the Sinai Peninsula) would be released right on the spot. Those captured on Egyptian territory would be kept. Most captured on Egyptian territory were pilots and were transferred to Alexandria, as far away from the front lines as possible.[4] Egypt's message was rather reassuring, ostensibly predicting the early release of the POWs. However, at least one Israeli pilot became an exception: the pilot of a French-made fighter jet had to abandon his plane on June 5 during the first wave of an attack and was taken prisoner off the waters of Gaza.[5] This is clearly further evidence of the Egyptian interest, like that of every fighting actor, in having the best chips available for further negotiations. The list delivered by the ICRC headquarters in Geneva on June 13, marking its early efforts to secure the release of all prisoners, reveals nine Israeli names in all—three pilots and six naval commandos[6]—without including a word about their medical conditions. All of the pilots were what any party to a conflict would label "quality POWs."

A secondary effort during those early post-war stages was reflected in a couple of messages conveyed from Israel to the ICRC stating that Israel was ready for an immediate exchange with all Arab countries.[7] However, that offer stood alone and was not accompanied by any humanitarian gestures nor any political context. In short, this was a declarative move intended to call attention to the issue rather than trigger a process. Those two endeavors seemed to be aimed at all Arab players, probably assuming that all parties were playing by the same rules. However, that was not to be the case. The first news of Israeli pilots being hanged in Syria arrived in Israel on June 12, was verified, and became part of the Israeli public position presented on the 15th.[8] Unfortunately, that was not the only incident of its kind.

Within the context of the war Israel not only took uniformed enemy personnel, but also a few Arab diplomats from countries involved in the fighting: three Iraqis, two Egyptian, one Syrian, and one representing the Arab League.[9] At the time of their capture they all stayed at the Belgian Consulate in (Jordanian East) Jerusalem, sparking close interest in their condition within the government in Brussels.[10] Some of the diplomats, among them Syrians and Iraqis, were particularly significant for Israeli efforts to secure its own. Iraq at the time held two pilots downed during the war, whereas Israel had no captured Iraqi military personnel.[11] However, it did come into possession of the Iraqi Consul General to (Jordanian) Jerusalem, whose mission came to an abrupt de facto end on June 8 with the surrender of the city to Israel. In spite of Turkey's request, along with those of other nations, to release the diplomat, the inner correspondence of the Israeli Foreign Ministry reveals a more complicated picture.[12] The idea was that the diplomat, along with his other Arab counterparts, would be released only after the two Israeli pilots from Iraq and the others from Syria were returned home. Later, with the prospects of a deal with Jordan—to include Israeli pilots in Iraqi hands—Israel somewhat changed its internal guidelines in this regard and insisted on releasing the diplomats only upon the return of the Israeli civilians in Arab hands.[13] The very brief written words exchanged between Israeli officials did not address the main issue: Was the Israeli behavior legal under international law, notwithstanding the fact that the Arab diplomats were housed in a jail? The answer to that is inconclusive: according to Article 29 of the Vienna Convention on Diplomatic Relations 1961: "The person of a diplomatic agent shall be inviolable. He shall not be liable to any form of arrest or detention. The receiving State shall treat him with due respect and shall take all appropriate steps to prevent any attack on his person, freedom or dignity."[14] Obviously, the key phrase here is "the receiving State," which was Jordan and not Israel. The Israeli interpretation of this article was that because none of the captured Arab diplomats, with the Iraqi being only one of several representatives, were accredited to Israel, and because they all belonged to enemy countries, Israel had the right to detain them—but clearly only under the best conditions possible, as diplomats were citizens of enemy countries, but not members of the armed forces.[15]

With the hours passing since the cessation of hostilities and the post-war issues taking over, more and more components of the Israeli strategy in regard to enemy prisoners began to surface. Strangely enough, the long and tedious paper chase for this book has not revealed any minutes of any authoritative body that made decisions on the POW issue—concerning either Israelis in enemy hands or enemy POWs in Israeli hands. If indeed such a high-level forum never took place, it stands to reason that the military commanders had to grapple with that issue, at least during the first stages of the post-war period.

Contemporary documents reveal several tactical and perhaps strategic guidelines emerging along with the way Israel reconstructed its POW policy vis-à-vis Egypt.[16] Views from the Israeli side:

1. Numbers do not matter; quality matters—that is, only officers and NCOs are to be taken. All in all, on June 15 Israel detained several Egyptian Generals, ten Colonels, and three hundred more officers.[17] Israel reported these numbers in public, but left out a small number of POWs,[18] probably for these two reasons: to be able to interrogate them without being pressed for time and in order to be able to "discover" them at critical junctures in any exchange process.
2. Wounded Egyptian soldiers, civilians, bodies, and those not useful for intelligence purposes are to be released unconditionally, perhaps in order to create something of a positive atmosphere and some asymmetry between the Israeli adherence to international conventions and the Arab side's ignoring of the same instruments.[19] That process began on June 15 and continued up to the last day of the main POW body exchange. Egypt responded in kind and released one pilot whose plane had been shot down in the Gaza area; later, after its sinking of an Israeli destroyer in October, Egypt agreed to return more bodies to Israel.[20] Israel added to the process by inviting all foreign military attaches to visit the hospital in which Jordanian and Egyptian POWs were being treated.[21]
3. All others are not to be taken into POW camps but are to be given a canteen or water container and perhaps transportation to the canal; they should also be allowed to cross into Egyptian territory.[22]
4. The once prosperous Jewish community of Egypt that the Egyptian government placed in two concentration camps at the first indications of an imminent war[23] are to be included in the exchange process. The safety and well-being of the Jewish communities in the Arab world, probably referring to Syria primarily, are to be improved in exchange for the safe return of the Arab POWs.[24] Furthermore, while negotiating with the Arab parties the release of "civilians" from Egypt, Syria, and Lebanon, the implications of

those discharges on the fates of the remaining Jewish communities in their respective countries are to be calculated very cautiously.[25]
5. The ICRC is to be given priority over any other mediator in the process.

The Egyptian side, meanwhile:

1. Cut off the main water pipeline to the Sinai without respect for the humanitarian needs of its troops wandering in the desert.
2. Started shooting at its own troops attempting to cross back home.

These points serve to redraw a picture of Israeli policy during the first days after the war. Israel clearly did not wish to use the POW issue in order to gain anything politically from any other player. However, as this was a humanitarian issue, the emerging policy reflected Israel's interest in gaining global support on it—in spite of a hostile world (the Arab world, Muslim countries, and the Eastern Bloc countries took a strong anti-Israel position in the wake of the war). The separation of POWs/MIAs from any other foreign policy agenda served Israel well, at least on the declarative level, with the passing of UN Security Council Resolution 237 on June 14 "that recommends," inter alia, in Article 2 "to the Governments concerned the scrupulous respect of the humanitarian principles governing the treatment of prisoners of war and the protection of civilian persons in time of war contained in the Geneva Conventions of 12 August 1949."[26]

One week after the ceasefire and an attempt to collect all information available, Israel had quite a clear idea of the numbers of POWs on the Arab and on the Israeli sides. All in all, Israel possessed POWs from three countries: Egypt (4,000, including 300 officers, among whom were four lieutenant generals, six major generals, and eleven colonels)[27]; Jordan (424, including seventeen officers)[28]; and Syria (578, including eighteen officers).[29] This list did not include one Israeli POW who was murdered in cold blood in the (then) Syrian town of Quneitra and two pilot POWs murdered by Egyptian citizens upon reaching ground.[30] The small number of officers hampered any Israeli attempt to present them as quality POWs and demand much for them. However, Israel saw that period of adjustment to the new Middle Eastern realities as a golden opportunity to devise a package deal through which all humanitarian issues, whether civilian or military, could be resolved. To that end, Israel acted on several interwoven levels, each influencing the other and each generating an Arab player's reaction; yet there is no evidence that any of these efforts was the result of a concerted or agreed upon cabinet decision. That would come with the growing frustration over the deadlock between Israel and Egypt in the fall of 1967. The impression created is that all negotiating Israelis, whether military or diplomatic, were operating under vague, assumed policy guidelines until the cabinet had made resolutions to guide them. Consequently, the handling of the POW issue, as had been the case in the past and would be for years to come, was the outcome of collective and spontaneous actions taken by all echelons of government. Those actions fall under several groups of interests and lines of action:

1. Perhaps the most obvious was the Israeli interest in getting the boys back as soon as possible. Being a close-knit society fed that interest, along with Israel's partial ignorance regarding the full list of POWs, its ignorance as to their medical conditions, and the need to cut short the supply of fresh intelligence to the enemy. It is noteworthy that as of November 5, 1967, responsibility for the POW camps in Israel moved from the Israeli general command to the IDF northern command, indicating that interrogations of internees changed from a matter of routine to some sporadic questioning on random issues. This in turn suggests that even the most basic information that could be extracted from the prisoners was not considered worthy by Israel five months after the outbreak of the war.[31]
2. Much less obvious were other levels of the POW situation: perceptions and misperceptions by the Israeli leadership regarding the true intentions of the enemy on the prisoners' issue. No one drew the right conclusions from Egypt's shooting at its own troops attempting to cross back home, as mentioned above.[32] With the desired impression lost on Israeli leaders, further signals were sent: based on testimony by the Belgian Foreign Minister's chief of staff, Israel realized that Egypt was not interested in its own troops—that is, in its officers getting back home. As far as they were concerned, the Egyptian POWs were not welcome in their homeland. This posed a major problem for Israel, as it badly wanted its own POWs back as soon as possible but apparently had no real bargaining chips, probably with the minor exception of the captured Arab diplomats.[33] In this context the Israeli ambassador to Belgium pressed for keeping the Arab diplomats in Israeli hands in order to use them to induce the Arab parties to make an exchange. That approach might be supported by two additional observations: Nasser, being the self-proclaimed "leader of the Arabs," could not afford to be seen by his fellow Arab leaders as failing to secure the release of Arab diplomats from other countries, while he perhaps considered himself accountable for the fate of his fellow countrymen only to himself and to his close circle of aides. An additional element concerned the fact that Arab diplomats, at least at that time, were usually seen by their respective leaders as their personal emissaries, and serving in such positions meant close ties between the diplomat or his family and the ruler. In this configuration of power, not working for the release of the diplomats could

be interpreted by fellow Arab leaders and regimes simply as an insult. It is fascinating to note that the ambassador who called the attention of the Israeli decision makers to that dimension was one of the most familiar among Israeli diplomats with the Arab culture. That understanding prevailed over a more traditional diplomat's different, more Western type of viewpoint that took in only the damage inflicted on Israel due to its detaining of foreign diplomats.[34]

3. Another level of analysis concerned the very basic issue of who was a prisoner of war for the purpose of an exchange deal. Israel had to deal with that problem on three fronts: the "civilian" members of the sabotage cells in Egyptian prison, all of whom were Egyptian residents[35]; an Israeli citizen, Wolfgang Lotz, who was believed by the Egyptians to have worked for Israel while he was a German citizen; the body of an Israeli spy executed in Syria in 1965 and his living assistant in a Syrian jail; and a former Israeli secret agent in Lebanon. Another genuine civilian issue had to do with Israelis who had disappeared along the Syrian-Israeli border or elsewhere and who were presumed kidnapped by Syria. That government had admitted—always on the eve of their return to Israel—that it held such persons in the past. Syria has always been hesitant to admit that it held these people because any such admission would mean confessing to a crime. Therefore, before the 1967 War, whenever these civilians were allowed back home, there was a reason for Israel to allow as little publicity as possible. The evolving situation in late June 1967 provided Syria an opportunity to return Israelis, but once again Syria wanted to avoid bad press. In line with that traditional policy, its envoys dealing with the ICRC conveyed to Israel the message that the only pilot they held would be returned along with "civilians imprisoned in recent years."[36]
4. An additional element related to the very definition of Israel as the homeland of the Jewish people, hence Israel's insistence on the release of or at least easing of conditions for the Jews living in the Arab countries. Here again the Red Cross was asked to assist Israel even though those Jewish communities did not fall at all within the Geneva Convention on prisoners. They could probably be included in the Fourth Convention.[37] That indeed was the approach adopted by the ICRC in the wake of the war. Actually, the ICRC de facto declared some symmetry between the civilian population in the newly acquired territories and the condition of the Jewish communities in the Arab lands.[38] Formally, however, there was no reason to include in the diplomatic exchange the Jewish communities in Arab countries because they were not in occupied territories. Yet once Israel did include them, it did not do so in a systematic way or draw any symmetry between them and the Arabs liv-

ing in the newly acquired territories of Israel.[39] Egypt agreed to ICRC visits to non-Egyptian Jews in Egypt as part of the process, but insisted on not letting any citizen meet with foreign diplomats.[40] That position obviously did not satisfy the Israeli authorities, who asked the ICRC to request such visits in Egypt and Syria, but for a long time to no avail.[41] With time passing without any movement on the Egyptian and Syrian fronts, Israel got impatient and, with the almost full backing of the ICRC, pressed on the Jewish communities' issue. The final goal of the Israeli diplomats, guiding their decision makers behind the scenes, was the creation of a clear-cut linkage between the release of Israeli POWs and the granting of permission to the local Jews to immigrate to Israel.[42]

The Israeli insistence on speaking on behalf of the Jewish communities, along with the existence of a sizable Arab population under Israeli occupation as of June 10, led eventually to the ICRC taking a similar position. Whether that was the immediate result of Arab governments' requests or of an ICRC decision did not matter. The end result, any way it is analyzed, was the creation of a clear symmetry between the conditions of the Jews in the Arab lands and the Arabs in the territories newly occupied by the Jewish land.[43] The main point made by the ICRC on behalf of the Arab countries was that Israel was violating Article 63 of Convention (IV) Relative to the Protection of Civilian Persons in Time of War, Geneva, August 12, 1949, which reads:[44]

> Subject to temporary and exceptional measures imposed for urgent reasons of security by the Occupying Power:
> (a) recognized National Red Cross (Red Crescent, Red Lion and Sun) Societies shall be able to pursue their activities in accordance with Red Cross principles, as defined by the International Red Cross Conferences. Other relief societies shall be permitted to continue their humanitarian activities under similar conditions; (b) the Occupying Power may not require any changes in the personnel or structure of these societies, which would prejudice the aforesaid activities.The same principles shall apply to the activities and personnel of special organizations of a non-military character, which already exist or which may be established, for the purpose of ensuring the living conditions of the civilian population by the maintenance of the essential public utility services, by the distribution of relief and by the organization of rescues.

On top of the uniformed POWs and the Jews living in the Arab countries, a third group existed—apprehended Israeli intelligence agents. On June 17 Egypt agreed to the principle of general exchange of POWs but would not approve the release of "the six civilians" it held.[45] The Egyptian position was that these people were not entitled to be covered by the stipulations of the Geneva Convention because they were civilian citizens of Egypt and not members of the Israeli armed forces—despite the fact that Israel granted them all military ranks and treated them accordingly. Unfortunately, that Israeli interpretation did not work in any case of an Israeli citizen caught while serving Israel on any Arab land.

5. Another level of analysis has to do with the issue of Arab state national interests as opposed to Pan-Arab interests. The first days after the war witnessed the breakdown of one united Arab strategy. This clearly showed on the POW frontlines: each and every country took a different path in dealing with its own POWs A series of meetings between Israel and the ICRC representatives that took place in the wake of their sessions with representatives from the combatant Arab countries also reflected the shift from a Pan-Arab approach. Those meetings were the scene of indirect negotiations between the parties regarding the release of their respective POWs. These talks were held under the auspices of the ICRC—a strong indication that all parties, whatever quid pro quo they were hoping for, saw this particular issue as separate from all other issues on the table. That situation would be dramatically changed after the 1973 War, for reasons related to the War of Attrition and the October War.

EGYPTIAN INTERESTS IN ACTION

Egypt held the largest number of Israeli POWs: eleven uniformed and six Jewish Israeli agents, including a couple of Israelis who the Egyptian authorities were led to believe were German by citizenship. Two of the Israeli POWs were members of the Israeli navy who were caught after the war in an abortive attempt, sanctioned by the then Israeli Minister of Defense, to establish a presence on the Suez Canal and eventually to divide its operations between Israel and Egypt.[46]

Of all Arab parties to the conflict, Egypt was the one that, as "leader of the Arabs," had to perform as a role model for other parties to some degree. Moreover, as one of the leading members of the nonaligned countries organization, it had to adhere to some degree to accepted international norms. That had no bearing on Egypt's attitude toward Israel, a perennial foe of the Arab coalition, but at least it had to show that it was treating its own citizens in captivity in an acceptable way. Consequently, about one week after the ceasefire and after documented cases in which Egyptian troops had been prevented from returning to their homeland, Egypt changed its attitude.

Starting in mid-June, Israel's practice on the ground was to provide transportation for the improvised border crossing over the Suez Canal to

Isma'ilia (south of the Canal) on the west bank of the Suez Canal and to Qantara (north of the Canal) on the eastern side of the Suez Canal. The crossing to Isma'ilia was closed by the Egyptians a few days after its opening, but the exact location is of no great significance. In principle both countries agreed to set up a temporary arrangement by which each trapped Egyptian soldier could freely cross into Egypt, be welcomed by an Egyptian doctor, and if necessary be rushed to a hospital.[47]

That ground operation included Egyptian troops who were not formally labeled POWs—whom Israel, that is, was unable to verify as either officers or pilots. Consequently, their exchange value was rather low and their intelligence value was limited to that of the lower tactical units. Holding them just meant more mouths to feed on the Israeli side. The prisoners in the Israeli POW camps were a different matter altogether. Their value was obviously higher and Israel wrongly believed that holding onto them would expedite the exchange process. In any case, the request for an exchange that Israel put on the ICRC table was rather simple: all reported Egyptian officers in Israeli custody in exchange for the eight Israeli uniformed POWs and six civilians that Egypt had imprisoned in connection with the 1954 failed Israeli espionage and sabotage cells.[48] Egypt did not put any counter proposal on the table, with the exception of their request that their POWs be allowed to write home.[49] The position that Israel presented also included an agreement that its six civilians be flown out of Egypt to Europe and released there with no publicity.[50] Obviously, that was intended to save Egypt the embarrassment of their sending off their residents convicted of serious charges while letting Israel start the process of rehabilitating its own citizens. Moreover, the open and uncensored reporting of the release of the civilians might have sparked another round of political squabbles within Israel due to the Israeli domestic debate regarding the responsibility for the 1954 affair, bringing back the tension between the two cliques of the social-democratic ruling elite. Egypt's unwavering position of resisting any inclusion of the Israeli agents in late June left no room for any compromise with Israel on the fate of Israel's people in captivity. On the other hand, out of keeping with its traditional policies of not caring for its own, Egypt suggested that Israel set the wounded Egyptians free with no quid pro quo. Had this been accomplished, Egypt would have received good publicity, as Israel would have, but the latter would not have benefited in any tangible way.[51] In spite of the Egyptian position regarding the agents, Israel agreed to such an exchange of the wounded (not to include officers), while delaying the issues of the civilians and of the Jewish community. The Israeli position in this instance is clear: any returning prisoner is worth the political/diplomatic loss to Israel.

About one month after the ceasefire, all Arab parties, with the exception of Jordan (see below) were, either through an early agreement or a unilateral decision, united in setting their rules for any Jews to be exchanged: uniformed personnel—yes; Jewish communities—no; nonlocal Jews—yes; and definitely a "no way" no to the release of captured Israeli espionage agents.[52] From an Israeli perspective that position was a nonstarter. Yet, appreciating the difficulties and the national pride issues involved in returning the civilians and perhaps with less diplomatic language, Dayyan devised a plan by which most Egyptian-recognized POWs, that is no agents included, would be publicly exchanged for all Israeli military men; the rest of the Egyptian personnel would be released at a later date along with the civilians. None of that would be put in writing, but the president of the ICRC would give his own personal written commitment to Israel (and probably to Egypt as well).[53]

Essentially, by late July 1967 the negotiations with Egypt were put on hold.[54] Whereas Egypt agreed to the principle of "all uniformed for all uniformed," Israel insisted on the return of the civilians and the departure of the remaining Jews in Egypt. Realizing the deadlock, the Israeli cabinet, in its capacity as the Ministerial Committee on Security Affairs, approved the following resolution on October 1: The exchange with Egypt will be delayed until the civilians and Jewish community issues are resolved; the delay is limited to three months and the cabinet will reconvene on that matter at the expiration of that deadline.[55] Concurrently, Israel tried to no avail to launch a campaign in which the Israeli-held POWs would complain that it was time for them to get back home.[56]

As if to make the tense relations between Israel and Egypt more dangerous, in late October Egypt attacked an Israeli destroyer sailing along the Israeli-held Sinai Peninsula coastline, inflicting heavy losses on the crew. One of the main issues bothering Israel after the attack was whether Egypt held any Israeli prisoners. The ICRC, which all along had done a remarkable job initiating new approaches in its effort to secure a deal, took it upon itself to inquire of the Egyptians whether it held any new Israeli POWs.[57] That incident, however, was treated by all parties as being separate from the big POW picture, therefore no compromise could be reached. By mid-December Egypt agreed to a full and comprehensive exchange of uniformed personnel, whereas Israel upheld its nonbudging position on the release of its agents. That position, even though partially supported by the ICRC, was not fully based on the principles of the Geneva Convention—a point very well known to the Israeli authorities.[58] However, realizing the ordeal of the agents, who had not been released in the aftermath of the 1956 campaign and who were at the heart of one of the most intricate civil-military scandals in the history of Israel, the then chief of Israeli security services insisted on no deal without his agents. That stumbling block led Israel at the three months deadline to try another approach: a new cabinet resolution (December 28, 1967) carried out by the UN special envoy Gunnar Jarring, probably coinciding with a conciliatory message from Egypt, ordered the release of one or two generals, very much in line with the road not taken earlier based on the belief that quality mattered more than quantity, which would carry a personal message to the UAR president, Nasser. The Israeli message included, inter alia, a direct appeal to Nasser's honor as an officer and a gentleman: We will return yours for your word to release ours.[59] The hopes in Jerusalem were low because Nasser had made the issue of the Israeli spies almost a diplomatic casus belli. However, behind the back of the ICRC and through at least two distinct channels, Nasser conveyed to Israel his message that the Israeli path was acceptable and that once Israel gave up its prisoners its civilians would be flown out of Egypt to Europe and to freedom. The deal was finalized around January 6, 1968, almost seven months after the end of hostilities and on the verge of another round.[60] The agreement was so classified that it was personally handled by a small number of ministers, officers, and civil servants—resulting in some of those who usually handle such matters continuing to resist the emerging deal once it became final without their knowledge.[61] Right away Israel notified the ICRC that an agreement for an exchange had been reached with the UAR. The language of the note was rather succinct and mentioned only the uniformed personnel.[62] The exchange was possible for several reasons:

1. Circumventing the ICRC in this context and allowing the UN mediator Gunnar Jarring to deal with the issue suggested an Israeli separation between the military POWs and the "civilians." This Egyptian move could be partially interpreted as a gesture to Mr. Jarring, creating an atmosphere of sympathy in the UN corridors, which might come in handy during the upcoming diplomatic process. Because Israel shared a similar motivation, it too had to add more assets to the deal, including all diplomatic personnel left in Israeli hands and several Egyptians trapped under Israeli occupation in the wake of the war.[63]
2. This approach allowed Egypt to save face and avoid any clear public linkage between the uniformed deal and the civilians deal.
3. The release of the Egyptian high-ranking officers—who were among the closest comrades-in-arms of the Egyptian president—indicated an Israeli acknowledgment of Nasser's personal interests.
4. Finally, the Israelis placed trust in the military man who had become the supreme leader of Egypt as a man of military honor.

With that secret agreement in place, the exchange process could go ahead in full swing, unhampered by the flaring up of a new war of attrition between Israel and Egypt and in spite of many doubts of the agreement's architects, among them Jarring personally.[64] The third week of January saw the exchange process coming to public fruition, while the secret part materialized a couple of weeks later away from the media.

THE CONSISTENTLY BELLIGERENT SYRIAN POLICY

As had happened many times in the past, Syria took a different path from that of Egypt and withheld vital information on the POWs: no lists were transferred to Israel and no Red Cross visits were allowed. That policy, ostensibly uncoordinated with Egypt, was probably heralding Syria's departure from Egyptian leadership or its trip from Pan-Arabism to Syrian nationalism, a process that is usually dated back to the end of the 1967 War.[65] Syria's policy became evident to the negotiating Israelis during their meetings with the ICRC personnel on June 19 and 22.[66] Israel demanded that all POWs be released (the exact number and the division between dead and alive was not clear to Israel), as well as fifteen civilians who had disappeared or been abducted along the Israeli-Syrian borders in the years preceding the 1967 War, the jailed "Renee," and the remains of Eli Cohen.[67] A couple of days after the first meeting took place Syria informed Israel through the Red Cross that it held only one live pilot and that he had been visited by the organization's representative on June 15.[68] That was at least a strange statement considering that the alleged meeting took place a few days before the ICRC delegate met the Israeli negotiators and divulged no such information to the Israelis. The Israeli position presented at that meeting included the following elements: early return of the bomber pilot who had been captured alive; the bodies of two pilots who were known to be dead; and information on the fate of one pilot. One of the missing pilots was presumed killed by a Syrian lynch mob upon parachuting from his downed plane.[69] During that initial meeting, Israel added to the list of uniformed personnel the names of several civilians who had been missing for years and were presumed held or killed by Syria. At the top of that list Israel put the return of the body of the best known Israeli spy, Eli Cohen, who had been executed in May 1965, and the release of a female involved in the case, "Renee," who was still in a Syrian jail by the conclusion of the June 1967 War. The Syrians requested on their part that Israel allow reunification of families: some from the Israeli-held Golan Heights into Syria and some in the opposite direction. At that point no Syrian request for the return of their POWs was conveyed to Israel. One of the more remarkable issues addressed at the meeting raised by the ICRC was that of the Jews in Syria. That serves to prove that the organization did see Israel as responsible for the fate of the Syrian Jewish community and that an ICRC representative tried to provoke Israel into creating some quid pro quo, while the Syrians were trying to use the humanitarian issue of the Golan families' reunification. The latter issue in this very context would become much more central in the POW negotiations in the aftermath of the 1973 War. And once again, in 1973 Israel would fail to create some sort of case to balance the Syrian reunification humanitarian issue.

The second meeting, on June 22, saw the first response by both parties to the issues raised a few days earlier. Syria admitted to having one live pilot in its hands and only one civilian of the fifteen that Israel was looking for. The Israeli assessment of the information from Syria was highly negative, and the Israeli UN delegation was looking for new ways to pressure Syria—including delaying the negotiations once it came to a substantial point.[70] Obviously, this was a mistaken approach to a country that had not to that point demonstrated (nor did it demonstrate later) any interest in getting its POWs back, with the possible exception of a small number of officers. Israel insisted on getting a response regarding each and every missing person—and if that person was not alive, the circumstances of his death. Regarding the missing pilots that Syria listed as dead, Israel would not accept their deaths without clear-cut proof. Finally, Israel was not going to give up on the release of the female involved in Cohen's case. All in all, by about two weeks after the termination of hostilities, the only regional player that had not moved on in the negotiations was Syria.

Indeed, with the absence of any incentive from Israel, Syrian efforts continued to be in limbo. With the exception of a few minor concessions, perhaps in order to manifest to the ICRC some movement on its part, Syria agreed to some small gestures.[71] Being so well aware of the Israeli insistence on getting back the remains of Cohen, a symbol of national bravery in Israeli eyes and an icon of failure for Syria, Damascus agreed "to present" to the ICRC Syria representative Cohen's gravestone and the burial certificate signed by a local rabbi. Israel did not understand that language and insisted on getting back Cohen's remains. Likewise, the Syrians were not forthcoming on the issue of "Renée." And to add insult to injury the Syrians did not allow the ICRC to visit the (one and only, as they claimed) Israeli POW or POWs (as the Israelis alleged). Based probably on intelligence material, the Israeli representatives labeled Syria's stance all across the board—Israeli POWs, remains of Cohen, and the female agent—as "lies." The fact that Israel had seized a Syrian file containing documents concerning the interrogation of an Israeli missing since September 1966, whose very presence in Syrian hands had been denied time and again, did not bolster any trust in the Syrian position either.[72] Perhaps the only ray of hope came from the ICRC representative who informed the Israeli delegation that he would meet the Syrian Foreign Minister the next day to discuss the situation of Syrian Jewry. Moreover, considering that the Syrians specified the release of the remaining Arab diplomats as their own requirement after their three Iraqi counterparts were released by Jordan (on the 26th), Israel and Syria might have worked out a tradeoff—a possibility that was missed by the Israeli side that saw the propaganda value of the Syrian move but not its potential contribution to a solution.[73]

With continued communication the borders of agreement and disagreement with Syria were clearly drawn: Israel demanded and the Syrians agreed to the exchange of those who were clearly POWs—that is, who were in uniforms at the time of capture; the return of the bodies of the fallen Israeli pilots and the body of an Israeli abducted in September 1966. One of the pilots was murdered on the ground and, with the passing of time, identifying marks could perhaps have been obscured. Both sides also agreed that an ICRC representative would visit Syrian prisons in an attempt to verify whether they were holding Israeli citizens.[74] The wide field of disagreement included the remains of Eli Cohen, the living "Renee," the fifteen abducted Israelis, and anything whatsoever that had anything to do with the Jewish community in Syria.[75] At that point the ICRC position was that Israel might release one Syrian spy imprisoned by Israel in exchange for the living "Renee." Later Israel added a couple more Syrian espionage agents to be returned to Syria in this context.[76]

For obvious reasons, mainly the mutual interest of both actors in not embarrassing Syria, the agreed upon parts came to a successful end on July 17. Israel returned to Syria 591 POWs, including 18 officers, 343 soldiers, and 290 civilians (whose exact types were not detailed in the internal MFA documents). Israel received one pilot of an Israeli bomber, whose navigator managed to parachute himself onto Lebanese territory, the bodies of two other pilots, and that of one civilian.[77] The exchange process continued out of public sight. It included "Renee," who was released with no publicity whatsoever. The remains of Eli Cohen have never been returned to Israel.

LEBANON'S INTERESTS RELATED TO ISRAEL AND SYRIA: BETWEEN A ROCK AND A HARD PLACE

On the Lebanese flank Israel began its POW negotiations from a rather inferior position: Israel had no Lebanese POWs but Lebanon had Israeli uniformed and ununiformed personnel that Israel wished back. Lebanon manifested a dramatically different approach from Syria from the beginning of the negotiations until their conclusion[78] and the August 1967 two-stage exchange: by June 18 the one Israeli uniformed POW they were holding, a first lieutenant pilot of a fighter plane, had already been visited by the ICRC representatives. In exchange, Israel notified the Lebanese through the ICRC that it was holding eleven Lebanese citizens who had been captured in the West Bank once Israel had taken it over. Even though the status of those detained Lebanese citizens was not known to the Beirut government, Israel presented their names in order to create some symmetry between them and an Israeli citizen in the Lebanese prison. All eleven names did indeed represent humanitarian cases of civilians separated from their families due to the breaking war.[79] The

Israeli citizen Shula Cohen (no connection to Eli Cohen), on the other hand, was one of the leading Israeli spies ever employed in an Arab country, and Israel insisted on her release at any price but did not insist on making her release public or simultaneous with the release of the pilot. That was in line with the policy regarding civilians in Egyptian hands.[80] Apparently, at that juncture the major stumbling block was not the Lebanese government but rather the ICRC Tel Aviv representative, who seemed to the Israeli delegates to be trying to slow down the exchange process for reasons unclear to the Israelis. A possible explanation might be that he wished to work out a three-way exchange including Syria so as not to alienate the Syrian government.

In spite of the ostensibly shared interest in finalizing a deal, even the Jordanian conclusion of the exchange on June 26 did not expedite the process with Lebanon. The lack of outstanding issues between Israel and Lebanon gave way to the interests of the Syrian menace. Syria pressured Lebanon persistently to have Shula Cohen, once she was released, turned over to Syria to stand trial in Damascus for "her crimes against Syria."[81] Lebanon's precarious position—refusing any exchange deal with Syria—among the Arab nations probably delayed any positive result on the Lebanese end. Israel, intent on breaking the deadlock, adopted some bizarre rules. It suggested that on top of the already agreed upon exchange of the Israeli aviator and one innocent Israeli who crossed the border demarcation line by mistake for eleven Lebanese citizens, Israel would add to the deal five Lebanese citizens convicted for treason in Israel who were serving time. All of that, in Israel's view, would guarantee the release of Shula Cohen.[82] After about a month of behind-the-scenes negotiations in Europe, mainly between Israel and the ICRC, which became the "honest broker," the terms of the exchange were agreed upon. However, not too much could be accomplished without securing the tacit approval of Damascus. One way of accomplishing that was through a Lebanese move against foreigners engaging in subversion and espionage activities against Lebanon after their serving time. In early August 1967 Beirut announced the expulsion of 132 foreigners after they had served time and been convicted of illegal entry into the country and running suspicious activities.[83]

Against that background of de facto patron-client relations between Syria and Lebanon, the Israeli-Lebanese exchange deal had to be executed in a rather cautious way. Consequently, the main exchange took place on August 9 with thirty-three Lebanese civilians leaving for home versus one Israeli pilot and three innocent civilians who had crossed to Lebanon by mistake. Shula Cohen was included in the deal but not in the exchange. Beirut promised the ICRC that a fortnight after the main event she would be freed along with her family.[84] Indeed, all parties kept their word and Shula along with her family finally landed in Israel on August 23.[85]

JORDAN

Of all the warring nations Jordan was an exception. Jordan's foreign policy during the war, and more so after losing the West Bank to Israel, was based on three pillars: close ties with the United States approaching a "moral commitment" by the latter,[86] continued close cooperation and coordination against enemies shared with Israel—itself in a process of becoming an ally of the United States—and deep hatred for and fear of Egypt. With the early indications that the power of the "Leader of the Arabs" was waning and the need to convince Israel that mutual cooperation can and should continue, Jordan needed any marginal complications to be removed. Moreover, the Jordanian king Hussein had to sign a humiliating mutual defense pact with Egypt on May 30 that he wanted to render null and void once the war was over.[87] Additionally, prior to the 1967 War, Israel and Jordan shared highly secret channels of communication that had secured the continued existence of the Kingdom in spite of its defeat.[88] The Jordanian monarch had every interest in the wake of the war in reviving his direct line to Jerusalem. Dealing separately with Israel on the POW matter perfectly served that interest. Jordan's motivation was evident to the Israeli side with the launching of the POW exchange negotiations process. That bilateral process was particularly brief in consideration of Israel's traditional policy of early return of all prisoners and the abovementioned Jordanian interests. Lest that policy fail for Israel, Jordan went the extra mile and conveyed to Israel through the ICRC their wish to expedite the process.[89] Even the fact that Jordan took it upon itself to represent Iraq, which originally held two captured Israeli pilots and later transferred them to Jordan, did not complicate the fast progression of the negotiations. Strangely enough, even though the monarchy in Iraq had been overthrown in the 1958 revolution, the new regime followed in the footsteps of the Baghdad *ancien régime* by refusing to deal directly with Israel and to entrust Jordan with that task.

The Israeli demands from Jordan were rather simple: to get back the two pilots formerly in Iraqi custody and to receive the bodies of four dead pilots shot down over Jordan and Iraq. One of those had been murdered upon reaching ground by members of the Jordanian 60th Armored Brigade. Jordan did not ask for the return of its POWs, which was very much in line with most of the other Arab actors; however, it did ask for free passage for eighty-nine (later to be changed to 150)[90] children who were in an educational institution in the West Bank before and during the fighting and who needed to be reunited with their families in the East Bank. Israel for its part had no problem with that request and, perhaps as a gesture of goodwill, had thirty-seven children from that group returned to Jordan right on the day of the June 21 meeting.[91] Even though Israel and Jordan did not hold any direct dialogue and communicated only through the ICRC representatives, it is clear that the instructions from Amman were in line with Jordan's interest in reconstructing bridges to Israel. That was observed in letters from Israeli POWs that were seemingly uncensored and that revealed humane treatment of the Israelis by the Jordanians.[92] Moreover, Sa'ad Jum'ah, the Jordanian prime minister, personally indicated to the ICRC representative that he preferred a rapid exchange. The Jordanian request was simple: the return of all Jordanians held by Israel, an Iraqi POW, and a few Iraqi civilians. All in all, the impression conveyed to Israel by the ICRC mediator was that the Jordanian side was ready, perhaps even eager, to reach an agreement that would be implemented in the very near future. The deal was concluded in two Israel-ICRC meetings on June 25 and 26, and a parallel signing by Jordan of the agreement.[93] This last point, that the exchange was finalized by simultaneous instruments between Jordan and the ICRC concurrent with an Israeli-ICRC agreement, is perhaps an additional indication of the public enmity between the parties, side by side with a continued secret dialogue that had begun long before the war and would continue in spite of the war.[94]

The exchange took place on June 26 and included about four hundred uniformed and ununiformed personnel as well as three Iraqi diplomats.[95] The only part of the agreement not to be fulfilled at that time was the return of the bodies of the fallen Israeli pilots shot down over Jordan and Iraq, which were returned in early August.[96]

The accumulated experience of the 1967 POWs in regard to the Arab players can teach a few lessons: while not recognizing the Arab side's lack of interest in its prisoners and the respective governments' willingness to pay a price for ignoring the Geneva Convention, Israel continued to follow the international instruments to the letter.[97] In addition, the Arab governments did not reciprocate the concern of the rest of the world with the larger issues of borders, refugees, and the possibility of using the war as a springboard for a lasting regional settlement.

Israel throughout all the years has had mounting, major reservations regarding international organizations. This is due to some extent to what Israel perceives as the automatic anti-Israeli majority within these bodies. However, the activities of the ICRC, which did not necessarily reflect its global makeup, had at least to rouse Israel's appreciation. The wealth of documents in the aftermath of the war did not disclose any major slant by representatives of the organization. There were some deviations from the neutral line expected of this body, but those never negatively influenced the outcome of negotiations. True, Israel did whatever it could to satisfy the humanitarian demands of the international community as embodied by the ICRC. Consequently, with no one to please except the human beings behind the numbers of prisoners and dislocated people, the ICRC responded in kind to Israel. A fascinating example of their cordial relations is found in a memo distributed to all Israeli delegations overseas reporting on the meeting between Dayyan and Gaillard, delegate general of the ICRC representative in the Near East.[98] The ICRC position was crystal clear: there is a linkage between the treaties on POW treatment and the conditions for civilian populations under occupation. On this latter point the ICRC adopted the Israeli interpretation that included Jewish communities in Arab countries that are under the protection of the Fourth Convention, even those that did not participate in the 1967 fighting, such as Libya.[99] On the POW issue per se there was full agreement between the two actors:

1. A distinction must be made between wounded and healthy POWs.
2. The term *POW* is to include civilian as well as uniformed personnel (probably a hidden reference to Shula Cohen, "Renee," and the remains of Eli Cohen). As far as the Israelis were concerned, in the aftermath of the war and in light of prospects for gaining the release of all Israelis in hostile jails, the preferred term was just *prisoners*, not *prisoners of war*.[100]
3. Family reunification is part of the negotiations, referring to both Jewish communities as well as Arab families from the newly acquired territories.
4. All parties should have all pertinent information in spite of any interest in keeping it for future bargaining purposes.[101]

With that correct or mistaken worldview Israel continued its negotiations through the Red Cross with the Arab players. That approach was not to the liking of the Arab parties, which led to an abortive Egyptian attempt to get the Holy See as an honest broker. Israel did not wish the papal authority to be involved for two main reasons: the traditional uneasy relations between the Jews, Israel, and the Vatican; and second, the ICRC mediation was fair and balanced.[102] Perhaps the only exception to the rule—relying only on ICRC mediation—was the Israeli approach to Jarring, who was called in for help in late 1967 during the period of deadlock over Egypt's refusal to free the Israeli civilians.[103] In any case Jarring's intervention in the process did not contribute to the process and was abandoned a short while after its beginning.

One of the major hurdles in getting the POWs back was the blurred lines among all players active in the process regarding the identities of the requested prisoners and the prices for their release. This was not only a matter of lacking an agreed upon policy, but went far beyond that[104]: at least three separate bodies were involved, along with difficulties in exchanging findings and minutes of meetings. The following serves to illustrate these blurred lines:

1. The negotiating team with the ICRC in the Middle East was led by an Air Force helicopter pilot, a captain who was promoted to major during the negotiations, and his team included two more (reserve) officers (both majors) under the command of the Manpower Direc-

torate of the IDF. His own commanding officer was the Air Force commander, whereas the majors under his command reported to the Manpower Directorate.[105] However, that was only one dimension of the hastily put together ad hoc apparatus dealing with the POWs.

2. Being an international organization and a party to many international instruments, the ICRC team had their own counterparts at the MFA. The dialogue went on mainly in Geneva between the Israeli delegation and the ICRC headquarters, often without bringing into the picture the MFA people in Jerusalem, who for their part did not always share their data with the diplomats in Switzerland.[106] The ministry had a full-fledged department charged with the ongoing dialogue with the ICRC during times of peace and war. However, in the post-war era they only were briefed by the military people dealing with the ICRC and did not participate in any meeting with the organization.
3. To make things even worse, the *Foreign Ministry* as a term indicating an integrated and comprehensive foreign policy did not exist: The Israeli delegation to the international organizations in Geneva was not fully briefed by Jerusalem, leading to many misunderstandings among Jerusalem, Geneva, and the ICRC. That coupled with deficiencies in the flow of information between the IDF and the MFA caused each and every organ of the Israeli system to draw somewhat different conclusions about the prospects for deals and the true reasons for the delays in the exchange.[107]
4. As if all that was not enough, the Israeli supreme command took it upon itself to make an unprecedented move in international relations by approaching the ICRC on its own. That was at least a major infringement of international treaties because the State of Israel was the signatory to the Geneva Convention; consequently the only body responsible for the dialogue was the MFA and nothing but.[108]
5. Because Israel insisted on getting back some of its captured agents from the Arab countries it stands to reason that the Israeli security services, through the Minister of Defense, Dayyan, used back channels that are not reflected in contemporary documentation. This might provide the only logical explanation of the gradual change in the Arab countries' position regarding the Israeli ununiformed personnel who were eventually included in the concluded deals.

The lingering post-war exchange process perhaps exposed a major deficiency of the Israeli POW policy: the lack of a clear-cut list of targets intended for bargaining. The negligible interest of any of the Arab countries in the fate of their fallen in captivity went hand in hand with old Soviet doctrine that any lost POW is useless; once returned home, he or she is sometimes considered a traitor to his or her homeland as well. The Egyptian side, for instance, not only shot at its own troops attempting to cross the Canal on their way home during the first days after the war, but it did whatever it could to prevent an exchange of letters between the POWs and their families back in Egypt. That clearly violated their own troops' rights and obviously caused Israel to apologize for its own alleged attempt to prevent the letters from getting to the families.[109] Even the ICRC felt that it should adopt the Israeli position while reporting on the disturbances at the refugee camp—it cited the frustration of the POWs and their prolonged captivity as some of the reasons for their restlessness.[110] Under such harsh conditions, the traditional approach—"all your POWs for mine"—does not usually work, unless the subjects in question are national assets, that is, members of leading families, very high-ranking officers, leaders of an intelligence community, etc. Inasmuch as these circumstances present an Israeli decision maker with an almost unsolvable issue, they also might provide a way of staging a propaganda victory by declaring the unconditional return of unessential personnel, or by not even trying to negotiate a deal once a number of people such as those at the abovementioned refugee camp fall into Israeli hands. That, for instance, was the case when a group of forty-two Algerian students were apprehended by the Israeli authorities after the ceasefire and no Algerian voiced any interest in their return. Eventually, Israel took the right humanitarian course, which did no harm to Israeli interests or to the students, and handed them over to the ICRC.[111]

The 1967 POW issue marked the first time that Israeli POWs were shown on enemy TV. True, past prisoners had been brought to radio studios, either by force or willingly, whenever Israeli deserters or convicts crossed into enemy territory. However, the first TV appearance on Egyptian TV in mid-July signaled to Israel a form of exploitation of the POWs for propaganda purposes.[112] The mistaken Israeli concept would be corrected in the aftermath of the 1973 War with Israel's realization that such TV presentations, though intended for propaganda, were at times the only way to verify the capturing alive of an Israeli.

The lessons of the 1967 War are multidimensional: Israel respected the Geneva Convention for whatever respect toward POWs it demonstrated; however, Israel did see any Israeli in enemy hands, whatever the conditions of his being taken prisoner, as a POW contrary to the Convention's definition of POWs. The prisoners of the other side were treated accordingly: in spite of other international instruments, whoever could serve as a "bargaining chip" was kept in Israeli hands. The fact that the prisoners in question were diplomats did not mean that the policy applied was very different from that of the 1950s.

Additional lessons in the aftermath of the war contributed only a new layer to an already old insight: there was no point in taking prisoners under the level of NCOs. They were too costly to keep in POW camps in relation to their exchange and intelligence value, and above all, no Arab country was genuinely interested in getting them back. That meant—from a balance sheet sort of viewpoint—that Israel not only had a humanitarian duty to collect wounded enemy soldiers, but doing so also provided an opportunity to treat them well and to send them away after they recovered with no quid pro quo. It was not only the right thing to do, it also provided Israel with tangible diplomatic benefits.

In discussing the issue of indirect negotiations among belligerent countries, the UN and its respective organs were practically nonexistent. The ICRC on the other hand did its utmost in spite of the traditional Israeli suspicion. Israel benefitted from the realization of the ICRC that it was the "Jewish State" and should be addressed as the representative of all Jewish communities in danger. Nevertheless, that came with a price tag: the ICRC spoke on behalf of the civilian Arab communities in the territories to the chagrin of Israel.

That observation should be supplemented by the observation that even though all Arab countries agreed at the end of the exchange process to the principle of "all for all," some lingering doubts did continue where Syria was concerned. It never created the impression of being open and welcoming to all Israelis in its jails. Actually, reflecting on the four processes of exchange, one is left with the impression that the Arab players were not coordinated and that each and every one of them conducted its own POW policy. It is indeed astonishing to find that even Israel found it difficult to put together one clear tactical approach to the issue, considering the large number of decision makers and advisors involved without any clear central decision maker. It is obvious that they all wanted all prisoners back but it is unclear how much the inner competition among many players delayed the actual return of the Israelis.

NOTES

1. ISA/FM/4085/1, June 6, 1967.
2. ISA/FM/1508/6/1965–70/, June 10, 1967, from Paris, to Jerusalem; identical text: ISA/FM/4085/1, June 10, 1967.
3. Major general (retired) Yeshayahu Gavish , commander, Southern Command during the June 1967 war, personal interview, August 12, 2014; ISA/FM/4085/1, from Geneva, to Jerusalem, July 7, 1967.
4. ISA/FM/1508/6/1965–70/280; ISA/FM/4085/1/280.
5. http://www.iaf.co.il/Shared/Library/Controller.aspx?lang=HE&docID=12803&docfolderID=923&lobbyID=40.
6. ISA/FM/4085/1/correspondence between the Israeli second secretary and the ICRC, Geneva, June 13, 1967; ISA/FM/4085/1/65, from Jerusalem, to Geneva, June 16, 1967.
7. ISA/FM/4085/1/823, from Jerusalem, to Israel delegation in New York [the UN] and Washington, June 12, 1967; ISA/FM/4085/1/51, from Geneva, to Jerusalem, June 14, 1967; ISA/FM/1530/9/1063, from Jerusalem, to Katmandu, June 17, 1967.
8. ISA/FM/4085/1/300, from Jerusalem, to Paris, June 12, 1967; ISA/FM/4085/1/92, June 15, 1967, from Brussels, to Jerusalem.

9. ISA/FM/4085/1/67, from Jerusalem, to Israel delegation in New York [the UN] and Washington, July 2, 1967.

10. ISA/FM/4085/1, June 22, 1967, from the Turkish Consul General in Jerusalem, to the Foreign Ministry, June 22; ISA/FM/4085/1/143, from Brussels, to Jerusalem, June 22, 1967; ISA/FM/4085/1/91, from Jerusalem, to New York, June 22, 1967.

11. ISA/FM/4085/1/143, from Geneva, to Jerusalem, June 23, 1967.

12. ISA/FM/4085/1, June 13, 1967, June 15, from Brussels, to Jerusalem, no. 814, from Jerusalem, to New York, June 21, 1967.

13. ISA/FM/4085/1/949, June 24, 1967, from Jerusalem, to New York, June 24.

14. Vienna Convention on Diplomatic Relations, 1961, http://legal.un.org/ilc/texts/instruments/english/conventions/9_1_1961.pdf.

15. ISA/FM/4085/1/837, from Jerusalem, to New York, June 22, 1967.

16. ISA/FM/4085/1/100, internal correspondence, June 13, 1967; ISA/FM/4085/1/39, from Jerusalem, to Geneva, June 13, 1967; ISA/FM/1530/9/ 22, from Jerusalem, to Katmandu, June 14, 1967.

17. ISA/FM/1530/9/1060, from Jerusalem, to Katmandu, June 15, 1967.

18. ISA/FM/4085/1/130, from Jerusalem, to Geneva, June 26, 1967.

19. The first fifty wounded Egyptian POWs were returned to their country on June 15, ISA/FM/4085/1/ 55, from Geneva, to Jerusalem, June 15, 1967; ISA/FM/4086/7/8–12/67, report on the repatriation of the mortal remains of an Egyptian pilot, September 4, 1967; ISA/FM/4085/1/1065, from IDF/Manpower Directorate, to numerous addresses, October 18, 1967.

20. ISA/FM/4085/1/1065, from Jerusalem, to all Israeli representations, June 13, 1967; IDFA, 117/1970/61/5806-(13)2, from IDF Operations Directorate, to numerous addresses, November 1, 1967; IDFA, 117/1970/61/5877-(15)2, from IDF Operations Directorate, to numerous addresses, November 1, 1967; ISA/FM/4085/1, from IDF/Operations Directorate, to numerous addresses, December 17, 1967.

21. ISA/FM/4085/1/107, internal correspondence, June 15, 1967.

22. ISA/FM/1530/9/921, 1062, from Jerusalem, to Katmandu, June 15, 16, 1967; ISA/FM/4085/1/934, from Jerusalem, to New York, June 23, 1967.

23. ISA/FM/4085/1/55, from Geneva, to Jerusalem, June 15, 1967.

24. ISA/FM/4085/1/622, from Jerusalem, to New York, June 16, 1967; ISA/FM/4085/1/56, from Jerusalem, to Geneva, July 13, 1967.

25. Cf. ISA/FM/4085/1/395, from Washington, to Jerusalem, June 26, 1967.

26. http://unispal.un.org/unispal.nsf/0/E02B4F9D23B2EFF3852560C3005CB95A.

27. ISA/FM/4085/1/150, from Tel Aviv [Israel Defense Forces HQ], to Jerusalem, June 27, 1967.

28. ISA/FM/4085/1/152, from Tel Aviv [Israel Defense Forces HQ], to Jerusalem, June 27, 1967.

29. ISA/FM/4085/1/105, from Jerusalem, to Geneva, June 21, 1967; IDFA, 535/2004/2799: "Syrian Casualties in the Six Day War," in Basic Study 3/68, The Syrian Army in the Six Day War, "Secret," December 1968, 157.

30. ISA/FM/4085/1/837, from Jerusalem, to New York, June 22, 1967.

31. IDFA, 117/1970/61/5823-(12)2, from IDF Operations Directorate, to numerous addresses, November 2, 1967.

32. ISA/FM/4085/1/100, internal correspondence, June 13, 1967; ISA/FM/4085/1/39, from Jerusalem, to Geneva, June 13, 1967; ISA/FM/1530/9/22, from Jerusalem, to Katmandu, June 14, 1967.

33. ISA/FM/4086/9/6–7/67, memorandum on the meeting with the ICRC representative in Syria, July 5, 1967.

34. ISA/FM/4085/1/74, from Brussels, to Jerusalem, June 17, 1967; ISA/FM/4085/1/928, from New York, to Jerusalem, June 23, 1967.

35. Even though they formally recruited to the Israeli Defense Forces prior to their arrest, that fact was concealed from the Egyptians all throughout their ordeal in order to prevent further complicating their situation. The Egyptian authorities learned of

that fact only toward the end of the negotiations for their release in late 1967. ISA/FM/7455/11, from Geneva, to Jerusalem, January 3, 1968.

36. ISA/FM/4085/1/86, from Brussels, to Jerusalem, June 21, 1967.

37. http://www.icrc.org/ihl/INTRO/380.

38. ISA/FM/4086/7/8–12/1967, minutes of a meeting between the leaders of the U.S. Jewish community with the Middle East leadership of the ICRC, no date [probably early December], 1967.

39. *Davar*, June 16, 1967, 2.

40. ISA/FM/4085/1/83, from Jerusalem, to Geneva, June 21, 1967.

41. ISA/FM/4085/1/86, from Brussels, to Jerusalem, June 21, 1967.

42. ISA/FM/4085/1/423, from Washington, to Jerusalem, June 27, 1967.

43. ISA/FM/4085/1/143, from Geneva, to Jerusalem, June 23, 1967.

44. http://www.icrc.org/applic/ihl/ihl.nsf/Treaty.xsp?action=openDocument&documentId=AE2D398352C5B028C12563CD002D6B5C.

45. ISA/FM/4085/1/75, "continuation" of #75, from Brussels, to Jerusalem, June 17, 1967.

46. Major general (retired) Yesha'ayahu Gavish, commander, Southern Command during the June 1967 war, personal interview, August 12, 2014, http://www.navy.idf.il/1288-he/Navy.aspx; ISA/FM/4086/9/ handwritten memo, from an IDF negotiator (?), to MFA, July 20, 1967.

47. ISA/FM/1530/9/1075, from Jerusalem, to Katmandu, June 19, 1967.

48. ISA/FM/4085/1/346, from Jerusalem, to Washington, June 27, 1967.

49. ISA/FM/4086/9/6–7/67, memorandum on the meeting with the ICRC representative in Egypt, June 21, 1967.

50. ISA/FM/4086/9/6–7/67, memorandum on the meeting with the ICRC representative in Lebanon, June 21, 1967.

51. ISA/FM/4085/1/133, from Jerusalem, to Geneva, June 26, 1967; ISA/A/7461/7/67, from Geneva, to Jerusalem, July 19, 1967.

52. ISA/FM/4085/1/26, from Geneva, to Jerusalem, July 7, 1967; ISA/FM/4085/1/26, from Geneva, to Jerusalem, July 7, 1967.

53. ISA/FM/4085/1/26, Internal MFA memo, Jerusalem, July 21, 1967

54. Cf. ISA/FM/4085/1/26, from Rome, to Jerusalem, October 23, 1967.

55. ISA/FM/4085/1, "top secret" resolution of October 1, 1967.

56. Cf. "4,700 Egyptian Prisoners Wait," *The Standard*, October 19, 1967.

57. ISA/FM/4086/7/26, from Geneva, to Jerusalem, October 23, 1967.

58. Cf. ISA/FM/4085/1, from Geneva, to Jerusalem, December 19, 1967.

59. ISA/G/6692/9, Cabinet resolution 52B, December 27, 1967; Yedioth Aharonot, Israel, Hebrew daily, September 12, 1976; ISA/FM/7455/103, from Jerusalem, to New York, January 4, 1968.

60. ISA/FM/30/3/49, internal MFA memo, January 7, 1968.

61. One striking example: ISA/FM/4096/1 internal MFA memo, [no date] probably around January 9–10, 1968.

62. ISA/FM/30/3/52, internal MFA memo, January 7, 1968.

63. ISA/FM/7455/103, "top secret," from Jerusalem, to New York, January 4, 1968.

64. ISA/FM/7455/333, from New York, to Jerusalem, January 24, 1968.

65. Cf. "Pan-Arabism's retreat began in 1967 after the Six Day War, which marked the Waterloo of Pan-Arabism," in Fouad Ajami, "The End of Pan -Arabism," *Foreign Affairs* 57, no. 2 (Winter 1978): 357.

66. ISA/FM/4086/9/6–7/67, memorandum on the meeting with the ICRC representative in Syria, June 19, 1967; memorandum on the meeting with the ICRC representative in Syria, June 23, 1967.

67. ISA/FM/4085/1/346, from Jerusalem, to Washington, June 27, 1967.

68. ISA/FM/4085/1/83, from Jerusalem, to Geneva, June 21, 1967.

69. Cf. ISA/FM/4085/1/311, from London, to Jerusalem, June 27, 1967; ISA/1392/12/1967/no number, June 27, 1967; a list of Israeli Air Force air crew fatalities indicates

that he was murdered upon reaching ground: http://sfile.f-static.com/image/users/134771/ftp/my_files/KIA/KIA%20name.pdf?id=16275667 .

70. ISA/FM/4085/1/997, from Israel delegation in New York [the UN], to Jerusalem, June 24, 1967; Jerusalem did not share that view because negotiations satisfactory or not were already in motion: ISA/FM/4085/1/979, from Jerusalem Israel delegation in New York [the UN], to Jerusalem, June 24, 1967.

71. The following paragraphs are based on ISA/FM/4086/9/6–7/67, memorandum on the meeting with the ICRC representative in Syria, June 26, 1967.

72. *Ma'ariv*, July 19, 20, 1967, 8.

73. ISA/FM/4085/1/1187, from Israel delegation in New York [the UN], to Jerusalem, June 28, 1967; ISA/FM/4085/1/1187, from Jerusalem, to Israel delegation in New York [the UN], Jerusalem, June 28, 1967.

74. ISA/FM/4086/9/6–7/67, memorandum on the meeting with the ICRC representative in the Middle East, July 8, 1967.

75. ISA/FM/4086/9/6–7/67, memorandum on the meeting with the ICRC representative in Syria, July 5, 1967; ISA/FM/4085/1/468, "top secret," from Israel delegation in New York [the UN], to Geneva, July 7, 1967.

76. ISA/FM/4086/9/6–7/67, memorandum on the meeting with the ICRC representative in Syria, July 9, 1967.

77. ISA/FM/4085/1/104, from Tel Aviv [IDF Liaison], to Jerusalem, July 17, 1967.

78. ISA/FM/4086/9/6–7/67, memorandum on the meeting with the ICRC representative in Lebanon, June 18, 1967.

79. The list can be consulted at ISA/FM/4085/1, from MFA, to the Director of the RCAC Delegation, Tel Aviv, June 20, 1967; ISA/FM/4085/1/137, from Jerusalem, to Geneva, June 27, 1967.

80. ISA/FM/4086/9/6–7/67, memorandum on the meeting with the ICRC representative in Lebanon, June 21, 1967. Ms. Cohen was granted the highest Israeli honor by being invited to be one of the twelve people lighting the traditional beacons indicating the beginning of the 2007 Israeli Day of Independence. http://lib.cet.ac.il/pages/item.asp?item=22595; http://malam.cet.ac.il/ShowItem.aspx?ItemID=7f1e021f-ad99–470f-a150–160ad3a53a5c&lang=HEB; ISA/FM/4085/1/115, from Jerusalem, to Geneva, June 23, 1967.

81. Ambassador Isaac Lebanon, son of Shula Cohen, personal interview, August 17, 2014.

82. ISA/FM/4086/9/6–7/67, memorandum on the meeting with the ICRC representative in Lebanon, July 3, 1967; ISA/FM/4085/1/468, "top secret," from New York [the UN], to Geneva, July 7, 1967.

83. *al-Safaa'*, Lebanon, Arabic daily, August 8, 1967.

84. Ambassador Isaac Lebanon, son of Shula Cohen, personal interview, August 17, 2014; ISA/FM/4085/1/33, from Jerusalem, to Geneva, August 9, 1967; *Ma'ariv*, August 10, 1967, 2; *Davar*, August 10, 1967.

85. Ambassador Isaac Lebanon, son of Shula Cohen, personal interview, August 17, 2014; ISA/FM/4086/7, from Geneva, to Jerusalem, October 10, 1967.

86. [UK] NA/FCO17/226/EJ2/5/May 12, 1967, FO internal correspondence (overtaken); [UK] NA/FCO17/225/EJ2/4/January 20, February 27, 1967/, from Washington and the Foreign Office, respectively.

87. Full text of the joint defense treaty: *al-Watha'iq al-Urduniyyah 1967*, 19–21.

88. USNA/RG59/POL32–1 ISR-JORDAN/11368/November 13, 1966/, from Tel Aviv; USNA/RG59/POL ISR-JORDAN/83785/November 13, 1966/, from Department of State; USNA/RG59/POL JORDAN -ISR/9566/December 11, 1966, from Amman; USNA/RG59/POL 32–1 ISR-JORDAN/4875/December 6, 1966/, from Amman.

89. ISA/FM/4085/1/124, from MFA, to Geneva, June 24, 1967.

90. ISA/FM/4086/9/6–7/67, memorandum on the meeting with the ICRC representative in Jordan, June 23, 1967.

91. ISA/FM/4085/1/149, from Jerusalem, to Israel delegation in New York [the UN], June 21, 1967; ISA/FM/4086/9/6–7/67, memorandum on the meeting with the ICRC representative in the Middle East regarding POWs in Jordan, June 21, 1967.
92. ISA/FM/4086/9/6–7/67, memorandum on the meeting with the ICRC representative in Jordan, June 23, 1967.
93. ISA/FM/4089/5, June 26, 1967; ISA/1392/12/1967/486, June 26, 1967.
94. The two parties along with the United States were signatories to a 1965 de facto limited demilitarization of the West Bank agreement. Cf. USNA/RG 59/POL 32–1 ISR-JORDAN/13051/November 15, 1966, from Amman; ISA/FM/4085/1/145, from Jerusalem, to Geneva, June 28, 1967.
95. ISA/FM/4085/1/330, from MFA, to Geneva, June 26, 1967.
96. ISA/FM/4086/9/6–7/67, memorandum on the meeting with the ICRC representative in the Middle East, July 8, 1967; ISA/FM/4086/9/ handwritten memo, from an IDF negotiator (?), to MFA, July 20, 1967; ISA/FM/1530/9/1009, from Jerusalem, to Katmandu, August 7, 1967.
97. *Ma'ariv*, Israel, Hebrew daily, June 18, 1967, 7; ISA/FM/1530/9/1, from Jerusalem, to Katmandu, July 2, 1967.
98. ISA/1392/12/1967/484, July 1, 1967; ISA/FM/1530/9/1, from Jerusalem, to Katmandu, July 2, 1967.
99. ISA/FM/4085/1/14, from Geneva, to the MFA Affairs, July 4, 1967.
100. ISA/FM/4085/1/224, from Jerusalem, to New York, July 5, 1967.
101. ISA/FM/4086/9/6–7/no number, memorandum on the June 30, 1967, meeting with the ICRC pilot assigned by ICRC with carrying returning POWs, July 2, 1967.
102. Ernest Evans, "The Vatican and Israel," *World Affairs* 158 (Fall 1995): 88–92; ISA/FM/4085/1/65, "immediate" MFA memo, July 5, 1967.
103. ISA/FM/4085/1/70, from the foreign minister, to the mother of the captured pilot Dan Manor, December 18, 1967.
104. Major general (retired) Yesha'ayahu Gavish, commander, Southern Command during the June 1967 war, personal interview, August 12, 2014.
105. ISA/FM/4085/1, internal MFA memo, July 21, 1967.
106. ISA/FM/4085/1/not numbered, from Geneva, to Jerusalem, June 28, 1967; ISA/FM/4085/1/467, from Jerusalem, to Geneva, July 7, 1967.
107. ISA/FM/4086/7/no number, from Jerusalem, to Geneva, August 8, 1967.
108. ISA/FM/4086/7/internal Geneva delegation memo, August 1, 1967.
109. ISA/FM/4086/7/, from IDF Manpower Directorate, to MFA, November [no date], 1967; ISA/FM/4085/1/904, from Jerusalem, to New York, December 11, 1967.
110. ISA/FM/4086/9/, from Geneva, to Jerusalem, December 12, 1967; ISA/FM/30/3/41 internal MFA memo, January 5, 1968.
111. ISA/FM/4085/1, internal MFA memo, September 5, 1967.
112. ISA/FM/4085/1, internal MFA memo, July 23, 1967, in reference to a July 18 letter that was not available at the time of preparing the manuscript.

Part III

Israel, the State Actors and the Subnational Players: New Rules, Parallel Systems, and the Merging of the Two—the Fourth Generation

EIGHT

The 1967–1970 Crucial Interregnum

The Challenging Legacy of the War of Attrition

With the end of hostilities, a new stage in Israeli-Arab relations began. The realization that each and every Arab country had its own unique set of interests replaced the concept of Egypt and Nasser as "leader of the Arabs." At times those interests served as bases for ad hoc cooperation and at times they were used by the respective national leaders as sources of friction among themselves. These years also saw some ideological and political soul searching and the rise of new methods and approaches in regard to confronting Israel. One of the newly strengthened actors in the arena resulting from the winds of change was the Palestinian organizations. Each and every Arab leading actor was involved in one way or another with the Palestinian semi-military activity that began prior to the 1967 War but overshadowed parts of the changing Arab-Israeli conflict after the war.

At the end of June 1967 War all had gone according to the Israeli plan, including POW exchanges. It even managed to retrieve its agents captured in Egypt and Lebanon in the 1950s and 1960s. All who were captured in the armed conflict were returned, without distinction between officers and soldiers and those in sensitive positions and regular troops. The Arab armies' defeat led to a relatively short negotiation process involving almost all Arab uniformed and nonuniformed personnel and citizens. The last POWs were returned in January 1968.

Those years also saw terrorist attacks fully supported by the Arab countries. The distinctly different regular and irregular military activities were united on two purposes: eroding the amazing 1967 Israeli victory and securing a Geneva-based POW status for the terrorists. Israel for its part continued to demonstrate full adherence to the Geneva Convention in its POW treatment clauses, whereas Arab violations continued unpunished by the international community.

Two domestic developments and one foreign and security process marked the era between June 1967 and the outbreak of the Yom Kippur October 1973 War: the Israeli prime minister, Levi Eshkol, died in February 1969 and was replaced in March by Mrs. Meir. Later that year in October Mrs. Meir was chosen in general elections to form a new coalition government, which she presented later that year. Meanwhile, in March 1969, Egypt and later Jordan launched a War of Attrition against Israel, which came to an end with a U.S. ill-brokered deal that was violated by Egypt one day after it came into effect on August 9, 1970.[1] That violation probably marked the pre-1973 stage during which the Arab players prepared for the upcoming imminent showdown while Israel, immersed in its post-1967 euphoria, believed that no Arab party would dare to attack. Furthermore, during the six years between the two wars, substate actors joined the fold creating new precedents regarding hostages, kidnapped, and prisoners taking the lead from the Arab state players in forcing a new exchange policy upon Israel. Across from the Arab players stood a national unity Israeli coalition government that operated through three cabinets (two only part of the time) from June 5, 1967, to August 6, 1970. That tenure between the outbreak of the June war and the ceasefire ended the War of Attrition and was responsible for all Israeli policy decisions made during that time—partially explaining the Israeli opposition's inability to develop its own POW policy in the aftermath of the 1973 War, thus paving the way for a civil society activity in that context.

Israel was not only on the losing side, militarily and diplomatically, from day one of the 1973 conflict, but also had to grapple with its challenging legacy of POW policy from the War of Attrition. In that war, Israel suffered a relatively large number of casualties and prisoners, leaving it too weak and exhausted to retaliate against Egypt's violation of the August 8, 1970, ceasefire. Israel's desire to bring the boys back at any price negatively affected its diplomatic standing—the media and other opinion shapers added to the emerging picture of an unnecessary war during the War of Attrition as long as the attrition battles were going on. By three to four years after the 1967 War of survival, Israel's resilience had completely eroded. On the Arab side, it became clear that POWs were Israel's Achilles' heel and that Israeli POWs could and should be used as pawns on the diplomatic chessboard.

In terms of POWs, 1968 was essentially a quiet year except for a growing number of border clashes with Egypt heralding the imminent War of Attrition, and one serious flare-up between the Jordanian army and the Palestinian organizations on one side and Israel on the other on Jordanian soil. This clash caused a large number of casualties on both sides—including prisoners[2] —and its aftermath was complex: Israel and Jordan lost prisoners and MIAs, whereas Israel captured seventy-eight members of al-Fatḥ.[3] Israel took twelve Jordanian soldiers and officers, who were returned a week after the incident.[4] The Israeli release of only Jordanian POWs further complicated the issue of the status of the captured enemy fighters. Because all Arab combatants were apprehended during the same battle by the same army, the Israeli Defense Forces, they all deserved the same status according to the ICRC. That was the matter at the heart of the voiced and public Israeli position: enemy troops had that status because they belonged to a legal and recognized army of a sovereign enemy country, whereas the terrorist organizations led by al-Fatḥ did not meet any of the criteria to be considered a legal enemy force. With that March 1968 Karameh incident an issue that had only been alluded to since before the June 1967 War came into the limelight. The lines were clear: Israel would not recognize al-Fatḥ members as POWs at any cost. On the other hand, with the continued insistence of the ICRC on a position recognizing all Arab captured combatants as POWs, Israel had to give up a little and adopted the position that the Fourth Geneva Convention, which dealt with protection of civilians during war, would be used in this case instead of the Third Convention, in order to enable ICRC visits with the al-Fatḥ members.[5] However, Israel made it crystal clear that applying the Fourth Convention in this particular context did not mean the adoption of the Convention because Israel, according to its official position, did not occupy the territories. Israel's position allowing ICRC visits to the incarcerated al-Fatḥ members did not provide any long-term solution to the issue of the Palestinian fighters—which has not been resolved one way or another to this day. It only offered an ad hoc solution for this case in order to provide a legal basis for ICRC visits. The visits did take place and were de facto subject to the regular rules of the ICRC regarding visiting POWs.[6] The March skirmish left the door wide open for further attempts by the subnational player, the Palestinian organization, to try and gain POW status through other means.

The nonstate combatants issue was not the only one to upset Israeli decision makers in the wake of Karameh. The vast gulf between the Jordanian leadership under King Hussein, who was already dealing directly and indirectly with Israel, and Jordan's military, devoted to fighting the enemy of the nation, Israel, was never more apparent than in the following incident. Because the Jordanian military could not find the bodies of the Israeli MIAs, they handed over to Israel two coffins containing sand and no trace of any human remains, very much to the chagrin of the Jordanian deputy prime minister and the ICRC representatives.[7] Jordan for its part tried to deflect the Israeli and ICRC criticism by serving as the voice of all Arab prisoners in Israel and accusing Israel of torturing its detainees and drawing their blood.[8]

Nothing along the Israeli borders with any of the Middle Eastern nation-states provided any indication of the change to occur after only a few months of the diplomatic skirmish with Jordan resulting from the March Karameh incident. Two unrelated developments changed the rules of engagement regarding POW exchanges. In May 1968 Israel inaugurated its first television channel enabling Israelis to follow human dramas live, including the falling of POWs and taking of hostages as well as other kinds of military and semi-military activities on live broadcast. About a couple of months later, in July, the first hijacking of an airplane in the Middle Eastern/Arab-Israeli conflict took place. Some effects of the media on the POW issue will be dealt with in the next chapters because it reached its temporary zenith in combination with POW-related civil society activities that influenced the formation of the Israeli policy in the aftermath of the October war. The immediate effect was felt during the hijacking of an Israeli civilian plane to Algiers in July 1968 and the demand that was finally met to release convicted terrorists in exchange for the passengers.

One of the chief Israeli exchange negotiators observed years later that that incident changed the rules of the game.[9] In a nutshell, an El Al airplane en route from Rome to Tel Aviv was hijacked in midair in the early hours of July 23, 1968, by a cell of George Habash's Popular Front for the Liberation of Palestine (PFLP) and was forced to land in Algiers. Of the thirty-six original passengers, only twelve were not released, including the aircrew, with the intention of the organization being to hold them as bargaining chips against Israel. Through a process of indirect negotiations, the hostages were returned to Israel after about six weeks in exchange for a number of convicted terrorists not involved in any murder cases.

The clashing interests of the protagonists were clear: Israel needed to get the crew and the passengers back home as quickly as possible through international pressure on the Algerian government, which represented the PFLP, without any hint of recognition of the organization and without any other diplomatic achievement. The organization's interests were almost a mirror image of Israel's: as much international recognition as possible, including giving POW status to Palestinians in Israeli jails, sympathetic media all over the world, and as much damage as possible to the no-negotiating policy of Israel.[10]

Diplomatically, Israel had no significant experience in dealing with civilian hostages: in most previous cases the "civilians" were sent one way or another by Israel. This time around none of them were on any official or clandestine missions. Furthermore, legally speaking, the Geneva Conventions, which had served in the past as the legal basis for ICRC involvement, were not applicable in this case. Even the Algerian government debated whether the adult male hostages could fit the definition of POWs and decided against it.[11] Actually, in spite of defining the Israeli air carrier El Al as a "military tool," which makes it a legitimate target, there were no clear-cut indications of treating the hostages as POWs.[12]

Attempting to secure the release of the civilians, Israel had to grapple with several fundamental issues and eventually give up its policy, which had held up to that point, of not negotiating with terrorists. The significance attached by this writer to the El Al incident stems from the variety of dimensions of the PFLP action.

The stage on the Arab side was set for two players who differ on the benefits they could extract from the hijacking. Algeria had an interest in clearing itself of any charges for being a party to air piracy, yet was also interested in taking charge of the Palestinian issue heretofore the domain of only Egypt and Syria. After all, the Algerian regime defined itself as being revolutionary as well. On the other hand, it was a legitimate member of the family of nations through its membership in the UN. That duality was somewhat demonstrated by the brief, military nature of the interrogations that the Israelis underwent after landing in Algiers.[13] Indeed, there was no active conflict between Israel and Algeria in the summer of 1968, and maybe there never was one, with the exception of Algeria making some anti-Israeli statements on a sporadic basis. Moreover, no Algerian force had participated in the June 1967 War. Consequently, and in order not to be drawn into the conflict any further, Algeria, a signatory to the Third Convention (upon its independence in 1962), refrained from declaring the Israelis POWs.[14] Quite to the contrary, Algeria was interested in being recognized by all other involved parties, led by Israel, as a legitimate negotiator, while advancing Palestinian interests and contributing to their cause at least as much as Egypt and Syria.

The PFLP had a rather conflicting interest in mind: securing POW status for its people once apprehended by Israel was its first priority. Legally, the Third Geneva Convention specified the following in Article 4(A):

> (5) Members of crews, including masters, pilots and apprentices, of the merchant marine and the crews of civil aircraft of the Parties to the conflict, who do not benefit by more favourable treatment under any other provisions of international law [would be considered POWs].[15]

That wording did not allow for defining the Israeli hostages as POWs, just as there was no reference to people like PFLP members being apprehended as POWs. That might in the mind of the PFLP leadership serve as the basis for some agreement between Israel and themselves. Because neither group was included in the Convention, they could perhaps enjoy a similar focus on securing the release of all held people and use that as a precedent in later hijacking and kidnapping incidents. Having failed to reach an agreement on that basis due to Algeria's lack of interest helped Israel avoid the formal status question but did not give it any strategic advantage over the Arab side. This hijacking incident signaled the addition of a new dimension to the old issues relating to POW issues: the legal framework to be employed in trying to secure the release of civilian hostages. Lacking the Geneva context, the Arab side had to be satisfied with a smaller trophy: getting Palestinians convicted by a court of law for various terrorist-related crimes released. In this way, the Palestinian organization could point to two main accomplishments: overruling binding Israeli court decisions against Israeli citizens and some of the neighboring Arab countries and getting as many members as possible of several organizations out of jail—making the releasing organization the leader, at least temporarily, for staging a Palestinian victory and promoting unity against Israel. Out of the twenty-four released, some just preferred to get back home instead of joining the ranks of any Palestinian organization: five Israeli Arab citizens to their original homes, eight to Egypt, two to Jordan, and one to Lebanon.[16]

Along the way and for the first time, the Israeli cabinet had to grapple with the fundamental difficulty arising from the need to talk to a terrorist organization. Moreover, because the stated policy of Israel at the time was that of not negotiating with terrorists, doing exactly that would grant the organizations an additional layer of victory in a zero sum game with its perennial enemy. In an attempt to pursue its policy, Israel approached the Italian government from whose sovereign territory the plane took off. Among the many appeals made to many countries and international organizations, the only effective one was that of the Foreign Minister of Israel, Abba Eban, known for his dovish ideology, to the Italian government—asking them to serve as intermediary between Jerusalem and Algiers.[17] It is important to note that at this point, a little over a year after the June 1967 War, the atmosphere of mutual trust and cooperation between Israel and the ICRC—which had contributed so much to that war's successful conclusion with the release of the June POWs—no longer existed by the summer of 1968, bringing to an end a short period of combined efforts.[18] Perhaps the most obvious explanation for that worrying development was the link, apparent to the ICRC but totally ignored by Israel, between the Third Convention dealing with POWs and the Fourth Convention dealing with civilian populations under occupation. Israel has never acknowledged the territories captured in 1967 as "occupied" and consequently if and when it applied any of the Fourth Convention clauses, it was a humanitarian gesture rather than out of adherence to that international instrument. The ICRC for its part felt much less obliged to help Israel in its continuous quest to get its POWs and hostages back considering what the organization saw as a lack of goodwill on the part of Israel.

On top of Israel losing ground with the ICRC, the hijacking and the diplomatic moves in its wake represented to Algeria a major breakthrough for the Arab players in the POW context, as a strategic defeat to Israel. The main victor was the PFLP: unlike all fighting Arab armies that had been defeated only a year earlier, a relatively small organization, not officially affiliated with any Arab country, managed to lower Israel to its knees as it struggled for a diplomatic solution while being unable to devise a military one.[19] Indeed, the hijacking took the Arab-Israeli conflict into a new, broader arena far away from the immediate borders of Israel and added the air traffic dimension to the conflict. The distance, the lack of intelligence on Algeria, and the reliance on large tank and infantry fighting rendered the mighty Israeli army useless against a small organization holding Israeli citizens in a faraway country. Some of the lessons would be drawn later; the Entebbe raid in 1976 partially attested to that but did not eradicate the political and diplomatic fallout of the El Al hijacking.

No Israeli activities post-Algeria could reverse the precedents set. With no military operation possible and a policy of not negotiating with terrorist organizations, Israel found itself in limbo at first and at the losing end once the crisis was over. Not only did the PFLP stage a surprising move against an unprepared Israel, it also managed to get the Palestinian issue into the Middle Eastern political equation—an issue ignored altogether by the Arab nation-states exchanging their POWs only months ago.

That distinction between military POWs and civilian hostages would in a few years disappear and aspects of the two would mutually affect each other. In real time, the El Al Algeria incident came as a surprise to the Arab state actors as well; consequently, it took their respective governments some time to study its ramifications. Back in August 1968 the nation-states' behavior was still totally divorced from that of any organization, as the case of the August 1968 Syrian pilots indicated. Toward the conclusion of the indirect communications about discharging the El Al crew and the remaining passengers, two Syrian pilots landed their pair of MiG-17 planes in a semi-deserted airstrip in northern Israel. In spite of media demands that their fate be linked to the release of the hostages in Algeria, noting its close diplomatic relations with Syria, official Israel refrained from creating such a connection.[20] Strangely enough, Syria, which did not have any interest in Algeria taking the lead in the Palestinian issue, approached the ICRC on August 14, a couple of days after the Israeli landing of its pilots, declared its pilots POWs, and demanded their release.[21] That did indeed lead to ICRC involvement in the context of securing the rights of the pilots as POWs and visiting them from time to time in the Israeli jail.[22] Yet this time around and perhaps based on one of the lessons of the past war, Israel insisted on not releasing the Syrians—in all probability waiting to use them as "bargaining chips" in any future incidence of Israelis falling into Syrian hands.

July 1968 signaled the beginning of attempts by Palestinian organizations to disrupt civilian transportation to and from Israel while taking hostages. That eventually came to an end with the military operation that led to the release of the Air France Israeli hostages from the Entebbe, Uganda, airport in July 1976. In between and especially between July

1968 and August 1970, Israel was the target of low-intensity warfare by the Arab countries that were its immediate neighbors, while also involved in a confrontation with the Palestinian organizations. That combined campaign involved uniformed and nonuniformed Israelis: those taken by a regular enemy army and those taken by subnational actors.

With the massive artillery attack on the Israeli outposts along the Suez Canal on March 8, 1969, a new stage in the regular armies' Arab-Israeli conflict commenced: no more total wars, but instead small warfare intended to wear down Israeli morale and cause some dissatisfaction among the Israeli population, which would eventually achieve the results desired by the Arab side. That warfare was quite different from the kind in June 1967: it manifested a long military effort on the tactical level by three Arab armies—Egypt, Syria, and to some degree Jordan—including stretching out the conflict overseas and into typically civilian fields, as well as full participation. All of that meant that as of March 1969, the POW issue facing Israel was threefold: Israeli troops apprehended while operating on enemy territory; troops kidnapped from Israeli positions by Egyptian commandos; and civilians captured by the Palestinian organizations within and outside of Israel.

Fighting along the Israeli-Egyptian demarcation lines spread onto the Syrian front, and the Jordanian army, assisted by Iraqi expeditionary forces, some of whom were leftovers from the June 1967 War, followed suit. On top of the regular armies exchanging fire and the Palestinian organizations attempting to stage their own successful path to international diplomatic recognition, all Arab parties were keen on trying to accomplish their goals by, inter alia, capturing Israeli POWs. The lessons of the June 1967 War and later were not lost on any Arab actor: Israel would do almost all in its power to release its people, whatever the price. The POW issue and the potential for new updated intelligence on the most recent Western-made armaments could not have been lost on the Soviet Union either. As of late 1968, its Kavkaz operation got underway. That operation meant the deployment of organic military units in Egypt for the purposes of helping Egypt during its confrontation with Israel and collecting through that process any military and diplomatic dividends available.[23] Launching that operation almost automatically meant that the Soviet intelligence effort aimed at Israel had to be stepped up. Indeed, intelligence ships monitored Israeli signal traffic and probably kept a close watch on current developments. However, that could not satisfy the new kid on the block. With little appreciation of the Arab intelligence effort, the Soviets had to reconstruct the military echelons, the decision-making processes, the makeup of the IDF units, and above all the war doctrines of the Israeli army. All of that could only be accomplished by capturing Israeli officers—especially those belonging to the highest ranks possible. Consequently, it is safe to assume that each Israeli POW in Egyptian or Syrian hands between late 1968 and at least mid-

1974 was either interrogated by Soviets or asked questions put together by Red Army intelligence officers. Considering the need for that strategic and basic information, none of the Arab players had any interest in returning the Israeli POWs right away. If the issue had been fresh intelligence that might have been the case, but the effort of extracting the very basics of the Israeli system was a much longer process. Moreover, it called for some rather careful raids into Israeli-held territories so as not to harm potential sources. That view also explains to some degree the increasing number of Egyptian commando raids from late 1968 to the summer 1970 ceasefire. Having said that, it is important to remember the extraordinary price tag that Israel put on its POWs, guaranteeing the highest quid pro quo possible from exchange deals.

The War of Attrition not only saw early indications of the reinternationalization of the Arab-Israeli conflict, but also accentuated the already present perennial enmity among the warring regional nations and their soldiers. On top of shooting dead Israeli pilots parachuting themselves from falling planes during the 1967 War, the conduct of the local inhabitants and troops at the sites where they fell was cruel and betrayed any internationally accepted norm. One such case occurred on July 10, 1969. An Egyptian commando unit raided an Israeli tank encampment on the Suez Canal, killed an entire tank platoon, and took back across the Canal what they believed to be a POW. Upon getting back to their base they discovered that the soldier was dead and they expressed their frustration with unacceptable behavior.[24] Considering that loud protest to the ICRC would obviously make its way to Egypt and might harm present and future Israeli POWs, Israel decided to file a rather mild protest to the organization but to refrain from any publicity. Remembering that the ICRC has no sanction power on any nation and that its power is derived precisely from the publicity given to violations of the international treaties, the Israeli decision was problematic at the very least. That decision was probably made by Israeli diplomats on an ad hoc basis and was not the result of a cabinet discussion. In this case, as in many others documented elsewhere in this study, the lack of a comprehensive procedure (that could have been modified from time to time based on changing conditions) led Israel to abandon the discussion of other options. The Israeli reaction in this case did not deter Egyptian authorities from repeating similar behaviors in the case of a living POW. However, Israel changed its response and not only filed a complaint with the ICRC, but also launched a mass media campaign hoping to score some diplomatic success.[25]

While Israel was busy with POW issues, the War of Attrition went on, and in August 1969 a new precedent was created: a united Arab front against Israel aimed at gaining equal status between a legitimate POW and a terrorist enjoying POW status due to political and diplomatic maneuverers. The trigger for such a united front was supplied by the Popular Front for the Liberation of Palestine (George Habash), the same organization that had hijacked the El Al plane a little more than a year earlier This Arab stance was somewhat successful and came at the end of the following drama that took place in December 1969. Briefly stated, a TWA plane en route from Rome to the Tel Aviv airport was kidnapped in midair by a cell belonging to the PFLF and forced to land in Damascus. The hijacking demonstrated a process of drawing all possible conclusions from the earlier El Al capture. Perhaps the most significant lesson was that El Al planes were no longer a possible target due to the extra Israeli security for air traffic. Yet that lesson was still lost on most other carriers, including TWA. Concurrent with the Israeli effort to get the two civilians freed, Egypt had its own two Israeli POWs. It attached high value to both—one was a squadron commander whose plane was shot down on August 19 and the other was the IAF champion at shooting down enemy planes, who was shot down on September 11.[26] Both might have been perceived by the Egyptians not only as possible bargaining chips in future deals involving hostages, but also as quality intelligence sources. These two elements, on top of the traditional Egyptian treatment of Israeli POWs, might explain their refusal to let the ICRC visit the pilots until a later date.[27]

Upon the hijacking of the plane, the PFLP people released all female and young passengers and were left with only two male adult Israeli citizens, one a Hadassah hospital/Hebrew University professor of neurobiology, captured on board a plane belonging to a noninvolved third party registered in the United States. The initial Israeli reaction was to voice in a sense a sigh of relief, hoping that the influential Americans and the media would side with Israel and, combining all of their resources, create enough pressure on Syria to induce it to release the hostages.[28] The PFLP, sensing their approaching success, continued their attacks on Israeli air traffic, albeit in a different form. In September and November, the PFLP attacked El Al offices in Brussels and Athens. The pressure on Israel was building without a military Israeli response in sight—possibly even signaling a break with the past's almost automatic discussion of the military option. That option, along with the dramatically different circumstances along the Canal and their interest in not linking the two situations, led Israel not only to frustration but to open threats against Egypt. Israel's decision makers felt that it had a strong case in terms of international law and norms and that consequently—if it used the lack of visits and threw in some threats as well—Israel could effect a change.[29] Egypt correctly read the Israeli intentions and one day after the Israeli semi-official daily signaled Israel's frustration and alluded to its willingness to take harsh action, the first ICRC visit materialized with the squadron commander on October 4, to be followed by visits on October 28 and November 27. The other pilot was visited on October 26 and November 27; the TWA hostages were visited by the ICRC representative three times.[30] The ICRC also supported Israel's tough attitude toward Egypt; it felt that Egypt did indeed violate the rights of the captives and planned to publicly reprimand Egypt.[31]

With the visits stumbling block out of the way, Egypt was ready for its next move: suggesting an exchange deal. Through the ICRC it offered to return the Israeli pilots for soldiers and civilians that Israel held. Israel responded positively, offering to return fifty Egyptians, uniformed and not uniformed.[32] The Egyptian counter-proposal included all Israelis, just two, for all Egyptians. Then, within that message to the ICRC in the context of the indirect negotiations, Egypt presented a strict ultimatum: no deal without the two Syrian pilots (captured on Israeli soil in August 1968 and kept for future negotiations). The clear-cut Israeli position requiring all of its POWs for all Egyptian POWs and civilians was complicated by the Red Cross siding with Egypt and suggesting that Syria be involved in a deal as well.[33] This came in response to President Gamal Abd al-Nasser trying to represent the Arab side and acting as the "leader of the Arabs" and possibly prior consultations with the Syrian president.[34] Egypt's public diplomacy during the summer and autumn of 1969 revealed a wide range of considerations. During the War of Attrition, Israel had captured Syrian POWs; in August 1969, the two kidnapped TWA passengers, Israeli citizens, were still in a Syrian prison. Thus Egypt suggested a "package deal" in which all parties would exchange all of their "prisoners." The benefits for Egypt were clear: it would again prove that it spoke for all Arab players and that Nasser was indeed the "leader of the Arab world." Moreover, it would free Syria from any foreign pressure emanating from TWA and the air traffic industry to get the exchanges over with.[35]

For Israel, such a deal posed the negative precedent of blurring the lines between legitimate POWs and hostages taken by subnational actors. The Israeli position, however, was not set in stone. Israel was willing to countenance any Arab move as long as all or even some of the persons in question were returned to Israel.[36] The only exception was that releasing Israeli pilots was made a precondition for any deal. The upshot was that Israel could be satisfied with the return of the military personnel without the TWA hostages or any other unspecified contingent of the claimed Israelis, either from Egypt or from Syria. Israel's weak position was magnified by the ICRC, which was at that time in a rather low diplomatic position stemming from its failure to make a humanitarian effort in the context of Biafra and its humanitarian crisis. These inferior cards in the hands of those two relatively weak players only provoked Egypt to delay any deal, against the interests of all other players, including Syria, while trying to demonstrate its success to the Arab world and the world at large.[37] That meant that Israel accepted de facto the implicit Arab position that any Israeli concession was only a prelude to further concessions. Another concession in the context of the late 1969 deal was Israel's agreement to negotiate with two Arab countries acting as one, concurrent with their representing a terrorist organization. That directly contradicted Israel's paradigm of attempting to separate its enemies and bargaining with each separately on whatever subject.

With the exchange of bodies on November 19 and the main exchange on December 6, it emerged that all of Israel's complaints about the physical treatment of its pilots in Egypt, involving repeated violations of the Geneva Convention, were confirmed.[38] However, for lack of clear evidence and not wanting to cause the POWs further harm, Israel had avoided any countermeasures as long as Egypt held the pilots. This November 19 deal was perhaps the precedent for the aftermath of the 1973 War and, years later, for other deals. All in all, in December 1969 Israel returned seventy-one Egyptian and Syrian military personnel and got back two pilots from Egypt and the two civilian hostages from Syria.[39] Once again, Egypt realized that Israeli society's Achilles' heel, and perhaps the key to overcoming Israel, was through creating internal opposition to the fighting on the grounds of not wanting to lose more POWs or face more casualties.[40] While the Israeli media was still celebrating the return of all involved in the TWA-POW deal, Egypt embarked on a new stage. On December 14, 1969, its commandos raided the Israeli line of fortifications along the Canal, targeting IDF officers to be taken. One was captured, and in Egypt's eyes, he was the one that might have tipped the balance between the two armies. That reserve officer was the son of one of the legendary commanders of the 1948 War on the Egyptian front and was part and parcel of the highest Israeli elite at the time.

The Palestinian organizations contributed their share. With the ongoing War of Attrition on the Egyptian and Syrian fronts and repeated Palestinian terrorist attacks, the POW issue remained very much on the agenda.[41] In January 1970 a night watchman was kidnapped from his post in northern Israel by al-Fatḥ; later that year several pilots had to abandon their planes over hostile territory and were taken prisoner by the Egyptian army, while others continued to be held by Syria.

The kidnapping of an Israeli civilian marked yet another development in the kidnapping policy of the Palestinian organizations: on their way back from placing a mine inside Israel, the organization encountered that civilian and, in spite of any possible planning on the Israeli's part, forced him into Lebanon with them.[42] Post factum that improvised decision contributed to a change in the modus operandi of the organizations that is still valid as these lines are being written. As of that night, the arsenal of Israel's enemies included, on top of air jacking, deliberate attempts to kidnap Israelis from their own territory—inflicting damage to Israeli morale as well as tangible political and diplomatic losses. That was exactly the lesson that Israel did not want its enemies to learn from that civilian kidnapping incident, especially because the War of Attrition involved a deliberate attempt to take POWs, and any surrender to that tactic could have wreaked havoc on the generations-old Israeli approach of all POWs for all POWs. Obviously the main hurdle in the 1970 kidnapped night watchman case was that he was not a POW and Israel definitely did not see the Palestinian terrorists as deserving POW status. Actually, the formal Israeli position claimed that had the Arab side been in adherence to international conventions, it would have had to follow the 1949 Geneva Fourth Convention, since the person in question had nothing to do with military activity of any sort.[43]

Against that background Israel reactivated its policy of gaining "bargaining chips"; about twenty-four hours after the kidnapping Israeli forces crossed the border into Lebanon and captured twenty-two people: eleven Lebanese troops and eleven civilians suspected of collaborating with the Palestinian organizations. Israel assumed that because it had taken Lebanese and non-Lebanese as well, the Beirut government would step in and lead a process of negotiated exchange. The Israeli approach, including insistence on negotiation with the government of Lebanon and no other actor, was publicly announced by the Israeli Minister of Defense and conveyed to the ICRC.[44] The Lebanese reaction was rather confused for a good reason: official Lebanon was at the time torn between the supporters of the Palestinian activities from Lebanon against Israel and those who strongly resisted that on the grounds that it might expose the country to more Israeli attacks. That public debate was very similar in its dividing lines to the traditional division in that country between Muslims and Christians. The former not only supported the Palestinian activities, but also resisted any Lebanese negotiations with Israel, believing that any Israeli-PLO talks, whether direct or indirect, would promote the organization's status and constitute a step ahead in its efforts to be recognized by Israel or at least in getting POW status for its captured people. The matter was further complicated by the fact that the hostage was transferred a short time after his abduction from the border area, perhaps even to somewhere outside of Lebanon, and no Lebanese person as far as Israel was able to substantiate had any knowledge of his whereabouts. Lebanon had no impact on the PLO's diplomatic or military activities at any point since the person was kidnapped. On the other hand, in attempting to gain international recognition, any Palestinian body affiliated with the PLO would contact the ICRC through the Palestinian Red Cross and arrange for a couple of visits by its representatives with the hostage.[45] Apparently the close involvement of the ICRC in this matter did satisfy the immediate PLO interest: a de facto recognition by an international organization. Consequently after exhausting that issue and without any intelligence value being attached to the prisoner, the PLO approached the ICRC through the Beirut government in late January, informing it that "they may be able to hand over Mr. Rosenwasser against one or more Palestinian prisoners."[46] That message conveyed in effect three veiled messages: Israel should once again forfeit its policy of not negotiating with terrorists; the PLO adhered to international covenants; and finally, the PLO was a responsible player in Lebanese politics and was moving Lebanon during its domestic strife away from a confrontation with Israel.

For Israel the POW/hostage issue was much more complex. The Lebanese subject was not the only one of its kind on the diplomatic plate of Israel. The one Israeli POW in Egypt presented an ongoing challenge with no solution in sight. The prisoner, a reserve infantry officer, was a member of the Israeli social and political elite and the Egyptian side made every effort possible to increase his price for an exchange, including the denial of visits by the ICRC. No ICRC intervention influenced the Egyptian authorities to change that position or even to discuss an Israeli proposal for an exchange.[47]

The obstinate Egyptian position along with the continued frustration of the Israeli ambassador to the international organizations in Geneva—combined with the fruitless Israeli policy on POWs—led the ambassador to ask his superiors to consider a change in policy.[48] That policy was identical with regard to Egyptian POWs to the policy followed with any other fighting Arab player, whether recognized as POW (regular armies) or not (members of Palestinian organizations). Moreover, the ICRC pressured Israel to ease the conditions of the irregulars, to grant them detainee cards, and to report to the ICRC on a regular basis the names of the detained and allow regular visits to them. Clearly, these requirements when put together created a de facto status of Protecting Power to the ICRC and consequently meant recognizing the irregulars as de facto POWs.[49] Very much in line with the Israeli tradition of not making decisions according to a well-devised system, no cabinet session was called, and not even the a-formal inner cabinet was convened to discuss the dual dimensions of the issue: the Egyptian and the Palestinian. The document summarizing the Israeli position on the Palestinians in Israeli custody makes the following points[50]:

1. There will be no limit on the number of ICRC visits to the detainees.
2. Once the interrogation is complete any detainee can enjoy an ICRC visit.
3. The ICRC can drop by in order to pay a visit. No more than a thirty-minute notice is necessary.
4. No detainee list will be presented to the ICRC (connects to the protecting power issue discussed above).
5. Israel will not necessarily inform the ICRC of the existence of new detainees upon their capture if operational considerations justify that.
6. No detainee cards will be issued.

It is significant to note that the distinction between regulars and others was accepted by the ICRC and that in addition to its own frustration with Egypt, the ICRC agreed with Israel that its intervention on behalf of the night watchman apprehended by a Palestinian organization should not be interpreted as any degree of recognition of the organization.[51] In spite of the Israeli impression to the contrary, the ICRC did try its best to facilitate humanitarian exchanges of prisoners, whatever their formal status might be. It even went as far as to suggest to the warring armies of Israel and Egypt that they implement Article 109 of the Third Convention dealing with the repatriation of seriously wounded and seriously sick prisoners of war. That was clearly in response to the Israeli interest in getting back the wounded officer whom Egypt tried to keep for future bargaining on the grounds of his poor health. Implementing Article 109 might still save face for Egypt, as it wanted a high price but was probably concerned that the officer might pass away while in their jail system. That ICRC gesture was well intended but did not convince Israel of the organization's fair policy, especially after it was rejected by Egypt.[52]

Worsening security conditions along the Suez Canal coupled with the deterioration in the public morale in Israel led the IDF to launch a major commando raid on an Egyptian fortified outpost at the Shadwan Island, twenty miles southwest of the (then) Israeli held town of Sharm al-Shaykh on the Sinai Peninsula on January 22, 1970. One of the objectives of the operation (codenamed Rhodes) was the capture of Egyptian officers and soldiers who would serve as bargaining chips in the Israeli attempts to advance the cause of prisoners exchange.[53] Indeed, part of the outcome of the event was the capturing of 41 Egyptian military personnel.[54] It took Israel less than forty-eight hours to unofficially convey to Egypt through the ICRC in Geneva a proposal for the exchange of one imprisoned officer for the forty-five POWs in Israeli hands. Previously, with only four Egyptians in Israel, Israel would not even consider an exchange; now it was a totally different issue.[55] Egypt for its part did not rush to respond, yet spread rumors that the release of the Israeli POW in Egyptian hands was nearing.[56] The Egyptian indifference was also manifested by the fact that the one-week Israeli delay in conveying the names of the Egyptian prisoners to the ICRC did not provoke any reaction from the Egyptian side.[57] Egypt responded in kind by delaying by a week the confirmation to Israel through the ICRC of the capture of the pilot on February 2.[58] Was it a general feeling of indifference concerning the Egyptian POWs as opposed to strict adherence to diplomatic protocols as already seen in the past or was it the apparent low intelligence value of the prisoners? Impossible to answer.

Concomitant with the POW issue, the War of Attrition intensified and escalated. In February, Soviet-operated ground-to-air missiles along with Soviet combat and reconnaissance airplanes made their debut along the Israeli-Egyptian confrontation lines. In terms of the narrow POW angle, the intensified Soviet presence meant that any Israeli taken prisoner might have been interrogated directly or indirectly by the Soviets, and Israel might have found itself in the awkward position of taking Soviet POWs with the prospects of a direct confrontation with that superpower. Having said that, it is not at all clear that the Soviets had not been involved previously in such interrogations, albeit in an indirect way. The ICRC shared the Israeli concerns and consequently tried to establish some new ground rules in case more POWs were taken by any of the sides—a rather logical assumption considering the developing circumstances. The Israeli response to the ICRC initiative could be described as "cautiously positive": the Israeli mission to Geneva was all for the initiative while Jerusalem, which obviously shaped the official Israeli position, was much less enthusiastic. The position presented by the Geneva delegation was not different from those previously presented. The only exception was the suggestion to stop using the term *POW exchange* because that term does not exist within the Geneva Convention. Instead Israel spoke in line with Article 139 of repatriation without any reference to terms previously used by Israel: unilateral or unconditional.[59] The Geneva diplomats probably believed that using that language might separate the issue from any diplomatic context and that such usage might be interpreted as not belonging to any diplomatic process or be seen by the Arab players as even a remote recognition of Israel. The Jerusalem position was much more detailed and practical.[60] That position preferred to defer any fundamental issues until the status of the current POWs was cleared up. On the issue of unilateral release Israel was adamant that it could not trust the Arab side; consequently, the initiative was deemed impossible to accept. On the issues closer to Israel it was much stricter: notify immediately of a capture and include the health condition of the captive; first visit and first letter within seven days of capture; and finally simultaneous release. In a system of total mistrust and the use of POWs as bargaining chips, these directives could not work. Indeed, no documents have been found indicating that Egypt even considered that approach. The War of Attrition continued unabated, under growing opposition in the Israeli domestic arena, until a U.S.-brokered ceasefire came into effect. That included, inter alia, Article F: "Both sides will abide by the Geneva Convention of 1949 relative to the treatment of prisoners of war and will accept the assistance of the ICRC (International Committee of the Red Cross) in carrying out their obligations under that convention."[61]

On top of the Israeli casualties it lost between February 9, 1970, and the August ceasefire, there were eight POW pilots, including one murdered while in captivity.[62] Three of the planes were shot down during one week in early July 1970,[63] making a ceasefire more necessary than ever. Israel's position at that point was so desperate that it did not condition its agreement on the release of the POWs in Egyptian hands. It was satisfied with only vague U.S. language in Article F allowing Egypt in effect to disregard its commitment if one existed at all and to continue its denial of visits and certainly refusal to release the prisoners.[64]

With the conclusion of the War of Attrition, Egypt held thirteen Israelis (one badly wounded pilot returned to Israel about a week after cease-fire),[65] including seven pilots, and Syria held three pilots.[66] One Israeli pilot was murdered in jail.[67] Israel held seventy-one Egyptian POWs and forty Syrians POWs. However, all efforts to work out a release of all POWs with no preconditions failed; even the wounded prisoners were not returned in violation of the Geneva Convention, and the Israeli authorities were not informed of their condition by the ICRC. The international organization, trusted by all if only to a certain degree by Israel, could only secure regular visits to the Arab POWs held by Israel with no parallel luck on the Arab side.[68] The already existing seeds of friction between Israel and the organization were nourished by the failure of Israel to put together a unitary POW policy, including the appropriate reaction to the ICRC's partial success and the growing disenchantment with its failures. As already indicated the Israeli MFA and the military were entangled in a confrontation over the issue of responsibilities regarding POWs. Even though the ICRC was an international organization and consequently fell squarely within the MFA jurisdiction, the military tried time and again to maintain its direct channels of communication and to approach the organization on its own. These efforts took place without proper guidance from the MFA and at times without the military being fully aware of diplomatic protocols. This situation led to a vocal confrontation between the IDF commander of the Manpower Directorate and the ICRC's Israel delegate, leading in turn to another explanatory conversation between the ICRC representative and the Israeli diplomat in charge, all of which resulted in a milder Israeli position as reported to Geneva.[69] The main issue between the two Israeli bodies was crystal clear: the military was concerned with its POWs and the strict adherence of Egypt to the Third Geneva Convention. Official Israel as embodied by the MFA considered any friction with the ICRC as negatively impacting the latter's position on the status of the Arab civilians in the territories—namely the Fourth Convention. Similar friction between these two bodies on other occasions led as well to difficulties in putting together a clear and comprehensive POW policy by successive Israeli governments.

The War of Attrition presented Israeli decision makers with a variety of issues to confront. Perhaps the most demanding was the extra-parliamentarian opposition demanding withdrawal from the Sinai Peninsula for the sake of peace. Through their activities members of the opposition, mainly within the ruling party, created the impression that the war was not justified and by association that the POWs were captured fighting an undesirable war. Reacting to that viewpoint, which was not shared by most Israeli citizens (the "Alignment" leading party, a coalition of the ruling party with other social-democrat parties, won 56 out of 120 parliament seats in the 1969 general elections), the leaders felt that they had to adopt a clear policy of doing almost all in its power to release its people at whatever the price. One element, however, was consistent in the Israeli policy: releasing Israeli pilots was made a precondition for any deal. That did not mean in any way giving away the release of all others—uniformed and nonuniformed Israelis, those taken by regular enemy armies and others taken by subnational actors.

Even though the ground rules for dealing with state actors were more or less known, the emergence of the Palestinian organizations heralded a new era that would one day soon lead to a competition over the price extracted from Israel for its people in captivity. In 1967 and during the attrition time it was Egypt that realized that the Achilles' heel of Israel's open and democratic society could lead to successful dealings with Israel by creating domestic opposition within Israel via public opinion.

That lesson was not lost on the Palestinian organizations, which used the natural concern for human lives within Israeli society, while kidnapping Israelis and negotiating with them—all aimed at getting some degree of diplomatic recognition with full recognition of their people as legitimate POWs. One of the results of that period was the blurring of lines between legitimate POWs and hostages taken by subnational actors. Israel dealt with them all as legitimate POWs and paid for them as if the deals with the organizations were just more deals with legitimate state actors. Within that context Israel agreed—and that precedent would be used many times in the future—that a binding Israeli court decision would be overturned in order to secure the release of captured Israelis. By their actions and precedents, the Palestinian organizations, especially in the period under discussion, managed to present themselves as the victors after the 1967 Arab defeat and sparked a competition among themselves for the highest achiever from Israel.

In contrast to that Palestinian policy, official Israel presented a frustrated and confused leadership. There was no comprehensive procedure on how to diplomatically and militarily react to a kidnapping or capturing, and the diplomats and military men continued their traditional wriggling, rendering any policy decision impossible. As bad as it was, the situation did not trigger any cabinet meeting or any prime ministerial instruction indicating the need for one clear POW policy. As usual, the operations people drew their own conclusions and installed a new defensive aviation policy making the Israeli national carrier safer than before.

To turn from the domestic and Palestinian levels, Egypt and Syria continued their policies of delaying exchange negotiations as long as the intelligence was not fully extracted, or so they believed, from the prisoners. On the international level, the linkage between the Third and the Fourth Conventions continued to mar relations between the ICRC and Israel. At the end of the attrition period, the degree of mutual mistrust was such that in spite of the ICRC efforts to mend fences with Israel, it could not serve at that point as an "honest broker." In a word, in August 1970, Israel could not have been very optimistic with regard to getting back its own through a trusted mediator.

NOTES

1. For a thorough analysis of the war, see R. Bolia, "Israel and the War of Attrition," *Military Review* 84, no. 2 (March 2004): 47–51.
2. For further details, see PRO/FCO17/633/ [ET2/8]/March 24, 1968, "Report on Operations in Karama"; PRO/FCO17/633/ET2/8/April 1, 1968, "The Karama Raid"; Abu Iyyad, *Lelo Moledet* [Hebrew: Without a Homeland] (Tel Aviv: Mifras, 1979), 89; PRO/FCO17/222/EJ1/21/March 25, from Amman, April 2, 1968.
3. ISA/FM/30/3/11, from Jerusalem, to Washington, April 2, 1968.
4. *al-Milaff al-Watha'iqi l-Ma'arakat Karameh, al-Khamis, 21 Adhar 1968* [Arabic: The Documented File of the Karameh Battle] (Amman, 1998), 59; ISA/FM/30/3, from Jerusalem, to Geneva, April 18, 1968.
5. ISA/FM/30/3/11, from Jerusalem, to Washington, April 2, 1968.
6. ISA/FM/2717/26/68–69, ICRC information notes 106, May 2, 1968; ISA/FM/30/3/41, from New York, to Jerusalem, May 2, 1968.
7. ISA/FM/30/3/9975–747/68–14, from Israeli Police HQ/Investigations, to Military Rabbinate, April 4, 1968; ISA/FM/30/3/159–9, from Judea and Samaria regional HQ, to IDF manpower directorate, April 15, 1968; ISA/FM/30/3, from Jerusalem, to Geneva, April 18, 1968; ISA/FM/30/3/344, from Jerusalem, to Geneva and New York, April 24, 1968.
8. ISA/FM/30/3/23, May 9, 1968, internal memo; ISA/FM/30/3/334, from MFA, to IDF/Manpower Directorate, July 3, 1968; IDF response: ISA/FM/30/3/3405/ (3101)/512, July 16, 1968.
9. Shmuel Tamir, *Ben ha Aretz ha Zot* [Hebrew: The Son of this Country, Autobiography] (Lod: Zmora-Bitan, 2002).
10. Cf. ISA/FM/30/4, "secret," from Geneva, to Jerusalem, June 19, 1969; ISA/FM/2717/26/68–69/504, from Jerusalem, to all representations.
11. *Davar*, July 28, 1968, 1–2.
12. *Davar*, July 25, 1968, 1.
13. ISA/FM/6455/1–4/85, from Geneva, to Jerusalem, July 1968.
14. https://www.icrc.org/applic/ihl/ihl.nsf/vwTreatiesByCountrySelected.xsp?xp_countrySelected=DZ.
15. https://www.icrc.org/ihl/WebART/375–590007?OpenDocument.
16. *Ma'ariv*, October 22, 1968.
17. ISA/FM/2717/26/68–69, from Geneva, to Jerusalem, February 18, 1969.
18. ISA/FM/2717/26/68–69, ICRC notes, October 28, 1968; cf. ISA/FM/27/10/1966, from Geneva, to Jerusalem, February 1, 1966.
19. ISA/FM/4300/5–11/1, Cabinet minutes, August 1968.
20. *Ma'ariv*, editorial, August 13, 1968.
21. *Ma'ariv*, editorial, August 15, 1968.
22. ISA/FM/2717/26/68–69, ICRC notes, October 28, 1968.
23. Dima Adamsky, "Zero-Hour for the Bears: Inquiry into the Soviet Decision to Intervene in the Egyptian-Israeli War of Attrition, 1969–70," *Cold War History* 6, no. 1 (2006): 119.
24. This incident is reconstructed here based on ISA/FM/30/4/576, "top secret," from Jerusalem, to Geneva; IDF soldier testimony, http://www.fresh.co.il/vBulletin/showthread.php?t=27963#post159848; http://www.izkor.gov.il/HalalView.aspx?id=46990; ISA/FM/30/4/572, "secret-urgent," from Jerusalem, to Geneva, August 6, 1969.
25. ISA/FM/30/4/604, from Jerusalem, to Geneva, August 15, 1969; ISA/FM/30/4/137, from Jerusalem, to Geneva, August 18, 1969; *Ma'ariv*, August 29, 1969.

26. ISA/FM/2717/26/68–69, from Jerusalem, to Bern, September 12, 1969; ISA/FM/2717/26/68–69/42, from Jerusalem, to Bern, September 12, 1969.
27. Cf. ISA/FM/2717/26/68–69/42, from Jerusalem, to Bern, September 12, 1969.
28. ISA/FM/3216/10/246, from Washington, to Jerusalem, August 30, 1969; ISA/FM/3216/10/677, from Jerusalem, to Israeli representations, August 31, 1969; ISA/FM/3216/10, MFA "secret" memo, August 31, 1969.
29. *Ma'ariv*, September 23, 1969; *Neue Zürcher Zeitung*, September 29, 1969; *Davar*, October 3, 1969.
30. ISA/FM/3902/4, several ICRC visit reports; ISA/FM/3902/4/121, from Geneva, to Jerusalem, October 27, 1969; ISA/FM/3902/4/226.70, from Geneva, to Jerusalem, October 28, 1969; *al-Ahram*, Egypt, daily, October 27, 1969; ISA/FM/3902/4/226, from Washington, to Jerusalem, October 28, 1969; ISA/FM/3902/4/214.12.3(3), from Geneva, to Jerusalem, November 19, 1969; cf. "241. Paper Prepared by the NEA Working Group in the Department of State Operations Center, Washington, September 15, 1970", in *FRUS*, 1969–1976, Volume XXIV, 678, Original: National Archives, Nixon Presidential Materials, NSC Files, Box 330, Subject Files, Hijackings. Secret. Received in the White House Situation Room at 8:45 a.m.
31. *Ma'ariv*, October 19, 1969; ISA/FM/3902/4/107, from Geneva, to Jerusalem, October 23, 1969.
32. ISA/FM/3902/4/175, from Jerusalem, to Geneva, October 31, 1969; *Davar*, November 3, 1969.
33. ISA/FM/3902/4, from Geneva, to Jerusalem, November 3, 5, 1969.
34. Cf. the language in U.S. ambassador telegram 4196 to State on November 6, 1969: "new Egyptian proposal approved at quote highest level." USNA/YR POL27–7 ARAB-ISR.
35. ISA/FM/3902/4/241, from Jerusalem, to Washington, November 28, 1969.
36. ISA/FM/3902/4/214.12.3/ (3), Internal MFA correspondence, November 24, 1969; director-general's recommendations to the Minister [November 25, 1969], from Jerusalem, to Geneva, November 28, 1969.
37. ISA/FM/4299/4/141, from Jerusalem, to Geneva, November 30, 1969; ISA/FM/4299/4/497, from Jerusalem, MFA, to Geneva, November 30, 1969; ISA/FM/2717/26/68–69/1, from Jerusalem, to Geneva, November 30, 1969.
38. ISA/FM/3902/4/214.12.3/ (3), from General Eyyal, chief manpower officer, IDF, to the director-general of the Foreign Ministry, December 14, 1969.
39. ISA/FM/4299/4/21, from Tel Aviv [IDF HQ], to Jerusalem [MFA], December 6, 1969.
40. W. S. Lind, K. Nightengale, J. F. Schmitt, J. W. Sutton, and G. I. Wilson, "The Changing Face of War: Into the Fourth Generation," *Marine Corps Gazette* 85, no. 11 (2001): 24.
41. ISA/FM/33/7.
42. *Ma'ariv*, January 1, 1970.
43. ISA/FM/33/7/8, from Geneva, to Jerusalem, January 16, 1970.
44. ISA/FM/33/7/8, from Jerusalem, to Geneva, January 3, 1970; *Ma'ariv, Davar*, January 4, 1970; *Davar*, January 12, 1970.
45. ISA/FM/33/7/439, from Jerusalem, to Geneva, January 20, 1970; ISA/FM/33/7/66, 70, 111, from Geneva, to Jerusalem, January 21, 22, 1970.
46. ISA/FM/33/7/125, from Geneva, to Jerusalem, January 25, 1970.
47. ISA/FM/33/7/5, 14, 16, from Geneva, to Jerusalem, January 5, 7, 16, 1970.
48. ISA/FM/33/7/14, from Geneva, to Jerusalem, January 7, 1970.
49. Cf. Articles 8 and 10 of the third Convention, https://www.icrc.org/applic/ihl/ihl.nsf/INTRO/375?OpenDocument; FM3–218—Chapter 6-Section V- Enemy Prisoners of War and Detained Persons, in *U.S. Army Field Manual 3–21.8*, http://www.infantrydrills.com/fm-3–21–8-chapter-6-section-v-enemy-prisoners-of-wars-and-detained-persons/.

50. ISA/FM/33/7/ [GM-42], from Brig. Gen. Gazit, in charge of the committee running the political, security, and economic affairs in the territories, to The Minister of Foreign Affairs via the Minister's policy advisor, January 8, 1970.

51. ISA/FM/33/7/28, from Jerusalem, to Geneva, January 7, 1970.

52. ISA/FM/33/7/59, from Geneva, to Jerusalem, January 19, 1970.

53. IDFA/1726/192/1974, *Rhodes Operation [Complete] De-Briefing;* IDFA/1723/192/1974, *Rhodes Operation [Tactical] De-Briefing*, 3.

54. *Ma'ariv*, *Davar*, January 23, 1970; strangely enough all secret correspondence of the Israeli ministry of foreign affairs spoke of sixty-two captured. Nowhere is there an explanation for that discrepancy.

55. ISA/FM/33/7, from Geneva, to Jerusalem, January 23, 1970.

56. ISA/FM/33/7/87/132, from Jerusalem, to Geneva, January 27, 1970.

57. ISA/FM/33/7/159, from Jerusalem, to Geneva, January 29, 1970.

58. ISA/FM/33/7/39, from Geneva, to Jerusalem, February 10, 1970; ISA/FM/33/7/62, from Jerusalem, to Geneva, February 10, 1970.

59. ISA/FM/33/7/6, from Geneva, to Jerusalem, February 6, 1970.

60. ISA/FM/33/7/61, from Jerusalem, to Geneva, February 10, 1970.

61. Robert H. Baraz [Bureau of Intelligence and Research, Office of Research and Analysis for USSR and Eastern Europe, Defense Department], "The Arab-Israeli Ceasefire of 1970," CIA-RDP76B00734R00020005000–6, CIA records search tool (CREST), National Archives and Records Administration, College Park, MD.

62. His picture upon being captured alive: *al-Ahram*, daily, Egypt, August 4, 1970; ISA/FM/33/12, from Geneva, to Jerusalem, September 21, 1970.

63. *Ma'ariv*, July 6, 1970.

64. ISA/FM/33/11/100, from Jerusalem, to Geneva, August 21, 1970; ISA/FM/33/11/194/214, from The IDF UN Liaison Officer, to several addresses, August 25, 1970.

65. *Ma'ariv*, August 16, 1970.

66. ISA/FM/33/11/Formal Israeli protests to the ICRC, August 4, 12, 1970.

67. *Ma'ariv*, August 4, 9, 1970; *Davar*, 4, 16, 17, 1970.

68. ISA/FM/33/12/118, from Geneva, to Jerusalem, August 30, 1970; ISA/FM/33/12/143, from Jerusalem, to Geneva, August 30, 1970; ISA/FM/33/12/6, from Jerusalem, to Geneva, September 1, 1970; ISA/FM/33/12/193, from Jerusalem, to Geneva, September 17, 1970.

69. ISA/FM/33/12/535, Internal MFA correspondence, September 7, 1970.

NINE

Black September, Subnational Actors, and the Early Internationalization of the Hostage/POW Issue, 1970–1973

The events of September 1970 ("Black September") about a month after the War of Attrition ended turned out to be the materialization of one of the worst scenarios possible in the context of exchanging Israelis, under whatever definition: POWs, hostages, etc. All throughout the years since 1949 Israel tried to limit the scope of negotiations so that any contacts regarding Israelis in hostile prisons would be with the capturing players and would lead to a "prisoners for prisoners" deal. Any third-party intervention, so that logic goes, might lead to a confrontation with a major power or, even worse, press Israel for unwanted concessions that might lead to deals requiring Israel to change paradigms on a wide range of issues. Thus it stands to reason that Israel captured Soviet bloc experts who were in the service of Egypt and Syria, but Israel never admitted that. Rumors regarding Israelis in Soviet prisons swept the country at times, and yet Israel consistently removed that international dimension from any discussion—public or secret. However, "Black September" created a precedent that would wreak havoc on the traditional Israeli POW policy during the 1973 October War. During those days the POW issue was on the agendas of the superpowers that, moreover, accepted the principle of "other than POWs (or territory) for POWs." The early seeds of those policies were present in the "Black September" hostages crisis.

In February 1970, while Israel was still engaged in a brutal standing war with its state neighbors, Jordan entered the early stages of the civil war that reached its peak in September 1970 (and finally ended in July 1971). On September 6 and 9, four civilian planes carrying scores of European and American passengers were hijacked by the Popular Front for the Liberation of Palestine in the context of the Jordanian civil war. One of the planes was flown to Cairo where it was blown up by the PFLP. A short while after the hijacking, the exact number and identity of the travelers involved were established: U.S. citizens and Europeans from Germany, Switzerland, and the United Kingdom. Of these people about thirty to fifty were either Israelis or held dual citizenship.[1] The hijacking plunged the area, including Israel, into an international crisis. The first contact by the PFLP command was made on the day of the initial hijacking. It conditioned the release of the aircrafts and the passengers in Jordan on four demands: 1) the release and return to Amman of three PFLP commandos imprisoned in Switzerland; 2) the return to Amman of the commando killed in the abortive El Al hijacking and the release of his female accomplice; and 3) release of three *fedayeen* being held in West Germany. A fourth demand, relayed by the PFLP office in Beirut, called for the release of all *fedayeen* held in Israel.[2]

On the diplomatic level the countries involved created an informal group of four, also known as the Bern Group for their usual meeting venue. They were the United States, Great Britain, the Federal Republic of Germany, and Switzerland. Israel was not included because it had no formal exclusive representation among the hostages. Moreover, the Israeli position, based on lengthy experience and the lack of Israelis among the kidnapped (as Israel initially believed), led Israel to the most clear-cut position among the five nations: no negotiations and no deal. Israel did not become aware of the Israeli dimension of the demands until September 10, from a wire report—or at least that was the public impression that Israel wanted to create.[3] Documents available to this author gave no indication of any other direct communication with Israel on the subject. In any case, it is unclear whether Israel was kept in the dark by supposedly friendly countries so that it would not intervene in the process? Or was it an indication of an Israeli policy trying to get away from active involvement it?

Soon enough the hijacked passengers took up all main headlines all over the world because that was a major news story—unlike the lingering bilateral POW issue between Israel and its neighbors. The national affiliations of the kidnapped compelled their respective governments to intervene. With these governments' interest in not involving themselves in the Jordanian civil war, they picked the neutral ICRC to negotiate on their behalf with the PFLP and "in effect [were] buying time and providing a vehicle for the Red Cross to begin negotiating."[4] Strictly speaking, the ICRC was not legally supposed to play a major mediating role because the people in question were not POWs by any definition. It is even doubtful whether the ICRC role fell under the Fourth Convention. The victims were innocent passengers kidnapped along a civilian route on personal business. However, the organization's two main undertakings in the crisis were the representation of the U.S.-European front in its negotiations with the PFLP and the humanitarian dimension of the kidnapping. The latter duty was probably accomplished one way or another, although as seen through the Jewish and Israeli prism the ICRC was at least tasked with interviewing the passengers and providing them with basic necessities—such as food that would meet the requirements of the kosher Jewish dietary laws, at which the international organization failed.[5]

The former issue of representation was no less complex. Four conflicting groups of players were involved in the attempt to resolve the situation:

1. An ad hoc multinational coalition of the United Kingdom and the Federal Republic of Germany, under the leadership of the United States.
2. Israel, while kept in the dark and not invited to join the coalition, along with the Hashemite Kingdom of Jordan—the two most obvious partners that unknown to all other players at the time kept an open channel of communications throughout the crisis.
3. Each and every European player that tried to promote the release of its own through back channels to the PFLP.
4. The ICRC in its attempt to preserve its status in a turbulent region in which at least one player, Israel, was losing patience with its approach relative to the Fourth Convention and to the people living in the areas captured in 1967.

This picture of overlapping and conflicting interests presented itself from day one of the crisis. Each government was concerned first with its own, whereas the ICRC believed, based on its vast experience in humanitarian cases, that it was the right body for the tasks ahead: not only humanitarian aid but negotiations as well. However, its activity depended on the full support of the coalition. Had they decided to go their separate ways, the ICRC would have once again been downgraded to a messenger capacity rather than the chief negotiator. In this case the Red Cross representatives "will withdraw completely and leave the place."[6]

In the early stages of the crisis Israel adopted a cautious wait-and-see position. After all, the only foiled attempt at hijacking a plane was that of the Israeli national air carrier. Moreover, it was not evident right after the forced landing of the planes that Israelis were involved at all. From that position Israel could insist in spite of the PFLP demands that no terrorists be released from Israeli jails, considering that they would definitely go back to attacking Israeli and Jewish targets.[7] Israel actually ignored, while voicing that position, the fact that at that time it had one hostage in the hands of another Palestinian subnational actor—the night watchman. At that same time Israel also held two Algerian citizens who had been apprehended on August 14, 1970, while on a layover on board a BOAC plane flying from Tehran to London.[8] The reason Israel gave for their detention was that Algeria was an enemy country, had participated in the 1967 War, and at the time of the arrest was supporting the Palestinian organizations. Official explanations notwithstanding, it was a clear case of capturing potential bargaining chips in case the Palestinian organizations, well supplied and financed by Algiers at the time, held onto the night watchman kidnapped in early 1970.

In its first assessment of the crisis the Israeli government realized its lack of policy intelligence and misreading of the overall picture. The ministers believed that they saw the emergence of two distinct coalitions: the governments of Switzerland, the Federal Republic of Germany, and the United Kingdom, which agreed to release all terrorists requested by the PFLP,[9] on one side, and on the other, a looser coalition of the United States and Israel.[10] While keeping lines of communication with Israel open, the United States continued its dialogue with its European allies. A short while after the numbers and identities of the hostages became known to the allies, they made an initial proposal to the PFLP through the ICRC. Its basis was the demarcation of what was possible (a "package deal" including all passengers, no less, for the seven hijackers and a small number of people in Israeli hands) and what was not (a total release of terrorists by Israel, without its being notified in advance of their identities). On September 10 the PFLP responded. It proposed permitting the immediate evacuation of all women, children, and the sick from their holding place in return for the release of the *fedayeen* held by the British, Germans, and Swiss (seven persons plus one corpse). The remaining male hostages would be released only in exchange for a yet unspecified number, believed to be around six hundred, of *fedayeen* held by the Israelis.[11] On the face of it, it looked like a positive move expediting the full release of all captives. However, a closer look would reveal that if such a deal were enacted, Israel would be directly responsible for the next stage and any failure would be its own fault.

Compared with the initial PFLP initial demands calling for the release of all *fedayeen* in Western hands, the new position did mark a positive change and was one the United States could relate to. Originally, the Unite States had several reasons for its position unequivocally rejecting the Palestinian demands. First, it had been the traditional U.S. policy for years not to negotiate with terrorists. This policy is still in effect as this book is being written. Secondly, the United States had an obvious symbolic reason for refusing to release the person demanded by the PFLP: he was the assassin of Senator Robert F. ("Bobby") Kennedy, an American icon of freedom and liberalism. Israel resisted the release of any terrorists for three reasons: it was the traditional Israeli position; no Israeli plane had been hijacked; and any release would endanger "Jews"[12] in the future.

From Israel's point of view, it preferred against the background of a divided front without any significant ICRC involvement that all relevant parties would agree to insist on the release of all hostages without exception. Israel for its part contributed the two Algerians, only on condition that delaying the release of the night watchman would be a sacrifice for the larger good.[13] Obviously Israel was not aware of the intense deliberations taking place in Washington; had it known, Israel's policy decisions might have been different. However, the Combined Washington Special Actions Group and Review Group met in Washington on September 9 and 10th and one of their suppositions was that it was quite possible that Israel would not give up and would not surrender the requested guerrillas/terrorists in exchange for the hostages.[14] The team also considered the possibility of Israeli intervention in Jordan for a "surgical operation" intended to rescue the hostages, but eventually decided that such action would come only third, after a Jordanian and American operation. If Israel did intervene, the United States would support it in order to help what looked at the moment like the possible crumbling of the Hashemite regime. Indeed, the discussion on September 10 just underlined the fact that the hostages' crisis was only one segment of a much larger showdown between the Hashemite Jordanian regime and the Palestinian organizations. All five Western players had a common interest in resolving the crisis at the earliest possible time and removing the people in question from the battle zones. The PFLP, at loggerheads with other Palestinian organizations over the leadership of the Palestinian movement, had a clear interest in keeping the hostages in their hands for as long as possible and if necessary using them as human shields against the Jordanian military.

The united front was clearly not to the liking of the PFLP. They insisted on releasing all except for the Israelis. Apparently, after their interrogation of the passengers and in spite of repeated Israeli denials, the PFLP determined that they had what they labeled forty "prisoners of war" (twenty-three with dual citizenship, six Swiss, six Germans, and five British).[15] Consequently, on September 12, 350 passengers were released—not including, however, those labeled "Israelis" by the PFLP. They numbered fifty-four or less according to U.S. and Israeli assessments: twelve dual nationals (Israel believed that only two were Israelis), sixteen to eighteen Jewish, and four U.S. government employees.[16] Apparently, the PFLP interpretation of the term *POW* was broad and did not correspond with the accepted definition of that term—any Israeli citizen, whether that was his or her only citizenship or one of two, was considered POW by the PFLP. They included within that definition a seventy-five-year-old woman and two breastfeeding mothers of three- and four-month-old babies, all holding Israeli citizenship.[17] Once again, the Palestinian side, the PFLP in this case, used a wide definition of POW, attempting to broaden it as far as to finally get international recognition of the POW status of its captured people and simultaneously be considered a legitimate participant in the international arena.

With the release of a large number of hostages, the Palestinian organization scored a diplomatic success: it presented itself as humanitarian and ready in the second phase of the crisis to negotiate with one or all of the hostages' countries of origin, while keeping an ample number to allow further pressure on Israel. Now with fewer hostages, it changed its definition and labeled only five Israelis as POWs, whereas all other nationals were just bargaining assets with the United States and the European players.[18] Clearly, the idea of "divide et impera" returned to center stage with a twist: because all countries except Israel and the United States agreed to separate deals the outcome could only benefit the PFLP. Any U.S. involvement in Jordan would lead to the execution of the U.S. hostages[19] and consequently the United States, so this logic goes, would refrain from intervening, and the PFLP triumph would still be great because it deterred a superpower from military action. That leaves Israel as the only country breaking ranks with the rest, and it would find itself isolated from the rest of the world. The new revised PFLP position did indeed put Israel in a rather uneasy position. The other players pressed Israel for concessions, believing that Israeli submissiveness would almost instantly affect the U.S. position. That clearly contradicted the Israeli position as voiced from day one of the crisis: "[Israel] would refuse to acquiesce in any blackmail." [20]

Considering the Palestinian moves and the Europeans' positions, the U.S. State Department indirectly indicated that the preferred and revised U.S. position at that point was to keep the Bern Group as one diplomatic actor through movement toward the European positions. That included three main elements:

1. Bringing back the ICRC to play a mediating role between the group and the PFLP. The organization refrained at that time from playing its traditional part because the British and the Germans went, or at least tried to go, their separate ways, leaving very narrow leeway for the organization. Swiss sources suggest that Switzerland was perhaps the most advanced, reaching a resemblance of a diplomatic cooperation agreement with the Palestinian organizations in exchange for the release of its own hostages in Jordan.[21] The British insisted on a certain ICRC figure, the Swiss diplomat Marcel Andre Boisard, whom they believed would be the best figure to negotiate with the PFLP considering his long field experience. The United States adopted Britain's position, indicating that the ICRC was the only international player to gain credence by all pertinent parties.
2. A reinforced role for King Hussein, whose army was engaged anyway in fighting the organizations and already on the verge of being assisted by Israel.[22] This meant that the outcome would either reflect the allies' success in giving the local players the necessary

diplomatic backing or demonstrate that blame, in case of a catastrophe, belonged squarely on the shoulders of Israel and Jordan.

3. Finally, pressing Israel—although not a party to its development—to accept any agreed upon solution. However, the longstanding Israeli policy of not giving in to terrorists was taken into consideration—the Americans cited two prerequisites that would let Israel act: "(a) the Palestinians make precise demands, and in particular submit a specific list of *Fedayeen* prisoners, and (b) they can cite overwhelming pressure (especially from U.S.) forcing them to take part in the exchange."[23]

That American position did indeed lead to securing ICRC agreement to dispatch their figure to Amman; however, that organization tried as much as possible to slow down its being dragged back into the process, probably for fear of failure. The PFLP already criticized the "biased role"[24] of the ICRC, which obviously did not contribute much to its chances of getting an acceptable agreement. Besides, in spite of their agreement to the dispatch of the ICRC official to the region, the British did not put an end to their independent effort.[25] That in turn only spurred the PFLP to toughen its position. In two September 15 statements the organization said that " the [Western] front has closed the door to all mediation; their stand is simply the release of *fedayeen* detained by the states concerned and that any attempt to free hostages by force would endanger their lives." The PFLP demanded a prompt exchange: "we will not wait forever." Their position at that point was crystal clear: separate agreements, full surrender by Israel, no ICRC mediation.[26]

As mentioned, concurrent with the Bern Group deliberations, the European actors were negotiating with the hijackers in efforts to reach separate solutions. The only obstacle they could see was the inflexible Israeli position, insisting on getting a list of Palestinian individuals to be released, as opposed to a general agreement to the principle of an exchange. In the Israeli mind that would be tantamount to accepting the Palestinian members of a subnational guerrilla group as equal to the Israeli POWs and kidnapped civilians and being forced to release about six hundred Palestinians as the PFLP demanded.[27]

Israeli internal correspondence reveals the Israeli predicament at that juncture.[28] In a nutshell, Israel found itself fully justified in its position of not releasing convicted terrorists responsible for scores of civilian casualties. At the same time, Israel was being almost brutally forced to accept a general exchange agreement through pressure by friendly countries led by the United States and indirectly joined by the ICRC, which had suspended its mission.[29] Yet, predicting that kind of pressure and realizing that the loss of currency that would result from giving in to the PFLP demands would be too much for Israel to bear, Israel arrested about 450 family members (about 125 were released shortly after their detention) of leading PFLP members on September 11 through 14, described by several Arab media outlets as hostages and possible bargaining chips.[30] To parts of the U.S. intelligence community, the rather radical Israeli move looked harsh but necessary:

> The remaining forty passengers became a source of great contention. Moshe Dayyan ordered the Shin Bet to round up all known relatives of the senior PFLP leadership who lived on the West Bank. Essentially, the Shin Bet took them as counter-hostages. All told, several hundred Palestinians were taken into custody and held during the crisis. To alert the PFLP's leadership that their families were now at Israel's mercy, the Shin Bet allowed a small group of them to cross the border into Jordan to carry the news directly to their relatives. As brutal as Dayyan's response was, it proved extremely effective.[31]

Toward the end of the first week of the crisis Israel did indeed start to manifest signs of flexibility under friendly pressure: the new not yet publicly declared position was that Israel was willing to release detainees before trial; the language was ambiguous enough to be interpreted as indicating that recent detainees would be freed, not necessarily those who already had been in Israeli prisons for a while. For the receiving side, Israel added to the deal the night watchman and the return to Lebanon of the Lebanese soldiers captured in the same context.[32] That indicated Israeli willingness not only to fully involve itself in the negotiations and to release a significant number of detainees, but also to broaden the scope of the deal to include the Palestinian organizations as indirectly representing the Beirut government. That meant a de facto recognition of the Palestinian organizations as part and parcel of the Lebanese political system, very much to the chagrin of Lebanon's Christian-led government. Amazingly, while voicing concern over the European efforts at establishing independent and separate paths to the PFLP, Israel followed suit and dispatched its own emissaries to Jordan in order to discuss a deal.[33] Another development, rather disturbing for Israel at that point, was the emergence of new terminology used by the other non-Arab players: "hostages" was replaced by "prisoners of war."[34] Thus the separation and the gradual release did contradict the narrow Israeli definition of POWs, strictly in line with the Geneva Convention. Considering that some of the pertinent correspondence did not reach this author, it is possible to speculate based on the available material that the Israeli approach to the PFLP was kept a secret from the other allies, including King Hussein, but had the blessing of the United States, as the latter wanted Israel to agree to any separate settlement by the Europeans. Yet simultaneous with that path, the British pressed the United States very hard to conclude a deal in which all hostages except the Israelis would be freed.[35] Considering the range of common interests between Israel and the United States, the United States needed a solution that would not place it in opposition to any of its allies or, even worse, lead to a confrontation between two allies at the time the Cold War was still raging on.

Meanwhile, the escalating domestic circumstances in Jordan, coupled with the failure of all international attempts to secure the release of the endangered remaining fifty-four passengers, led the United States to ask for Hussein's intervention in the crisis.[36] It was a timely appeal because on September 16 the king appointed a military cabinet; the next day that new administration launched a new offensive against the Palestinian organizations. At that moment the foreign powers' appeal to Hussein probably reflected their hope that the Jordanian offensive might yield some positive movement. For the first time since the hijacking, Hussein became a legitimate player in the context of the events taking place on his sovereign territory. With the exception of the plea to the Jordanian monarch and considering his faltering attack on the Palestinian organizations, the main players were at a loss. The PFLP insisted on a "package deal" and maintained their demands from Israel.[37] Israel for its part did indeed start a process of retreating from its original position, giving more impetus to the Palestinian organization that was less yielding than before in its demands. Within that deadlocked picture a new—yet old—player represented itself as a possible go between: the ICRC. The main motivation of the organization was not to be seen as indirectly standing aloof while all other players were giving in to the PFLP demands. That might have created a precedent to be followed later, although the ICRC would not be a party to any future exchange deal. The ICRC position became even more precarious in the international arena because Switzerland, the home of the ICRC, not having hostages of its own on Jordanian territory, took it upon itself to steer an international committee that would find a solution.[38]

The variety of channels used by all five nations involved in the crisis ignored to some extent the missing player: King Hussein of Jordan. Even though he was entangled in a bitter civil war with the Palestinian organizations, some of which were responsible for the hijacking, his very well-trained ground and intelligence forces could have been asked by the five nations to be more involved in the process. Similarly, in spite of a generation-long Western guarantee of the continued existence of his regime, the European players negotiated with Hussein's archenemies as equals and also pressed Israel for moves that would eventually bolster the organizations' international recognition. Only Israel, an ally of Jordan since the early 1960s, used the good services of Jordan and dispatched members of the 325 "counter-hostages" to meet with PFLP leaders on Jordanian soil and sent humanitarian convoys to the Palestinians in Jordan with units of the Jordanian army accompanying them. These two allies, Israel and Jordan, coordinated their moves on the eve of the Syrian invasion of Jordan and finally semi-publicly closed ranks with the blessing of the United States in stopping the invasion that started September 18, 1970.[39] There is no evidence to suggest that the Israeli assistance was connected in any way to a demand from Hussein to militarily intervene in order to enable the release of the hostages. The main attention of all players shifted between September 17 and 23 from the stalled release dialogue to two interconnected main theaters of activity: the failing counterattack by the Jordanian army on the Palestinian forces that was launched on the 17th and the Syrian invasion that started on the 18th and ended with the Syrian retreat into their homeland on the 23rd. The Syrian withdrawal damaged the Palestinians organization's military and morale, which led them to a temporary ceasefire on the 24th.[40]

The military decline of the Palestinian organizations was a diplomatic success for the Hashemite regime. However, the chaotic mood in the streets of Amman and the refugee camps around it, along with the lack of information regarding their locations, raised genuine concern for the lives of the remaining hostages.[41] The already released passengers, especially air crews, moved from one European capital to another begging for any unilateral action to free the endangered remaining passengers. Consequently, the governments of Switzerland, Britain, and Germany that had insisted all along on acting separately and been rebuffed by the United States applied harsh pressure on the United States in hopes of it pressing for a change in Israel's unyielding position and providing a last chance for a united deal. Meanwhile, the Jordanian forces cut off of lines of communication, raising doubts as to whether the PFLP would deliver, if and when a deal was struck with them at the venue of the PFLP headquarters.[42] Israel and Jordan clearly standing side by side and the fact that these two countries bore the burden, the larger part on Jordan, of confronting Syria and the Palestinians not only strengthened their bilateral relations. It also allowed Israel to appeal to the United States, and probably to Jordan through a secret channel, to include in any exchange the Palestinian leaders imprisoned in Jordan. Hence extending the scope of the quid pro quo would induce the PFLP to bring down the price for each country involved.[43] However, the outcome of the civil war was far from being decided at that time. Pressure continued to build on Israel to accept the PFLP's conditions—that is, for Israel to publicly announce its acceptance of the principle of an exchange without verifying the identities of the Palestinians to be released. This time the advocates of this line of action were the family members of the hostages, probably encouraged by the U.S. State Department.[44] The U.S. motivation was obvious: their main concern was the humanitarian aspect, whereas Israel was concerned with the possibility of creating a precedent that would have created a snowball effect.

On the 25th the Jordanian army in the course of recapturing one of the refugee camps around Amman freed fifteen hostages, and one more emerged after the battle. At that point, the number of hostages was down to thirty-eight.[45] The deteriorating military position of the Palestinian organizations, the blow to their morale from Jordan's occupation of the Amman refugee camps, along with the military release of several hostages, led the PFLP to hastily sign an agreement with the ICRC. On September 26, thirty-two hostages were released and later flown out of Jordan, and six more were moved to the Egyptian (at that time United Arab Republic [UAR]) embassy in Amman. Britain in return released the plane hijacker who was detained in London.[46]

With the conclusion of the crisis several changes in Israel's viewpoint regarding hostages emerged:

1. The working definition of people within the Israeli cabinet's scope of decision making is up to the detaining player: in this case decisions regarding Jews of whatever nationality and dual nationals were to be made by the Israeli government. The PFLP did not care at all about the fact that no passenger whatsoever carried an exclusive Israeli citizenship.
2. Israel did change its traditional policy of not negotiating with terrorists. However, it did it with a twist: the principle is acceptable as long as Israel determines its quid pro quo. Blackmailing the PFLP by detaining hundreds of Palestinians was indeed compatible with the rules of the PFLP (civilians for civilians; women for women; etc.) and therefore put extra pressure on the organization.
3. The five nations united front, at times maintained only thanks to the United States, prevented separate deals through which some of the hostages would have stayed behind. However, every member of the coalition would have been ready to leave this ad hoc coalition had the PFLP offered it an exceptional deal. Differently put, each player of the five obviously preferred its own interests to those of other players. Yet they all shared the belief that Israel was the weakest link; it was not invited to all consultations and was asked time and again for a "contribution."
4. Finally, the Jordanian military effort, and the Israeli support for that, proved once again that regional alliances tend to jealously maintain their sovereignty and shy away from any foreign intervention, be it by a friend or a foe.

Jordan's crushing of the Palestinian organizations gave Israel only a short break from its two-front struggle—that is, with the national and subnational players. The former continued to challenge Israel on the POW issue. Egypt held twelve of them and Syria three. The Israeli diplomatic correspondence is replete with messages among many Israeli representations all looking for a magic formula to bring the prisoners home.[47] Two breaks changed that gloomy picture: one tactical and one that perhaps marked one of the turning points in the Israeli approach to its own POWs.

The tactical development occurred with the 1972 Israeli kidnapping of five senior Syrian officers aimed at exchanging them for the Israelis held in Syria. That episode, to be analyzed later in this chapter, was in line with standing Israeli policies adopted in the 1950s. In a nutshell, the Israeli policies as projected to its allies and foes alike included a persistent effort to make sure that badly wounded prisoners be medically treated and that they, along with all other POWs, be allowed to see ICRC representatives on a regular basis and to receive letters and packages from Israel. Israel also complained to the ICRC about the killing in jail of some of its POWs. Nevertheless, with the exception of these moves, passive in nature, there is no indication of any exchange negotiations taking place between Israel and Egypt or Syria, at least until May 1972 when communication with the Syrians entered another phase due to the kidnapping of its officers. This picture of inactivity on the part of Israel was not the result of its abandoning its own. It was the overall feeling of the military and policy makers that all avenues had been exhausted and that a new approach was necessary. That atmosphere, along with undiminished interest in getting the boys back, led some officials at the Israeli Foreign Ministry to suggest that Israel propose an exchange of the badly wounded Israeli POWs for the civilian Egyptian taken by the Israeli military during the January 1970 raid on the Shadwan Island. If anything, this plan only demonstrated Israeli weakness and exposed it to more pressure: under Articles 109 and 110 of the Geneva Convention the following shall be repatriated directly:

1. Incurably wounded and sick whose mental or physical fitness seem to have been gravely diminished.
2. Wounded and sick who, according to medical opinion, are not likely to recover within one year, whose condition requires treatment, and whose mental or physical fitness seems to have been gravely diminished.
3. Wounded and sick who have recovered, but whose mental or physical fitness seems to have been gravely and permanently diminished.[48]

These articles speak only of the return of the wounded and sick and are not conditional on any exchange. Consequently, any Israeli proposal to that effect would in fact contradict the spirit of the Convention, thus shaking the Israeli position. Moreover, the Israeli and Egyptian interest in the prisoners was clearly symmetrically opposed to each other: Israel would have paid dearly for its own, whereas Egypt did not indicate any interest whatsoever in its own.[49] This "boys back at any price" approach continued to be discussed by Foreign Ministry officials, but no definite action was decided upon based on it. The continued failure to get the prisoners back only added to already tense relations between the diplomats and the military men. That in turn led the military to try and act on its own by submitting a complaint to the ICRC, in clear and undisputed violation of diplomatic protocol, embarrassing their diplomat colleagues.[50] The Israeli decision makers' feeling that they had exhausted all avenues and were at a dead end led them to one of the most painful decisions in their approach toward Israel's own POWs: at a meeting with the participation of the prime minister (Meir), Minister of Defense (Dayyan), and the military chief of general staff (Bar-lev), it was decided to ask the French government to intervene with the Egyptian authorities for the release of the four badly wounded POWs. The others were not included in that exceptional and humanitarian request.[51] These efforts failed completely as a result of the Egyptian military leadership's staunch opposition to any release of any kind under any circumstances.[52] The reason for that opposition was crystal clear: President Sadat was preparing his people for an imminent war with Israel[53] and any move that could be seen by any party whatsoever as "capitulation" or "concession" could not be made at that juncture. Israel meanwhile decided to return to the UN-brokered peace negotiations with Egypt[54] and mistakenly believed that a humanitarian gesture by Egypt would help create the right atmosphere for negotiations.[55] Looking at the total collapse of their release offer, Israel went into uncharted territory: until December 1970 it looked for any mediation effort available in an attempt to get to Egypt. However, with doors closing everywhere, it turned to the United States to request an unprecedented act—that the United States intervene on Israel's behalf by asking the Soviet Union to persuade its main Middle Eastern client, Egypt, to release the Israelis on humanitarian grounds.[56] That move meant in no uncertain terms dragging the Soviets into the Israeli POW issues and opening the door for any concessions the USSR might ask of Israel through the United States. At this stage the POWs were not released; consequently no political price tag was presented to Israel. Yet Israel soliciting help from the Soviets in 1970 would serve as a precedent in the wake of the 1973 War. But that was yet to come. The Israeli action almost immediately drew it into the Cold War and opened it to new pressures. The full significance of this ominous development became evident during the meeting between a senior Israeli diplomat in Washington and the president of the USRC.[57] The latter saw in Israel's search, as presented to him for ways to involve additional players in the international arena, a unique opportunity for the USRC to improve its relations with Egypt in the absence of formal U.S.-Egypt diplomatic relations. The United States was entangled at the time in the Vietnam War and was looking for ways to get its own GIs out of POW camps in North Vietnam. A formal Israeli request for USRC intervention could have provided a venue to reach Egypt and, under the guise of negotiating on behalf of Israeli POWs, use the Egyptian Red Crescent as a mediator in the Vietnam context. This way two protégés of the Soviet Union, North Vietnam and Egypt, could be indirectly and directly involved in the U.S. effort.

This scenario was probably the first consequence of the new Israeli position: internationalizing the POW and putting it on the agenda of the international system instead of staying within the much narrower regional system.

There is no document available to indicate that such a turn in the changing Israeli POW policy was the result of a cabinet or parliament resolution. Considering the lack of a single authority to take care of the issue and the inner struggle between the diplomats and military officers, it stands to reason that a strategic move of that magnitude was the result of some bureaucratic initiative taken without consideration of the possible effects of this new policy. Meanwhile, on the individual POW front, the interrogations subsided because of the relatively long time the POWs had been in captivity and the fact that whatever intelligence they might have had was by that time, about six months since their capture, outdated. In late December 1970 and early January 1971 the ICRC representatives who visited Israeli POWs in Egypt and Cairo announced that such visits would be allowed on a regular basis.[58] Yet Egypt insisted that the exchange issue not be discussed at all.[59] The reason for that Egyptian position in the context of high-level negotiations, involving the United States, on the possibility of Israel-Egyptian peace talks under the UN special envoy, Gunnar Jarring, was fairly obvious. It would have served Egyptian interests to use the POWs to extract diplomatic concessions from Israel, knowing well the importance attached to the issue by Israel. In essence, for Israel it was a humanitarian concern whereas Egypt considered it one more item on a diplomatic agenda.

That intricate web of conflicting interests from within and without, together with the prolonged captivity of the POWs in Egypt and the lack of even the slightest contact with Syria, led the Israeli prime minister to make an unprecedented administrative move. On March 1, 1971, the prime minister announced in a "secret" letter to the government's legal advisor that he was appointed to chair the interdepartmental committee on the Israeli POWs. The other members of the committee were the Prime Minister Office's director general, an army general, and the deputy director general of the MFA.[60] From the minutes of the three meetings that are recorded in the Israeli archives emerges the following picture:

1. As of March 1971, Egypt held twelve Israeli POWs and Syria held three. By August 1971, the prisoners in Egypt were allowed regular ICRC visits but no exchange proposal was accepted; the three in Syria were not allowed ICRC visits and no exchange was possible.[61]
2. Israel held seventy-two Egyptians, forty Syrians, ten Lebanese, and one Jordanian.
3. Israel was willing to release with no quid pro quo some wounded POWs (Egyptian and Syrian) for the purpose of creating good pub-

licity. It did so in August 1971 without any Egyptian reciprocity. Four months later Egypt returned an additional badly wounded Israeli POW.[62] The Jordanian was returned to his country in exchange for four Israeli civilians in April 1972.[63]

4. Israel would launch a public campaign in the media and through notable figures aimed at getting the POWs back or at least at making the Israeli case the subject of world public opinion.
5. All of the above pertains only to the Egyptian front. The Syrian front would be dealt with only through the Red Cross.
6. Even though the Red Cross insisted on handling all activity related to Egypt itself, Israel would use other means depending on the opportunities available.[64] That decision was later reversed by the prime minister, leaving the field open for only two bodies to act on behalf of Israel: the Red Cross and the United States, which supposedly had an obligation to Israel in that matter based on Article F of the August 1970 ceasefire agreement.[65]

In the summer of 1971 Israel had a POW exchange proposal but no partner for negotiations. It requested the return of only three badly wounded (the fourth had been released in March 1971)[66] in exchange for nine Egyptians including six civilians. The deal proposed to Syria was more lucrative, but Syria did not even consider it: three Israelis in exchange for all Syrians, the two pilots and their MiG planes that had been in Israeli custody since 1968, and the Golan Heights Druze leader apprehended for espionage for Syria earlier in 1971.[67] Clearly, on top of the already mentioned reasons for the Syrians and Egyptians avoiding any talks with Israel on any deal, at that point, a few months after the end of the War of Attrition, the Arab POWs in Israeli hands became assets rather than liabilities for the Arab armies. Their intelligence value was none, but their frustration with their prolonged incarceration made them take a confrontational attitude toward their captors. In mid-April two Syrian POWs escaped prison, and Egyptian POWs staged riots against the camp authorities with one Egyptian dead.[68]

The low morale of the POWs on both sides and the potential danger to their well-being led Israel in May 1972 to once again reverse its position: it still accepted the idea of partial release but agreed to delay the pilots' exchange and to be satisfied for the time being with the return of only four people, none of whom were air force personnel.[69] In regard to Syria, Israel was ready to accept regular ICRC visits as long as there was no dialogue regarding a return.[70]

Israel's consistent attempts to get back the military POWs represented in the early 1970s only part of the issue of Israelis captured by the enemy. The lessons of the 1967 Arab defeat and the need for new ways to confront Israel led the Palestinian organizations to look for new tactics. In the early 1970s, terrorist organizations launched repeated attacks within and outside of Israel for various political purposes, including the capture of hostages for use in future negotiations. Two major incidents took place in May 1972, both at Israel's national airport near Tel Aviv: a Sabena (Belgian) plane hijacking and forced landing in Israel and a massacre at that location. The Sabena hijackers were unsuccessful in taking hostages. The Red Cross, much to Israel's chagrin, called them "commandos" and criticized the Israeli rescue mission, claiming it had been executed despite Israel's request that the ICRC conduct negotiations with the hijackers.[71] Israel was already disenchanted with the ICRC and now only resented the organization more. As the Israeli inner circle of decision makers saw it, the ICRC went from a helpful operation, as demonstrated in the post-June war days, to an inept one that concentrated too much on the Arab civilian population in the territories and sided with the Arab players on other occasions rather than investing much effort in the POW and hostages issues.[72] Even the Israeli cabinet's legal adviser, who was known for his strict adherence, chapter and verse, to the law, suggested that the episode had further contributed to blurring the lines between legitimate acts of war and terrorist activities.[73]

Frustration with the ICRC, which Israel saw as using delaying tactics regarding Israel's POWs to retaliate for the Sabena affair, combined with Damascus's refusal even to allow doctor visits to the POWs, led Israel to act.[74] Israel viewed the Syrian prison conditions as harsher than Egypt's. Syria had held three pilots since 1970, keeping them isolated from the outside world and allowing them almost no prison yard walks.[75] Moreover, Israel could not persuade the Syrians to perform an exchange. That, along with continued terrorist activities, served as the foundation for a commando raid of the type that had been rather popular in the 1950s. In June 1972, an Israeli unit operating in Lebanon seized five senior Syrian officers and brought them to Israel. On top of their seniority and their potentially bettering the chances of an exchange, the officers were senior enough and privy enough to military secrets that Israel believed they would become sources of vital and timely intelligence.[76] Israel now held forty-four Syrian POWs including the officers, while Syria held the three pilots.

Israel's decision makers wanted the successful operation, which sparked intensive diplomatic activity, to be a springboard for a package deal involving Egypt. The partial documents available today suggest that Syria quickly agreed to a prisoner swap. Israel, surprised by this response, went one step too far by openly, though cautiously, proposing the general Israeli-Syrian-Egyptian deal, which did not materialize. The Syrian reaction to the raid was swift: not even twenty-four hours after the raid the ICRC contacted Israel, probably on behalf of Syria, suggesting a deal.[77] Israel responded with clear interest in a deal.[78] Even though the actual exchange did not take place until June 3, 1973, it stands to reason that it was the direct result of the negotiations following the Israeli kidnapping of the officers. This episode established several precedents that might have been useful in the future had it not been that the post-1973 decisions were made by a failing leadership suffering from the October 1973 trauma.

Perhaps the most revealing lesson was that the Syrians did not care about any POW who was not a close associate of the regime. The five senior officers were not just high up in the military hierarchy, but had probably reached their positions because of special allegiance to the regime. There are no indications in the contemporary documentation that the Syrian authorities cared about the nonsenior officers. Yet that lesson was not applied in the context of the 1973 War. Two more lessons pertain to the international arena and the functioning of international organizations. All indications available today are that the ICRC tried to be fair to all.[79] Even the ICRC's not assertively pursuing the rights denied to the POWs in Egypt and Syria can be understood in light of its concern that the Arab actors would not accept it as an "honest broker." That does not mean that Israel had to satisfy the organization at all costs. Indeed, Israel created a clear asymmetry between the conditions of the Arab POWs it held and those of the Israeli POWs. Israel allowed visits by the ICRC a short time after taking prisoners, provided regular medical care, and enabled postcard communications between POWs and their families. That policy was in line with the Geneva Convention but never generated any reciprocity.

Unlike the ICRC, the UN played a negative role that harmed not only Israeli but Syrian interests. Security Council Resolutions 316 of June 26, 1972, and 317 of July 21, 1972, gave Egypt the excuses it sought[80] not to join in the emerging deal and deterred Syria from concluding a speedy deal lest the Soviets and Egyptians accuse it of preferring its own interests to "world peace." Moreover, the timing of the kidnapping, unknown to the Israeli decision makers, coincided with Egypt's preparations for a break with the Soviets. Under these circumstances, Egypt had no interest in any accomplishment that would tangibly benefit the USSR's closest ally in the region—Syria. This probably explains Egypt's extreme indifference to the Syrian interest in a deal.[81]

The vote of the council on Resolution 316 (thirteen for condemning Israel, with the United States and Panama abstaining) was not only a setback for the exchange efforts, but also an indication of the international community's distinction between POWs taken in battle and officers on operational missions kidnapped from the sovereign territory of a warring nation. Israel and the ICRC[82] did not make that distinction; four Israeli POWs then in Egypt had been abducted from the Israeli side of the Suez Canal, yet it did not provide the UN Security Council with a reason to discuss it. Apparently the international community saw the difference as long as Israel was on the kidnapping side.[83]

One last lesson in the context of Resolutions 316 and 317 concerns the negative role of the UN and its subsidiaries, including the Security Council. The resolutions were so one-sided against Israel that they also harmed the interests of the Soviet Union's closest regional ally, Syria. Because of Resolution 316, indirect communications between Syria and Israel were slowed to the point of insignificance. That not only harmed the officers' families who were part of the regime's infrastructure, but probably also gave Israel enough time to extract the rich intelligence available to these senior figures. Actually, the most significant players to realize the mistake were the Soviets themselves, and after the 1973 War they ignored the Security Council as a forum for POW issues and partly accepted Kissinger's suggestions through bilateral negotiations.

The post-kidnapping episode also serves to show an interesting twist in which Israel post factum did not realize it had acted against its own interest. The Israeli insistence on a package deal and the release of all its POWs from Egyptian and Syrian jails looked rather rational at the time. However, perhaps one of Israel's mistakes, in addition to the now infamous belief that the Arab parties would not attack it, was that it saw Egypt and Syria as sharing identical interests.[84] Consequently it insisted on a deal that would not only include both, but would serve as a precedent in future conflicts. The lesson was finally learned in late August 1972, but by that time it was too late to initiate a new round of talks with Syria, which had to subordinate itself to the international consensus that favored a unilateral Israeli surrender in the June 1972 kidnapping case over any other option.[85] However, that policy in late 1972 and the first half of 1973 did not bear fruit and was eventually formally abandoned through a secret Israeli cabinet resolution on September 4, 1972—which essentially provided the vehicle for both Arab actors to separately negotiate the POW issue in the aftermath of October 1973.

In spite of the UN Security Council resolution the Syrian defense attaché in Ankara approached his British counterpart in mid-September 1972, suggesting a prisoner swap with Israel.[86] In a series of diplomatic contacts that involved asking British diplomats all over the region, as well as the Jerusalem and Damascus governments, for their opinions, it became evident that Syria was interested in a deal that would start with Israel releasing all prisoners captured in June 1972 in return for a continuation of the process in the future, which would include the Israeli POWs in Egypt and Syria. Israel responded with its old position: all Arab POWs for all Israelis. Syria, which was at the time engaged in an effort to mend fences between Egypt and the Soviet Union in the wake of the July 1972 Soviet expulsion from Egypt, had an interest in brokering a deal that would bring back its own. It did not want to be perceived by Egypt or the USSR as surrendering to the Israeli demands. Were they sincere in that effort? It is hard to determine. However, a unilateral Israeli release, even if followed later by a move letting the Israelis go home, would have given

Syria not only added prestige among the Arab nations, but would also have bolstered its image as a peace-loving nation in contrast to the deteriorating security situation along the border with Israel. Had such a deal been reached it would have probably tied Israel's retaliating hands, at least until the return of its own. Eventually, in mid-October 1972 it became clear that the mutual lack of trust on the part of Israel and Syria would not have allowed a multiphased deal.[87]

In retrospect the year 1973 was no different from the previous years: Egypt continued to reject any idea of an exchange; even when discussing a peace process with the President of the United States, a senior Egyptian said, "a prisoner exchange might be possible"—that is, official Egypt did not at that point consider a POW exchange to be an essential element of peace between Egypt and Israel.[88] Moreover, the feeling in European and to some extent American diplomatic corridors was that Israel had to make conciliatory gestures toward the Palestinians in order to get its POWs back.[89] Syria for its part was not as interested in the Palestinian issue as Egypt was in the spring of 1973. The Syrian leadership was still interested in getting its senior officers back on two conditions: that a deal would not be linked to Egyptian-Israeli POW discussions, if any, and that Syria would gain Arab legitimacy to the highest degree possible. Obviously, neither of the two was expressed verbally, but Syria's stance suggested that very strongly. Their demands as conveyed to Israel included:

1. The release of all Syrians and Lebanese held by Israel, very much in line with their generations-old policy that they spoke for Lebanon.
2. The release of a Golan Heights leader arrested for espionage for Syria, clearly indicating that the Syrians were the legal spokesmen for the occupied Golan Heights.
3. The release of two Arab Israeli citizens from northern Israel, once again demonstrating their own leading role, even in regard to Arab citizens of the sovereign state of Israel.[90]

Unlike on previous occasions, the ICRC-brokered indirect negotiations did lead to an exchange, which took place on June 3, 1973. It is clear that Israel agreed to release the senior officers not as a part of a wider deal but as a stand-alone act, leaving the continuation of the process in Syrian hands, Damascus agreed. Apparently, the issue here was nothing more than how much trust Israel could place in the words of the negotiating Syrian officers and diplomats. Concurrent with the Israeli-Syrian negotiations, Israel and Egypt were on their own separate course that was supposed to lead to the return of one Israeli POW who was badly wounded and whose health was worse than that of all other Israeli POWs held by Egypt. The negotiations advanced to the point that his release in exchange for a number of Egyptians was set for June 8.[91] However, based on ICRC reports from Cairo, the exchange did not go through due to the extensive media coverage in Israel of the exchange with Syria and Egypt's concern that it would also be followed during that exchange. In this instance Israel made a major concession while agreeing to an exchange of a gravely ill prisoner, whose release was mandatory under clauses 109 and 110 of the Geneva Convention. Israel de facto accepted the Egyptian violation of the Convention, agreed to refrain from any formal complaints to international bodies, and, above all, agreed to minimal media coverage. In spite of all that, Israel was frustrated to learn that no exchange took place.[92] Throughout August and September the Israeli Minister of Foreign Affairs and the prime minister continued their efforts at securing the release of that one sick POW. Unknown to the Israeli negotiators, all of their appeals were received in Cairo at a time of increased preparations for the October war. Egypt was probably preparing, inter alia, to keep the ten Israeli captives through the next stages. Indeed, they all did not return home until after the war.

Before addressing the 1973 October War, it is time to assess the development of the Israeli position between the attrition phase and the war. This was a period of complacency and arrogance for Israel and its leaders. During that fateful interregnum all POW-related decisions were made by Prime Minister Meir, with the participation of Defense Minister Moshe Dayyan and a close associate of the prime minister, Minister without Portfolio Yisrael Galili. Meir's twofold position was that all information available to the capturing party must be shared with its enemy and that the previous guidelines for POW exchanges would remain in force—which were not usually shared by the Arab side, whether Egyptian or Syrian. According to those guidelines, each side would return all POWs that it held and no party would distinguish between POWs according to military profession, significance to any of the players, or any other factors.

Mainly as a result of the War of Attrition and successive regular and irregular attacks on the borders and within Israel, along with the weakening of public morale, Israel abandoned its realist policy on prisoner exchange deals and adopted an inconsistent policy with no clear-cut criteria. That process peaked in the months preceding the 1973 War and became a norm. Linking the return of POWs in ways different from those envisioned by the Geneva Convention became common practice.

Because Israel suffered a relatively large number of casualties in prisoners and dead during attrition, and because it was too weak to retaliate against the Egyptian violation of the August 8, 1970, ceasefire, it clearly experienced mental attrition and wanted an end to the bloodshed and the boys back at any price. The media and some public opinion shapers added to the emerging picture the aura of an unnecessary war. The overall national consensus started to shift three to four years after the 1967 War from a concept of a war of survival to a war to be concluded as early as possible at any price. Clearly, the attrition period helped erode Israel's resilience. On the Arab side, once the Israeli POW Achilles' heel was defined and its willpower was eroding, the road was clear for using the Israeli POWs as pawns on the Arab-Israeli chess table.

Because the attrition years also saw some terrorist activities fully supported by the Arab countries, these two distinctly different military efforts, the regular and the irregular, were united on one point: securing for the terrorists a Geneva-based POW status. That would have bolstered their effort to gain international support and recognition on behalf of Israel. In addition, Israel demonstrated full adherence to the Geneva Convention, whereas the Arab violations continued unpunished by the international community. That discouraging picture stood in sharp contrast to the realities of a little more than six years earlier.

The main pressures shaping the Israeli POW/hostage policy on the eve of the 1973 October War were:

1. War of Attrition and military pressure outside and public pressure inside.
2. Accumulation of terrorist activities and growing numbers of casualties.
3. Possible impact of witnessing the return of POWs and hostages on the general public and active duty soldiers.

The War of Attrition left a challenging heritage that later, in the context of the 1973 War, would affect the Israeli POW policies. The intermission between the 1967 and 1973 Wars marked yet another precedent—a positive one for a change. This was the realization that Israel and Jordan shared many strategic interests and that the POW issue should not overshadow that. Hence Jordan was not part of the Egyptian-Syrian effort in this context during the attrition or later during the 1973 War, in which Jordan did not participate.

Perhaps one of the most edifying lessons of the period from 1970 to 1973 (until the October War) was that Israel should insist on clear and simultaneous moves by all actors so that each move is reciprocated by the release of some of the POWs held by the other side.

The Israeli policy regarding its own people held against their will in hostile hands went into a new phase. Once again, as a result of the plane hijacking in early September 1970, Israel reconfirmed its longstanding policy that it was responsible for the lives of Israeli citizens and Jews all over the world, whatever citizenship they held. In spite of being a strong supporter and follower of the Third Geneva Convention, or perhaps because it held so much respect for it, Israel expanded its clauses in order to encompass all pertinent populations as it found appropriate.

In this short period Israel was caught time and again without any clear-cut policy guidelines. True, the prime directive of getting all prisoners back at any price still held, but early cracks in that approach were becoming evident. Amid the deadlock with Syria and Egypt and international pressure relating to the planes, Israel agreed to gradual exchanges, in effect giving away for an indefinite time the released prisoners/hostages. Yet Israel did not abandon its traditional tactics of gathering "bargaining chips," whether the families of PFLP leaders or senior Syrian officers. That approach clearly strengthened Israel's efforts. The backing of that tactic by the government legal adviser obviously helped Israel to put it in the right legal context.

The Arab actors for their part continued to use POWs as the winning ace in order to stop Israel from taking military steps and to contribute to the already spreading civil society and media opposition to the continued presence in the Sinai Peninsula. The same was true for Syria, which manifested almost total obliviousness to the Geneva Convention and to its own commitments under that. The only ray of hope was Jordan, as it continued behind the scenes to cement its strategic alliance with Israel and did not need any POW issues to interrupt that. The only power to extract concessions from Israel was the PFLP, not a signatory to any international instruments, which continued its drive to be internationally recognized, have its people defined as POWs, and force Israel into a dialogue. In all three areas, the organization scored partial successes.

One of the PFLP's accomplishments was contributing to the internationalization of the September 1970 crisis, which in turn exposed Israel and Jordan to brutal pressures from all Western actors involved, led by the United States. They did not care the price for the hostages as long as the two Middle Eastern nations paid.

Wherever international organizations were involved Israel realized that the UN was only a disrupting force, whereas the ICRC was the least of all evils. Clearly, that period encouraged Israel to try to find new "honest brokers" in the future. However, none were available at that time.

NOTES

1. All figures citing "213. Memorandum From the President's Assistant for National Security Affairs (Kissinger) to President Nixon, Washington, September 9, 1970, 9 a.m.," in FRUS, 1969–1976, Volume XXIV, 617, Original: National Archives, Nixon Presidential Materials, NSC Files, Box 330, Subject Files, Hijackings. Secret. Sent for information. The time is hand written at the top of the page. A stamped notation on the memorandum indicates that the president saw it.

2. "204. Paper Prepared by the NEA Working Group in the Department of State Operations Center, Washington, September 7, 1970," in FRUS, 1969–1976, Volume XXIV, 607, Original: National Archives, Nixon Presidential Materials, NSC Files, Box 330, Subject Files, Hijackings. Confidential. The NEA Working Group was formed to coordinate information and responses to the hijacking crisis.

3. ISA/A/7430/4/283, from Jerusalem, to all Israeli representations, September 11, 1970; cf. Document 6: Senior WANG meeting, Summary of decisions, September 10, 1970, The National Security Archives, George Washington University, http://www2.gwu.edu/~nsarchiv/.

4. "207. Memorandum From the President's Deputy Assistant for National Security Affairs (Haig) to President Nixon, Washington, September 7, 1970, as of 3:30 p.m.," in FRUS, 1969–1976, Volume XXIV, 608, Original: National Archives, Nixon Presidential Materials, NSC Files, Box 330, Subject Files, Hijackings. Top Secret; Sensitive. Sent for information. The time is handwritten at the top of the page; "213. Memorandum from the President's Assistant for National Security Affairs (Kissinger) to President Nixon, Washington, September 9, 1970, 9 a.m."

5. David Raab, "Terror in Black September: An Eyewitness Account," *Middle East Quarterly* (Fall 2007): 33–42.

6. "213. Memorandum from the President's Assistant for National Security Affairs (Kissinger) to President Nixon, Washington, September 9, 1970, 9 a.m."

7. ISA/A/7430/4/299, from Jerusalem, to New York and Washington, September 11, 1970; "213. Memorandum from the President's Assistant for National Security Affairs (Kissinger) to President Nixon, Washington, September 9, 1970, 9 a.m."

8. *Davar*, August 20, 1970.

9. That was a correct impression: "213. Memorandum from the President's Assistant for National Security Affairs (Kissinger) to President Nixon, Washington, September 9, 1970, 9 a.m."

10. Shabtai Teveth, *Moshe Dayyan: Story of my Life* (Jerusalem and Tel Aviv: Schoken, 1976), 539.

11. "221. Memorandum From the President's Assistant for National Security Affairs (Kissinger) to President Nixon, Washington, September 10, 1970, 3 p.m.," in FRUS, 1969–1976, Volume XXIV, 640–41, Original: National Archives, Nixon Presidential Materials, NSC Files, Box 330, Subject Files, Hijackings. Secret. Sent for information. The time is handwritten at the top of the page.

12. ISA/A/7430/4/299, from Jerusalem, to New York and Washington, September 11, 1970.

13. ISA/A/7430/4/414, from Jerusalem, to Geneva and Bern, September 12, 1970.

14. "214. Minutes of a Combined Washington Special Actions Group and Review Group Meeting, Washington, September 9, 1970, 11:40 a.m.–12:35 p.m.," in FRUS, 1969–1976, Volume XXIV, 621, Original: National Archives, Nixon Presidential Materials, NSC Files, NSC Institutional Files (H-Files), Box H–114, WSAG Minutes (Originals) 1969 and 1970. Top Secret; Nodis. This meeting took place in the White House Situation Room. Kissinger is not listed as a participant, but he chaired the meeting; "222. Minutes of a Washington Special Actions Group Meeting, Washington, September 10, 1970, 3:15–4 p.m.," in FRUS, 1969–1976, Volume XXIV, 642–43, Original: National Archives, Nixon Presidential Materials, NSC Files, NSC Institutional Files (H-Files), Box H–114, Washington Special Actions Group, WSAG Minutes (Originals) 1969 and 1970. Top Secret. The meeting took place in the White House Situation Room. Kissinger is not listed as a participant, but he chaired the meeting.

15. "233. Transcript of a Telephone Conversation between President Nixon and the President's Assistant for National Security Affairs (Kissinger), Washington, September 12, 1970, 6:15 p.m.," in FRUS, 1969–1976, Volume XXIV, 665–67, Original: National Archives, Nixon Presidential Materials, Kissinger Telephone Conversations, Box 30, Chronological Files. No classification marking. All brackets are in the original; *Davar*, September 16, 1970.

16. "235. Memorandum from the President's Assistant for National Security Affairs (Kissinger) to President Nixon, Washington, September 13, 1970, 10:30 a.m.," in FRUS, 1969–1976, Volume XXIV, 668–69, Original: National Archives, Nixon Presidential Materials, NSC Files, Box 330, Subject Files, Hijackings. Secret. Sent for information. Haig initialed the memorandum for Kissinger; "238. Telegram from the Department of State to Certain Diplomatic Posts, Washington, September 13, 1970, 2220Z," in FRUS, 1969–1976, Volume XXIV, 672–74, Original: National Archives, RG 59, Central Files 1970–73, AV 12 US. Secret; Immediate. Drafted by Davies and Beaudry, and approved by Davies. It was sent to Amman, Bern, Bonn, Beirut, London, Tel Aviv, and Geneva; "241. Paper Prepared by the NEA Working Group in the Department of State Opera-

tions Center, Washington, September 15, 1970," in FRUS, 1969–1976, Volume XXIV, 677–78, Original: National Archives, Nixon Presidential Materials, NSC Files, Box 330, Subject Files, Hijackings. Secret. Received in the White House Situation Room at 8:45 a.m.; ISA/A/7430/4/537, from Jerusalem, to major Israeli representations, September 17, 1970.

17. ISA/A/7430/4/222, from Jerusalem, to London, September 13, 1970.

18. ISA/A/7430/4/465, from Jerusalem, to all representations, September 14, 1970.

19. *al-Ra'id*, Lebanon, Arabic, daily, September 13, 1970.

20. "208. Paper Prepared by the NEA Working Group in the Department of State Operations Center, Washington, September 7, 1970," in FRUS, 1969–1976, Volume XXIV, 609, Original: National Archives, Nixon Presidential Materials, NSC Files, Box 330, Subject Files, Hijackings. Secret. Drafted by Albert A. Vaccaro (INR/RNA/NE) and Peter A. Sutherland (NEA/ARN) and cleared by Seelye.

21. On the September events through Swiss eyes and the agreement: *Neue Zürcher Zeitung*, December 27, 29, 30, 31, 2014; January 20, 21, 2016.

22. Cf. "246. Memorandum From the President's Assistant for National Security Affairs (Kissinger) to President Nixon, Washington, September 15, 1970," in FRUS, 1969–1976, Volume XXIV, 684, Original: National Archives, Nixon Presidential Materials, NSC Files, Box 331, Subject Files, Hijackings. Secret. Sent for information; "250. Memorandum From Samuel Hoskinson of the National Security Council Staff to the President's Assistant for National Security Affairs (Kissinger), Washington, September 16, 1970," in FRUS, 1969–1976, Volume XXIV, 693, Original: National Archives, Nixon Presidential Materials, NSC Files, Box 615, Country Files, Middle East, Jordan, Vol. V. Secret; Nodis. Sent for information. Kissinger initialed the first page of the memorandum.

23. "236. Telegram From the Department of State to Certain Diplomatic Posts, Washington, September 13, 1970, 1808Z," in FRUS, 1969–1976, Volume XXIV, 670–71, Original: National Archives, RG 59, Central Files 1970–73, AV 12. Secret; Immediate. Drafted by Sisco and Beaudry (EUR) and approved by Sisco. It was also sent to Bern, Bonn, London, Geneva, Amman, Beirut, and Tel Aviv.

24. "246. Memorandum From the President's Assistant for National Security Affairs (Kissinger) to President Nixon, Washington, September 15, 1970," in FRUS, 1969–1976, Volume XXIV, 684, Original: National Archives, Nixon Presidential Materials, NSC Files, Box 331, Subject Files, Hijackings. Secret. Sent for information.

25. "244. Telegram from the Department of State to the Embassy in Switzerland, Washington, September 15, 1970, 1757Z," in FRUS, 1969–1976, Volume XXIV, 681, Original: National Archives, RG 59, Central Files 1970–73, PS 7–6 JORDAN. Confidential; Flash. Drafted by Scotes; cleared by Seelye and Beaudry (EUR); and approved by Sisco. It was repeated Immediate to Amman, Beirut, Bonn, London, Tel Aviv, and Geneva.

26. "242. Memorandum From the President's Assistant for National Security Affairs (Kissinger) to President Nixon, Washington, September 15, 1970, 9 a.m.," in FRUS, 1969–1976, Volume XXIV, 679, Original: National Archives, Nixon Presidential Materials, NSC Files, Box 331, Subject Files, Hijackings. Secret. Sent for information. The time is handwritten at the top of the first page. Another notation indicates the president saw the memorandum; "243. Telegram from the Department of State to the Embassies in Switzerland and Jordan, Washington, September 15, 1970, 1710Z," in FRUS, 1969–1976, Volume XXIV, 680, Original: National Archives, RG 59, Central Files 1970–73, AV 12. Secret; Flash. Drafted by Seelye and Scotes; cleared by Beaudry (EUR); and approved by Sisco. It was repeated Immediate to Bonn, London, Tel Aviv, and Geneva, and also repeated to USUN.

27. "238. Telegram From the Department of State to Certain Diplomatic Posts, Washington, September 13, 1970, 2220Z," in FRUS, 1969–1976, Volume XXIV, 672–74, Original: National Archives, RG 59, Central Files 1970–73, AV 12 US. Secret; Immediate. Drafted by Davies and Beaudry and approved by Davies. It was sent to Amman,

Bern, Bonn, Beirut, London, Tel Aviv, and Geneva; ISA/A/7430/4/537, from Jerusalem, to major Israeli representations, September 17, 1970; *Davar*, September 14, 1970.

28. ISA/A/7430/4/501, from Jerusalem, to all representations, September 15, 1970; ISA/A/7430/4/121, from London, to Jerusalem, September 15, 1970, reporting a rather aggressive indirect message from the Prime Minister of Great Britain; on the French pressure, see ISA/A/7430/4/537, from Jerusalem, to major Israeli representations, September 17, 1970.

29. ISA/A/7430/4/321, from New York, to Jerusalem, September 18, 1970; "235. Memorandum from the President's Assistant for National Security Affairs (Kissinger) to President Nixon, Washington, September 13, 1970, 10:30 a.m.," in FRUS, 1969–1976, Volume XXIV, 668–69, Original: National Archives, Nixon Presidential Materials, NSC Files, Box 330, Subject Files, Hijackings. Secret. Sent for information. Haig initialed the memorandum for Kissinger.

30. "251. Airgram from the Consulate General in Jerusalem to the Department of State, Jerusalem, September 16, 1970," in FRUS, 1969–1976, Volume XXIV, 695–97, Original: National Archives, RG 59, Central Files 1970–73, POL 27 ARAB–ISR. Confidential. Drafted by John T. Wheelock (POL); cleared in ECON and POL; and approved in draft by Consul General Stephen J. Campbell. It was repeated to Amman, Beirut, and Tel Aviv; *Ma'ariv*, September 13, 1970.

31. Chapter 12 of *Chasing Shadows;* https://wikileaks.org/gifiles/docs/36/365045_chasing-shadows-edits-to-chapters-10–18-and-epilogue-.html.

32. ISA/A/7430/4/78, from Bern, to Jerusalem, September 17, 1970; ISA/A/7430/4/125, from London, to Jerusalem, September 18, 1970.

33. "251. Airgram from the Consulate General in Jerusalem to the Department of State, Jerusalem, September 16, 1970."

34. ISA/A/7430/4/537, from Jerusalem, to major Israeli representations, September 17, 1970.

35. "255. Transcript of a Telephone Conversation among the President's Assistant for National Security Affairs (Kissinger), the Assistant Secretary of State for Near Eastern and South Asian Affairs (Sisco), and the Permanent Under Secretary in the British Foreign Office (Greenhill), September 17, 1970, 8 a.m.," in FRUS, 1969–1976, Volume XXIV, 714–15, Original: National Archives, Nixon Presidential Materials, Kissinger Telephone Conversations, Box 30, Chronological Files. No classification marking. Kissinger and Sisco were in Washington and Greenhill was in London. The conversation was on the "secure phone."

36. ISA/A/7430/4/326, from New York, to Jerusalem, September [18?], 1970.

37. "267. Minutes of a Washington Special Actions Group Meeting, Washington, September 19, 1970, 9:25–10 a.m.," in FRUS, 1969–1976, Volume XXIV, 747, Original: National Archives, Nixon Presidential Materials, NSC Files, NSC Institutional Files (H-Files), Box H–114, Washington Special Actions Group, WSAG Minutes (Originals) 1969 and 70. Top Secret; Sensitive; Nodis. The meeting took place in the White House Situation Room.

38. ISA/A/7430/4/134, from Geneva, to Jerusalem, September 19, 1970.

39. *Moshe Dayyan: Story of my Life*, 540; Naphtali Lau-Lavie, *Am caLavi* [Hebrew: Nation as a Lion] (Jerusalem: 1994), 251.

40. A Jordanian version of the events, dramatically belittling the hostages' crisis: Musa S. Braizat, *Jordanian-Palestinian Relationship; The Bankruptcy of the Confederal Idea* (London: British Academic, 1998), 141–42; ISA/A/7430/4/177, from Bern, to Jerusalem, September 21, 1970; cf. Directorate of Intelligence, *Central Intelligence Bulletin*, CIA-RDP79T00975A01720001001–9, CIA records search tool (CREST), National Archives and Records Administration, College Park, MD, 2.

41. ISA/A/7430/4/103, from Bern, to Jerusalem, September 22, 1970.

42. ISA/A/7430/4/75, from Bern, to Jerusalem, September 21, 1970; ISA/A/7430/4/91, from Bern, to Jerusalem, September 21, 1970.

43. "319. Telegram from the Embassy in Israel to the Department of State, Tel Aviv, September 23, 1970, 1500Z," in FRUS, 1969–1976, Volume XXIV, 903, Original: Nation-

al Archives, RG 59, Central Files 1970–73, AV 12. Secret; Immediate. It was repeated to Amman (Immediate), Beirut, Bonn, Bern, London, and Geneva; ISA/A/7430/4/673, from Jerusalem, to Washington, Bern, London, September 23, 1970.

44. ISA/A/7430/4/223, from Washington, to Jerusalem, September 23, 1970.

45. "328. Memorandum From the President's Deputy Assistant for National Security Affairs (Haig) to President Nixon, Washington, September 26, 1970, 9 a.m.," in FRUS, 1969–1976, Volume XXIV, 916, Original: National Archives, Nixon Presidential Materials, NSC Files, Box 615, Country Files, Middle East, Jordan, Vol. V. Secret; Nodis. The time is hand written. A stamped notation indicates the president saw the memorandum.

46. "330. Memorandum From the President's Assistant for National Security Affairs (Kissinger) to President Nixon, Washington, September 28, 1970," in FRUS, 1969–1976, Volume XXIV, 920, Original: National Archives, Nixon Presidential Materials, NSC Files, Box 615, Country Files, Middle East, Jordan, Vol. V. Top Secret; Sensitive. Printed from an unsigned copy.

47. ISA/FM/33/12, 13.

48. Convention (III) Relative to the Treatment of Prisoners of War, Geneva, 12 August 1949, Case of Repatriation and Accommodation. https://www.icrc.org/applic/ihl/ihl.nsf/Article.xsp?action=openDocument&documentId=3884B4927CA7CB55C12563CD0051B3E5.

49. ISA/FM/33/13/25, from Geneva, to Jerusalem, November 9, 1970.

50. ISA/FM/33/13/unnumbered (226.81), from Geneva, to Jerusalem, November 17, 1970; ISA/FM/33/13/unnumbered (226.81), from Jerusalem, to Geneva, November 27, 1970.

51. ISA/FM/1508/6/1965–70, December 16, 1970; also see a large number of diplomatic cables between Jerusalem, Paris, and Geneva in that context in the same file during the following days.

52. ISA/FM/1508/6/1965–70/139, from Paris, to Jerusalem, December 20, 1970; ISA/FM/1508/6/1965–70/176, from Paris, to Jerusalem, December 23, 1970.

53. Cf. *New York Times*, December 13, 21, 1970.

54. *New York Times*, December 29, 1970.

55. Cf. ISA/FM/33/13/817, from Jerusalem, to Geneva, December 9, 1970.

56. ISA/FM/33/13/98, from Jerusalem, to unspecified destination, December 24, 1970.

57. ISA/FM/33/12/1742, from Washington, to Jerusalem, December 30, 1970.

58. *Davar*, January 22, 1971.

59. *Ma'ariv*, February 23, 1971.

60. ISA/A/7428/27, March 1, 1971.

61. ISA/A/7428/27, August 9, 1971.

62. *Davar*, November 29, December 16, 1971.

63. [UK] NA/FO17/1756, from Tel Aviv, to London, April 18, 1972.

64. ISA/A/7428/27, March 22, June 23, 1971.

65. ISA/A/7428/27, Note by the legal advisor, April 26, 1971.

66. *Davar*, March 29, 1971.

67. *Davar*, June 6, 1971; the Minister of Defense suggested, probably due to tactical considerations, that the Druze leader issue would be raised at the negotiations table by Syria and not by Israel. ISA/A/7240/2/00494/Q, June 8, 1972 at the interdepartmental committee on the Israeli POWs, session 4.

68. [UK] NA/FO17/1756, from Tel Aviv, to London, April 18, 26, 1972; *Davar*, April 20, 1972; ISA/A/7041/11/98, from Jerusalem, to Geneva, May 7, 1972.

69. ISA/A/7041/11/98, from Jerusalem, to Geneva, May 7, 1972.

70. ISA/A/7041/11/822/H, from Jerusalem, to New York, Geneva, May 7, 1972.

71. ISA/FM/5241/1/932, May 13, 1972, FM Eban interview to Israel Radio, as reported in major Israeli representations overseas, and other cables in that file. Regarding the ICRC position: ISA/FM/5241/1, Israel ambassador to Geneva letter of May 15, 1972, sheds more light on the issue.

72. See above and cf. ISA/FM/33/7, from Stefan Svikovsky, ICRC, Tel Aviv, to Israel Ministry of Defense, January 11, 1970; ISA/FM/33/7/121, from Jerusalem, to Geneva, January 14, 1970; ISA/FM/5241/1/72/421, May 15, 1972, from Geneva, to Jerusalem.

73. ISA/FM/5241/1, Government Legal Adviser Shamgar letter to the director-general of MFA, May 23, 1972.

74. ISA/FM/5241/1, from Geneva, to Jerusalem, May 16, 1972; ISA/A/7240/2, interdepartmental committee on the Israeli POWs, file 1, 11.1971–9.1972, minutes of discussion 4; June 8, 1972, from the military secretary to the minister of defense, to the government legal adviser, June 8, 1972.

75. ISA/A/7240/2, interdepartmental committee on the Israeli POWs, file 1, 11.1971–9.1972, minutes of discussion 4; June 8, 1972, from the military secretary to the minister of defense, to the government legal adviser, June 8, 1972.

76. *Ha Modiyin be milhemet Yom Kippur; Arbaim shana aharei* [The Israeli Intelligence in the Yom Kippur War; Forty Years Later] (Intelligence Heritage Center 2013), 43.

77. ISA/A/7240/2, June 22, 1972, from Guy Deluz, ICRC, Tel Aviv, to Israel ministry of Defense.

78. ISA/A/7240/2 [130], June 25, 1972, from Israel ministry of Defense, to Guy Deluz, ICRC, Tel Aviv.

79. Cf. [UK] NA/FO17/1756, from UK UN mission, to London, July 12, 1972.

80. ISA/A/7240/2. That was the impression of the ICRC representative to Cairo, from director-general, MFA, to the Minister, July 5, 1972; [UK] NA/FO17/1756, from Cairo, to London, July 10, 1972.

81. ISA/FM/5241/1/unnumbered, July 5, 1972, from policy advisor, to the FM.

82. [UK] NA/FO17/1756, from Tel Aviv, to London, July 6, 1972.

83. [UK] NA/FO17/1756, from Tel Aviv, to London, July 3, 6, 1972.

84. A view not shared by at least the British, [UK] NA/FO17/1756, from Beirut, to London, July 11, 1972.

85. ISA/A/7240/2/ [186], August 30, 1972, "top secret," at the interdepartmental committee on the Israeli POWs, session 8.

86. [UK] NA/FO17/1757, from Ankara, to London, September 21, 1972.

87. [UK] NA/FO17/1757, from London, to Cairo, September 22, 1972; from Tel Aviv, to London, September 23, 1972; from Cairo, to London, September 25, 1972; from Tel Aviv, to London, September 25, 1972; from Cairo, to London, September 26, 1972; from Ankara, to London, October 12, 1972.

88. "26. Memorandum for the President's Files by the President's Deputy Assistant for National Security Affairs (Scowcroft)," in FRUS, 1969–1976, Volume XXIV, 83, Original: National Archives, Nixon Presidential Materials, NSC Files, Kissinger Office Files, Box 131, Country Files, Middle East, Egypt/Ismail, Vol. III, Feb. 23–26, 1973. Top Secret; Sensitive. The meeting was held in the Oval Office. Brackets are in the original. There is a presidential tape recording of this meeting ibid. White House Tapes, Oval Office, Conversation No. 862–10.

89. Cf. ISA/FM/6807/4/112, from Geneva, to Jerusalem, March 24, 1973.

90. ISA/FM/6807/4/, minutes of a meeting between the Israel ICRC representative and Mr. Kidron, MFA, May 30, 1973; internal unnumbered MFA memo, May 31, 1973; from MFA, to the government's legal advisor, May 31, 1973.

91. ISA/FM/6807/4/, "top secret-personal" memo, June 5, 1973; "secret" memo, June 7, 1973; "secret," from IDF liaison, to MFA, June 13, 1973.

92. ISA/FM/6807/4/88, 89, from Jerusalem, to Geneva, June 16, 1973; USNA/RG59/ Bureau of Near Eastern and South Asian Affairs. Office of Israel and Arab-Israel affairs/Records relating to Israel and Arab-Israel Affairs, 1951–1976, Box 22, Internal memo, July 2, 1973.

TEN

The 1973 War as a Watershed Line and the Dramatic Shift to Defensive POW Policies

The 1973 Yom Kippur War put the POW matter distinctly on the national agenda because of the large number of prisoners and MIAs involved. A series of questions arose, such as how to retrieve the POWs, and whether it would be possible or desirable to do so at any cost. Domestic actors included the victims' families, parts of the media, and civil society bodies. The external dimension of the war involved Israel's foreign relations more than ever, including U.S.-Israeli relations, the already sensitive relations with Germany that took upon itself some mediation efforts, and, obviously, international organizations, led by the ICRC.

The number of Israeli POWs in the 1973 War was unprecedented during the years following the 1948–1949 War of Independence.[1] In the 1973 War, Israel lost 242 POWs to Egypt, 68 to Syria, and 4 to Lebanon.[2] About 90 POWs were killed during captivity by the Egyptians and Syrians.

The POW issue in the 1973 context is significant because it reflected most of Israel's cumulative experience up to that point. During the war and in its wake the issue affected Israeli decision making in four intertwined ways:

1. The immense shock caused by the surprise attack shattered the popular belief in the military establishment and sparked popular participation in the POW exchange process, which would become a lasting component of Israeli civil society.
2. For the first time since 1948, Israel lost hundreds of POWs/MIAs, many of whom were on active reserve duty. That reinforced the Israeli estimation that there is no significant difference between a

soldier and a civilian; hence the price paid for both should be similar.

3. Because Israel was caught unprepared for the war, with no coherent POW policy, it had no clear ground rules necessary for a relatively beneficial exchange. The Israeli confusion and panic combined with the absence of a policy led to a "land for prisoners" exchange with the Syrians, creating a lasting precedent.
4. The concern lest more soldiers be captured led Israel to abandon its old directive of not negotiating with hostage takers and instead moving militarily to free prisoners. The war saw the demise of that policy, with a few exceptions (Entebbe rescue operation, 1976—successful; Nahshon Waxman, 1994—failure). Since the war, Israel has preferred the diplomatic track to attempts to release POWs and/or hostages militarily.

Prisoner treatment and the exchange processes for situations of symmetrical warfare were established either by the 1949 Geneva Convention or by the two recognized nation-states before or just after the end of such a conflict. Because of these established procedures, it is possible to forgo exploring the decision-making and value assessment processes involved in prisoner exchange situations in the context of the 1973 War, both during fighting and after the ceasefire on October 24, 1973. The accumulated precedents prior to the war served as the basis for the war exchange deals—which in turn were among the most significant lessons of 1973. Those deals have served ever since as the baseline for any prisoner exchanges with national and subnational enemy players.

The Israeli ethos of bringing back all POWs prevailed for decision makers until 1973. But in needing the mediation efforts of the United States, Israel deferred to the United States demands in that context. In mediation efforts throughout the years, the United States, like other mediators, has tried to devise compromises among the protagonists while having its own set of convictions on POW questions. In 1973 the almost inevitable result was a compromise between the United States—not the Israeli—and the Arab positions.

The U.S. tradition of insisting on full implementation of the Geneva Convention was shaped by the Cold War and its interest in preventing minor Soviet violations from leading to superpower confrontations. More closely associated with the 1973 Israeli experience was probably the double need of the United States to follow Vietnam precedents and to establish that the U.S.-Vietnam April 1973 peace agreement, including its POW clauses, was indeed a perfect instrument (which would eventually lead the Nobel Peace Prize Committee to jointly award the prize to Secretary Henry A. Kissinger and Le Duc Tho, who declined it, in 1973). With Kissinger's personal stake in the outcome, it was no wonder that the tactics applied during his talks with the Vietnamese were used in the post-1973 War negotiations in the Middle East.

Yet Israel, a relatively small, close-knit society, could not afford to accept such a reality—if any nation could. Did the Vietnam legacy affect the POW negotiations in the Middle East? It may have, especially because in both cases the main U.S. actor was Secretary Kissinger. Did he prefer a settlement of the issues between Israel and its neighbors along lines similar to the U.S. end of conflict agreement in Vietnam? Was his method of mediation rational and fair to both sides? There is no way to answer that question, but the historical record compels any student of POW issues at least to raise the question.

One major concern of democratic and nondemocratic societies alike is that the decision-making process regarding whether or not to exchange prisoners is rational and that it bears in mind tactical or strategic goals. A decision that is merely desirable may not be welcome to one or more parties involved. In any case, POWs are not neutral, passive observers on the sidelines. Decisions on retrieving POWs can either positively or negatively affect both sides of a conflict, and states must take contextual factors into account. In this case, anti-Israeli terrorism between the 1967 and 1973 Wars blurred the lines between war and peace and between combatant and noncombatant. Israeli decision makers were unsure how to apply even the most basic laws on POW exchanges to prisoners taken in fighting terrorism. That confusion enabled the Arab side to secure the release of nonsoldiers in their deals with Israel.

The Arab players had their own concerns. They feared that freed Israeli prisoners would not comply with Article 117 of the Geneva Convention, which forbids repatriated prisoners from returning to active military service.

On the other hand, Israel had to take into account threats to repatriated Arab prisoners. Such detainees, whether full-fledged POWs or convicted terrorists, came from states with poor human rights records where they would likely face imprisonment, torture, or execution for falling into captivity. The United States has pursued releasing prisoners to third countries as a possible solution, an approach never adopted by Israel. However, that system clearly might decrease Israel's enemies' interest in taking back their released POWs lest their torture be made public and harm their public image. This idea has a historical basis, as Article IV, Section 1 of the Geneva Convention permits detaining states to release POWs into the care of neutral third powers, albeit for medical reasons. Much like the U.S. government itself, the governments of many potential host states feel unwilling to accept the risk or the domestic political cost of publicly allowing former prisoners to live freely within their countries.[3]

The attitude toward POWs upon their capture and especially after their release marks another asymmetry between Israel and its Arab enemies. Whereas Israel is concerned with its POWs from the moment of capture to the end of the process and their reunions with their families, the Arab side acts in line with foreign policy realism. That means the value of prisoners must be evaluated in light of strategic and tactical considerations. In a rational decision-making process, only when the greatest advantages and fewest possible disadvantages are attainable is a trade reasonable. Hence the most valuable prisoners are not just those of highest rank, but those who are available at an opportune time. Moreover, the value assigned to certain individuals will vary among the different organizations involved. For Israel, "the principle of returning POWS, MIAs, kidnapped and fallen IDF personnel has been sacrosanct since the IDF's inception in 1948."[4] A unit in the General Staff Personnel Directorate, the Unit for IDF Soldiers Missing in Action, was created following the 1973 Yom Kippur War in order to locate MIAs from all of Israel's wars and military operations. The unit uses both overt and covert means in its search for information and is in contact with international governmental and nongovernmental organizations to obtain information regarding MIAs and POWs. A special civilian negotiating team employed by the Prime Minister's Office works with the unit in order to obtain information and to negotiate eventual releases. On the operational level, the Ministry of Foreign Affairs emphasizes that the IDF does not spare any effort to free hostages.

Rationally speaking, there is no reason for a larger power to engage in prisoner exchange negotiations unless the exchange values for the two sides are equal in proportion. Otherwise there is no immediate advantage to an exchange; the only advantage then is in capturing enemy combatants. Strategically, the only advantage rests with the side of the actor that is willing to sacrifice its own fighters for a higher cause. The strikingly disproportionate values assigned by Israel and perhaps other Judeo-Christian nations to their soldiers allows enemies who do not share those values to make long-term gains. Ultimately, for the larger power, Israel in the case of the 1973 War, prisoner exchanges harm deterrence, encourage future kidnappings, endanger the lives of those who are taken hostage by terrorist groups, and encourage additional recruitment, donations to, and support for enemy armies and organizations. A rational and correctly proportional decision-making process renders the strategic value of taking prisoners nearly negligible. Through the use of a rational policy when approaching the decision as to whether or not to take or exchange prisoners, nearly every benefit, either tactical or strategic, is nullified for the non-Judeo-Christian power. There are very few tactical advantages to exchanging prisoners for Israel in the first place; however, the strategic concerns remain in effect even after the rational exchange policy has been adopted.

The political value associated with prisoners also affects their exchange value. Since the introduction of TV broadcasts in Israel in 1968,

Israeli soldiers appear to have a high political value in general. Popular concern about captured soldiers is yet another factor leading to irrational policies. The influence and interaction of civil society organizations and the media further augment the political value placed on captured combatants or the remains of such combatants. An exchange can help political leaders regain popularity, especially with an election imminent, as was partly the case in 1973.[5] Clearly, all that reflects only on Israel because the constraints placed on the nation-state regarding prisoner treatment, such as the Geneva Convention, cannot be applied to countries that are signatory to the Convention but that ignore it when it suits their needs.

The evidence of violations of the international laws governing the exchange of POWs mentioned previously in this volume begs the question of why. Why would any nation continue to secretly hold POWs after hostilities have ended, and why would any nation ignore the fact that some of its POWs have not been repatriated? The reasons are intelligence related and political. In the intelligence-related category, states decide to hold POWs illegally to gain the benefit of intelligence from them. This includes not only information gained from interrogations, but also, as is suspected in the case of the Korean War POWs sent to the Soviet Union, information about POWs' lives that states can use as cover stories for its intelligence agents.[6] Similarly, a state may choose to ignore the fact that an adversary holds members of its military if acknowledging those POWs would jeopardize intelligence operations. This reasoning may have factored into the U.S. decision to deny the existence of POWs captured during illegal missions carried out in Cambodia and Laos during the Vietnam War. When considering the benefits of not returning a POW to his or her homeland, it is important to bring into the equation quite the opposite factor: releasing a POW who had become an intelligence asset to the Syrians or the Egyptians, for instance, might prove destructive for these countries because the released prisoners might inform Israel of all the compromised intelligence and lead it to take steps to repair the damage. On the other hand, releasing prisoners of high value would add to the chaos in the rank and file of the adversary's intelligence and send it into a long rehabilitation effort instead of concentrating its efforts on the enemy. This line of thought was probably the main factor behind releasing to Israel an intelligence officer who, as rumor had it, went far beyond betraying his top secret position details and shared with his Syrian captors his broad and deep knowledge of the Israeli intelligence community.

In the politics-related category, states may illegally hold POWs to gain some political, diplomatic, and/or strategic advantage vis-à-vis their opponent. Variations include withholding the names of POWs and, after a long delay, asking for a political quid pro quo, then later delaying or altogether denying medical assistance to those POWs. The aim is to extract diplomatic gains in post-war negotiations or, in the case of not releasing POWs at all, to deny the enemy high-ranking, well-trained officers or just to inflict morale damage.

Thus the Egyptians briefly delayed releasing the names of the 1973 Israeli POWs, and the Syrians took much longer to do so. That tactic has subsequently developed to the point that Israel is sometimes forced into a deal while totally ignorant of the returning POWs' conditions—dead or alive. In adopting that policy, the Syrian and Egyptian behavior in 1973 was only the continuation of historical precedents set by other countries after studying that behavior on the part of the Soviet Union, directly or through proxies.

Along these lines, China proposed to hold 20 percent of all U.S. POWs during the Korean War, whom they hoped to use as diplomatic leverage against the United States.[7] This purpose also seemed to motivate the decision by Vietnam and Laos to continue to illegally hold U.S. POWs; as Quang stated in his briefing, they "could be used to blackmail the 'stubborn' Nixon Administration and extort U.S. economic reparations."[8] Of course, if the North Vietnamese government did intend use POWs to pressure the United States, why they never did remains an open question. One possibility is that after the unexpected fall of Saigon in 1975, they no longer felt it necessary to play this card.[9]

States might also decide against demanding that POWs be returned if they feel the political, diplomatic, and/or strategic cost would be too high. In the case of the Korean War POWs, the United States felt the political costs of a confrontation with China and the Soviet Union outweighed any benefit to the United States in the chance that the Soviet Union would return the POWs.[10] Political concerns also appear to have persuaded the United States not to press the North Vietnamese government on the issue of missing POWs. Strong domestic opposition to the war, culminating in the passage of congressional legislation in 1973 prohibiting further U.S. military action in Vietnam, convinced the United States that it could not afford to jeopardize the success of the Paris Peace Accords and the U.S. withdrawal over the POW issue. As former Secretary Kissinger warned, if the United States had continued the war because of the possible continued imprisonment of POWs by North Vietnam, "American society would have blown apart."[11] Also, as previously noted, many POWs were captured while on secret missions that violated Cambodian and Laotian sovereignty, the public acknowledgment of which would have proved politically embarrassing to the United States both domestically and internationally. Thus the POW cases from the Korean and Vietnam Wars began to degrade the strict, formalized rules governing the exchange of POWs codified in the Geneva Convention.

Strategically, the advantage remains with the power prepared to violate international instruments. Taking a rational approach does not change such a power's policy with regard to prisoner capture, but only affects its prisoner exchange policy. In order to gain the most advantageous position, a nation-state must ignore political pressure and the affinity felt with its combatants and strive for a rational approach to prisoner exchange that precludes emotional and biased evaluation of a prisoner's value. The substate actor should take advantage of this disproportionate exchange rate whenever possible in order to gain the best long-term tactical advantage. Because of the lack of restraints placed on actors in war situations, the prisoner exchange process must be examined by outside observers in order to generate critical new views on the process of conflict as it has evolved in modern society. Through this process it is possible to observe how a government, and even a substate organization, values its people in general and combatants in particular.

The 1973 War involved two asymmetrical players. Egypt, Syria, and other Arab actors formed one side, which sought to cause maximum damage to the Jewish state at any price, including disregard for international documents. That side was helped by the Soviet Union, which sought to bolster its regional position after its partial estrangement from Egypt and the expulsion of its military experts in the summer of 1972. Soviet support for the Arab side was complete and unconditional. On the other hand, Secretary Kissinger hoped to bring the Arab actors into the U.S. sphere of influence and score a major diplomatic victory after the Vietnam fiasco. Moreover, the U.S. administration, then at the apex of the Watergate scandal, saw the war as an opportunity to divert world attention to an international success. Kissinger was then perhaps the only one in the administration dealing with global strategy and he acted accordingly.

The October 6 attack that incited the war found an Israeli cabinet in disarray. The policy that had been in place since the early stages of the War of Attrition and after 1970 proved to be wrong. The attrition stage turned into a trenches war in a complete break with the Israeli tradition of short and decisive wars. The public felt in retrospect that in overlooking Egypt's violation of the ceasefire agreement that had ended the War of Attrition, Israel had made a crucial mistake, and the lack of preparation for the imminent war sparked a wave of protests against the government. Morale was also low among the highest echelons; that, along with general Israeli disappointment in its leaders, meant that there was no way to put together any comprehensive strategy related to the war. Obviously, the same was true of POW policy as well. The inevitable outcome was that the Israeli cabinet shaped its POW policy according to Secretary Kissinger's original interests. That translated partly into giving in to Arab demands that had never been raised before but that would become standard ones in future POW exchange deals.

Right from the first public indication that any of the warring parties held POWs, the war of concepts started on an asymmetrical footing. Israel believed that by strict adherence to the Geneva Convention it would gain world sympathy, leading to an early exchange. Clearly, Israel played the civilized world game: play by the internationally accepted rules and you will be rewarded by an early exchange resulting from a legitimate and rational foreign policy. Four days into the fighting, the semi-official Israeli daily *Davar* published a short piece on the hospitalization of what was presented as Egyptian and Syrian officers in an Israeli (civilian) hospital, heralding continued reports along these lines until the Israeli POWs were returned.[12] However, that mistaken move, along with others to follow, including a daily report to the ICRC on the numbers, names, and conditions of the Arab POWs,[13] served to present Israel as a Western country that provided the best possible treatment to POWs to an unimpressed audience. Once captured, so this Israeli logic goes, they are human beings. That concept was totally alien to the Arab decision makers. For them, until the very moment of exchange, all POWs were pawns on a foreign policy chessboard. Even releasing their names and allowing medical care was a political accessory for extracting more concessions from the other side.

The Arab players missed no opportunity to parade Israel's POWs during the initial stages of the fighting, while managing to keep Israel in the dark. No information was provided on the numbers and identities of the captured troops.[14] Israel learned its POWs' identities only right before the actual exchange, and the negotiations were prolonged by bargaining over the price of the names and medical visits. Throughout the dealings Israel committed yet another mistake by blocking the transmission of detailed information, through public channels, to its own citizens, ostensibly to prevent any possible blow to morale—yet giving rise to rumors of all kinds.[15]

During the first days of fighting, Israel had a strong interest in an early exchange: it would minimize the damage to Israel's image and what was left of its already shattered deterrence. Moreover, the sooner the captured troops returned, the less intelligence damage would occur. Yet there is no record of any cabinet discussion on guidelines for the POW policy in the coming days and weeks. The POW issue provided yet another cause for panic among the decision makers.

The first appearance of any component of POW policy took place in an October 12 telephone conversation between Meir and the ambassador to Washington, Simcha Dinitz. The ambassador asks for instructions regarding a possible ceasefire and, within that context, whether Israel insisted on a general POW exchange, including the attrition POWs. The prime minister's response included these words: "the most important [element] for us is to get our boys out of captivity."[16] Later in the conversation she details several scenarios for a ceasefire and basically agrees to any route to one, as long as there is a general POW exchange. Since the first reference to the issue was only in response to a direct question from Dinitz, and because Meir was in essence giving him the "green light" to any policy move as long as the prisoners were returned, she was giving up any possibility of a political maneuver. This major policy decision—that only the POW issue was important—had never been approved by any Israeli administration and opened the door to any conditions the enemy might impose on release of the troops. That quid pro quo of POWs for any political concession continues to affect Israel's POW issues to this day. It is doubtful whether Kissinger even bothered to convey the message to the Arab parties. Indeed, no Arab player has yet exhausted the huge potential in benefits that the Israeli POWs, especially in Syria, represent. Moreover, despite the lessons from the capture of the senior Syrian officers, Israel was now too overextended militarily even to consider such an operation. Given that Syria did not care about its POWs unless they were very high in the hierarchy, it had no incentive to continue with any exchange process.

It took Israel four days after the outbreak of hostilities to admit that it had lost Mt. Hermon with the initial Syrian strike. It did not admit on that occasion the number and quality of soldiers taken POW by the Syrians. The mountain was commonly known in Israel as "the eyes of the country" because its location enabled Israel to detect movements deep inside Syria. The way it was reported showed once more Israel's failure to comprehend the minds of enemy leaders: while admitting that the fate of the Hermon soldiers was unknown to Israel, the report once again mentioned its abiding by the Geneva Convention.[17]

It took Meir about a week to forswear a perhaps emotional approach to the POW issue and to take a different tack. In a draft letter intended to eventually reach Kissinger, she suggested a comprehensive Israeli position. It included an immediate exchange of POWs, agreement on the procedure for peace negotiations, and a return to pre-war lines. Clearly, no party including the United States could consent to this proposition, but at least Israel moved from making the POW issue equal to all others to making it a precondition for any long-term arrangements.[18]

Whereas Meir perceived the issue as simply a humanitarian one that needed to be included in any settlement as a precondition, the Soviets and the United States did not agree. Part of the outcome of Kissinger's talks in Moscow (October 21, 1973) was "Brezhnev's pledge that he will produce the Arabs on a prisoner exchange."[19] This in effect made the USSR a full participant in POW exchange negotiations, fully commandeering the issue from the regional arena and making it yet an additional item on the international plate. That led President Nixon to promise Meir that "the Soviets have agreed to join us in strongly urging an immediate exchange of prisoners of war."[20] But that Soviet expression of sympathy contained no definite commitment and was subject to the Syrians', and ostensibly the Soviets', time constraints for learning all that could be learned from the Israeli captives. Additionally, it is clear from the wording that Nixon's message, like the Soviet statement, did not include any specific commitment to directly and speedily intervene on this humanitarian issue turned topic of superpower discussion.

The declarative nature of the Soviet-American agreement on the POWs emerged during the October 22, 1973, meeting between the Soviet foreign minister and Kissinger: "The Secretary offered a second written understanding [Tab B] to confirm the agreement to use maximum influence with the parties to ensure an exchange of prisoners of war within 72 hours of the ceasefire. 'This will help me in Israel,' Kissinger said. After a brief private conversation, it was agreed that a formal written understanding was not necessary."[21] The only possible reason for that was that Israel was the sole party genuinely interested in the exchange.[22] The Arab players were either disinterested or opposed it for tactical reasons already explained above. Under these circumstances the Americans saw no point in taking a position that might be interpreted as one-sided. Kissinger repeated his evasive wording in his meeting with the Israeli prime minister and chief of staff, but to give his position some credibility, because even Meir could see the holes in that formula, he said the matter could not be discussed publicly.[23]

Actually, Kissinger probably did not then comprehend the magnitude of the leadership crisis in Israel. At that stage, forty-eight hours before the full cessation of hostilities, Meir was willing to appease him at any price; given her eroding support among the Israeli public, she needed some backing. Moreover, from their losing position, both Meir and Dayyan led the Israeli nation to believe that no ceasefire would be acceptable unless the POWs were returned. On the eve of the scheduled parliamentary elections (originally set for October 31 and later moved to December 31), the political issue and the pressing need to show some results probably mattered more to Meir than anything else—an assessment that Kissinger shared.[24] That is probably why she abandoned her request for a prisoner exchange and implored Kissinger to speak publicly of the U.S.-Soviet formula before she addressed the parliament on October 23.[25]

Now based on a rather vague formula, Israel not only agreed to a ceasefire, but also committed to release the Arab POWs without any parallel commitment from the Arab actors. Moreover, Arab bargaining did not center on an exchange deal but rather on amending their violation of the Geneva Convention and conveying to Israel the names of its POWs. Clearly, Meir and Kissinger were playing on two distinct fields: he was seeking an agreement with the USSR that would maintain world peace and she was moving from attempting to satisfy her potential voters to easing the pain of the POW families.[26] Whatever the motivations, both sides expressed their views but failed to recognize the pressing needs of the other side.[27] Despite the difficulties in the dialogue, it marked a major change in Israel's modus operandi regarding its prisoners. It came in the form of a statement by Meir: "There is one other matter I want to ask you [Kissinger] about. There are 4,000 Jews left in Damascus, who are living in terrible conditions. We would like the Red Cross to come in and take them out."[28] In a sense that was a repetition of the 1956 Israeli effort on behalf of the Jewish community in Egypt. This time around, with a different outcome, it was no more than a desperate Israeli attempt at a face-saving deal due to the prices Israel was willing, or perhaps forced, to pay.

At first glance, Meir's statement might mean that the issue of the Syrian Jews was yet another humanitarian one for the prime minister, but indeed it indicated a major shift in the Israeli attitude toward its prisoners: Israeli POWs were from then on only one element of its position. It was no longer a stand-alone issue that preceded all other discussions. This opened the door to consideration of many more issues not connected with the POW question. The change was not lost on the Syrians, and the eventual exchange deal included a territory: the town of Kuneitra, the regional capital of the Golan Heights. Kissinger, realizing the implications of the new Israeli position, simply indicated that he would raise with the Russians two things: the prisoners of war and that. His response indicated that he probably did grasp the full meaning of the prime minister's statement above, which further indicated the Middle Eastern parties' inability to resolve any pending issue on their own.

Apparently, this episode marked the first time an Israeli POW issue was knowingly internationalized. Instead of a deal between the two protagonists with the ICRC or other international organization as mediator, the POWs became another discussion point between the two superpowers, opening the door to U.S. concessions to the Soviets because of that humanitarian issue.[29] That position granted both Arab and Israeli sides equal standing, the adherence to the Geneva Convention notwithstanding. Israel saw itself as the sole country that was interested in its own POWs as such; however, that was not recognized by the international community. Israel's view was reinforced by the debate preceding the adoption of UN Security Council Resolution 338—no representative except the Israeli one spoke about POW exchanges.[30] The Israeli position that the implementation of the resolution was subject to "POW exchange before ceasefire becomes effective" sounded at best pathetic.[31]

The Israeli views did not inject any new thinking about the return of POWs. The war continued past Resolution 338 of October 22 and despite Resolution 339 of October 23. When hostilities ended on the 24th, Israel laid siege to the Egyptian Third Army that was deployed within the Sinai Peninsula with no way of linking up with the rest of the Egyptian forces. Under other conditions, that is, with two adversaries respecting the Geneva Convention, that would have been the turning point. However, with a player like Egypt that did not care about its besieged troops, it meant nothing. Not realizing the complexities of the situation, the Israeli cabinet approved on October 24 "top secret" resolution number 69, specifying, inter alia: assemble POWs who are (Egyptian) officers in order to increase "our bargaining power" (Article 2) and later in Article 5: "maximum effort in order to bring about the immediate release of [our] POWs will continue."[32]

It was not only a conservative resolution but rather meaningless, a defensive, passive action. How would the Egyptian officers be used to expedite the exchange process while the cabinet refused to acknowledge that Egypt was far from interested in retrieving all of its POWs or even the officers among them? One right move, which may not have led to the desired deal but that would have shown that Israel had finally begun to grasp the rules of the game, would have been to collect a small group of the most valuable officers to Egypt—the highest ranking and those connected to top figures in the government and military. Meir's repetition of the number of Egyptian POWs meant nothing to Egypt and convinced the enemy that Israel did not understand the game. Likewise, on the day of the resolution, Meir also divulged to Kissinger, through Dinitz, that Israel had only partial knowledge of the number and identities of its POWs in Egypt. Up to that point, on the eve of an end to actual fighting, Israel had lost about eighty POWs to Egypt, but did not know the whereabouts of about 290 more. In addition, Egypt had been holding ten more POWs since the War of Attrition.[33] By sharing her information with Kissinger during his meeting with the Soviet ambassador to Washington, Meir inadvertently gave Kissinger and ambassador Anatoly Dobrynin an additional tool in their attempts to rescue the besieged Egyptian Third Army.

The guns fell silent on October 24. Israel was clearly at a loss in formulating a policy that would retrieve its imprisoned fighters. Israeli morale remained extremely low, and the public was not sure the leaders were doing enough to get the boys home. Once some of the military censorship was lifted after the ceasefire, it emerged that Israel did not even know the number and identities of some of the POWs and casualties. That led to two more developments that further eroded Israel's already low bargaining power.

The Syrians launched a public war of nerves against Israel, realizing that with the price tag Israel attached to its POWs, Syria could get much more than its POWs back in any future bargaining. And on the domestic front, Israeli citizens started to form civil society organizations promoting the idea that its POWs should be brought back at any price.

By coincidence, these two campaigns began simultaneously on October 25. Syria unofficially announced that it had fifty Israeli prisoners from the Mt. Hermon outpost, and "mothers and wives of POWs" called on the Israeli government to immediately exchange POWs.[34] For Syria, the move was only one stage of an endeavor to maximize their quid pro quo for the Israeli POWs. For the Israeli group, it was a genuine attempt by people totally ignorant of the government's efforts to retrieve their dear ones. They could not know at the time that most of the policy that was devised piecemeal was mistaken and that they were only worsening Israel's inferior position.

Many more actors began by October 24 to advance their respective causes and to try to benefit from the process. Some, like the Israeli administration, had quite a bit of experience in retrieving POWs yet had no preplanned scheme for the inevitable eventuality of losing some troops as POWs. Organized administrations usually prepare for rainy days during calm times, an especially advisable practice in a country like Israel that in spite of its victory in June 1967 could not secure recognition and peace with its neighbors. However, for reasons discussed so much in the literature dealing with the 1973 War, it is now common knowledge that the euphoric atmosphere in the wake of the 1967 War continued up to the minute that hostilities broke out on October 6, 1973. That general mood among decision makers was also reflected in the POW issue. Israel did have a number of POWs in Egypt since the War of Attrition; the three POWs in Syria had been released as a direct result of the Israeli kidnapping of the Syrian officers; and with the passage of time POWs became more and more a humanitarian issue per se. By October all intelligence that the Egyptians could extract from the POWs was in their possession; no Israeli move could convince them to exchange the prisoners; and a rather uneasy status quo continued on that front until October 6. This is not to say that Israel did not care for its POWs—it was quite the contrary, but all efforts were in vain. Actually, with passing time and increasing public calls for one form or another of giving up the Sinai, the fighting put out by the IDF troops was portrayed by parts of the Israeli media as less and less legitimate. In a sense it was a creeping mirror image of the Vietnam syndrome in the United States at that same time.

And yet the established print media, the major news outlets at the time, did not circumvent Israeli military censorship that forbade any mention of the Egyptian and Syrian concentration of forces along their respective borders with Israel. In a desperate attempt to withhold that information from the public eye and in spite of the leaks from Secretary Kissinger's entourage, not only was news regarding the Israeli POWs kept from the public eye, but all newspapers published only official versions, ignoring any leaks from other sources.[35] Some information was even concealed from the Knesset, the Israeli parliament, and its Foreign Relations and Security Committee charged with overseeing the cabinet's policies and decisions on these matters.[36] In pursuing that policy Meir and her government continued a traditional Israeli course of action—ignoring the participation of civil society organizations and enhanced public participation in the public discourse regarding the POW issue. Indeed, Israel has lost scores of POWs since its war for independence in 1948–1949. In spite of the human interest in their fate and the (limited) media coverage, the issue has never made the headlines—always in prominent locations but not in the main headlines. Furthermore, reports on almost every contact with the ICRC or any other third party serving as a mediator were blocked from publication through harsh military censorship. That wall of silence was partially broken due to public activity in the post-1973 War period. In retrospect it would be quite safe to conclude that the Meir government's elaborate policy of not sharing information with the public eventually backfired and might have been one of the reasons for the switch from POW for POW deals to POWs for POWs and land deals.

That mistaken censorship policy coupled with strong rumors of a major Israeli defeat, heavy casualties, and insufficient war materials gave credence to the Arab players' claims that they held a large number of POWs. Even when the numbers were officially revealed, that sense of a major catastrophe did not fade. Israel had not seen such a large number of pilots, officers, and field personnel taken prisoner at any point in its history. Some air personnel had been lost to captivity during the War of Attrition, many civilians had been captured by the enemy in 1948, and a number of field officers had been lost to the enemy during the attrition period. However, this time Israel reached a stage of public shock: a number of an elite intelligence unit were captured by the Syrians, leading to permanent unbearable damage to Israel's intelligence capabilities; high level pilots, some of whom had knowledge beyond their formal duties, were apprehended by the enemy; and on top of all that, as mentioned, an unprecedented number of Israel's finest were taken prisoner. In the public mind it was no longer a case of losing a senior pilot or officer as occurred during the War of Attrition. The bare number became a key concern and a symbol of the lessons of attrition: Israel, tired as it was of attrition, got into a much wider conflict as the result of domestic exhaustion and leadership complacency combined.

Right from the chaotic outbreak of hostilities on October 6, Israel had had to deal with unprecedented issues: How to verify the fate of a missing ground soldier? A pilot who was seen leaving his plane deep inside hostile territory? How to try and get the troops back when their identities were unknown? The chaos and surprise of the first couple of days and the last minute preparations for the imminent war on October 5 without any written records in many cases left Israel very few ways of knowing the locations of these missing soldiers. Even the enemy was shocked by the large number of Israeli casualties; despite knowing the fate of the POWs in its hands, the enemy knew little regarding some of the MIAs. Some of these MIAs are still missing to this day.

The Syrians and Egyptians, in any case, aimed to put together a large enough contingent of captured troops that Israel would pay as much as possible for them after the intelligence in their possession was extracted. The War of Attrition could have played a negative role here for Israel: Israel did not find the right formula to get its own back for what could be interpreted by the Arab actors as lack of motivation to pay the highest prices possible. The Egyptian, and much more the Syrian, interest at the cessation of hostilities was twofold: to use the POWs for intelligence and propaganda purposes and then impose on Israel the highest price possible in terms of a strategic accomplishment. All of that on top of their traditional violations of the Geneva Convention led the Arab actors to not even release the POWs' names.

The mirror image of that picture consisted of the efforts by the families of the missing in action to follow, with the help of the IDF, all available news items in order to identify their family members. That Sisyphean effort produced the first lists of Israelis held in Egypt and Syria.[37]

The families' exertions along with the overall Israeli sense of despair and defeat—even though the conditions on the ground during the second and third weeks of fighting signified otherwise—led to another negative precedent. For the first time in wartime, Israel underwent a rift between the government—interested in publicly playing down the POW issue as a symbol of the failure of the first forty-eight hours—and the families that had lost all confidence in the government and had begun to try their own media searches and later their own diplomatic activity. Even though building up pressure on the government was not new, because it had already happened during the times of attrition, the difference lay in the magnitude of the pressure. With the help of extra-parliamentarian protest movements, the formal decision makers appeared more and more to be incapable of even bringing the prisoners back home. Not only that—all Israeli diplomatic moves were shrouded in secrecy because Israel did not really know what it was asking for: Scores of POWs? Hundreds of them? All without figuring out the right formula for negotiations or realizing that the United States was not on Israel's side but was naturally pursuing its own interest, which was to become Egypt's major ally, not the early release of the Israelis in Syrian and Egyptian prisons.[38]

Meanwhile, Israeli Foreign Minister Abba Eban advised the U.S. ambassador to Israel that his country had practically no names of prisoners, except for forty in Egypt out of "some hundreds," and that he wished the United States would try along with the Israeli government "to keep all aspects of the POW issue under wraps."[39] He also informed the ambassador that some Israeli POWs were murdered at the Mt. Hermon outpost. His request to deal with the issue behind closed doors could reflect first ignorance of the fate of POWs and even their names, and second worry that the outcome of future indirect talks might be negative and that the "boys," much like the attrition POWs, would have to spend a long time in Arab prisons.

The War of Attrition had established that the ICRC could insist on making regular visits to the Israeli POWs, but always subject to the diplomatic and strategic balance sheet. The organization had failed to secure the release of the attrition POWs or to get updated information on their health in the first stages of their captivity. Those failures, coupled with the issue's elevation to a strategic one, downgraded the ICRC's role in the 1973 War's aftermath. Senior ICRC officials even complained to Israel about their de facto exclusion from discussions on the topic.[40] By doing so, they were trying to motivate Israel, the only party interested in an exchange, to try to persuade the United States to bring them (the ICRC) in. Apparently, like other players, they did not realize the depth of the Israeli government's crisis and its almost total inability to make its voice heard in the superpower talks. Yet the government was able to convey that if there was one issue that united the exhausted people, it was the POW issue. That point was not lost on Kissinger and his colleagues, who suggested to all interested parties that there was no progress on the matter Israel might stall the diplomatic process.[41]

Given Israel's intense concern about its POWs and Egypt's lack of interest in its own, Kissinger found the one and only strategic benefit that he could offer the Egyptians at that moment: not their POWs who were in Israeli hands and not the removal of the Israeli siege of the Egyptian Third Army, but rather a creative solution that would further remove Egypt from its traditional ally, the Soviet Union. The United States would supply the Third Army with forty tons of food and Egypt would undertake to (the following is from Ismail Fahmi, Egypt's Acting Foreign Minister): "A) [provide] the list of wounded to the Israelis in the next military meeting, B) give the same list to the Red Cross, C) we are ready to negotiate regarding the exchange of wounded POWs, D) we are ready to give the list of POWs to the Red Cross, E) we have already permitted the Red Cross to visit the wounded POWs."[42] That was a winning proposal due to Egypt's lack of interest in getting their own back. Had they been returned the prisoners might have spread the word of their whereabouts or information on how a battlefield victory turned into a defeat. On the other hand, removal of the Israeli siege of the Third Army would prove that in spite of Israeli pressure, Egypt was able to take care of its own; after being supplied by the United States, its troops would even look refreshed and fit, further disproving Israeli claims. That moral victory was about to be given to Egypt in exchange for movement on the POW dimension.

Meanwhile, Israel still struggled to find the right formula to free the POWs. Kissinger, for his part, preferred indirect Israeli-Egyptian talks so that both parties would realize that, absent the United States in general and Kissinger in particular, no agreement on either POWs or the Third Army was attainable.

While keeping its contact with Kissinger secret, the Israeli government still had one major arena to take care of: Israeli public opinion. With the parliamentary elections due on December 31, protests started to escalate. Hence Israel chose to create a mock confrontation with the ICRC by prohibiting it from searching for Egyptian soldiers who were left behind in the Israeli-occupied areas along the Suez Canal as long as Israel did not get the lists of its POWs.[43] Moreover, simultaneous with Kissinger's talks with the Egyptians that Israel was not made privy to, Israel announced that, in clear contravention of Kissinger's agreements with the Egyptians, no wounded Third Army soldiers would be allowed to leave the besieged area.[44]

That small gesture for the sake of Israeli public opinion was not enough. On October 29, a little over three weeks after the outbreak of hostilities, a group of parents of POWs wrote an open letter to Meir asking how she could renege on her promise not to agree to a ceasefire without the POWs' return. They further demanded that the government declare the ceasefire null and void, and in addition that it cease any contact with the enemy and with international organizations.[45] That letter from concerned parents marked the beginning of antiwar and antigovernment civil society organizations that would try, sometimes successfully, to turn policy in new directions. The parents, however, could not comprehend the pressures the government was under. On the one hand, the government was losing political ground due to its responsibilities during the war and its aftermath; on the other, the ministers could not withstand Kissinger's pressure and they were not fully aware of his commitments to Egypt. Thus they were in no position to reveal details to the parents. They were also embarrassed about their functioning since late September 1973 and they simply did not know what Kissinger's next ultimatum would be. The overall impression was that the government was evading the public's questions and had something to hide, further intensifying public anger and civil activity. In a rather pathetic attempt to square the circle, Meir traveled to the United States to attempt to find out "what is being planned between the parties."[46] As already indicated, Kissinger revealed only part of the picture to each Middle Eastern adversary, making Meir's efforts futile.

The prime minister was undoubtedly under pressure: twenty-five days after the outbreak of hostilities, Israel had no definite list of its POWs in Egypt and in Syria, and with the fast approaching general elections, the demonstrators could not wait any longer for a word regarding their loved ones. The families felt betrayed because all government promises to make the release of the prisoners a precondition of any agreement, no matter how temporary, were violated. At that point the trust of the people in their representatives was low enough to attract more people to the emerging protest movement. In her meeting with Kissinger, Meir acknowledged that "what is in jeopardy now is the greatest thing we have, the confidence of our people in us. We promise to them, and we find twenty-four hours later we can't deliver."[47]

It was probably the first time in Israel's history that its decision makers had to take into account the views and activities of an extra-parliamentary group, later to be joined by protest movements demanding the government's resignation. The precedent set on November 1, 1973, would later affect Israel's negotiations with Egypt and the Palestinians. Meir found herself at that stage of the negotiations caught between a rock named Kissinger and a hard place in the form of the families and emerging protest movements. Whereas the families demanded the POWs' immediate release, Kissinger demanded that Israel withdraw to the October 22 lines in accordance with Security Council Resolutions 338, 339, and 340, which entailed lifting the Israeli siege of the Third Army. These two opposing political factors only served to illustrate the dead end that Meir and her cabinet reached within a month after their failure to prepare and correctly respond to the combined Arab attack on October 6.

However, U.S.-Egyptian relations were improving and the United States was replacing the Soviet Union as the main superpower backing Egypt, while Syria at the war's end found itself in a much worse position than Egypt. Whereas the latter could claim it had reoccupied some of the land lost to Israel in 1967, Syria not only lost to Israel all of the 1967 occupied lands, but also new territory that had not been in Israeli hands prior to October 6. On the other hand, it had quality Israeli POWs, first and foremost an intelligence officer who divulged his wide-ranging information. Syria held other intelligence personnel and high-ranking officers as well, including the most senior Israeli pilot ever taken prisoner. Given Syria's total contempt for the Geneva Convention, many if not all other POWs were subject to murder; about twenty-eight were killed in prison or while under torture. Even the Saudi Foreign Minister, when requested to do so by an American official, said that he would try to persuade the Syrians to be less brutal.[48]

In any case, both Syria and Egypt again demanded that Israel uphold Security Council resolutions, which meant returning to the October 22 lines. Israel claimed these could not be verified; the Arab actors claimed they meant full Israeli withdrawal from Mt. Hermon, giving the Syrians an outpost Israel had occupied in the 1967 War and a full lifting of the siege on the Third Army. That is, both countries demanded strategic benefits for launching the POW exchange process. Egypt now sought to become a full-fledged member of the U.S. camp and was willing to pay some price for that; Syria was sure of Soviet support and hence was much less open to compromise with the United States. Not only that, but in addition, President Sadat of Egypt started, upon succeeding President Nasser in 1970, a process of Egyptianizing his country—that is, building its character as a nation state that is part of the Arab heritage. His Egypt was more Egyptian than Arab, while the Syrian leaders preferred to present their country as the cradle of Arabism and therefore as the pace setter for the nation. That ideological approach probably led them to be less open to concessions than Egypt considering their special "Arab" duty.

By early November the lines were fully drawn. Israel and Egypt conducted direct negotiations with American participation. The POW issue seemed to matter less to all players and became just another topic on the agenda, while the mounting popular pressure in Israel rendered Meir incapable of making any concessions but subject to Kissinger's pressure and dictates. Egypt now enjoyed full access to the Third Army and was in no hurry to see it reunited with the rest of the army. Syria, for its part, was still striving to extract intelligence from the Israeli POWs and wanted to regain not only territory occupied by Israel in this latest war, but some of the 1967 losses as well. These points became the basis for the Israeli-Egyptian interim agreements of November 1973 and January 1974 and the May 1974 interim agreement with Syria. Under these agreements, Israel withdrew from parts of the Sinai, eventually restoring all of it through the March 1979 Israeli-Egyptian peace treaty. Israel and Syria gradually exchanged their POWs, completing the process in May 1974, and Israel withdrew from the Syrian town of Kuneitra, which it had occupied in 1967. In this way Syria gained back some of its lost prestige and manifested its Arab commitment to the full liberation of all Arab occupied lands.

In June 1974 Golda Meir resigned, largely because of the growing protest activities of groups demanding that she take responsibility for the war and her failure to retrieve the POWs earlier, and also in response to the report of the Commission of Inquiry that was seen by many Israelis as an appropriate context in which to force the prime minister out but that did not blame her directly for the 1973 disaster.

The 1973 War served to demonstrate the irrational nature of modern prisoner exchange policies. The tactical and strategic concerns as to who to take prisoner and when were tested by the Arab players but not necessarily by Israel. A lesson can be drawn that in order to gain the most advantageous position, a nation-state must ignore the extra political pressure and affinity felt with its combatants and strive for a rational approach to prisoner exchange that precludes emotional and biased evaluation of a prisoner's value.

For Israel, the Yom Kippur War was a watershed line regarding policy on POWs. Leaving the arena to the Israeli public became customary in the years to come, as did blurring the lines between POWs and hostages. Subnational players were not bound by international instruments, and they followed previous behavior on the part of the national Arab players.

Perhaps the most outstanding change resulting from 1973 was twofold: the POW issue was no longer a bilateral issue but an international one and the principle of prisoner for prisoner disappeared forever to be replaced by prisoners for whatever price the enemy presses for.

NOTES

1. http://www.mia.org.il/idfhxheb.html.

2. http://www.mia.org.il/idfhxheb.html.

3. Cf. Later concerns regarding illegal combatants: Michael Crowley, "Prisoners Dilemma," *The New Republic* 17 (June 2009): 9.

4. Israel Ministry of Foreign Affairs, "Background on Israeli POWs and MIAs," January 26, 2004, November 23, 2009.

5. Even though PM Meir empathically denied it, see, ISA/Meir's testimony before the Agranat Commission of Inquiry, February 2, 1974, http://www.archives.mod.gov.il/Pages/Exhibitions/Agranat2/%D7%A2%D7%93%D7%95%D7%AA%20%D7%92%D7%95%D7%9C%D7%93%D7%94%E2%80%8F%20%D7%9E%D7%90%D7%99%D7%A8%20-%20%D7%A8%D7%90%D7%A9%20%D7%94%D7%9E%D7%9E%D7%A9%D7%9C%D7%94/mywebalbum/index.html.

6. Melinda Liu, "Counting the Ghosts," *Newsweek* 5 (October 1992): 50

7. Ibid., 49.

8. "Hanoi's Smoking Gun," *National Review* 24 (May 1993): 16.

9. Morris Stephen, "Quangmire," *The New Republic* 31 (May 1993): 18.

10. Liu, "Counting the Ghosts," 50.

11. Ibid., 49.

12. *Davar*, October 10, 26, 1973.

13. *Davar*, October 25, 1973, quoting the Israeli Foreign Minister at a press conference.

14. Wikileaks/U.S./Jerusalem cable 1169 to State, Washington, October 19, 1973, Wikileaks/The Kissinger Cables/U.S./Jerusalem cable 1169 to State, Washington, October 19, 1973, https://search.wikileaks.org/plusd/cables/1973JERUSA01169_b.html.

15. Wikileaks/U.S./Cairo cable 2995 to State, Washington, October 8, 1973, https://search.wikileaks.org/plusd/cables/1973CAIRO02995_b.html; *Davar*, October 8, 1973; *Ma'ariv*, October 24, 1973.

16. ISA/G/6695/phone conversation PM-Washington ambassador, October 12, 19:00, 3, 6.

17. *Davar*, October 16, 17, 1973.

18. ISA/A/7049/25/October 19, 1973, 19:45.

19. "222. Telegram From Secretary of State Kissinger to the President's Deputy Assistant for National Security Affairs (Scowcroft)," FRUS, 1969–1976, Volume XXV, 642, Original: National Archives, Nixon Presidential Materials, NSC Files, Kissinger Office Files, Box 39, Kissinger Trip Files, HAK Trip—Moscow, Tel Aviv, London, HAKTO, SECTO, TOSEC, Misc., October 20–23, 1973. Top Secret; Sensitive; Exclusively Eyes Only; Flash. Sent to Scowcroft for President Nixon.

20. "228. Letter From President Nixon to Israeli Prime Minister Meir," FRUS, 1969–1976, Volume XXV, 648, Original: National Archives, Nixon Presidential Materials, NSC Files, Kissinger Office Files, Box 136, Country Files, Middle East, Dinitz, June 4–October 31, 1973. No classification marking. A handwritten notation reads: "Hand delivered to Amb. Dinitz, 11:00 a.m., 10/22/73."

21. "229. Memorandum of Conversation, Moscow, October 22, 1973, 8:45–9:45 a.m.," FRUS, 1969–1976, Volume XXV; Original: National Archives, Nixon Presidential Materials, NSC Files, Kissinger Office Files, Box 76, Country Files, Europe, USSR, Kissinger Trip to Moscow, Tel Aviv and London, October 20–22, 1973. Top Secret; Sensitive; Exclusively Eyes Only. The meeting was held at the guest house of the U.S. delegation in Lenin Hills, Moscow.

22. A striking example can be found in the deliberations at the Security Council preceding the adoption of Security Council Resolution 340 with the Israeli permanent representative, Tekoah, being the sole speaker to raise the POW issue. Wikileaks/U.S./Washington cable from the Secretary of State 211133 to embassies and consulates, October 24, 1973, https://search.wikileaks.org/plusd/cables/1973STATE211133_b.html.

23. ISA/A/7047/15/minutes of the meeting of the Israeli PM and the chief of staff with Kissinger, October 22, 1973, 9.

24. ISA/A/7047/15/minutes of the meeting of the Israeli PM and the chief of staff with Kissinger, October 22, 1973, 11; "261. Memorandum of Conversation, Washing-

ton, October 24, 1973, 1:05–2:42 p.m.," FRUS, 1969–1976, Volume XXV, 722–27, Original: Ford Library, National Security Adviser, Memoranda of Conversation, Box 2. Secret; Nodis. The luncheon meeting was held in the White House Map Room.

25. Indeed, the department's spokesman made that statement on the 23rd. Wikileaks/U.S./Department of State cable 208876 to Cairo, Tel Aviv, October 23, 1973, https://search.wikileaks.org/plusd/cables/1973STATE208876_b.html.

26. ISA/A/7047/15/minutes of the meeting of the Israeli PM and the chief of staff with Kissinger, October 22, 1973; "230. Memorandum of Conversation, Tel Aviv, October 22, 1973, 1:35–2:15 p.m.," FRUS, 1969–1976, Volume XXV, 657, Original: National Archives, Nixon Presidential Materials, NSC Files, Kissinger Office Files, Box 76, Country Files, Europe, USSR, Kissinger Trip to Moscow, Tel Aviv and London, October 20–22, 1973. Top Secret; Sensitive; Exclusively Eyes Only. The meeting was held in the Guest House in Herzliyya near Tel Aviv.

27. "230. Memorandum of Conversation, Tel Aviv, October 22, 1973, 1:35–2:15 p.m."

28. Ibid.

29. Cf. "251. Message From Secretary of State Kissinger to Soviet General Secretary Brezhnev, Washington, October 23, 1973," FRUS, 1969–1976, Volume XXV, 701, Original: National Archives, Nixon Presidential Materials, NSC Files, Kissinger Office Files, Box 69, Country Files, Europe, USSR, Dobrynin/Kissinger, Vol. 20, [October 12–November 21, 1973]. Secret. A handwritten notation at the top of the page reads: "Rec'd Moscow 0141Z, 10/23/73, dispatched from WH at 5:15 pm, 10/23."

30. Wikileaks/U.S./Tel Aviv cable 8467 to State, Washington, October 22, 1973, https://search.wikileaks.org/plusd/cables/1973TELAV08467_b.html.

31. Ibid.

32. ISA/A/7049/25, from the cabinet secretary to the PM, Defense Minister, Minister of Foreign Affairs, October 25, 1973, "top secret."

33. ISA/A/7792/3, Dinitz-PM phone conversation, October 24 at 3:40 p.m. (Israel time).

34. *Davar*, October 25, 1973.

35. ISA/Meir's testimony before the Agranat Commission of inquiry, February 2, 1974, 65, http://www.archives.mod.gov.il/Pages/Exhibitions/Agranat2/%D7%A2%D7%93%D7%95%D7%AA%20%D7%92%D7%95%D7%9C%D7%93%D7%94%E2%80%8F%20%D7%9E%D7%90%D7%99%D7%A8%20-%20%D7%A8%D7%90%D7%A9%20%D7%94%D7%9E%D7%9E%D7%A9%D7%9C%D7%94/mywebalbum/index.html.

36. Shmuel Tzabag, "Termination of the Yom Kippur War between Israel and Syria: Positions, Decisions and Constraints at Israel's Ministerial Level," *Middle Eastern Studies* 37, no. 4 (2001): 192.

37. *Davar*, October 26, 1973.

38. Wikileaks/U.S./Tel Aviv cable 08686 to State, Washington, October 27, 1973, https://search.wikileaks.org/plusd/cables/1973TELAV08686_b.html.

39. Ibid.

40. ISA/A/7049/25/367, from Geneva, to Jerusalem, October 26, 1973.

41. Wikileaks/U.S./Department of State cable 212609 to all pertinent representations, October 27, 1973, https://search.wikileaks.org/plusd/cables/1973STATE212609_b.html; Wikileaks/U.S./Tel Aviv cable 8714 to several representations, October 28, 1973, https://search.wikileaks.org/plusd/cables/1973TELAV00001_b.html, containing the translation of the summary of Deputy Prime Minister Allon's interview to Israeli TV on October 27; "296. Backchannel Message From Secretary of State Kissinger to the Egyptian Presidential Adviser for National Security Affairs (Ismail)," Washington, October 28, 1973, FRUS, 1969–1976, Volume XXV, 782, Original: National Archives, Nixon Presidential Materials, NSC Files, Kissinger Office Files, Box 132, Country Files, Middle East, Egypt/Ismail, Vol. VII, October 1–31, 1973. No classification marking. A handwritten notation on the message indicates that it was sent for delivery by the Situation Room at 1:00 p.m.; Wikileaks/U.S./Tel Aviv cable 8779 to Secretary of State,

summary of meeting with Israeli FM, October 30, 1973, https://search.wikileaks.org/plusd/cables/1973TELAV08779_b.html.

42. "298. Memorandum of Conversation, Washington, October 29, 1973," Washington, October 28, 1973, FRUS, 1969–1976, Volume XXV, 790, Original: National Archives, RG 59, Central Files 1970–73, POL 27 ARAB–ISR. Secret; Nodis. A handwritten notation indicates that this is a first draft.

43. Wikileaks/U.S./Geneva cable 05717 to all pertinent representations, October 29, 1973, https://search.wikileaks.org/plusd/cables/1973GENEVA05717_b.html.

44. *Davar*, October 29, 1973; Wikileaks/U.S./Tel Aviv cable 8780 to all state and pertinent representations, October 30, 1973, https://search.wikileaks.org/plusd/cables/1973TELAV08780_b.html.

45. *Davar*, October 30, 1973.

46. "305. Memorandum of Conversation, Washington, November 1, 1973, 8:10–10:25 a.m.," FRUS, 1969–1976, Volume XXV, 808, Original: National Archives, RG 59, Central Files 1970–1973, POL ISR–US. Top Secret; Sensitive; Exclusively Eyes Only. The meeting was held at Blair House.

47. Ibid.

48. Wikileaks/U.S./Jeddah cable 4792 to State, Washington, Tel Aviv, Beirut, November 1, 1973, https://search.wikileaks.org/plusd/cables/1973JIDDA04792_b.html.

Part IV

Fourth-Generation Approaches Taking Over: POWs and Hostages as a Means for Smaller Powers to Gain Parity with Israel

ELEVEN

The Palestinian Substate Actors Taking Over

From POWs to Hostages? The Effect of Fourth-Generation Players on the Making of POW Policies, 1974–1985

On June 6, 1974, all Israeli POWs in Syria in the last stage of the post-1973 War exchange were returned to Israel along with three Arab Muslim Israeli civilians.[1] The POWs in Egyptian hands, from the attrition time and the war, had all been reunited with their families in November 1973. In June 382 Syrians also returned home. All left the country of their imprisonment by air because the two warring countries had not agreed on the exact demarcation of the new disengagement line and could not establish a crossing point.

Not long after the exchange a group of terrorists infiltrated a collective community (*kibbutz*) in northern Israel, killing three female civilians.[2] That violence was followed by a series of terrorist attacks aimed at times at killing civilians and at other times at taking hostages for bargaining with the Israeli authorities over the release of their own. Unknown to anyone at the time, although it is clear in hindsight, these incidents marked the crossing of an implicit watershed line. The 1973 War marked the end of the regular armies' confrontations in the Middle East. All of the following military flare-ups would be either entirely carried out by subnational players or, as in the 1982 limited Israeli-Syrian confrontation, those players would supply the detonator for the conflict. That meant that in the aftermath of 1973 the era of symmetrical wars gave way to a long series of a-symmetrical confrontations. In the context of POW and

MIA issues that translated into dealing with organizations that did not adhere to any international understandings, and in light of the 1973 POW-related precedents they had a larger degree of independence in their actions. Obviously, that does not mean that the Arab nation-states, on the other hand, did live by any POW-related international traditions, legal or otherwise. Yet they could be approached by international organizations like the ICRC or UN bodies. With regard to the Middle Eastern organizations, however, it has been impossible to use those avenues, which have been giving way to individuals and NGOs.[3]

Moreover, the very nature of combatting subnational actors/terrorist organizations is unlike that of encountering national actors. It is possible to speculate, based on the work of Andrew Mack, that with the eventual Israeli victory over its enemies in 1973, its public lost interest in lesser wars than those of survival.[4] His main thesis is that because the survival of larger states would not depend on the outcome of a conflict, they tend to invest less in that kind of challenge compared with the smaller state. Indeed, for a nation that has had to fight its neighbors several times, the smaller organizations have been, at least in the mind of many Israelis, no more than nuisances. Moreover, with the gradual Palestinian turning into a blend of diplomacy and terror, domestic Israeli concern with countering those organizations' activities moved from the realm of full consensus on security affairs into a debate over the right approach to the Palestinians—with a "two states" solution becoming the predominant, official Israeli approach. The traditional policy regarding a quasi-equal POW exchange was turning into Israel's de facto abandonment of the old paradigm of equal exchange along with its gradual willingness to release many more Palestinians than the number of Israelis being released. For the first time, it would also include convicted murderers in the process, contradicting past stated positions.

All of that coupled with Mack's thesis leads to a subnational actor paradox: its interest is in the larger power committing fewer resources than necessary, which would lead to at least tactical achievements for the smaller power. Yet investing too little in confronting terrorist organizations would obviously lead to their political demands receiving less attention. The way out of this predicament was already in effect in the late 1960s—taking hostages. One of the best known foiled cases involved an attempt by the DFLP to take hostages in order to exchange them for a Catholic bishop convicted of terror-related offenses and a few members of Palestinian organizations in Israeli hands. It was perhaps the first time that a Palestinian group also requested the return of their own killed in activities inside Israel.[5] That September 1974 incident was followed by a series of Palestinian terror actions aimed either at killing the largest number of Israelis possible or at taking hostages. The former peaked in 1974–1975 and most of those activities ended with a large number of Israeli casualties; however, almost all of the terrorists were also killed, bringing them only short-lived media attention but no long-term accomplishments. A former leader within the Popular Front for the Liberation of Palestine (PFLP), Wadi[c] Haddad, who had left the organization in 1973 to establish his own PFLP-External Operations (EO) organization, broke that chain by repeating the September 1970 air hijacking in which he had taken part—he initiated a hijacking in late June 1976 of an Air France plane from Tel Aviv to Paris, with a layover in Athens. The Israeli rescue operation to be analyzed later in this chapter did not put an end to the terrorists' old modus operandi, but rather extended the repertoire of all organizations into more types of operations not necessarily limited to hijackings.

The conditions in 1976 were utterly different from those of 1970 that included a strong Israeli coalition government. The cabinet was not in any position to make any decisions unless forced to. That is the usual status of any Israeli cabinet. However, even within that unholy tradition, the 1974–1977 Israeli seventeenth cabinet was an exception. This particular cabinet was formed in the wake of a high-level Commission of Inquiry for the 1973 War whose findings led to the resignation of the wartime prime minister and along with her the cabinet at large. The call of the day was to bring in only public figures who had not been involved in the 1973 decision-making process. Hence a significant number of its 1976 ministers were not members of the legislative branch and consequently lacked some of the bench's support needed to perform their duties. Rumors of alleged ministerial corruption were common, leading to a succession of criminal investigations and eventually to the resignation of the prime minister. Additionally, the public morale was low, considering Israel's perceived defeat in the 1973 War and continued terrorist activities against Israeli citizens. Overall, again, the 1976 Israel was very different from its September 1970 version. Back then Israel just barely ended the War of Attrition by a bleeding tie. Cooperation at that time with other international players in the wake of the U.S.-brokered August 1970 ceasefire could only bolster Israel's position among the nations and demonstrate that it was a legitimate participant in the War on Terror. In 1976 the hijackers unknowingly committed a strategic mistake by releasing all non-Israeli, non-Jewish hostages. In 1970 the hostages belonged to different nationalities; therefore no country could move without the consent of its partners in trouble. In 1976 Entebbe, Israel was able to take unilateral action in line with its self-assumed responsibility for all Jews, whether citizens or noncitizens of the country, because no third-party interests were involved. However, realizing that Israel was under international scrutiny, the chief military advocate prepared a legal document regarding the (future at that time) operation for the release of the hostages.[6]

Aside from security and foreign relations considerations, one should not underestimate Prime Minister Rabin's background—he had been Israel's ambassador to the United States (1968–1973) immediately after concluding his tenure as the military chief of staff (1964–1968), all of which familiarized him with the unyielding U.S. policy not to give in to hostage takers. Likewise, his ambassadorial term coincided with the U.S. war in Vietnam and the U.S. military effort to bring back its own without giving in to the other side.[7]

All of that and perhaps Israel's lost deterrence in the wake of 1973 strengthened the prime minister's basic ideology,[8] leading him to press for military action once the airplane was hijacked. In the absence of precautionary measures usually taken today (usually referred to as deterrence by denial) and the clear and immediate danger to the lives of 105 Israelis and non-Israeli Jews aboard the Air France plane hijacked to Entebbe, Uganda, Israel had no alternative but to deter by punishment: convincing would-be or potential attackers that the future cost to them would outweigh their advantages.[9] Giving in to the demands of the hijackers was not ruled out by the Israeli cabinet, but it would involve not only full Israeli surrender to their demands, but also international humiliation because the hijackers demanded the release of fifty-three of their own imprisoned in Israel and in four other countries.[10] The hijackers also prohibited any international organization's involvement, probably believing that they would ask the hijacking organization to implement some or even all international treaties governing such cases.[11] And yet, until the July 3 Israeli commandos' takeoff for a rescue operation, the cabinet was closer to surrender than to a military operation for lack of operational intelligence.[12] Two lines of pressure were building up between the hijacking and the military operation:

1. The military intelligence, using old operational planning in that area, spoke of the need to update the old information and planning through means available after a number of non-Jewish, non-Israeli hostages were released. That intelligence effort was carried out within the responsibilities of the Israeli intelligence community and did not necessitate any special permission.
2. The Israeli Air Force that was preparing in the post-1973 War period for any eventuality, far away or nearby, was confident of its ability to perform a combat mission far away from the Israeli borders.

In spite of all that, only minutes before the forces had to take off from Israel the special small ministerial task force gave its approval for the operation. The decision to negotiate with the terrorists that had been passed by a clear majority in the cabinet plenum had indeed been genuine. All ministers with the exception of the prime minister, circumventing the Minister of Defense, were confident that there was no other way. The prime minister, as mentioned, a former military man himself, assessed the risks involved and made his Minister of Defense a partner once he was convinced of the feasibility of the operation.[13] The IDF was unsuccessful until July 1, 1976, in its attempts to convince the Minister of Defense of the probability of a successful operation. Consequently, the minister continued to support a negotiated resolution of the crisis. The turning point came about on July 2, 1976, during a short meeting between the IDF Chief Infantry and Paratroopers Officer and the prime minister. Even without any declassified meeting records, it is evident from the speeding up of preparations that the senior officer got his conditional "green light," meaning that the Minister of Defense had abandoned in effect the negotiations approach. However, unknown to his colleagues, while approving the military approach the prime minister continued to publicly support the diplomatic track. In that way, he not only deceived the enemy but, under the utmost pressure to keep the operation secret until executed, he also misled his ministerial colleagues, a necessary move in light of the time-honored Israeli tradition of leaking secrets.

All throughout the Entebbe crisis a phenomenon reminiscent of the 1973 POW development accompanied the Israeli decision makers: a spontaneous organization of the families of the hostages who demonstrated at the gates of the Tel Aviv governmental-military compound (*hakiryah*), demanding that the government give in to all of the terrorists' demands, surrender, and bring back their loved ones.[14] It is hard to assess the effect that these demonstrations had on the decision makers, but clearly they had their effect on the personnel within the compound, who relayed the families' demands to the Israeli top echelons. The Entebbe operation concluded with a significant Israeli success: all hostages and troops returned home except for three civilians and one senior officer killed during the extraction battle. Yet considering the scores of hostages, the Entebbe incident became a turning point in post-1973 Israel. Its beaten self-esteem was cured to a large extent and consequently, in a reverse effect, Israel was once again perceived by friends and foes alike as a deterring power. Its readiness and ability to carry out daring activities reminiscent of the 1950s efforts in rescuing its own—and probably much more—spoke volumes. The Israeli cabinet's self-assurance is all the more admirable considering intelligence was lacking in spite of the massive Israeli intelligence community effort. After all, Uganda had never been an enemy country. Moreover, judging by the contemporary media and the cabinet ministers' attitudes, Israel, in a rare incidence of acting in its own interest as the ministers interpreted it, proceeded against a strong current in Israeli public opinion that pushed for giving in to get the hostages back.[15] The Entebbe success clearly foiled one of the main goals of Israel's adversaries: to undermine the enemy psyche, in this case Israel's, so that they would abandon their will to fight against the organizations and to stand as one in that confrontation.[16]

The impression of victory and deterrence did not last long. Terrorist activities, mainly from south Lebanon, began to take their toll on Israel. As the number of such activities grew, they became more and more daring and included all kinds of maneuvers intended to impose on Israel their diplomatic and military interests. In early April 1978, in the wake of the Litani Operation (Operation Forebear of Wisdom), a reprisal operation for the worst terror activity to be committed on Israeli soil with thirty-seven dead, five Israeli soldiers went missing in an area controlled by subnational actors: al-Fatḥ under Arafat's PLO and Jibril's organization. A few days later rumors surfaced that one of the missing, a reservist, was in the hands of the PFLP-GC, an organization not included under the PLO umbrella and thus dedicated not only to fighting Israel, but also to manifesting its lead over the PLO. The remaining soldiers were killed or managed to escape the scene without harm. Although unknown at the time, that capture would lead Israel into yet another modification in its policy: instead of attempting, unsuccessfully at times, to maintain the principle of a military rescue effort or at least a "one for one" approach, that incident would lead to the release of a large number of Palestinian organizations members from Israeli jails.

The timing of that incident and the following release negotiations were extremely significant. In May 1977, Israel elected a new prime minister of the central right Likud party. Unlike his public image as a warmonger and perhaps because of that, he took unprecedented moves in many areas a-typical of his previous public image. One of those concerned the issue of the Israeli reservist. His release about eleven months later created a series of precedents that, put together, symbolized a break with the past and that would serve in time as the foundation for future exchange deals that gradually raised the price Israel had to pay for its own. That particular deal, like those to follow, was first and foremost unlike any others in the past. Those deals with national actors were intended to bring about a relative success: bringing back the POWs while paying the least possible. Put differently: attempting to minimize the price while showing the other side that there had been no point in taking the Israeli prisoners. In this 1978/1979 episode (the soldier was kidnapped April 5, 1978, and exchanged March 14, 1979)[17] Israel was probably not looking for any diplomatic accomplishment. Behind the scenes, the Israeli Minister of Defense, a famous former commander of the air force, even conducted direct negotiations with the most violent of all Arab groups, Abu Nidal, in order to secure Abu Nidal's tacit agreement to the deal.[18] Concurrent with that, Israel continued its dialogue with all Palestinian groups through the mediating efforts of the ICRC. Israel even raised the issue of the bodies of the Israelis killed in action, but not MIAs, from the 1978 operation, which would resurface in 1982 in the context of the PLO withdrawal from Lebanon agreement.[19] In 1978 the only Israeli goal was to get the soldier back "to his mom."[20] Consequently, from the capture incident on, it was an asymmetrical game between a subnational player intent on a tangible accomplishment and a player interested in the humanitarian achievement of bringing back the soldier, nothing more.

That little known kidnapping episode in 1978/1979 tilted the balance in favor of the Lebanon-based Palestinian organizations. This time it was the combination of the audacity of the Palestinian organizations that would once again be demonstrated in 1982. In 1978/1979 it was the first kidnapping not to take place under the old Labor leadership, with the new administration clearly abandoning the military option first policy that had been the trademark of the Israeli policy up to 1977.

The exchange process was rather atypical of the subnational player as well because it involved the ICRC. Indeed, all players, the PFLP-GC, Israel, and the ICRC, had a clear interest in cooperating with the international organization. However, the indirect negotiations involved for the first time a dialogue between Israel and a substate actor, contrary to the traditional Israeli policy. The involvement of the ICRC only gave the international stamp of approval to that unprecedented step in the development of the Israeli POW policy. Actually, it was much more than that: Israel did try to impose an embargo on the details of the deal—but the embargo did not hold for long and became public with the government's tacit approval. The initial Israeli desire to withhold information was crystal clear: it was the first time that convicted terrorists were released, and as far as can be judged from contemporary evidence, no military action of any kind was contemplated. Moreover, the kidnapping took place only a few months after the historic visit of the Egyptian president to Jerusalem, and the deal was executed about ten days before the peace treaty between Israel and Egypt was signed in March 1979. All in all, the impression created was that the Israeli prime minister wanted a "clean slate" so that his mind would be free to deal with the emerging peace with Egypt.

Clearly, the prime minister's actions may indicate that he would take any step possible, whatever the price, in order to shed his image as a warmonger; he thereby put an end to the 1949–1977 policies in this regard. By putting humanitarian considerations first and pushing aside all national interests, he did perform a major service to the POWs' families, but he also managed to change Israeli policy and give away any power to deter or pose a threat as far as the enemy was concerned. The person in charge of POW affairs in the post-1982 Lebanon War stated years later that the 1979 deal projected weakness and constituted a mistake that would clearly affect future deals.[21] In spite of several attempts by future Israeli prime ministers to reverse that shift in policy, they did not succeed. Moreover, with the individual humanitarian approach prevailing, the field was opened for civil society organizations to press future cabinets not to abandon the new lines. The combination of an ever-growing exchange rate and assertive civil society organizations, in addition to aggressive public campaigns against the 1982 War and its consequences, would surely contribute to the steady erosion of Israel's undefined, fading, but very much present POW policy.

Against the backdrop of the deteriorating military and diplomatic Israeli position in relation to the PLO and other Palestinian organizations, in early June 1982 Israel launched the "Peace for Galilee" operation that turned within weeks into the "Lebanon War." That war led to over six hundred Israeli dead and an extended, bloody Israeli stay in parts of Lebanon until the complete withdrawal in 2000. During a series of Lebanon War–related incidents, Israel was forced to make a number of POW exchange deals. In the course of the Lebanon Wars (with the second being fought in 2006) and skirmishes, 1982 to 2011, several negotiations tracks developed:

1. With the Palestinian organizations, which can be divided into two tracks:
   a. the PLO
   b. the Popular Front for the Liberation of Palestine—General Command (PFLP-GC). The Palestinian Lebanese track ended with an exchange deal in 1991.
2. With Syria for the exchange of the 1982 POWs taken in the context of the Lebanon War.
3. With Shi'ite organizations since 1986.

During that period one POW case involved the Israeli-Hamas confrontation in the Gaza Strip.

Exchanging prisoners with the Palestinian organizations began during the actual fighting in 1982. Two Israelis, one of whom was a pilot captured by the PLO during the first stage of the war and the other an infantry reservist kidnapped from his position in August 1982, along with nine bodies, returned to Israel. In this case unlike most of the other POW exchange deals in the past Israel did have leverage with the PLO. It agreed to a U.S. proposal under which Israeli forces would withdraw from certain strategic locations in the Beirut area in exchange for a withdrawal of the fighting PLO members outside of Lebanon with the IDF taking no action against them. Considering the Israeli siege over parts of Beirut and the clear and immediate danger to the PLO forces, the organization had an interest in living up to the agreed upon conditions. Had Israel not been given back its own, the agreement might have been jeopardized, practically giving Israel an open pass to continue its activities against the Palestinian organization. Against that background Israel in a sense repeated the Syrian diplomatic maneuver of 1974 by threatening the PLO indirectly with total annihilation as long as the two prisoners were not returned.

Two episodes in the Lebanon context are still in a way affecting the Israeli decision-making process regarding POWs: the MIAs of the Sultan Ya'akub battle and the capture of eight soldiers in early September 1982.

The Sultan Ya'akub battle is to this day one of the mysteries haunting the IDF. It occurred on June 11, 1982, in the context of the Lebanon War and a military clash between Israeli and Syrian forces. At the end of the battle, six Israelis were declared MIA. The body of one of them was later returned to Israel, two were returned alive while three remain MIAs to this day. All Israeli efforts at exchanging its own since then have included the MIAs but to no avail. The two returned POWs were freed as part of larger deals (see below). The fate of the MIAs is still unknown; the late Syrian president Hafiz al-Asad was probably the only one who had the "key to the riddle."[22] This Syrian president passed away in 2000.

Not many days after the August 1982 exchange and the partial PLO withdrawal from Lebanon, a new chapter in the POW-related dialogue with the Palestinian organizations began. On September 4, 1982, a group of eight Israeli combatants deployed about fifteen miles east of Beirut surrendered to a PLO fighter without a single shot being fired.[23] It was perhaps the one and only case in Israel's POW chapter of military history in which high-ranking officers condemned the captured in strong language. The Israeli public uproar grew even stronger after the 1985 release of the six who had not been exchanged in 1983, when it became evident that the deal was almost singlehandedly accomplished through the efforts of the mother of one of the prisoners. To her he was her son; to the Israeli public he was one soldier whose price, hundreds of terrorists, might lead to more terrorist actions and grieving families. That short description should be supplemented here by the larger picture of players and their interests, at times conflicting, at times overlapping, which eventually produced the deal, whatever the price.

With the eight in PLO hands (two were later transferred to the PFLP-GC leaving the PLO with six), Israel continued its own collection of Palestinian prisoners in preparation for exchange negotiations. Through Israeli eyes, its own people wearing uniforms while being taken captive deserved to be defined as legal POWs. However, the thousands in Israeli hands were neither citizens of the country nor residents, and many of them were suspected of terrorist activities, though not convicted. Formally speaking, they did not match the Israelis held by the organizations. Convicted terrorists in Israeli jails were not equivalent either; therefore in spite of the Arab side's lack of interest in an exchange, the circumstances from 1982 on were different: the organizations were no longer keen on having their prisoners recognized as acting legally. The global recognition granted to the PLO starting in the summer of 1981 with a U.S.-brokered ceasefire between Israel and the PLO rendered such recognition useless. The summer 1982 evacuation from Beirut was also the result of American recognition, though only partial, of the PLO—full U.S. recognition would eventually come in 1988. Strangely enough, and very much in line with the Israeli position, that partial recognition was not extended to the status of the imprisoned PLO members. The chief U.S. military advocate informed Israel that the PLO prisoners did not meet the requirements for POW status.[24] However, the growing world recognition of the PLO made the matter of recognition through legalizing their captured members a rather marginal one. Furthermore, with the PLO headquarters moving to Tunis, the PLO campaign took a more diplomatic turn, aimed at presenting itself as the sole and legal representative of the Palestinian people. The organization's main focus shifted in the wake of the 1982 fighting to retrieving all Palestinians in Israeli jails, whether of Israeli, Jordanian, Lebanese, or any other citizenship, in order to demonstrate its role as Palestinian representative in the world arena. Considering the PLO's diplomatic and Israel's humanitarian interests, the Austrian Chancellor, Bruno Kreisky, volunteered to help. He was a true friend and ally of the PLO, having been a strong critic of Israel in spite of being Jewish himself. Yet he had, on humanitarian grounds, helped fleeing Soviet Jews arrive in Israel. His record led him to agree to mediate between Israel and the PLO in order to grant each side its wishes.[25] The Israeli prime minister, a known "hawk" and a strong supporter of the Israeli presence in the 1967 territories, appointed as his negotiator and personal representative a radical peace activist, Arieh Eliav, a former lieutenant colonel in the Israeli military who by that time advocated talks with the PLO. Ordinarily, that particular Israeli administration would have denied him any official position. Yet considering that the prime minister's main focus was humanitarian, not political, appointment was not only the right move, but also served to alleviate PLO concerns that the prime minister was planning some kind of last minute devious trick.

Between June and August 1982 as well as during the actual exchange with the PLO in November 1983, the captured Palestinians and foreign combatants were held in an improvised POW camp on Lebanese soil that was supervised on site by the ICRC.[26] One of the reasons for that particular location was the concern that their presence on sovereign Israeli territory would be an imposition on the Israeli government because the latter would have to apply Israeli criminal law instead of military regulations—a much easier system—in their treatment of the Palestinians. In early 1983 the Israeli government chief legal advocate (the chief civilian legal authority of the executive branch) visited the camp. Afterward he approved the delivery of the list of detainees to the ICRC as the initial step of a would-be deal.[27] The list was delivered in early April, sparking a wave of unfounded rumors of an imminent deal.[28] Judging from past deals, the list was not especially significant for the organizations, but it did provide a confidence-building measure intended to create the right diplomatic atmosphere for continuing the indirect negotiations.

One complicating element in reaching a deal was the fact that for "technical reasons"—not enough space in the PLO vehicle carrying the prisoners—two prisoners were handed over to representatives of the PFLP-GC. Relations between the two organizations were strained at best;

the PFLP-GC was not a member of the PLO and had actually initially refused to honor PLO commitments in regard to the 1981 temporary ceasefire with Israel.[29] However, because GC people in 1982 were probably closer to the scene, they received the two Israelis likely as a deposit until an exchange agreement was reached.[30] However, in spite of some messages from the GC to the PLO in May 1983 to that effect, eventually the organization opted for a separate deal with Israel. Perhaps at that point in time, in May 1983, the PFLP-GC interests did differ from those of the PLO. Whereas the latter aspired to a leadership role among all Palestinians, the former, under the inspiration and perhaps the guidance of Damascus, a perennial enemy of Arafat, was much more interested in demonstrating the superiority of its "revolutionary" way—that is, the armed struggle—over the PLO's approach. Moreover, because of the May 1983 Israeli-Lebanese agreement, Syria formed the National Salvation Front, composed of all anti-PLO players. Their main mission was to defeat the central Beirut government and present Syria and themselves as the true fighters for the Arab and Palestinian cause. Once again, the Israeli POW card was played.

As of November 1983 the PLO and the PFLP-GC had two separate delegations to Geneva for talks with the ICRC.[31] Even without any public statement reaffirming their official position, the international organization already de facto accepted both as legitimate partners in negotiations, to a large extent because Israel, having no alternative, was forced into that position. On the Israeli side the official talks were directed (as of July 1983)[32] by a Ministry of Defense emissary, Shmuel Tamir, an eminent Israeli lawyer and a former Minister of Justice, and by a representative of the IDF Manpower Directorate. Parallel to that Israel used the good services of Eliav, the left-wing politician, and the Austrian government. However, that channel was closed with the termination of Kreisky's term in May 1983.

Substantively, as he himself observed, there was not very much the Israeli negotiator could do. Contrary to his hopes, he found that the precedents hanging over Israel could not be modified diplomatically, and that they had a paralyzing effect when it came to negotiations for the release of POWs. The only issue to be resolved and the one to determine the fate of the POWs would not be price, because it had to be higher than before, but the nature of the convictions and the number and cruelty of the crimes.[33] Even though the negotiator saw that state of affairs as a mistake, there was nothing he could do about it. Giving away the people required by the other side became the rule. That approach, coupled with the Israeli assessment that they were in grave danger in northern Lebanon, their holding place, motivated Israel to conclude a deal.[34]

As expected, the November 1983 deal—six Israelis in PLO hands for the 4,500 imprisoned by Israel on Lebanese soil, and ninety-eight more in Israeli jails, exactly as demanded by the PLO—sparked once again an upheaval in Israeli public opinion. The Israeli government surrendered to all the PLO demands without extracting any political advantage whatsoever. Even the Israeli official explanation that its POWs were in grave danger in Lebanon did not help. The deal did mark a change from the past, considering the so-called quality and makeup of the returned Palestinians. First, the number of released enemy fighters rose from seventy-six (1979) to about six hundred; second, many were convicted terrorists who had committed multiple killings; third, many of them were at an age that made it evident to the Israeli authorities that they would be active again within their respective organizations; and finally, some of the released were from Israel, meaning that in an indirect way Israel accepted the PLO formula that it was representing the Palestinian "within"—namely Arab citizens of Israel. The feelings of frustration in Israel were not limited to the general public. They infiltrated and were echoed in the Knesset chamber on November 29, 1983, when its members discussed the deal.[35] Even though they voted to approve the move, it was clear from the session minutes that a majority of the house did indeed reject the deal, but obviously could not vote against the coalition government that they belonged to.

The deal did not include Syria, which had played only a marginal role during the first Lebanon War. It became directly involved again after the war by continuing to serve as the main backer of the PFLP-GC, from armaments and money to shelter for its own Israeli POWs. However, in the context of that war Syria came to hold six Israeli POWs and five casualties who died in combat.[36] They were all returned to Israel in late June 1984 after the usual torture by their captors, thanks to the mediation efforts of an Austrian negotiator and the ICRC.[37] As most of the documentation related to the 1982 through 1984 Israeli-Syrian exchange negotiations is still closed to the public, suffice it to say that the outcome was not too different from any past negotiations: all living POWs and the dead from both sides were fully exchanged. In exchange for the Israelis, Syria received 312 of its own who had been in captivity since June 1982 during the Lebanon conflict. At that time Israel held 5,907 prisoners (including the Syrians) from a variety of countries, including Bangladesh, Egypt, Pakistan, Jordan, and others.[38] All of them would gradually be released in the weeks and months to come.

In line with its separate approach, Ahmad Jibril's PFLP-GC let the two prisoners in its hands signal that they were alive by taping and later broadcasting a short clip on Austrian TV. The choice of Austria was first and foremost intended to grant the Austrian mediator working under the direct authority of the Austrian chancellor some leverage with Israel. Moreover, it was meant to help the mother of one of the Israelis in her public attempts to force the Israeli cabinet into paying whatever the price was for her son.[39] The Israeli reaction came on two levels: the Israeli negotiator expressed satisfaction at the release of the video clip, but mentioned that even though proof of life had been an Israeli condition it was still far from meeting any of the other (unspecified) demands of Israel.[40] Two other publicly known conditions were: first, the simultaneous withdrawal of the 40,000 Syrian troops and 10,000 Palestinian fighters as well as the 30,000 Israelis from Lebanon[41]; and second, the Israeli agreement to return the archives of the Institute of Palestine Studies captured in Beirut upon the return of the POWs.[42] The former director of the IDF Directorate of Manpower, in charge of the POWs on behalf of the IDF, was more specific. For the first time during the indirect negotiations, he indicated that Israel would agree to release six hundred Palestinians for each of its own held by the organizations.[43] The Israeli Minister of Foreign Affairs stated for his part from the Knesset podium that Israel was negotiating with the U.S. IDF deployment changes in Lebanon.[44] Considering that it was a first public step in what was expected to be a tough process, the officer's proposal actually offered almost ten times the price paid for the return of the reservist in 1978. That public position also meant that at least the military accepted the idea that each deal would mean higher prices than the previous one. That position triggered a public debate in Israel that has not ended to this day, while the quid pro quo for future deals did indeed increase from one deal to another.

In November 1983 in the wake of the Israel-PLO deal, Jibril charged that it had been conducted without his knowledge or participation because Arafat was more interested in his prestige than in representing all Palestinians held by Israel.[45] As expected, the interorganizational rivalry between the PLO and the PFLP-GC meant that the prices paid to the PLO in November 1983 would serve only as a new starting point for the next talks with the PFLP-GC. Unsurprisingly, that turned out to be the case. Clearly, the Israel-PFLP-GC negotiations developed on a separate track, totally independent from the Israel-PLO way. Considering that the PFLP-GC was a client of Syria and its long arm in confronting Israel (a position to be later taken over by Hizbullah), Israel believed that Syria might have information regarding the Sultan Ya'akub MIAs, and perhaps even living prisoners or bodies. The organization, in line with the traditional behavior of Israel's foes, kept its mouth shut. Only with the Israeli capture of the PFLP-GC's leader's nephew did its commander indicate in rather indirect language that his organization was holding one of the MIAs. But there was much more. That capture opened the door to intensified talks between Israel and the organization. Strangely enough, the next move was not only initiated by Israel, but it also came through a phone call from Israel to the direct and unlisted phone number of Jibril. The Israeli message was clear: Israel would release the nephew and his driver in exchange for the two soldiers (part of the group of eight; six returned by the PLO). The organization rejected the deal but did not rule out holding negotiations with Israel.[46] In the wake of the conversation Israel became more convinced, although not fully, that the two soldiers along with one of the Sultan Ya'akub's MIAs were in Jibril hands.[47] Later, in April 1984, in order to apply additional pressure to Israel, a spokesman for the organization announced in Damascus that a Druze soldier, declared MIA since April 1983, was also held by the organization.[48]

In June 1984 Israel and Syria exchanged prisoners, as discussed earlier, but the latter made it clear that it was acting on its own and had nothing to do with its protégé, the PFLP-GC. This way and in the wake of the November 1983 PLO deal, the three-front post–Lebanon War POW negotiations (PLO, Syria, and the PFLP-GC) was down to one: the PFLP-GC. Israel was anxious to complete the process and Jibril was only too intent on demonstrating his advantage over all other Arab parties—especially Arafat. Most of the dealings were carried out during the twenty-first Israeli cabinet (September 1984–October 1986) that was equally divided between the two leading Israeli parties, the center right led by Yitzhak Shamir and the center left led by Shimon Peres. With the participation of the former prime minister, Yitzhak Rabin, who was at the time the Minister of Defense, they formed what came to be known as "the Prime Ministers Club." All major decisions had to be approved by that forum, as well as instructions for the negotiators for the release of the people held by Jibril.

In July 1984 after continued efforts by the Austrian mediator, the PFLP-GC conveyed pictures of the prisoners. That was followed by a visit from an ICRC representative with the prisoners in Damascus. Within that context, a spokesman for the PFLP-GC declared that it was ready for an exchange, obviously on the organization's terms. The primary condition was that the released PFLP-GC members be allowed to return to their homes in the territories.[49] Those signals were well received by Israel and in September negotiations between the two antagonists began in Geneva with the participation of the ICRC. However, the positions were too far apart and within ten days the Israeli delegation left the table with no tangible outcome. Israel, in a rather unprecedented but creative way, let the detainees in its hands write to their families expressing their frustration with Jibril.[50] Moreover, Israel manifested at that point some united bipartisan appearance that meant that the Israeli media, so against the war in Lebanon, could not be successful in shifting the government policy in the PFLP-GC direction. That would happen later in the Hizbullah context but not in 1984–1985. It is difficult to impossible to know if that resilient Israeli position did affect the PFLP-GC. However, the Palestinian organization did behave as though it needed the exchange as much as Israel did. In October, Kreisky, the former Austrian chancellor, the person who guided the Austrian mediator, conveyed upon his return from Damascus the organization's interest in an exchange to include the three Israelis as well as four thousand Palestinians incarcerated in Israeli jails.[51] That marked a change in the organization's position: while offering Israel its wish, it challenged the Israeli judicial system. The organization demanded, in effect, that the verdicts of four thousand convicted Palestinians be overturned and that they be freed. In other words, granting Jibril his demands would mean that Israeli verdicts were only valid until the next round of exchanges, considering that any deal could serve as a precedent for the next one. It is evident that Jibril's demands could not be interpreted in any other way because at that time Israel held in its detention center on Lebanese soil only one thousand people. Whatever the calculation it had to include prisoners within Israel proper.[52]

It is evident that once the PLO deal was concluded the negotiations with Jibril were about the number of people to be released by Israel. That was also clear to Jibril who added some more demands to his list: opening a university in the territories and completely closing the detainees' camp in Lebanon.[53] Israel for its part insisted that all released would not be allowed to stay where they lived prior to their arrest, whether in Israel or in the territories. That precedent set in 1979 would be repeated in almost all future deals with Palestinian organizations. Another precedent, starting in 1979, was the release of convicted murderers. All in all, the 1985 Jibril exchange did not create new precedents. However, releasing 1,150 convicted terrorists, many of them responsible for lost lives in Israel under heinous circumstances, sparked public fury in Israel to the degree that to this day it is wrongly depicted as the most expensive deal ever. Indeed, the number and nature of the felonies were unprecedented, but otherwise it did not create any major precedents. That would happen in the next stage: the confrontation with radical Islam as embodied by Hizbullah and Hamas. Yet the repetition of past behaviors suggested that Israel did indeed abandon its declared but not implemented traditional policy of not negotiating with terrorists. That projected an image of a declining power in the war on terror and did show the PFLP-GC to be the clear victor in the deal.[54] The overall outcome of the deal left no alternative for the government representative in charge of POW affairs but to resign in protest. He did not necessarily oppose the price that, as mentioned, was not higher in number and quality from past deals, but he believed that Israel surrendered to all of Jibril's demands without even giving the appearance of some diplomatic or other accomplishment.[55] The internal Israeli debate has never stopped since 1985 regarding the logic of the "Jibril deal," which not only freed over one thousand terrorists, some of whom were Israeli citizens, but in effect caused the loss of those later killed by the released and contributed to the emergence of experienced Palestinian leadership that led to the 1987 uprising in the territories.[56]

By mid-1974 all known October War POW issues were resolved with the exception of the MIAs, some cases still lingering to this day. The theater of operations changed. No more symmetrical interstate conflict, but rather a war by proxy changed at times into an asymmetrical confrontation between Israel and Palestinian or Lebanese organizations—none a signatory to the Geneva Convention.

The years between 1974 and 1985 were marked by two processes:

1. An ongoing Arab effort to internationally embarrass Israel and through that to be recognized as a legitimate actor on the Middle Eastern front—including the right to get POW treatment for their captured members. The formal demand for POW status was relinquished during those years. The Israeli consent to deal with the Palestinian organizations, directly or indirectly, clearly meant a degree of indirect Israeli recognition of the organizations and clearly led the ICRC to create some symmetry between Israel and the organizations: their people were not POWs but their cases were treated as such.
2. A continued and yet reinforced effort to drag into the Middle East conflict more international players and to create conditions that would leave them no alternative but to adopt non-Israeli positions. The 1976 incident in Entebbe, Uganda, clearly falls into that category.

A 1978 meeting between the prime minister and the mother of a captured soldier, atypical of the years before 1973 and even unthinkable before 1967, probably had an effect on the decision to pay an unprecedented price for that POW. From that moment on, the slippery slope, namely the departure from old, continued. The principle of returning all for all so prevalent in deals with sovereign states, even though it took much military and diplomatic effort to extract it, was abandoned. Not only has the number increased, but so has the burden of the released, including people responsible for massacre reminiscent of atrocities during some of the bloodiest wars. More worrying to the Israeli government was the fact that because the talks, usually indirect, were held in secret, the Israeli public refrained from voicing its position in a democratic way, clearing a path for certain interest groups to voice their positions unchallenged. One of the reasons for that situation was the overall public and media frustration with the war and consequently the general rejection of anything associated with the war. To some extent it was a reminder of the political dimension of the post-Vietnam era in the United States. Under these circumstances a beleaguered administration not only had to defend itself for the Israeli presence in Lebanon, but also had, pushed by public opinion shapers, to pay any price to the other side. Those prices would as usual serve only as a springboard once Hizbullah became the main enemy of Israel in the Lebanese arena.

NOTES

1. *Davar*, June 7, 1974.
2. *Davar*, June 14, 1974.
3. Cf. Rex A. Hudson, "Dealing with International Hostage-Taking—Alternatives to Reactive Counterterrorist Assaults," Terrorism 12, no. 5 (1989): 321–78.
4. Andrew Mack, "Why Big Nations Lose Small Wars: The Politics of Asymmetric Conflict," *World Politics* 27, no. 2 (January 1975): 175–200.
5. *Davar*, September 5, 1974.
6. IDFA/22/2009/8, July 1976.
7. Cf. for instance, Jerry L. Thigpen, *The Praetorian STARShip: The Untold Story of the Combat Talon* (Maxwell Air Force Base, Alabama: Air University Press, 2001).
8. Rabin's speech in the Israeli Knesset, session 89, May 27, 1985, http://knesset.gov.il/tql/knesset_new/knesset11/HTML_27_03_2012_05–59–19- PM/19850527@ 19850527001 @ 001.html.
9. This terminology is borrowed from Janice Gross and Ron Levi, "The Social Psychology of Denial: Deterring Terrorism," *New York University Journal of International Law and Politics* 47, no. 2 (January 2015): 409–38; cf. Jeffrey D. Berejikian, "A Cognitive Theory of Deterrence," *Journal of Peace Research* 39, no. 2 (2002): 165–83.
10. ISA/K/225/4, minutes of the Knesset session 3, meetings 313–316, Prime Minister Rabin's speech, July 4, 1976; see also ISA/FM/8484/10.
11. IDFA/IDF Operations Directorate/History Division, *" Secret" De-Briefing of Operation Jonathan, 3–4 July 1976*, November 1977, 9, http://www.archives.mod.gov.il/pages/exhibitions/yonatan/yonatan.pdf; cf. Renée de Nevers, "Modernizing the Geneva Conventions," *Washington Quarterly* 29, no. 2 (2006): 99–113.
12. *" Secret" De-Briefing of Operation Jonathan*.
13. It is alluded to, but not stated in so many words, in the chronology annex of ibid.
14. ISA/FM/8484/14, from Jerusalem to all representations, media digest, July 1, 1976.
15. Cf. Robert Putnam, "Diplomacy and Domestic Politics: The Logic of Two-Level Games," *International Organization* 42 (1988): 427–60; Editorial, *Davar*, July 1, 1976.
16. William S. Lind, Keith Nightengale, Jhon F. Schmitt, Joseph W. Sutton, and Gary I. Wilson. "The Changing Face of War: Into the Fourth Generation," *Marine Corps Gazette* 85, no. 11 (2001): 24–68.
17. *The Globe and Mail*, March 15, 1979; *Davar*, March 15, 1979.
18. [UK] NA/FCO93/2231/NFX/054/1/January 26, 1977, from Tel Aviv, to London.
19. [State department correspondence], From U.S. ambassador, Tel Aviv, to Secretary of State, Washington, August 19, 1982, 82/9275974, CIA Records Search Tool (CREST), National Archives and Records Administration, College Park, MD.
20. *NRG*, July 8, 2006, http://www.nrg.co.il/online/1/ART1/445/660.html; *NRG*, February 27, 2014, http://www.mynet.co.il/articles/0,7340,L-4493162,00.html.
21. Shmuel Tamir, *The Son of This Country, Autobiography* [Hebrew] (Lod: Zmora-Bitan, 2002), 1501.
22. General Vilnai, *Ma'ariv*, June 27, 1986.
23. *Ma'ariv*, October 3, 2003.
24. *Davar*, January 13, 1983.
25. *Christian Science Monitor*, December 29, 1982.
26. *Divre ha-Knesset* (Hebrew: Israeli Parliament Minutes), session 29, December 10, 1984.
27. *Davar*, March 25, 1983.
28. *Davar*, April 10, 1983.
29. *Boston Globe*, July 26, 1981; *The Globe and Mail*, July 29, 1981; *Christian Science Monitor*, April 15, 1982; cf. Ali Sadeghi, "Lebanon and After: Whose Victory?," Millennium—Journal of International Studies 13, no. 1 (March 1984) : 7.
30. *Davar*, May 2, 1983.

31. *Davar*, November 25, 1983.
32. *Ha'aretz*, May 21, 1985.
33. Cf. Tamir, *The Son of This Country*, 1501.
34. *Yediot Aharonot*, June 29, 1984.
35. *Divre ha-Knesset*, session 252, November 29, 1983.
36. *Awake at Night*, Israeli Association for Released POWs, the story of Captain Gill Fogel, http://www.erim-pow.co.il/article.php?id=31.
37. *Philadelphia Daily News*, June 28, 1983.
38. Knesset, session 103, June 29, 1982, 43.
39. *Davar*, May 2, 1983; *Ma'ariv*, May 2, 1983.
40. *Davar*, May 3, 1983.
41. *Philadelphia Daily News*, June 15, 1983.
42. Minister of Defense, Arens, response to a parliamentary motion in the Israeli Knesset, *Divre ha-Knesset*, session 229, May 27, 1983.
43. *Ma'ariv*, May 30, 1983.
44. Shamir's speech in the Israeli Knesset, session 215, June 20, 1983.
45. *Davar*, November 25, 1983.
46. Tamir, *The Son of This Country*, 1519–20.
47. *Davar*, December 29, 1983.
48. *Ma'ariv*, April 4, 1984.
49. *Ma'ariv*, July 9, 11, 1984.
50. Tamir, *The Son of This Country*, 1528.
51. *Ma'ariv*, October 8, 1984.
52. *Divre ha-Knesset*, session 29, December 10, 1984.
53. Rabin's speech, *Divre ha-Knesset*, session 89, May 27, 1985.
54. Cf. *Christian Science Monitor*, May 30, 1985; from [CIA], Tel Aviv, to Director, Foreign Broadcast Information Service, Washington, June 1, 1985, MTA-6005, CIA Records Search Tool (CREST), National Archives and Records Administration, College Park, MD.
55. *Ma'ariv*, June 14, 1985.
56. See, for instance, *Ma'ariv*, May 8, 1986; Knesset session 201, May 19, 1986; *Boston Globe*, May 22, 1985; Assaf Sagiv, "Preface: The Significance of the 'Silver Plate,'" *Tchelet* [Hebrew: Azure] (Winter 2008): 7.

TWELVE

Subnational Actors Taking Center Stage in the POW Context

1986 to 2011

Perhaps the cumulative impact of the period from 1982 to 1985 was its contribution to an emerging picture in which Israel released increasing numbers of prisoners, more and more of whom were convicted of serious crimes. The last deal of that stage, the Jibril deal, was probably the last deal to this day with a Lebanon-based Palestinian organization involving Israelis captured in Lebanon. The extended Israeli stay in southern Lebanon, lasting eighteen years (1982–2000), resulted in several Israeli POWs and MIAs on top of hundreds of dead. The first in that chain of POWs/MIAs—and the first of its kind—was the 1986 abduction of two Israeli soldiers on a convoy-securing mission. All previous Israeli captured were lost during times of battle, even the eight who were captured in early September 1982 in a "kidnapping by opportunity" (see chapter 11). That means that the Palestinian organization had not planned the capture of the Israelis in advance. The opportunity presented itself and they took it. However, the kidnapping of the two soldiers in February 1986 was preplanned. A short while after that incident, an organization affiliated with Hizbullah claimed responsibility and demanded an immediate Israeli withdrawal from a certain part of Lebanese territory. Failing to meet their demand would result, the organization threatened, in the immediate execution of the two hostages.[1] As the two were captured only nine months after the Jibril deal, the fallout from that deal was still fresh. Because the cabinet was still based on a widespread national unity government, any public calls for action to effect the release of the two could be brushed off. Furthermore, the Shi'ite organization was very careful not to indicate to any foreign power whether the soldiers were alive or dead. Even though it caused the families agony, the cabinet was not eager to advance an exchange not only because of the preceding deal, but also because the Israelis were not willing to pay full price for bodies, as opposed to living human beings. The only immediate tactical response came from the military Northern Command, which adopted what it termed *the Hannibal Directive*. Later that directive became the general IDF code of action in cases of a soldier kidnappings. In short, it details the order of actions to be taken in the event of a kidnapping, including measures to be taken to avert smuggling of the hostage.[2] Those instructions have generated much discussion within and outside of the military—particularly as to whether they allowed a friendly hostage to be shot dead in order to prevent his or her falling into enemy hands.

Later that year, the case of the two soldiers became a cause célèbre when an air force navigator, Ron Arad, who had to leave his plane in October 1986 was captured in Lebanon. Even though the early stages of this particular crisis looked familiar, the identity of the capturing organization was known,[3] and the price was clear (all Lebanese citizens in Israeli hands), no deal was concluded. The reasons for that are shrouded with mystery to this day. The most common guess as to the navigator's whereabouts suggests that because Israel did not accept the conditions of the Shi'ite organization (Amal) in time, the navigator was transferred to a more radical organization (Hizbullah); since then, no clue has ever been found regarding his fate. None of the exchange deals with Hizbullah that followed included the navigator, and no concrete details about him have ever found their way to Israel.

As early as January 1987, Israel, lacking any information about the navigator, appealed to the ICRC, which also knew nothing about him—not even if he was alive or if he was possibly being held for future deals.[4] A partial answer would be provided with an Israeli counter-move, abducting, years later, one of the people who had been involved in the capture of the aviator. Contacting the ICRC in early 1987 was not surprising: by that time and based on its cumulative experience in dealing with the Palestinian organizations, the ICRC was already accepted as a convenient, although not fully trusted, partner for Israel in deals negotiations. The ICRC, while not recognizing any of the Lebanese organizations in a de jure fashion, accepted all of them as legitimate partners by that time. As mentioned above, that gave the Lebanese factions full benefits without any disadvantages; they were exempt from the stipulations of the Geneva Convention, yet their irregular combatants were granted equal treatment to that of Geneva signatories—including, most significantly, Israel.

In spite of the growing number of Israeli casualties in Lebanon, no Israeli prisoners were taken between 1986 and 2000. The two 1986 soldiers were abducted in an organized Hizbullah operation, but the navigator fell into Shi'ite hands by chance. His plane was not shot down from the ground because the organization had no such equipment—it was a technical difficulty that forced it down. It is clear even from open sources, because no classified material is still available, that Israel made every possible effort to verify the navigator's whereabouts.

Meanwhile, in early 1987, a previously unknown organization demanded that Israel release four hundred Arab prisoners in exchange for four U.S. citizens incarcerated in Lebanon. The demand was rejected right away by the National Unity cabinet Minister of Defense, who stated that Israel would not turn into a prisoners' bank. The leader of an Israeli-backed South Lebanon militia was not completely opposed to the idea and suggested a three-way deal under which he would release the Lebanese he was holding—which would also involve the navigator and the two other Israeli prisoners.[5] Strangely enough, Israel did not respond positively to that idea—perhaps because it had no independent confirmation that its two soldiers were alive and because it assumed the navigator was in the hands of the less radical Shi'ite organization, Amal, led by a Lebanese holding U.S. citizenship.[6] Pressure from this organization, later augmented by Iran, continued well into 1988 but was unsuccessful.[7] It is also quite possible that Israel's resistance was connected to the U.S. policy of not giving in to terrorists and that it was meant to show the organization that it could not benefit from its actions.[8]

From the time of the navigator's capture to the summer of 1989 (and even later, as will be explained below) Israel had no credible intelligence regarding its captives in Hizbullah hands. It did have some shreds of information with no operative meaning. It was also constantly in danger of being drawn into the issues of other prisoners in Lebanon who were less able to withstand international pressure. To counter these circumstances, the Minister of Defense, who had been prime minister and the galvanizing power behind the Ugandan rescue operation, seized the moment in an attempt to bring back the long gone bargaining chips policy. Under his guidance and the unequivocal go ahead of the prime minister—a veteran of the Israeli secret services—Israeli commandos abducted the spiritual leader of Hizbullah from his home, about twenty-five miles northeast of the border with Israel, in late July 1989. The kidnapping had two main purposes: acquiring intelligence related to the navigator and holding the Hizbullah leader for future deals.[9] That move was very much in line with Rabin's traditional policy that a military rescue operation was the best alternative, but if that was impossible the "chips" should be significant enough to ensure an acceptable deal for both sides. However, the U.S. president reacted somewhat unfavorably to the Israelis' kidnapping the Shi'ite leader from home. That led to a phone conversation between the prime minister and the president that ended without a reprimand by the president.[10] It was clear that neither party knew whether the prisoners were dead or alive and that the president, in spite of his continued strained relations with the prime minister, was much more forthcoming in this case than he was on any other Israel-related topic during his presidency.

The kidnapping operation bolstered the image of Israel for a while as a deterring power. However, the intelligence value of the prisoner was low, and efforts to free the three Israelis did not benefit from that episode. The first reaction to the kidnapping from the Lebanese side came in the form of an offer by the "Revolutionary Justice Organization," a front name for Hizbullah, and later by Hizbullah officials, to exchange a U.S. hostage for the spiritual leader and 450 Lebanese and Palestinian prisoners in Israeli hands.[11] For Israel that was a nonstarter; any deal had to include all missing Israelis, including the navigator. Moreover, almost four years had passed since the capture of the two soldiers and officially Israel had no indication whether they were dead or alive. At this juncture, with the Shi'ite prisoner refusing to compromise any information on the hostages, the U.S. administration felt that Israel had too much leverage and that perhaps this was the time to finally get Israel to agree to a deal that would involve the American hostages, ignoring the Israelis. As long as the National Unity coalition held, there was a unified front supporting the prime minister's opposition to such a move. The Minister of Defense was the Labor Party minister whom the prime minister most respected; he in turn provided a "safety net" for the prime minister—or his full backing.

All of that changed in March 1990 when Labor ended its alliance with the prime minister's party and dissolved the coalition. With that, Israel, lacking support for its prime minister from domestic players, was also exposed to continued pressure from a rather unfriendly U.S. administration. The almost immediate result of the 1990 political tremors was Israel's use of incarcerated Arabs as a political tool detached from POW issues. That led to the release of some four hundred Arab prisoners "as part of Arens's' [the new Minister of Defense] plan to coax Palestinians into peace talks."[12] In early August 1990 the Iraqi leader, Saddam Hussein, invaded Kuwait and POW/MIA issues went to the bottom of the list of priorities until May 1991, along with preparations for a conference intended to discuss peace in the Middle East that would eventually be held in Madrid (from October 30 to November 1, 1991). The preparations involved state actors, with the Palestinians participating as part of the Jordanian delegation. The Lebanese situation, including Iran's involvement through Hizbullah, was only marginally on the agenda. Consequently, Hizbullah and its Iranian patron continued their activity with regard to Israeli and Western hostages/prisoners on their own—trying, as in the past, to represent the Palestinian prisoners issue as well. Israel for its part was skeptical about the upcoming international peace conference, fearing a world tribunal against Israel. For a short time, the interests of Iran, its proxy, Syria, their proxy, Hizbullah, and Israel, were in accord. Realizing that in May 1991 a team of State Department and CIA counterterrorism officials visited Damascus, and at the end of the month leading to Hizbullah declaring its readiness to exchange POWs. Although not publicly stated, the CIA director clearly indicated that the deal would include thirteen Westerners held in Lebanon and two Israelis.[13]

As optimistic as it seemed, the three-way understanding did not include the third missing Israeli—the navigator. Careful reading of an interview with Admiral Stansfield Turner, a former director of the CIA (1977–1981), suggests that Israel's Shamir administration, lacking broad political backing at home and under heavy pressure by the unsympathetic President H. W. Bush, gave in and agreed in June 1991 to a three-way deal—which it found not entirely acceptable—involving only the two Israelis.[14] Considering that the U.S. administration put Israel at that time in a number of situations that made it uneasy and that the Israeli prime minister wanted to minimize any confrontation, it stands to reason that—because the current issues, in his view, could hardly compare to those of war and peace and the future of the Jewish state—he did indeed agree to a move that was inconsistent with his way of thinking and that he would not have agreed to under different conditions. Yet in spite of the prime minister's initial consent and the subsequent release of two more hostages in mid-August,[15] Israel ultimately stood its ground. Its main public precondition was information regarding the navigator.[16] That position was reinforced by a secret inner cabinet resolution "that no prisoner would be released unless Hizbullah provided solid information about seven Israeli servicemen captured in Lebanon."[17]

At that point, in mid-August 1991, with the international conference looming closer and closer, the date it would convene set for October 30, 1991, the UN secretary general embarked on a shuttle mission between Jerusalem, Tehran, and Geneva (the ICRC headquarters) and backed by the United States. His main point made in Jerusalem was that Israel should make a *gesture*. That term in prisoner exchange negotiations meant either releasing Arab and Lebanese prisoners without any quid pro quo or accepting the possibility of a partial exchange—partial meaning no physical exchange of the aviator or of information about him. For Israel that constituted no possible starting point whatsoever. The prime minister's position, supported by the leading opposition party, the Labor Party, and Israeli public opinion, was that Israel was not open to any deal without the navigator. The prime minister was concerned that building international pressure on Israel might negatively affect what he saw as the approaching court martial in Madrid, the venue of the international conference. He therefore let his chief negotiator, an old hand in Arab affairs, hold a press conference.

On September 12 the negotiator, who on most days served as the Israeli chief liaison to Lebanon, informed the international and local media of a new deal: Israel had received the body of a Druze captured in

March 1983 as well as the single piece of information that one of the soldiers kidnapped in 1986 was dead. In exchange, Israel released a senior member of the Democratic Front for the Liberation of Palestine (DFLP), allowing him to return to the territories in Israeli hands, in addition to nine bodies of Hizbullah members. It also authorized the release of fifty-one prisoners held by the Israeli-backed "South Lebanon Army." Still, there was no word on the fate of one abducted Israeli soldier and the aviator.[18] The deal continued to unfold for a while with the setting free of two more Western hostages in mid-November 1991.[19] That intricate deal was unique in that it involved a large number of actors all agreeing all on its unusual design, including the UN secretary general vying for a part in the ongoing diplomatic moves for future peace in the region; the United States, which wanted its own released while continuing its policy of not negotiating with hijackers and certainly not paying them for their criminal actions; Israel, which was eager for any prisoner to get home, whether alive or dead, and in great need of any intelligence regarding the navigator; and of course Hizbullah, which once again proved by securing the participation of the DFLP that it had become the leading spokesman for the Palestinians, at a time when the PLO, "the sole and legitimate representative of the Palestinian people," was struggling to secure an independent seat in the upcoming Madrid peace negotiations. That deal also marked a break between the DFLP leader, Hawatmeh, and his second in command, who in the changing atmosphere shifted his loyalty from the organization to the PLO. As the split above makes clear, the September deal confirmed the existence of two clear-cut factions and political camps among the organizations active against Israel in 1991: those who preferred going to Madrid and those who believed in the armed struggle and in using diplomacy only in order to extract more concessions from Israel.

The Madrid conference and the negotiations on the Palestinian issue that followed, the Labor victory in the June 1992 general elections, the Oslo accords in September 1993, and the subsequent peace treaty with Jordan (October 1994) all moved the public's attention from the POW issue to other highly significant events and processes. From time to time sporadic pieces of information about the missing soldiers surfaced, but the overall feeling on the Israeli side was that all three (the two abducted and the aviator) were dead and therefore the desired deal should include bodies on both sides. Israel also believed at that time that because Hizbullah was the long arm of Iran, that country should be approached directly. However, some seeds of future developments were planted during this period. The visit of the Iranian foreign intelligence service to Germany in October 1993 and his reception by the German chancellor presumably opened new doors for Israel.[20] German involvement in Israeli-related POW deals began in 1980 and continued until 2004,[21] undoubtedly providing Germany with some moral basis for its growing interests in the

Middle East and in Iran above all. On the one hand, Germany did carry on significant trade with Iran; on the other, it wanted the world, especially successive U.S. administrations until 2014, to know that its relations with Iran could serve as the basis for future agreements—not the least of which could generate humanitarian help for Israel in getting back its POWs.[22] That policy culminated in some indirect Israeli-Iranian talks regarding the navigator held in Bonn since 1993, and in spite of early encouraging indications did not produce a deal. At about that time, in the early 1990s, official Israel was close to concluding that the navigator did not survive his captivity. Whether an official decision has been made or not is unclear. However, it is evident from the bits and pieces of information available today that from the failure of successive attempts to locate and later to retrieve him, Israel concluded that he may not only have died in captivity, but also that the number of people responsible for his imprisonment was so small that perhaps most or even all of them had perished during the violent Lebanese domestic confrontations.

Israel believed that "snatching a tongue" (kidnapping someone in the know from a hostile territory in operational jargon) might resolve the doubts and lead to either finding the necessary operational details to enable a rescue operation or an exchange deal or to verify that the aviator was indeed dead and consequently, if possible, that his body would be included in a body-for-body deal. As usual, the last word had to be spoken by the prime minister, the same leader who was responsible for the Entebbe rescue operation and had tried since to lower the price of the deals while building up some Israeli deterrence in this context. Moreover, his warm relations with the U.S. president on top of the precedent set between the former prime minister and the former president, approving that policy retroactively, served in his favor. In late May 1994 Israeli commandos once again crossed into Lebanese territory, about fifty miles to the north of the Israeli border, and abducted the chief operations officer of the Amal organization who held the airman during his first couple of years in captivity. It was a daring operation but politically unsuccessful. By that time the Lebanese official had already transferred the navigator to another organization, probably to the Revolutionary Guards, the long arm in Lebanon of the Iranian regime. The prisoner was captured in 1986, moved to Iran by proxy in 1988 or 1989, and the Shi'ite leader Karim Ubayd when brought to Israel in 1994 only had old information regarding his whereabouts. Indeed, the operation once again boosted the deterrence aspect of Israeli capabilities and presented its fighters as courageous, but that was beside the point. Israel was no wiser after May 1994 than before. It tried to save face and waited for any future prisoners' exchange in order to get rid of what had become a political burden rather than an intelligence gold mine. It is significant that Ubayd was kidnapped during the term of a national unity coalition government led by Prime Minister Shamir of Likud and Rabin as his Minister of Defense; the

1994 kidnapping was carried out by a cabinet led by the prime minister and Minister of Defense, Rabin. He was also the motivating power behind the Entebbe raid previously discussed in this book. It is evident that Rabin's policies, not always aligned with changing public opinion, were clear-cut and consistent: as long as there was a viable military option, that was the option he preferred. Consequently, his instructions to the military in 1989 and 1994 were intended to reverse the ill effects of the policy that had been developing since 1979. However, his inclination to repeat the 1950s/1960s policies by securing "bargaining chips" ran into unexpected snags.

In another military act, Rabin ordered a rescue operation for a soldier, Nahason Waxman, abducted by Hamas and held at the outskirts of Jerusalem. The October 1994 operation turned into a disaster, costing the lives of the hostage and an officer from the commando force. Even though the Israeli public agreed with the use of force within the Jerusalem area, it did not agree to the price. That operation was, up to the time of this book's writing, the last of its kind for a variety of reasons—including most notably new undercurrents of acceptance among Israeli society of both the Palestinian struggle's legitimacy and of the exchange deal option, which, whatever the price, looked less bloody than military operations.

That unfortunate episode came on top of a new development on the legal level. In late August 1994 the two kidnapped Hizbullah figures appealed to the Israeli Supreme Court to reverse a lower court ruling requiring them to stay in prison as administrative detainees under the 1979 Law on Authority in States of Emergency.[23] That appeal was unique because these proceedings were usually used by people living in the territories under Israeli administration to dispute their detentions. The 1994 case involved people brought by Israeli forces against their will into Israeli territory in a move somewhat similar to suspected terrorists being brought by the United States to Guantanamo. It was also a unique case in that the Law on Authority in States of Emergency specifically cites security considerations as the basis for the continued holding of the detainees. The Hizbullah members' advocate petitioned for their release on the basis that there was no case for holding them because it was impossible to prove their even remote association with terror and the state's reasoning that they were intended to be used as "bargaining chips" for the release of the airman could not meet the legal definition of "Israeli security." The district court ruled against them—hence the appeal. The Supreme Court, without providing any explanation, scheduled the first hearing for a time some twenty months after it was petitioned. It is possible that it hoped that within that long time span Israel would be able to exchange the detainees for the airman. That did not happen. In spite of some signs indicating that the airman might still be alive, no tangible intelligence could be developed from that and no diplomatic moves followed. The detainees' verdict was announced in November 1997. All of this meant in effect a long timeout, from August 1994 to November 1997, more than three years, during which time Israel was free of any judicial constraints in its efforts to release the navigator.

Over three years is a long time in POW exchange deals, as has been demonstrated throughout the years. Yet the precedent set here had nothing to do with any period of time. It had to do with the formal recognition of the Supreme Court as a legitimate player on the Israeli side whenever an exchange was on the agenda. True, the Israeli chief advocate had been a player for years, but only as a member of the executive branch. The mid-1990s saw the introduction of a brand new player that viewed the rule of law as the prime directive, at times symmetrically contradicting the security concerns of the executive decision makers. A striking example was provided years later in a Supreme Court ruling minority opinion. It said in a nutshell that the benefit from an administrative detention is limited to the prevention of direct damage that might be inflicted by the individual detained and that even that had to be limited in time (see below).[24] That minority opinion in effect outlawed all past "bargaining chips" cases and labeled any future such activities as illegal. Initially it was, as mentioned, a minority opinion, but with the tendency of the Israeli judicial system to carve its own particular path among the three branches it was an ominous sign for future developments.

These developments had no bearing on the continuing effort to get back the bodies of Israeli MIAs. In the late 1980s the Palestinian radical Muslim organization Hamas kidnapped and killed a number of Israeli soldiers in the Gaza Strip, and the issue of the three Sultan Ya'akub battle MIAs was still pending. None of this was resolved, in spite of Israel using all avenues open to it. However, in the summer of 1996, Israel and Hizbullah concluded a deal reached through German mediating efforts,[25] the last of its kind with this organization: the bodies of the two Israelis kidnapped in 1986 were exchanged for the bodies of 123 Hizbullah people. Yet it was the first swap in which the German mediating role was great enough to enable a deal.[26] From that exchange on, Israel agreed to return living people for bodies of Israelis in what would become another step up the ladder toward establishing Israel's quid pro quo requirement.

All through the Israeli stay in Lebanon, an outspoken opposition demanded Israeli withdrawal at any price, and the Israeli presence in Lebanon became an election issue in the 1990s. In May 1999 a former chief of staff, Ehud Barak, won the direct election for prime minister in part due to his campaign promise to leave Lebanon. He failed in putting together a stable coalition government and witnessed a gradual disintegration of his coalition. That did not deter him from fulfilling his promise and in late May 2000, with insufficient preparation and against the backdrop of the Hizbullah taking positions, equipment, and war materials from the IDF, the Israeli forces crossed the border back to Israel. That move was followed by the disintegration of the local pro-Israeli militia—the South Lebanon Army—and the reemergence of clear and immediate danger to northern Israeli towns and villages. While expressions of satisfaction were heard among many Israelis, so were the drums of war. The prevailing issue involved the timing of the next Hizbullah attack against Israel and its army, not its probability. That indeed materialized in October 2000.

A blow to traditional Israeli POW practices came from within in April 2000 on the eve of the Israeli withdrawal from Lebanon. The Israeli Supreme Court issued its verdict on the legality of the continued holding of Hizbullah-connected people in Israeli hands. The case, or additional criminal discussion (7048/97) as it was called by the judicial system, involved three sessions of the court (January and June 1999 and January 2000) and produced its bottom line in April 2000. By a majority of 6 to 3 the court ruled that Israel is legally prohibited from using convicted terrorists after their jail terms and administrative detainees as "bargaining chips."[27] All of this occurred amid total silence by Hizbullah on the fate of the three missing soldiers and its continued refusal to allow any visits by any third-party players. The case had been initiated as explained above in the late 1980s; all of the prisoners it concerned had been convicted of being members of hostile organizations and of participating in terrorist activities against the State of Israel and its citizens. After their jail terms, Israel continued to hold them under administrative detention so that by 1994 all Lebanese citizens connected to Hizbullah shared the same status. Under Israeli law any administrative detention must be reviewed by a district judge every six months. Those half yearly sessions developed within time into full-scale court hearings leading to the verdict. Even though the two Hizbullah-connected senior detainees were not included in the original group, any verdict in the case would have affected their status.

The court case ended with a verdict based on two main points agreed upon between the prosecution and the defendants: the latter did not present any clear and immediate danger to Israel and the real issue at stake was their continued incarceration lest Israel use them as "bargaining chips." In legal terms the two issues to be addressed were first whether the Minister of Defense is entitled to issue an administrative detention warrant against individuals for the sole purpose of keeping them for possible future negotiations on the release of Israeli POWs and MIAs, and second whether the Minister of Defense acted within his authority while implementing his policy on the subject of administrative detention.

The ruling, as unsurprising as it was considering the mood of the Israeli Supreme Court since the 1990s, amounted to a death sentence for the traditional Israeli policy, especially in regard to subnational combatants taken against their will from across the border into Israel, but also in cases involving regular armies. The verdict was especially frustrating for the decision makers at times of uncertainty regarding the MIAs—the missing aviator in particular. Along with the May 2000 Lebanon withdrawal, this verdict led to a quick desertion of all past "red lines." Israel needed to put together a new approach to the dynamics of releasing its own POWs/MIAs but was deprived of effective tools. At about that time Israel released to the public the scanty information it had on the missing navigator and it also leaked its intelligence assessment that he was not alive anymore. In other words, the POW negotiators not only accepted the Supreme Court ruling as should be done in a democratic society, but they also indicated in no uncertain terms that the ruling did not really matter in the case of the aviator. At the same time, Israel also released five administratively detained Lebanese in line with the court ruling—but it tried to depict the release as a gesture to the main mediating power behind the scenes, Germany, that wished to rescue one of its citizens from the hanging tree.[28]

Those developments took place under the shadow of yet another set of Hizbullah-initiated kidnappings already underway. In early October 2000, after a week of clashes between Israeli security forces and Arab citizens of Israel all over the country, with dead on both sides and the outbreak of a new wave of violence in the territories, the Hizbullah made its move. It kidnapped three Israeli soldiers from a remote outpost under the cover of heavy fire and a mass gathering of Lebanese citizens on the border diverting Israeli attention from the actual event. The timing, as far as the organization was concerned, was perfect because the Israeli decision makers had been under a lot of pressure from within and outside and had lost many hours of sleep to crisis groups. Yet the Israeli military, once it discovered that three soldiers were missing, tried in vain to block the kidnappers' way up north within Lebanon.[29] The Israeli reaction in the aftermath of the kidnapping is best described as a "containment policy."[30] That meant that Israel had no interest in escalating the situation and acted accordingly, by extension opening itself to negotiations while abandoning the military option. Clearly, this approach did not rule out collecting intelligence but definitely did exclude operational intelligence intended to guide the IDF in a rescue attempt. Indeed, the campaign promise of withdrawal intended to ensure peace was fulfilled, but at a price.

The October 2000 incident put to the test the Israeli promises that Hizbullah would pay dearly if it provoked Israel. Three Israeli soldiers were kidnapped from a disputed area under Israeli control in south Lebanon—the only area not vacated in May 2000. A few days later, an Israeli reserve colonel was lured into a trap in the Gulf and was taken hostage by Iranian/Hizbullah elements. These developments meant that Israel not only needed a clear POW policy but that it lacked the basic tools it had previously depended on: hostile elements it had kidnapped. Moreover, with the exception of the colonel, the organization did not volunteer any information regarding the well-being of the three soldiers and barred any ICRC visits while raising what would turn out to be false hopes for their safety. The evolving dichotomy is clear: while Israel lost its few means for encountering the new conditions, the Hizbullah became more sophisticated; it was planning on trading dead bodies, as would be discovered later, as if they were live soldiers. All of this took place in the shadow of the new Israeli player, the judicial branch that with its August 2001 ruling enabled—actually imposed on the military authorities—ICRC visits with the detainees.[31]

With no possibility of direct negotiations with Hizbullah, no legal "bargaining chips," deprived of full popular support, and with public opinion demanding that the three soldiers and the colonel return home, the government turned to the last tool in its box: the continued readiness of the German Republic to help Israel on any humanitarian issue.[32] Realizing that Israel had no viable alternatives, it gradually became evident to the Israeli public that the price would be high, especially because the fate of the MIAs since October 2000 was unknown and the colonel had been lured into a trap and captured under questionable circumstances in October 2000[33] that did not justify the risk of freeing active combatants against Israel. The group most offended by the emerging deal in late 2003 was that of veteran Israeli Air Force aviators who blasted it as being counterproductive to their efforts to convince the younger generation to volunteer for the Air Force.[34] They claimed that by concluding a deal without any relevance to the missing navigator, Israel was in effect abandoning him, contrary to the generations-old tradition of not leaving casualties behind.

No public protests deterred the Israeli cabinet under Prime Minister Sharon, himself one of the developers of the "bargaining chips" approach in the 1950s, from implementing a two-phased exchange, the first part being executed on January 29 and 30, 2004, and the second on an unknown yet-to-be-determined date.[35] The first exchange took place on German soil and consisted of the Israeli colonel (res.) and the bodies of the three MIAs for the two Hizbullah-related figures along with nineteen more. Concurrent with that, Israel returned to the ICRC at the Lebanon border crossing fifty-nine bodies of Shi'ites and Palestinians. The ICRC's representative crossed into Lebanon and handed over the bodies to Hizbullah representatives. Still, as part of the same process, Israel allowed 401 convicted terrorists to return to the territories under its rule. The second phase, at the undetermined later date, was supposed to involve the release of the most heinous terrorist in Israeli jails, who in 1979 murdered a family in ways reminiscent of Israeli Holocaust atrocities in the minds of many. His release was conditional on supplying Israel with information, but not physical evidence, on the whereabouts of the missing airman. Germany, in an unusual gesture in international relations, agreed to add to the deal two Lebanese terrorists and one Iranian prisoner all serving time in its jails in order to secure the release of the aviator or his body.[36]

If Israel's conduct since 1978, with the exception of the Shamir and Rabin tactics, constituted a slippery slope, it probably hit its temporary lowest point in 2004. Indeed, Israel had already paid for bodies with live prisoners (1991, 1998), but this time the price was the highest—let alone the fact that Israel agreed during most of the negotiations to negotiate, through Germany, with Hizbullah—without a shred of evidence as to the condition of the MIAs. Indeed, toward the end of the negotiations, once the deal was basically agreed upon, it became evident that Israel was about to receive three bodies instead of three live soldiers and a questionable person. Moreover, Israel not only continued its policy of handing over convicted murderers, but it also agreed in principle to hand over the 1979 terrorist—not just a murderer, but one whose crimes evoke memories of the Holocaust. However, that handover was conditional on supplying Israel with clear evidence regarding the airman. Because that condition was not met the terrorist was released in 2008, mocking in effect a significant part of the Israeli ethos.

Perhaps the first regional player to correctly assess the significance of the 2004 exchange was Iran. Iranian TV, closely supervised by the regime, stated in a commentary only one day after the exchange that the "region thinks [that] Israel can be 'pulverized' following POW agreement"[37]—an attestation to the weak image Israel projected in the wake of the deal. Another rather explosive reaction came in the form of blowing up a civilian bus in Jerusalem in late January. This incident was carried out by the territories-based al-Aqsa Martyrs organization, which was probably trying to block the next phase of the exchange because once again Hizbullah was successful in getting Palestinians alongside Lebanese released, to the chagrin of the PLO, the "sole and legitimate representative of the Palestinian people."[38]

As already indicated in regard to the 1996 deal, the 2004 exchange was also the result of no less than eight years of German mediating efforts carried out by former, and perhaps active, figures within the German intelligence community using their Iranian assets.[39] The Germans' interest in keeping good trade and diplomatic relations with the patron of Hizbullah, Iran, along with their hope of securing a sympathetic atmosphere for their trade with Iran, at the time under U.S. embargo, led them onto that particular track.[40] It did guarantee them that Israel, the main regional protagonist of Iran, along with its supporters in the United States, would not sabotage the German standing with Iran. Moreover, it was an easy way to demonstrate its continued humanitarian stance in relation to Israel. Considering that until 2015 and the Iranian superpowers agreement, only Germany could mediate in earnest between Israel and its enemies, Israel had no other choice. Moreover, being dependent on Germany for war material and sophisticated submarines in the first place, the last thing Israel needed was strained relations with Germany. That might also explain why, given its inferior deals since the 1990s, Israel could not turn to any other foreign player. Nevertheless, the Germans felt that such deals, especially the 2004 swap, only encouraged continued kidnappings by subnational players, and they were bewildered by Israel's continuing to place itself at a disadvantage.[41] Even more ominous was the consensus among the Palestinian media outlets that "kidnapping Zionists" was the way to "set free the prisoners."[42] From that time on the Palestinian media was unanimous in its assessment that more Israeli soldiers should be kidnapped and that any diplomatic negotiations should be supplemented by kidnappings. These views became one of the recurrent motifs in the Palestinian media between the January 2004 deal and almost to the day of the 2011 Gaza kidnapping.[43] Even the national Commission of Inquiry that investigated the escalation leading to the unfortunate decision to invade Lebanon in 2006 ("the second Lebanon War") expressed its opinion that the Israeli POW policy before that war did encourage kidnappings by hostile players.[44]

Naturally the 2004 deal sparked a heated debate in Israel and in its parliament, the Knesset. With the swap scheduled for January 29 and the discussion one day before, all speakers were careful not to say a word that might jeopardize the deal, yet the general tone was somber.[45] The minister responding on behalf of the cabinet stated in rather unambiguous terms that in striking a balance between facing more difficulties in confronting the Hizbullah and Israel's continued commitment to bringing back any of its soldiers, the latter would prevail, indicating that may be the case even in the future . Yet in spite of his pessimistic but realistic views, he still managed to find a silver lining in that no returned terrorist would be allowed back into areas under Israeli control, thus averting a repetition of the 1987 Palestinian uprising that had been initiated by terrorists released in the 1985 deal.

The direct lesson of the 2004 exchange as well as growing dissatisfaction in Israel sparked a decision to draft a bill in 2005 at the Knesset calling for establishment of clear-cut criteria to be followed by any future government when the release of terrorists is on the agenda.[46] The bill was defeated in the House because the executive branch did not wish to be bound by laws and rules that would limit its ability to deal with Israel's enemies. Unsurprisingly, similar drafts continued to surface in the context of future deals with the same results.[47] Clearly that 2005 initiative was ahead of its time. As expected the second phase of the 2004 exchange never materialized because neither Hizbullah nor Iran supplied Israel with any tangible proof of the whereabouts of the navigator. Their continued refusal to do so is a mystery to this day because they could extract much from Israel if they supplied that proof. Three possible accounts might explain their behavior include:

1. They genuinely lost track of the navigator, which does not stand to reason considering they realized at an early stage that they had an Israeli asset that may prove instrumental in future showdowns with Israel, not necessarily regarding POW issues.
2. The circumstances of his death, assuming that he is indeed no longer alive, are so gruesome that they would not admit to it under any pressure.
3. Perhaps the most plausible explanation is that by making the aviator a top priority for Israeli, the organization tried and succeeded in demonstrating its edge over Israel by getting whatever it wanted without surrendering the most desired Israeli POW.

If indeed this is the case, it is only a repetition of old Syrian behavior of the 1960s. As explained earlier, Syria never bothered to inform Israel in real time of the identities of the Israelis they were holding, and Israel has never been completely sure of the names of the Israelis held against their will in Syrian hands. Some would assert that that Syrian policy is still their MIA policy in regard to Israelis. Considering the close relations between Hizbullah, Iran, and Syria as this book is being written may also strengthen this hypothesis.

The 2004 deal failed to produce the release not only of the navigator, but also of the "dean of prisoners in Israeli jails," the 1979 terrorist whose release was sought by the organization in the second phase of the 2004 deal.[48] With that the Hizbullah preparations for the next round of taking hostages began and it was only a question of time until the next kidnapping. In early June 2006 under the cover of a well-executed deception plan Hizbullah kidnapped two soldiers from Israeli territory. This followed another kidnapping in late June of an Israeli corporal from Israeli territory to the Gaza Strip. Seventeen days passed between the two kidnappings and in both cases Israel failed to develop operational intelligence according to the then Israeli chief of staff.[49] During both kidnappings the prime minister was new to the job and inexperienced (he served as the acting prime minister of Israel for 120 days and during the first kidnapping had been a full-fledged prime minister for only seven weeks). His Minister of Defense was a former trade union leader with no record of experience in security decision making. They both ordered the military to invade the Gaza Strip in search of the hostage, and in mid-July with the kidnapping to Lebanon, they initiated a military operation large enough to be defined as a war in Middle Eastern terms. In both cases the fighting forces could not locate the missing Israelis, opening the door to yet another round of POW exchange negotiations. Once again both organizations kept their mouths shut regarding the condition of the Israelis. Hamas, the Gaza Strip ruler in the wake of the 2005 Israeli withdrawal, broke its silence several times in order to deliver the message that the soldier was alive. Hizbullah did not follow suit. Probably drawing from its experience with Israel, it concluded that each piece of information could be separately priced and that a high price should be paid by Israel for concluding a deal.

On the domestic scene the Israeli decision makers were met by strong public opposition to the Lebanon incursion that would eventually lead to the appointment of a State Commission of Inquiry and the resignation, due also to some other domestic issues, of the prime minister and the Minister of Defense. Obviously that did not deter the higher echelons of the Israeli political system from conducting exchange negotiations on two levels: with Hamas, leading to the release of the hostage in October 2011, and with Hizbullah, leading to the return to Israel in July 2008 of the bodies of the two Israelis. Once again, the German secret services served as the main go between in both cases, however different they were from each other. The media coverage in the years following both kidnappings suggest that Israel might have believed, at least since 2007, that the Gazan authorities held a living Israeli, whereas the two kidnapped to Lebanon died on the day of their seizure. Consequently, the issue of price was much more pressing in relation to the Gaza case. In the north, the Hizbullah case was different: the organization was probably pressed for time because Israel could have received news confirming their deaths at any time. The Hizbullah at that point, in 2007/2008, wanted to negotiate as if its captives were alive and feared that at any moment Israel's suspicion of their deaths could be confirmed and consequently the price would drop.

The October 2011 swap of the corporal for 1,027 Palestinians in Israeli jails was not especially different in terms of the main players: had it not been for the German mediation, the process would have probably been longer and more frustrating. However, the corporal deal, like all previous deals with substate actors, proved that Israel's main difficulty was in getting its willingness to negotiate across to its adversary. Once the public's close following of the incident died down, usually a week to ten days after each kidnapping, Israel was left with one certainty and one question mark. The former meant that the price would have to be higher in the next exchange than in the last one. Moreover, because Hizbullah aspired to take on the representation of the Palestinians, in effect if not in title, it had to work for the release of Lebanese and Palestinians alike. Hamas, with its rule over the Gaza Strip since 2006 and the declining authority of the Palestinian Authority, had to bring home more Palestinians and better known ones than Hizbullah was able to produce. That not so concealed rivalry was obviously conducted for the benefit of Israel. However, Israel still had to find a negotiator accepted by both sides. Here again Israel held the lower hand: the Palestinian and Shi'ite organizations would not recognize Israel or negotiate with it; they were not members of any international body; and they were not signatories to any international treaty governing the treatment of prisoners/POWs/ hostages. Based on all of that and given that the list presented by any organization would include a larger number of people than were involved in the last deal, the best known prisoners in Israeli jails would be on the list in addition to female prisoners and a number of foot soldiers, intended to create the impression by their large number that once again Israel surrendered to their demands. That issue has been resolved since the early 1990s. The German intelligence community, for reasons explained earlier, would usually step in. However, as part of the bargaining process, the organizations would negotiate only after a period between several months to several years in line with their traditional policy of manifesting to Israel that it had no alternative but to pay the requested prices. In the meantime, there is a golden opportunity for Israeli civil society organizations to pool their efforts and demand an immediate release at whatever price—a tactic that obviously strengthened Israel's adversaries' hand. At times the prisoners' families would enlist the help of political bodies that opposed the political line of the incumbent government and sometimes would hire public relations specialists to help them out.

Throughout the indirect release negotiations all players tend to use psychological warfare tactics intended on the Israeli side to present its willingness to negotiate lest it be seen by the mediators as the intransigent party. Hamas/Hizbullah on the other hand would press Israel for more concessions indicating that an early release is dependent on Israel's willingness to "compromise"—meaning to add to the original list presented by the organizations. With the lack of operational intelligence as proved along the Lebanese border since the 1980s and the Gaza Strip since 2005 and with the Israeli Supreme Court ban on counter-kidnappings, the only quid pro quo available to Israel was the number of Palestinian/Hizbullah detainees and prisoners.

After months of uncertainty the Israeli chiefs of all branches of the intelligence community came to the conclusion in June 2008 that the two kidnapped from northern Israel in 2006 were dead. A few weeks later the chief military rabbi declared them dead, thus allowing the widows to remarry once they wished to.[50] That was also supposedly intended to lower the price for the imminent swap scheduled for late June. For some unclear reasons that are the subject of speculation, that decision preceded a June 2008 cabinet resolution that finally granted the Hizbullah its most wanted prisoner—the 1979 terrorist, on top of scores of bodies of anti-Israeli combatants, including only eight bodies of Hizbullah people; the rest were Palestinian. With the exception of some lip service, Israel did not include the fate of the navigator within that deal.[51]

That release left only one prisoner in enemy hands: the abducted corporal in Hamas-ruled Gaza. In the opinion of the Palestinian print media, he had to represent the Palestinian lessons of the 2008 deal. That meant that the overall Palestinian attitude regarding him and other future abductees was that kidnappings were the only way to resist the Israeli military superiority and that the price that Hamas should extract from Israel must be high.[52] Indeed it was. As of 2008, Egypt, under the leadership of President Mubarak, took upon itself a mediating effort that, in spite of its domestic ordeal, continued until the return of the corporal in mid-October 2011.[53] Egypt's interest in that role is fairly evident. The Hamas-ruled Gaza Strip has become since 2006 a hotbed of radical Muslim organizations, most of which have been affiliated one way or another with Egyptian-based radical Muslim opposition organizations. Staying on good terms with the leading Gaza Strip organizations might have proved to the organizations the significance of the Mubarak regime. However, that narrow view ignored two key elements: the Hamas Gaza rulers were only one segment of the radical Muslim movement, and their rule depended to a large extent, at least in the late 2000s, on keeping on good terms with their external leadership. That Hamas segment had more far-reaching interests, not the least of which was helping Egyptian radicals take over Egypt—as indeed happened in February 2011. In late May 2009 Cairo became the center of semi-secret negotiations among representatives from the Gaza Strip Hamas, the out-of-Gaza Hamas representatives, the Palestinian Authority, and obviously Israel and Egypt. In spite of the high hopes of all participants, the negotiations failed to produce an agreement due to one stumbling block: the Hamas delegates demanded the release from an Israeli jail of a PLO member convicted of five murder cases and serving five consecutive life sentences.[54] Once again the intra-Palestinian competition was evident: releasing that person would not have granted Hamas any tangible accomplishment, but it would have granted them the recognition that they were successful where all other past negotiators failed. Moreover, with the 1979 terrorist out of jail, this figure became the new Palestinian cause célèbre. The inability of the government to conclude a deal for the swap of the Israeli soldier held in Gaza was met by increased civil activity by the soldier's family and supporting organizations.

Concurrent with the increased civil activity within Israel on behalf of the captured soldier, the German intelligence intervened once more. Their representative persuaded Hamas, after investing much effort, that even though the requested PLO prisoner would not be released, Israel would set free the largest ever number of Palestinians, no strings attached. That meant that any convicted terrorist who was demanded, with a few exceptions, would be out of jail no matter what crimes he or she had been convicted of.[55] The Israeli soldier was returned from Gaza to Israel in October 2011 and 1,027 people were returned to Hamas in two rounds. The return of the soldier was obviously a festive day for the family and the civil society organizations working on its behalf. However, it harmed Israel in two ways: first, a growing number of released Palestinians started a process of reintegrating into the Hamas violent activities against Israel, and the Israel attorney general requested in June

2014 that a number of them go back to jail.[56] Many more within the Gaza Strip and the Arab countries became once again wanted by the Israeli authorities. Second, on the Arab side, the lesson that Israel had no workable solutions to kidnappings became the main paradigm in planning future strategic blows to Israel.[57]

Still, in 2008, after a series of prisoner swaps, the Israeli cabinet under the recommendation of its Minister of Defense, Ehud Barak, appointed retired chief justice Shamgar to head a committee to work out a code of behavior for the Israeli cabinets in future cases of prisoners falling into the hands of terrorist organizations.[58] His choice was no surprise because Shamgar was one of the main players shaping the Israeli POW guidelines during the late 1960s' War of Attrition until the 1973 War (see above). The two other members were a retired general and a professor of ethics. The final report of the committee was presented to the Minister of Defense, Ya'alon, in January 2012. As far as is known to the public, the final report, the identities of the experts consulted, and the reports presented are classified as "top secret" to this day and have never been debated by any decision-making body, whether from the executive or the legislative branch.[59] The only report that was made public was the one prepared for the committee by the Palestinian Media Watch that summarized the pertinent Arab and Palestinian media and called the committee's attention to the growing propaganda advantage of the organizations from one deal to another.[60]

The ambivalent attitude of consecutive Israeli cabinets to the committee's report is not different from that demonstrated by the executive branch to draft laws seeking to limit the leverage of the cabinet in cases of POW deals. Indeed, no limit is possible on future cabinets because circumstances do change and shift in the kaleidoscopic Middle East. The Israeli public at large, however, is more and more disenchanted and frustrated with the growing ransoms paid to terrorists; on the other hand, if this is the only way to get "the boys" back, who can stand a mother's tears and not pay?[61] As reconstructed from scarce news items, the committee recommended, inter alia, that the Ministry of Defense have a permanent body in charge of POW/MIA affairs under the direct supervision of the Minister of Defense and the policy guidance of the prime minister instead of the rotating special prime minister's emissary. It further recommends the creation within that body of a media liaison officer as well as a liaison to the families. On the issue of the quid pro quo to the kidnapping party, it suggests rather general definitions so as not to tie the hands of the negotiators.[62] It is possible to assess that the committee was established in part in order to vent some of the public dissatisfaction with the growing pressures and prices from one swap to another. It might come as a surprise if any future government would agree to limit its freedom of decision at such a strategic juncture as a POW exchange.

Since the 1986 kidnapping of two Israeli soldiers and later the capture of the navigator, the main adversary of Israel in the POW context was Hizbullah. The organization in effect declared its intention to become the leading Arab power fighting Israel, and that clearly showed in the make-up of the prisoners it demanded: members of all *muqawamah* (Arabic: resistance) organizations, including the Palestinian ones, as well as Israeli citizens convicted of terrorism. It also insisted on including people waiting for trial, administrative detainees, and convicted terrorists. When seen as a whole, Hizbullah aimed much higher than simply speaking for the Palestinians—it challenged the Israeli judicial system, forcing it to give up on convicts before their jail terms were up. That branch of government stepped into the political vacuum created by the collapse of all old guidelines and injected its own views into the POW equation. Even Israeli civil society organizations became much more influential and affected to some degree Israeli cabinet decisions regarding POWs.

Israel has chosen since the late 1990s to keep up with international norms and to adhere to the Geneva Convention stipulations even though there has been no reciprocity and there cannot be any. After all, the Hizbullah is only a subnational actor and cannot subscribe to the Convention; even if it could, it is doubtful whether it would have done so and submit to self-curtailment of its activities against Israel.

In line with developments in previous periods, the POW issues became during this period an international focal point. On top of international mediation efforts, Israel began to treat POWs as a diplomatic tool, releasing them at times in order to build its confidence in relation to the Palestinians. The United States, perhaps the most familiar international actor with Israel, in line with past political behavior of other international players, did not hesitate to pressure Israel to release enemy prisoners in order to satisfy its own political interests.

NOTES

1. *Ma'ariv*, February 19, 1986.
2. Niv Sofer, "Kidnapping from Inside," *Ma'arckhot* 446 (December 2012): 25–26.
3. *Ma'ariv*, October 22, 1986.
4. *Ma'ariv*, January 12, 1987.
5. *Christian Science Monitor*, February 3, 10, 20, 1987.
6. Minister of Defense, Rabin's interview, *Ma'ariv*, April 30, 1987.
7. *Ma'ariv*, March 24, August 21, 1987.
8. Cf. William H. Webster, Director of Central Intelligence, "Remarks at Anti-Defamation League of B'nai B'rith," Washington, DC, March 22, 1987, CIA Records Search Tool (CREST), National Archives and Records Administration, College Park, MD.
9. *Ha'aretz*, October 29, 2001.
10. The George Bush Presidential Library and Museum, Memorandum of telephone conversation with Prime Minister Shamir of Israel, August 9, 1989, https://bush41library.tamu.edu/files/memcons-telcons/1989–08–09--Shamir.pdf, retrieved November 28, 2015.

11. *New York Times*, August 7, 1989; *Newsday*, August 9, 1989; *New York Times*, August 12, 1989.
12. *The Ottawa Citizen*, July 2, 1990.
13. *New York Times*, May 26, 1991; "Webster Hopeful about Hostages," *Associated Press*, May 13, 1991, CIA Records Search Tool (CREST), National Archives and Records Administration, College Park, MD.
14. "Admiral Stansfield Turner Interviewed," *World Day*, CNN-TV, June 12, 1991, CIA Records Search Tool (CREST), National Archives and Records Administration, College Park, MD; ABC "Good Morning America" interview with Admiral Stansfield Turner," *UPI*, June 25, 1991, CIA Records Search Tool (CREST), National Archives and Records Administration, College Park, MD.
15. *New York Times*, August 12, 1991.
16. *The Washington Post*, August 15, 1991; *New York Times*, August 15, 1991.
17. *Los Angeles Times*, August 18, 1991.
18. *New York Times*, September 12, 1991; *Jerusalem Post*, September 12, 1991; *Toronto Star*, September 13, 1991.
19. *New York Times*, November 19, 1991.
20. Charles Lane, "Germany's New Ostpolitik: Changing Iran," *Foreign Affairs* 74, no. 6 (1995): 79.
21. Tamir Libel, "Hostage of Foreign Interests: German Intelligence Involvement in Arab-Israeli Hostage Deals, 1980–2010," *Journal of Intelligence History* 12, no. 2 (2013): 177.
22. Lane, "Germany's New Ostpolitik," 81.
23. Administrative Detention Appeal 10/94, http://www.nevo.co.il.mgs-ariel.macam.ac.il/PsikaSearchResults.aspx.
24. Supreme Court, 7048/97, *Lebanese Citizens v. Minister of Defense* http://www.nevo.co.il.mgs-ariel.macam.ac.il/psika_html/elyon/9707048.htm.
25. Paul Belkin, *CRS Report for Congress: Germany's Relations with Israel: Background and Implications for German Middle East Policy* (Washington, DC: Congressional Research Service 2007), 10.
26. Guido Steinberg, *From Ron Arad to Gilad Shalit: Germany's Role in the Middle Eastern Prisoner Exchanges*, American Institute for Contemporary German Studies, Johns Hopkins University, December 9, 2011, http://www.aicgs.org/issue/from-ron-arad-to-gilad-shalit-germanys-role-in-the-middle-eastern-prisoner-exchanges/.
27. *Lebanese Citizens v. Minister of Defense.*
28. *Ha'aretz*, October 29, 2001.
29. Niv Sofer, "The Next Kidnapping" [Hebrew], *Ma'arckhot* 439 (October 2011): 41–42.
30. Nadir Zur, "The Awareness Test: The Second Lebanon War and the Exposing of the Meanings' Crisis within the IDF and the [Israeli] Society" [Hebrew], *Military and Strategy* 2, no. 2 (October 2010): 5.
31. *Ha'aretz*, April 24, 2002.
32. Cf. "Germany Silent on Mediating POW Exchange between Hizbollah and Israel," *Middle East News Online*, July 1, 2002, http://search.proquest.com/printviewfile?accountid=40023; on the demand of media people to become part of the decision-making process, see Sari Makover-Belikov, "At Any Price?" *Ma'ariv*, October 3, 2003; Belkin, *CRS Report for Congress*, 10.
33. *Ha'aretz*, February 1, 2004.
34. *Jerusalem Post*, October 30, 2003.
35. Michele K. Esposito, "Quarterly Update on Conflict and Diplomacy," *Journal of Palestine Studies* 33, no. 3 (Spring 2004): 141–42.
36. *Ha'aretz*, January 26, 2004.
37. Iranian TV, *BBC Monitoring Middle East*, January 25, 2004.
38. Cf. *International Herald Tribune*, Paris, January 30, 2004.
39. Cf. Martin Klingst, "Der Schweiger," *Die Zeit*, December 1, 2005.
40. *Die Welt*, August 28, 2006.

41. Cf. Steinberg, *From Ron Arad to Gilad Shalit.*
42. *al-Hayat al-Jadidah*, April 17, 2004.
43. *al-Hayat al-Jadidah*, January 26,27, 29, 2004; *al-Ayyam*, August 17, 2004; *al-Hayat al-Jadidah*, August 21, 29, 2004; *al-Hayat al-Jadidah*, December 15, 2005; *al-Ayyam*, February 14, March 16, 2006; *al-Hayat al-Jadidah*, April 17, 2006.
44. The Commission for the Study of the Events of the Lebanon Campaign, "The Winograd Commission"; The Second Lebanon War, *Final Report* [Jerusalem] 1 (2008): 502.
45. The Israeli Knesset, session 100, January 28, 2004.
46. The Israeli Knesset, session 214, January 26, 2005.
47. See, for instance, a 2009 draft by MK Marina Solodkin, which did not survive the vote.
48. Steinberg, *From Ron Arad to Gilad Shalit.*
49. *Ha'aretz*, January 1, 2011.
50. *Ha'aretz*, June 24, 2008.
51. "The Deal Outlines of the Return of the Israeli Soldiers Kidnapped by the Hezbollah on July 2006," http://www.pmo.gov.il/Secretary/GovDecisions/2008/Pages/des3690.aspx.
52. *al-Ayyam*, September 5, 2006; *al-Risalah* (Hamas organ), July 13, 2006, April 16, 2007; *al-Hayat al-Jadidah*, April 18, 2007; *al-Risalah*, April 23, 26, 30, 2007.
53. *NRG Ma'ariv website, BBC Monitoring Middle East*, September 25, 2008.
54. *New York Times*, November 23, 2009.
55. *The Gazette*, Montreal, October 17, 2011.
56. *NRG Ma'ariv website, BBC Monitoring Middle East*, June 25, 2014.
57. A song along these lines appeared in a clip and was quoted in *al-Hayat al-Jadidah*, November 21, 2012.
58. It is also very much in line with recommendation number 5 in the Commission for the Study of the Events of the Lebanon Campaign, "The Winograd Commission"; The Second Lebanon War, *Final Report* [Jerusalem] 1 (2008): 581–82.
59. The Israeli Knesset, session 44, June 24, 2013.
60. Itamar Marcus and Ya'ara Firon, *The Implications of the Release of Palestinian Prisoners on the Palestinian Leadership and Society* [Jerusalem] (November 2008).
61. Cf. The Commission for the Study of the Events of the Lebanon Campaign, "The Winograd Commission"; The Second Lebanon War, *Final Report* [Jerusalem] 1 (2008): 503.
62. *Ha'aretz*, July 7, 2008, January 6, 2012.

Conclusion

Studying the prisoner exchange deals involving Israelis, especially the diplomatic and military moves behind the scenes, reveals three main eras in the emergence of Israeli patterns of behavior. It is no mistake that the term *policy* is not used here. All throughout the years, Israel has had no comprehensive policy as a general set of directives. It has shown some general approaches and general guidelines but never any more than that. That lack of a well-established policy was not just the result of the unstable nature of Israeli politics that for most of the years since its creation, and definitely since 1977, could not reach a consensus on many issues crucial to the future of Israel. It was to a large extent the result of the tendency of most Israeli cabinets to delay critical decisions for some undefined time in the future. Successive Israeli governments have witnessed three distinct periods requiring unique approaches: a confrontation with nation states, 1948/49 to the June 1967 War; a mixed challenge posed by national and subnational players, 1967 to the aftermath of the October 1973 War; and eventually the long battle with subnational actors, first Palestinians, later Shi'ite Hizbullah. With the disintegration of a number of Arab states in the wake of the "Arab spring," it is quite possible to assume that the last phase will continue for many years to come.

With the change in the nature of the enemy, the term *prisoner of war* has broadened—at times only extending old definitions and at times moving into new territory. During the first era discussed here, POW meant anyone captured by the enemy during battle. Yet even in those old days, Jews persecuted for their religion or people crossing the border were also treated as deserving official Israeli intervention. As first indicated in the second era and clearly seen during the third, all prisoners involved in the deals—whether Israelis, foreigners, Jews, Muslims, Christians, or Druze—belong in the same basket of POWs as long as they were taken by the enemy in the context of the conflict in its broadest possible sense. The only exceptions are deserters. Clearly, enemy activities against all categories of Israelis and Jews blurred the lines between POWs and hostages.

Getting back these people has always been a top priority for the Israeli decision makers. The higher echelons of the Israeli political and military systems, which at times in the 1950s were interwoven, preferred military action to any other approach to gaining the release of Israelis in hostile prisons. The best 1950s course was considered to be a direct rescue operation that would end up with the prisoners back home. Failing that, the second best would be to acquire enemy figures, preferably high up in the hierarchy, political or military, for the purpose of an exchange. Use of such enemy captives—who became known as "bargaining chips"—would, effective as it was, be outlawed by the Israeli judicial branch years later. When this approach failed, grave violations of international law might be committed (hijacking a civilian plane, for instance) for an exchange. Any analysis of the first years of POW and other prisoner issues cannot avoid the unpleasant conclusion that people operating for Israel, whether in disguise or in uniforms, were not prepared for a possibility of being imprisoned by the enemy. That phenomenon would be observed in a series of POW-related cases until it was corrected as a result of the 1973 War. Moreover, Israel has never been keen on admitting that it has employed certain people behind enemy lines. Many of these characteristics of the Israeli POW modus operandi are still valid today.

It is evident today, for instance, that a model of political behavior by Israel emerged during the 1973 War and in the weeks and months following the war. It did not exist until 1967 due to the short span of the wars and opposition by the enemy. The model proposed here should form the basis for any guidelines if and when Israel finds itself in similar situations with national actors in the future:

Stage 1—Chaos and battle fog; no way to determine who is dead, alive, or missing. The main task: finding out by name who is missing.

Stage 2—An attempt to distinguish the MIAs from the POWs.

Stage 3—Concurrent with stages 1 and 2, a concerted effort to find high-ranking enemy POWs and/or relatives of senior decision makers.

Stage 4—Defining the possible main strategic assets, not necessarily live POWs (for example, specific territories, road junctions, locations overlooking hills, etc.), that the enemy would be interested in and either keeping them for future negotiations or letting the enemy have them so that both sides have something to bargain for. The principle of POWs for land was accepted by Israel in its May 1974 agreement with Syria and would undoubtedly resurface once Israel exhausted its high quality, Hizbullah, and Palestinian prisoners.

Stage 5—Defining prices and trying to include the topic sufficiently on the diplomatic agenda.

Stage 6—Insisting on clear and simultaneous moves by all actors so that each move is reciprocated by release of some of the POWs.

This is only a blueprint of a possible approach to the release of Israeli POWs. The 1973 War was the first to present the issue not as a humanitarian one but as one more discussion item on the international agenda.

The picture is somewhat different in dealing with subnational actors. Such a player tries to apply a disproportionate exchange rate whenever possible, and usually succeeds, in order to gain the best long-term tactical advantage. The subnational actor is not bound by any restraints, not being subscribed to international instruments and having no public opinion to manage. Moreover, while Israel agrees a priori to any mediator, he cannot be sympathetic to Israel or the opponent will not agree to his involvement. All of that puts Israel in an inferior position once one of its people is captured.

It has become increasingly obvious that as long as these circumstances continue, Hizbullah will prioritize the capture of Israeli soldiers. These exchanges necessarily diminish the credibility of the Israeli government in the face of the rest of the world and thus damage its political capability. Although the tactical situation is being taken advantage of by Hizbullah, the strategic situation remains unchanged and favors the Israeli forces. Throughout the past thirty years, the exchanges have continued to get even more tactically disproportionate in favor of Hizbullah.

One of the means the Shi'ite organization uses to increase its reward for the Israelis in its hands is with a piecemeal approach: Israel is expected to pay every step of the way, for names, for ICRC involvement and visits, and for conveying messages from the captives if possible. All of that leads not to an immediate exchange but to a prolonged process involving the organization's attempts to extract intelligence from the prisoners and to collect benefits from Israel along the way.

That process should be carried out by a mediator. Without open lines of communication between Israel and its adversaries, a mediator has always been a necessity, except for short periods of time. The Arab side since 1948 has always preferred using a third party, basically as a result of their refusal to recognize Israel, even remotely. Participation of the ICRC and UN has only been welcome when a given Arab actor believes at a given point in time that the organization would side with it.

The interests on the Arab side have not changed much over the years in spite of changes in the identities of the main actors. They have wanted an international stamp of approval regarding their policies in the regional conflict along with maximum humiliation of Israel—either by forcing it to directly or indirectly recognize the other side or by infringing on its sovereignty (for instance, by imposing the release of convicted inmates).

Years of daily friction with Israel have led to a change in the Arab side's policies, especially in regard to the subnational players: they started to care about bodies of their own and of Israelis. Indeed, they have withheld in order to increase bargaining prices the fact that Israelis were dead—yet in the 1990s the Hizbullah and Palestinian organizations began to ask for their dead and bury them in public. Each funeral has been used to demonstrate continuation of the war with Israel.

The Israeli side, on the other hand, has presented no clear-cut policy, but rather rules of behavior moved from the field to the High Command. The accumulated Israeli experience of almost seventy years has taught Israel to try and aim high for valuable POW assets. With the lack of such targets at hand, Israel has tried to pursue a policy using the intelligence value of the prisoners, then returning them—no matter how many for one Israeli. The cost of keeping the prisoners in jail on top of enemy countries and, later, the organizations squeezing Israel into the least prestigious solutions have shaped Israeli policy for years. Nevertheless, those Arab positions could not prevent Israel from checking out the perceived intelligence value of POWs, based in classic military wisdom and crucial to modern theory on asymmetric warfare. Today, the potential intelligence value of POWs seems largely accepted. However, can states realize the potential advantage, and if so, how? This question remains a matter of significant debate, one which the necessity for secrecy and the influence of politics make difficult to objectively and scientifically analyze. Yet such analysis must be made, for this question is not merely academic. Failure to accurately assess the actual value of POWs as a source of intelligence could have real strategic consequences in war.

Israel has never had a unitary policy regarding this issue and the right strategy regarding its own and enemy POWs. The military would occasionally deal with it, mainly during the times of the MAC. After 1956, the MFA would be in charge, with significant participation of the IDF, especially when "bargaining chips" were called for. The change from state player adversaries to subnational ones in the wake of the June 1967 War instigated a new system: whatever governmental body could provide a negotiator would take the lead. In the aftermath of the 1973 War, with the superpowers of the time placing this topic on their global agenda, the leading role in Israel moved to the prime minister, assisted most of the time by governmental agencies, mainly from the intelligence community. In the wake of the 1982 Israeli incursion into Lebanon and the loss of POWs, Israeli prime ministers began appointing special assistants to deal with the other side through third parties. That practice continues as this book is being written.

Throughout the conflict, and especially since the early 1980s, the exchanges that have taken place have drawn an image of Israel as an irrational player. The Palestinians and later Hizbullah have managed to repeatedly take advantage of Israel's irrational attachment to its soldiers and turn each price paid in a deal into the springboard for the next exchange, extracting from Israel higher prices each time.

If the Israeli position was not easy to decipher considering that no clear-cut policy has ever been decided upon, two developments over the years have added input to the complexity of the subject: the emergence of formal and a-formal civil society organizations dedicated to POW issues and the introduction of the judicial branch into the POW-related de facto system.

This public participation process began in the late 1960s in the context of the plane hijackings and reached its temporary zenith with the efforts to get back the soldier kidnapped in 2006 in the Gaza Strip. Israel has taken public opinion into its own calculations starting with the erosion of trust as a result of the war of attrition, the public pressure that was used by Secretary Kissinger in the wake of the 1973 War. That participation has only grown with the dissatisfaction with the long stay in Lebanon. Other factors also contributed to this process, including organized domestic opposition within Israel, which stood on the foundations of the political bankruptcy of the Israeli 1973 leadership. These changes in the makeup of Israeli society as well as the change of Israel's status among the nations after the 1973 military shock were expressed by abandoning the policy of returning POWs for POWs and replacing it by POWs for land and POWs.

In late 1990s and the early twenty-first century the judicial branch claimed full standing within the process of exchanging prisoners and in a series of groundbreaking rulings it ordered the military to allow ICRC visits with enemy prisoners and detainees with no strings attached and that holding bargaining chips was not allowed any more, in effect stripping the bodies dealing with POW issues from perhaps the only constant element in the traditional Israeli decisions.

Clearly, these two added elements only served to underline the need to formulate clear-cut guidelines regarding future POWs. An attempt by the legislature to also participate in the process has been blocked time and again by the executive branch. It already had its hands tied by public opinion and the judicial and did not need an additional set of handcuffs.

Since the creation of the State of Israel, the IDF has been in charge of dealing with MIAs and POWs. It used to operate with their counter numbers within the Mixed Armistice committees with Egypt, Syria, and Jordan. At times, whenever the committees did not operate due to other Israeli or Arab considerations, the best avenue used to be the ICRC. After all, all the neighboring countries are signatories to the Geneva Convention. In cases that could not allow direct military contacts, the MFA through its worldwide representations acted among foreign governments and international organizations. Many times the initial Israeli task was to try and locate the missing Israeli, however, only with the large number of MIAs in the 1973 War did Israel decide to set up a military body to take care of locating the missing.[1] While this function exists to this day, it mainly deals with locating the 173 IDF MIAs since the 1948 War.[2]

Structurally speaking, as early as the mid-1950s Israel created a governmental body to follow on a regular basis all efforts to release its prisoners and to take active part in the release attempts. That early beginning would undergo a series of changes in the years to come, but one clear connection still exists among all these bodies: they have all been members of the intelligence community and therefore privy to all information available to Israel, no bars held. It is a further indication of the priority given to the POW issue among the Israeli decision makers to this day. However, that body and any governmental organ needs a policy leader embodied by a senior minister. When the leadership is damaged, no one outside the elected decision makers should be allowed to make decisions that may effect the foreign and security relations of the state for years. Issues of strategic deterrence and diplomatic effect have to involve accurate intelligence, longstanding procedures, and experienced people from all agencies involved.

All that necessitates a permanent intra-agency body that would plan for any possible eventuality, including preparing the high-value targets to be acquired in case a deal is to be worked out. Such a body has to take into account and prepare for the following model:

1. Once Israel knows of a kidnapping, it is usually too late to chase the perpetrators. Perhaps the first couple of hours might yield some traces that will help in determining the condition of the missing.
2. The next Israeli step should be the materialization of existing plans of getting strategic assets for an exchange.
3. Israel will not know for a long time whether the MIAs were actually kidnapped. It would assume so, but no confirmation would come from the kidnapping organization.
4. Confirmation would usually come along with some initial agreement to hold negotiations. The mediator would always be a public figure, possibly a foreign dignitary supplemented by an Israeli sympathetic to the kidnapping side.
5. All through the process the prisoners would be kept incommunicado. Any gesture of allowing visits would be followed by a demand for a price to be paid by Israel.
6. Once a negotiations process starts, it will be long, with the adversary ready to leave the table at any minute. This is usually a charade considering that without any deal it would for the short run be seen as giving up, but in the long run does provide the expected end result.
7. The demands of the organization, be it Lebanese or Palestinian, will usually include convicted terrorists alongside detainees, Lebanese and Palestinian, and many times Israeli Arab citizens serving time. Since the 1990s, bodies have been as important as live prisoners for the Arab side because they will be presented as martyrs and in the context of the large number of Hizbullah casualties in Lebanon they will represent the continued commitment to the war against Israel.

8. In terms of numbers: the last concluded deal is the starting point. In terms of quality, the better strategic assets Israel has, the lower the price it has to pay.
9. Once a deal is being signed, it should be concluded outside the Middle East considering the ever growing price for Israel.

In short, the emerging working definitions and suggested model allow the cabinet enough working space, in spite of the limits put on it by the Supreme Court. That approach is flexible enough to allow future negotiators with substate actors to trade all classes of prisoners for all classes of the other side.

Israel today is on the defensive and lacking any new thinking and planning on this humanitarian and strategic issue. Considering that the regional conflict is far from resolution and that the upper hand today is in the hands of subnational actors, Israel should look back to the 1950s and 1960s if it wants to improve its standing.

NOTES

1. IDFA/47/2003/81, Locating MIAs Center, Standing orders, January 1, 1973–January 1, 2000.
2. http://www.aka-idf.idf.il/Eitan/main/.

Bibliography

202nd Israeli Paratroopers Brigade Official Website. First decade. http://www.202.org.il/.

890th Battalion Report to General Staff: "Operation *Barukh*." June 1954. http://idfarchives.bloger.co.il/118164/.

Adamsky, Dima. "Zero-Hour for the Bears: Inquiry into the Soviet Decision to Intervene in the Egyptian-Israeli War of Attrition, 1969–70." *Cold War History* 6, no. 1 (2006): 113–36.

Ajami, Fouad. "The End of Pan -Arabism." *Foreign Affairs* 57, no. 2 (Winter 1978): 355–73.

al-Ahram, Egypt, Daily Newspaper, Arabic.

al-Ayyam, Bahrein, Daily Newspaper, Arabic.

al ha-Mishmar, Israel, Daily Newspaper, Hebrew.

al-Hayat al-Jadidah, Palestinian authority, Daily Newspaper, Arabic.

al-Ra'id, Lebanon, Arabic.

al-Risalah, Hamas organ, Palestinian authority, Arabic.

al-Safaa', Lebanon, Arabic.

al-Watha'iq al-Urduniyyah 1967.

Ambassador Isaac Lebanon. 2014, Personal Interview.

Amit, Meir. *Rosh be-Rosh* [Hebrew: Face-to-Face; Personal Look on Vast Events and Clandestine Matters]. Tel Aviv: Hed Artzi, 1999.

The Avalon Project. *Documents in Law History and Diplomacy*. http://avalon.law.yale.edu/.

Aviezer, Golan. *Mivtzah Suzanna* [Hebrew: Operation Suzanna]. As told by Marcelle Ninio, Victor Levy, Robert Dassa, and Philip Natanson. Jerusalem: Idanim, 1976.

Awake at Night, Israeli Association for Released POWs, the story of Captain Gill Fogel. http://www.erim-pow.co.il/article.php?id=31.

Bar-On, Mordechai. "Olive Leaves: The Raid at the Lake of Galilee on the Night of December 12, 1955." *Iyunim bi-tekumat Israel* 9 [Hebrew: Studies in Israel's Revival]. 1999.

———. *Shearei Azah: mediniut ha bitahon ve ha hutz shel Israel, 1955–1957* [Hebrew: The Gates of Gaza: Israel's Defense and Foreign Policy, 1955–1957]. Tel Aviv: Am Oved, 1992.

Barzilai, Naomi, ed. *Documents on the Foreign Policy of Israel. 9: 1954*. Jerusalem: Israel State Archives, 2004.

BBC Monitoring, Middle East.

Belkin, Paul. *CRS Report for Congress: Germany's Relations with Israel: Background and Implications for German Middle East Policy*. Washington, DC: Congressional Research Service, 2007.

Berejikian, Jeffrey D. "A Cognitive Theory of Deterrence." *Journal of Peace Research* 39, no. 2 (2002): 165–83.

Bolia, Robert. "Israel and the War of Attrition." *Military Review* [serial online] 84, no. 2 (March 2004): 47–51.

Boston Globe, United States, Daily Newspaper, English.

Braizat, Musa S. *Jordanian-Palestinian Relationship: The Bankruptcy of the Confederal Idea*. London: British Academic, 1998.

Burns, Lt. Gen. Eedson. L. M. *Between Arab and Israeli*. London: George G. Harrap, 1962.

Central Zionist Archive (CZA), Jerusalem, S6: Files of the Zionist Executive and Jewish Agency, Immigration Department.

Christian Science Monitor, Newspaper website.

CIA. KUBARAK Counterintelligence Interrogation. 1963. http://nsarchive.gwu.edu/NSAEBB/NSAEBB122/CIA%20Kubark%201–60.pdf.

CIA Research Tool. National Archives and Records Administration, College Park, MD, http://www.foia.cia.gov/collection/crest-25-year-program-archive.

The Commission for the Study of the Events of the Lebanon Campaign. "The Winograd Commission." The Second Lebanon War, *Final Report*. [Jerusalem]: 2008, vol. 1.

Constantinople Convention. October 29, 1888. http://www.suezcanal.gov.eg/sc.aspx?show=37.

Crowley, Michael. "Prisoners Dilemma." *The New Republic* 17 (June 2009): 6–17.

Davar, Israel, Daily Newspaper, Hebrew.

David Ben Gurion Archive (BGA), Correspondence Additions File, Addition 4.

———. Correspondence Files, September 1954–January 1967.

———. Chronological Documentation, June 1955.

David Ben Gurion Archive [BGA]/Shabtai Tevet Archive [STA], File 13, Container 2, group files.

———. File 40, Container 5, *Bat Galim*.

Dayyan, Moshe. *Story of My Life*. Tel Aviv: Idanim and Dvir, 1976.

The Deal Outlines of the Return of the Israeli Soldiers Kidnapped by the Hezbollah on July 2006. http://www.pmo.gov.il/Secretary/GovDecisions/2008/Pages/des3690.aspx.

De Nevers, Renée. "The Geneva Conventions and New Wars." *Political Science Quarterly* 121, no. 3 (2006): 369–95.

———. "Modernizing the Geneva Conventions." *Washington Quarterly* 29, no. 2 (2006): 99–113.

Detter, Ingrid. "The Law of War and Illegal Combatants." *George Washington Law Review* 75 (2011): 1049–104.

Die Welt, Germany, Daily Newspaper, German.

Die Zeit, Germany, Daily Newspaper, German.

Divre ha-Kneset [Hebrew: Israeli Parliament minutes], Session 29, December 10, 1984.

———. Session 89, May 27, 1985.

———. Session 103, June 29, 1982.

———. Session 201, May 19, 1986.

———. Session 215, June 20, 1983.

———. Session 252, November 29, 1983.

Dörmann, Knut. "The Legal Situation of 'Unlawful/Unprivileged Combatants.'" *International Review of the Red Cross* 849 (2003): 45–74.

Egyptian Ilyushin 14 Interception. http://www.sky-high.co.il/134771/%D7%94%D7%A4%D7%9C%D7%AA-%D7%90%D7%99%D7%9C%D7%99%D7%95%D7%A9%D7%99%D7%9F-14-%D7%9E%D7%A6%D7%A8%D7%99–1.

"Egyptian-Syrian Mutual Defense Pact (October 20, 1955). Egyptian-Saudi Arabian Mutual Defense Pact (October 27, 1955)." *Middle East Journal* 10, no. 1 (Winter 1956): 77–79.

El-Ad, Avri, with Creech, James III. *Ha-Adam Ha-shlishi* [Hebrew: The Third Man]. Tel Aviv: Special edition, 1976.

Eli Cohen chronology from birth to death, http://www.elicohen.org/resources/chronology.php.htm.

Eshed, Haggai. *Mi natan et ha horaha; parashat Lavon* [Hebrew: Who Gave the Order; The Lavon Affair]. Jerusalem: Idanim, 1979.

Esposito, Michele K. "Quarterly Update on Conflict and Diplomacy." *Journal of Palestine Studies* 33, no. 3 (Spring 2004): 141–42.

Evans, Ernest. "The Vatican and Israel." *World Affairs* 158 (Fall 1995): 88–92.

Foreign Relations of the United States, 1952–1954. The Near and Middle East (in two parts): Volume IX, Part 1. https://history.state.gov/historicaldocuments/frus1952–54v09p1.

Foreign Relations of the United States, 1969–1976, Volume XXIV, Middle East Region and Arabian Peninsula, 1969–1972; Jordan, September 1970. https://history.state.gov/historicaldocuments/frus1969–76v24.

Foreign Relations of the United States, 1969–1976, Volume XXV, Arab-Israeli Crisis and War, 1973. https://history.state.gov/historicaldocuments/frus1969–76v25.

Gavish , Major General (retired) Yeshayahu . 2014, Personal Interview.

The Gazette, Canada, Daily Newspaper, English.

The George Bush Presidential Library and Museum, Memorandum of telephone conversation with Prime Minister Shamir of Israel, August 9, 1989. https://bush41library.tamu.edu/files/memcons-telcons/1989–08–09--Shamir.pdf.

The Globe and Mail, Canada, Daily Newspaper, English.

Gross, Janice, and Ron Levi. "The Social Psychology of Denial: Deterring Terrorism." *New York University Journal of International Law and Politics* 47, no. 2 (January 2015): 409–38.

Gur, Colonel Mordechai. "Golani Operations, Tawfiq and Nuqeib." *Ma'arkhot* 174–175 (April 1966): 18–23.

Ha'aretz, Israel, Daily Newspaper, Hebrew.

ha-Boker, Israel, Daily Newspaper, Hebrew.

Hameiri, Yehezkel. *Shevuei Suria: sipuram shel israelim be tzinok suri.* [Hebrew: Captives in Syria: The Story of Israelis in Syrian Confinement]. Tel Aviv: Am Oved, 1965.

"Hanoi's Smoking Gun." *National Review* 45, no. 10 (1993): 16–18.

Har-Zion, Meir. *Pirkei Yoman* [Hebrew: Chapters of a Diary]. Tel Aviv: Levin-Epstein, 1968.

Headquarters, [U.S.] Department of the Army. "Enemy Prisoners of War and Detained Persons." *U.S. Army Field Manual* No 3–21.8 (FM3–218), (March 28, 2007).

———. "Human Intelligence Collector Operations." *U.S. Army Field Manual* No. 2–22.3 (FM 34–52), (September 6, 2006).

Herut, Israel, Daily Newspaper, Hebrew.

Hudson, Rex A. "Dealing with International Hostage-Taking—Alternatives to Reactive Counterterrorist Assaults." Terrorism 12, no. 5 (1989): 321–78.

[IDF] MIA Locating Branch. http://www.aka-idf.idf.il/Eitan/main/.

Israel Defense Forces Archive (IDFA)/IDF Operations Directorate/History Division. " *Secret" De-Briefing of Operation Jonathan, 3–4 July 1976*, November 1977, http://www.archives.mod.gov.il/pages/exhibitions/yonatan/yonatan.pdf.

———. 8/1956/46, Intelligence Interrogation report. [n.d.]

———. 22/2009/8, Documentation and cataloguing, observations, May 19, 1974–July 5, 1976.

———. 22/2009/16, A list of IDF POWs, October 13, 1973–December 31, 1974.

———. 46/1955/488, Prisoners of War. 1953.

———. 47/2003/81, Locating MIAs Center, Standing orders, January 1, 1973–January 1, 2000.

———. 49/2012/64, Integration of POWs, *Yom Kippur War*.

———. 57/2014/13, Virtual collection file, January 1, 1966–December 31, 1976.

———. 79/2007/37, Report on actions regarding MIAs. 1950–1951.

———. 117/1970/61, IDF Chief of General Staff office, operations, November 5, 1967–September 8, 1967.

———. 121/535/04, Special Intelligence Report, Including Special Intelligence Reviews. January 1, 1956–December 31, 1956.

———. 151/2006/79, POW interrogation reports, 1956.

———. 535/2004/321, IDF General Staff/Directorate of Intelligence, Arab broadcasts summary, Ramalla [Jordan] Radio, November 21, 1956.

———. 535/2004/543, Director of the Intelligence Directorate presentation to the General Staff of IDF, February 8, 1956.

———. 540/1955/114, Office of the General Chief of Staff Files, 1953.
———. 626/1957/29, Office of the General Chief of Staff Files. [n.d.].
———. 636/1956/33, Armistice problems, infiltration. September 5, 1954–December 23, 1954.
———. 637/1956/17, Operations Directorate. [n.d.].
———. 637/1956/18, Operations Directorate. [n.d.].
———. 644/1956/88, IDF, General Staff, Directorate of Intelligence, "top secret" intelligence dispatch: Syria-Egypt treaty.
———. 675/1974/178, Reprisal Activities, 1950–1953 (Until the Establishment of Unit 101). [n.d.].
———. 734/1034/1965, Director of Operations office, review of education officer duties, January 3, 1957–September 18, 1957.
———. 1087/2004/535, First Brigade Report in Concluding the Sinai Campaign and interrogation transcripts.
———. 1338/1979/3, Liaison to the UN unit, Returning POWs, The War of Liberation. [n.d.].
———. 1338/1979/200, Liaison to the UN unit, Jordan. January 1, 1955–April 5, 1955.
———. 1338/1979/717, Liaison to the UN unit, Progress report. [n.d.].
———. 1338/1980/210, POWs. 1956–1971.
———. 1723/1974/192, *Rhodes Operation [Tactical] De-Briefing.*
———. 1726/1974/192, *Rhodes Operation [Complete] De-Briefing.*
Israel Ministry of Foreign Affairs. *Background on Israeli POWs and MIAs.* January 26, 2004.
Israel Ministry of Foreign Relations publications.
Israel State Archives (ISA) A/7041/11, Material and telegrams to the Prime Minister regarding Israeli captives in Egypt and Syria. 1972.
———. A/7049/25, Telegrams, copies of letters and government decisions. 1973.
———. A/7074/15, Minutes of the meeting of the Israeli PM and the Chief of Staff with Kissinger. 1973.
———. A/7240/2, Interdepartmental committee regarding Israeli POWs. 1971–1972.
———. A/7428/27, Prime Minister's office, director, POW. 1971.
———. A/7430/4, Prime Minister's office, director, plane hijackings. 1970.
———. A/7455/1, Prime Minister's office, director general. 1967–1968.
———. A/7792/3, Ambassador Dinitz office, Phone conversations, October 12, 1973–October 25, 1973.
———. A/7934/8, Copies and Surplus. 1963.
———. FM/18/2, Israeli representation in Geneva, Switzerland, Prime Minister's office. 1953–1958.
———. FM/20/3, Israeli representation in Geneva, Switzerland, Refugees.1958–1959.
———. FM/20/24, Israeli representation in Geneva, Switzerland, Red Cross. January 1958–July 1959.
———. FM/20/26, Israeli representation in Geneva, Switzerland, Red Cross. October 1958–June 1959.
———. FM/21/11, Israeli representation in Geneva, Switzerland, Red Cross. 1957.
———. FM/21/14, Israeli representation in Geneva, Switzerland, Red Cross. 1960.
———. FM/22/4, Israeli representation in Geneva, Switzerland, Red Cross. 1961.
———. FM/27/9, Israeli representation in Geneva, Switzerland, Captives. 1967.
———. FM/27/10, Israeli representation in Geneva, Switzerland, The International Red Cross. 1966.
———. FM/28/1, Israeli representation in Geneva, Switzerland, The International Red Cross. 1965.
———. FM/30/3, Israeli representation in Geneva, Switzerland, Red Cross, Captives. 1968.
———. FM/30/4, Israeli representation in Geneva, Switzerland, Red Cross. 1969.
———. FM/33/7, Israeli representation in Geneva, Switzerland, Red Cross, Captives. [n.d.].

———. FM/33/11, Israeli representation in Geneva, Switzerland, Red Cross, Captives, Israeli Pilots Moshe Goldwaser and Ig'al Sohat. 1970.
———. FM/33/12, Israeli representation in Geneva, Switzerland, Red Cross. [n.d.].
———. FM/33/13, Israeli representation in Geneva, Switzerland, Red Cross, Captives. [n.d.].
———. FM/211/12, Israeli Captives. 1959.
———. FM/748/15, Israeli Captives. [n.d.].
———. FM/1392/12, Israeli Captives. 1966–1967.
———. FM/1508/6, Israeli Captives. 1965–1970.
———. FM/1530/9, Captives, and Captives Exchange. [n.d.].
———. FM/1987/18, The Red Cross, Arab Captives. 1956.
———. FM/2096/13, The Red Cross, Captives, Vol. A. 1957.
———. FM/2096/14, Nongovernmental Organizations, Social Help, The Red Cross, Captives Vol. A. August 1957.
———. FM/2096/16, Nongovernmental Organizations, Social Help, The Red Cross, Captives Vol A. August 1957.
———. FM/2717/26, The Red Cross, prisoners. [n.d.].
———. FM/3216/10, TWA Plane Highjack. [n.d.].
———. FM/3838/3, Israeli Captives Vol. A. 1966.
———. FM/3838/4, Arab Captives in Israel. [n.d].
———. FM/3902/4, Israeli Detainees in Arab Countries. [n.d.].
———. FM/4085/1, Emergency Stage, Captives. 1967.
———. FM/4086/9, Memorandum on the meeting with the ICRC representative. [n.d.].
———. FM/4089/5, Captives Exchange Agreement. [n.d.].
———. FM/4299/4, Prisoner's Exchange with Syria and Egypt. 1969.
———. FM/4300/5, Cabinet minutes. August 1968.
———. FM/5241/1, The Red Cross, Plane Highjacks. 1972.
———. FM/6178/2, Egypt-Foreign Relations with Israel, January 2, 1957–October 31, 1957, News for the Israeli Overseas Representations. no. 1276, February 20, 1957.
———. FM/6455/1, El-Al Plane Hostages in Algeria, Telegrams, volume A. 1968.
———. FM/6807/4, Israeli and Arab captives. 1972–1973.
———. FM/8484/10, Entebbe, MFA Director General Office, July–September 1976.
———. FM/8484/14, Uganda, Entebbe, January–July 1976.
———. G/5460/10, Correspondence between Security Officers, Foreign Ministry and Prime Minister's office. 1956.
———. G/6692/9, Captives Exchange. 1967.
———. G/6695/3, Prime Minister's office, Golda Meir and Yitzchak Rabin. [n.d.].
———. K/225/4, Minutes of the Knesset session 3, meetings 313–316, Prime Minister Rabin's speech. July 4, 1976.
International Committee of the Red Cross. Treaties and States Parties to Such Treaties. https://www.icrc.org/applic/ihl/ihl.nsf/.
International Covenant on Civil and Political Rights; Adopted and opened for signature, ratification and accession by General Assembly resolution 2200A (XXI) of 16 December 1966, entry into force 23 March 1976, in accordance with Article 49, http://www.ohchr.org/en/professionalinterest/pages/ccpr.aspx.
International Herald Tribune, Daily Newspaper, English.
Israeli Air Force. Wars and Operations. http://www.iaf.co.il/4693-he/IAF.aspx.
The [Israeli] Intelligence in the Yom Kippur War, 1934–1974; Forty Years Later [Hebrew]. Intelligence Heritage Center, 2013.
The [Israeli] Law of Disbursement for Border Area Affected People (1956) [In Effect 1956–1982], http://www.nevo.co.il.mgs-ariel.macam.ac.il/law_html/law19/BTL0225.htm.
Israeli Navy Association, Prisoner Exchange November 30 1963, http://www.amutayam.org.il/?CategoryID=617&ArticleID=1543, retrieved April 21, 2015.
Israeli Navy Legacy, http://www.hi-teach.com/infohub/Main.asp.
Iyyad, Abu. *Lelo Moledet* [Hebrew: Without a Homeland]. Tel Aviv: Mifras, 1979.

Jacobs, Andreas. *Deutschland und der Nahe und Mittlere Osten: Standortbestimmung und Handlungsempfehlungen*. Sankt Augustin: Konrad-Adenauer-Stiftung, 2001.

Jerusalem Post, Israel, Daily Newspaper, English.

Jost, Kenneth, ed. "Closing Guantanamo." *CQ Researcher* 27 (February 2009): 181–83.

Junio, Timothy J. "Military History and Fourth Generation Warfare." *Journal of Strategic Studies* 32, no. 2 (2009): 243–69.

Knesset Meeting 573. January 17, 1955. 594–90, http://www.knesset.gov.il/review/data/heb/plenum/kns2_170155.pdf.

la-Merhav, Israel, Daily Newspaper, Hebrew.

Lane, Charles. "Germany's New Ostpolitik: Changing Iran." *Foreign Affairs* 74, no. 6 (1995): 77–81.

Laskier, Michael M. "The Israeli *Mossad* and Muslim-Jewish Coexistence in Colonial Algeria: The Constantine Affair of 12–13 May 1956." [Hebrew]. *Pe'amim* 75 (Spring 1998): 129–43.

Lavie, Naphtali Lau. *Am caLavi* [Hebrew: Nation as a Lion]. Jerusalem: 1994.

Lehaci, N. "The Decision-Making Process—From First Generation Warfare to the Post-Cold War Revolution in Military Affairs." *Strategic Impact* 54 (2015): 106–12.

Lepri, Charlotte. "Obama's Intelligence Policy: Meeting New Challenges." In *National Security Under the Obama Administration*, edited by Bahram M. Rajaee and Mark J. Miller. New York: Palgrave-Macmillan, 2012.

Libel, Tamir. "Hostage of Foreign Interests: German Intelligence Involvement in Arab-Israeli Hostage Deals, 1980–2010." *Journal of Intelligence History* 12, no. 2 (2013): 177–89.

Library and Archives Canada, Ottawa, RG 2 Export of Military Aircraft; General Policy.

———. RG 25 Records of the Department of External Affairs.

Lillich, Richard B., and John N. More, eds. *The Use of Force, Human Rights, and General International Legal Issues. International Law Studies* 62 (1980).

Lind, William S., Keith Nightengale, Jhon F. Schmitt, Joseph W. Sutton, and Gary I. Wilson. "The Changing Face of War: Into the Fourth Generation." *Marine Corps Gazette* 85, no. 11 (2001): 24–68.

Little, Douglas. "Cold War and Covert Action: The United States and Syria, 1945–1958." *Middle East Journal* 44, no. 1 (Winter 1990): 51–75.

Liu, Melinda. "Counting the Ghosts." *Newsweek* 5 (October 1992): 49–50.

Lovelace, Douglas C. Jr. "Commentary on Interrogation Methods: State of the Debate." In *Terrorism: Commentary on Security Documents; Terror-based Interrogation*, edited by Kristen E. Boon, Aziz Huq, and Douglas C. Lovelace Jr., 321–488. Oxford: Oxford University Press, 2010.

Los Angeles Times, United States, Daily Newspaper, English.

Lotan, Orly. *Prisoners' Rights in International Law and Criticism of the Imprisonment Conditions in Israeli Jails* [Hebrew]. Jerusalem: Knesset Research and Information Center, 2006.

Ma'ariv, Israel, Daily Newspaper, Hebrew.

Mack, Andrew. "Why Big Nations Lose Small Wars: The Politics of Asymmetric Conflict." *World Politics* 27, no. 2 (January 1975): 175–200.

Marcus, Itamar, and Ya'ara Firon. *The Implications of the Release of Palestinian Prisoners on the Palestinian Leadership and Society*. [Jerusalem], (November 2008).

Mann, Joseph. "The Conflict with Israel According to Neo-Ba'ath Doctrine." *Israel Affairs* 13, no. 1 (2007): 116–30.

Matzpen, Israel, Daily Newspaper, Hebrew.

McNeilly, Mark R. *Sun Tzu and the Art of Business: Six Strategic Principles for Managers*. Oxford: Oxford University Press, 1996.

Melcher, R. A. "Pentagon Knew Soldiers Held After War, Panel Says." *Congressional Quarterly Weekly Report* 50, no. 26 (1992): 1896.

Middle East News Online.

al-Milaff al-Watha'iqi l-Ma'arakat Karameh, al-Khamis, 21 Adhar 1968 [Arabic, the Documented File of the Karameh Battle]. Amman, 1998.

Morris, Benny. *Israel's Border Wars, 1949–1956: Arab Infiltration, Israeli Retaliation, and the Countdown to the Suez War*. Oxford: Oxford University Press, 1993.

Mudrik, Oded. "Hahzakat 'muva'im' be-ma'azar minhali ke"klafe mikuh" [Hebrew: "Detaining 'Abducted' in Administrative Arrest as 'Bargaining Chips'], *Mishpat ve-Zava* [Justice and Military] 16, no. 813 (2003): 833–34.

National Security Council Intelligence Directive No. 3. Coordination of Intelligence production. January 13, 1948. Clause 3. https://www.fas.org/irp/offdocs/nscid03.htm.

The New York Times, United States, Daily Newspaper, English.

NRG, Israel, Newspaper website.

Neue Zürcher Zeitung, Switzerland, Daily Newspapers, German.

Nevo, Israeli Legal Database. http://www.nevo.co.il./.

Oren, Michael B. "The Diplomatic Struggle for the Negev, 1946–1956." *Studies in Zionism* 10, no. 2 (1989): 197–215.

———. "Escalation to Suez: The Egypt-Israel Border War, 1949–56." *Journal of Contemporary History* 24, no. 2 (April 1989): 347–73.

———. "Secret Egypt-Israel Peace Initiatives Prior to the Suez Campaign." *Middle Eastern Studies* 26, no. 3 (July 1990): 351–70.

The Ottawa Citizen, Canada, Daily Newspaper, English.

Philadelphia Daily News, United States, Daily Newspaper, English.

Prime Minister Meir's testimony before the Agranat Commission of Inquiry, 1974, http://www.archives.mod.gov.il/Pages/Exhibitions/Agranat2/%D7%A2%D7%93%D7%95%D7%AA%20%D7%92%D7%95%D7%9C%D7%93%D7%94%E2%80%8F%20%D7%9E%D7%90%D7%99%D7%A8%20-%20%D7%A8%D7%90%D7%A9%20%D7%94%D7%9E%D7%9E%D7%A9%D7%9C%D7%94/mywebalbum/index.html.

Private Papers Collections.

Putnam, Robert. "Diplomacy and Domestic Politics: The Logic of Two-Level Games." *International Organization* 42 (1988): 427–60.

Raab, David. "Terror in Black September: An Eyewitness Account." *Middle East Quarterly* (Fall 2007): 33–42.

Rabin's speech in the Israeli Knesset, session 89, May 27, 1985. http://knesset.gov.il/tql/knesset_new/knesset11/HTML_27_03 2012_05–59–19-.

Rabinovich, Itamar. *Syria under the Ba'ath 1963–66: The Army-Party Symbiosis*. Jerusalem: Israel Universities Press, 1972.

Ray, Alan. "Another Partition of Israel?" *New Republic* 132, no. 15 (April 11, 1955): 17–18.

Reuters Wire Service.

Roberts, Adam. "Role of Law in the 'War on Terror': A Tragic Clash." *Proceedings of the Annual Meeting (American Society of International Law)* 97 (2003): 18–23.

Ronen, Yaniv. *Asirim Bithonim be batei kele be Israel* [Hebrew: Security-Related Prisoners in Israeli Jails]. Jerusalem: Knesset Research and Information Center, 2009.

———. *Ma'amarim Academim be nose Asirim Bithonim be batei kele be Israel* [Hebrew: Academic Studies of Security-Related Prisoners]. Jerusalem: Knesset Research and Information Center, 2013.

Rosenthal, Yemimah, and Luiz Fisher, eds. *Moshe Sharett, the Second Prime Minister; Selected Documents Related to His Life Chapters (1894–1965)*. Jerusalem: Israel State Archive, 2006.

Rumney, Philip. "The Effectiveness of Coercive Interrogation: Scholarly and Judicial Responses." *Crime, Law and Social Change* 44, no. 4 (December 2005): 465–89.

Sadeghi, Ali. "Lebanon and After: Whose Victory?" Millennium—Journal of International Studies 13, no. 1 (March 1984) : 1 –15.

Sagiv, Assaf. "Preface: The Significance of the 'Silver Plate.'" *Tchelet* [Hebrew: Azure] (Winter 2008): 3–11.

Sammon, Richard. "No Proof that Prisoners Remain in Southeast Asia, Panel Finds." *Congressional Quarterly Weekly Report* 51, no. 3 (1993): 138.

———. "POWS: Pentagon Knew Soldiers Held After War, Panel Leaders Say." *CQ Weekly Online* (June 27, 1992).

Schwartz, Judy B. "The Last Will and Testimony of Uri Ilan." *Iyunim Bi-tkumat Yisrael* [Hebrew: Studies in Israel's Revival] 15 (2005).

Sharett, Moshe. *Personal Diary*, vol. 2 (1954–55) [Hebrew]. Tel Aviv: Ma'ariv, 1978.

———. *Personal Diary*, vol. 3 (1955) [Hebrew]. Tel Aviv: Ma'ariv, 1978.

Sharon, Gil'ad. *Sharon—The Life of a Leader*. Tel Aviv: Matar, 2011.

Sofer, Niv. "Kidnapping from Inside." [Hebrew] *Ma'arckhot* 446 (December 2012): 20–28.

———. "The Next Kidnapping." [Hebrew] *Ma'arckhot* 439 (October 2011): 40–47.

The Standard, United Kingdom, Daily Newspaper, English.

Steinberg, Guido. *From Ron Arad to Gilad Shalit: Germany's Role in the Middle Eastern Prisoner Exchanges*. American Institute for Contemporary German Studies, Johns Hopkins University, December 9, 2011, http://www.aicgs.org/issue/from-ron-arad-to-gilad-shalit-germanys-role-in-the-middle-eastern-prisoner-exchanges/.

Stephen, Morris. "Quangmire." *The New Republic* 31 (May 1993): 18–19.

Sun Tzu. "Laying Plans." In *The Art of War*. Translated by Lionel Giles. Internet Classics Archive: n.d. http://classics.mit.edu/Tzu/artwar.1b.txt.

Tamir, Shmuel. *Ben ha Aretz ha Zot* [Hebrew: The Son of this Country, Autobiography]. Lod: Zmora-Bitan, 2002.

Tayler, Letta. *No Direction Home: Returns from Guantanamo to Yemen*. New York: Human Rights Watch, 2009.

The Telegraph, United Kingdom, Newspaper website.

Teveth, Shabtai. *Moshe Dayan: Biography*. Tel Aviv and Jerusalem: Schoken, 1971.

Thiele, Gregory A. "Fourth-Generation Warfare." *Marine Corps Gazette* 97, no. 6 (2013): 53–54.

Thigpen, Jerry L. *The Praetorian STARShip: The Untold Story of the Combat Talon* . Maxwell Air Force Base, Alabama: Air University Press 2001.

Thornton, Rod. *Asymmetric Warfare; Threat and Response in the 21st Century*. Cambridge: Polity Press, 2007.

Translation of National Conventions. Index of Treaties. http://www.justice.gov.il/Units/TergomOmanotBimLeumi/Pages/Odot.aspx.

Tzabag, Shmuel. "Termination of the Yom Kippur War between Israel and Syria: Positions, Decisions and Constraints at Israel's Ministerial Level." *Middle Eastern Studies* 37, no. 4 (2001): 182–205.

ha-Tzofeh, Israel, Daily Newspaper, Hebrew.

UN General Assembly and Security Council Database. http://www.un.org/en/index.html.

UN Resolutions on Israel. Regarding the Question of Palestine. https://unispal.un.org/DPA/DPR/unispal.nsf/udc.htm.

[United Kingdom] National Archives, AIR2/Air Ministry and Ministry of Defense: Registered Files.

———. AIR40/Air Ministry, Directorate of Intelligence and related bodies: Intelligence Reports and Papers.

———. FCO17/ Foreign Office, Eastern Department and successors: Registered Files (E and NE Series).

———. FCO93/ Foreign and Commonwealth Office: Near East and North Africa Department: Registered Files (NF Series).

———. FO/371/Foreign Office: Political Departments: General Correspondence from 1906–1966.

———. FO1032/Economic and Industrial Planning Staff and Control Office for Germany and Austria and Successor: Control Commission for Germany (British Element),

Military Sections and Headquarters Secretariat: Registered Files (HQ and other series).
———. WO32/ War Office and successors: Registered Files (General Series).
[USNA] United States National Archives, RG59/Bureau of Near Eastern and South Asian Affairs. Office of Israel and Arab-Israel Affairs/Records Relating to Israel and Arab-Israel Affairs, 1951–1976.
U.S. 103rd Congress, 1st session, Senate report 103–1, POW/MIAs Report of the Select Committee on POW/MIA affairs, United States Senate, January 13, 1993, http://fas.org/irp/congress/1993_rpt/pow-exec.html.
[U.S.] Department of Justice, Office of Public Affairs. Special Task Force on Interrogation and Transfer Policies Issues Its Recommendations to the President. August 24, 2009. http://www.justice.gov/opa/pr/special-task-force-interrogations-and-transfer-policies-issues-its-recommendations-president.
U.S. Department of State. "Anglo-Egyptian Agreement Regarding the Suez Canal Base, Cairo, October 19, 1954." In *The Suez Canal Problem; July 26–September 22, 1956; a Documentary Publication.* Washington: Department of State Publication 6392, 1956.
U.S. Interrogation policy and executive order 13440. Hearing before the Select Committee on Intelligence of the United States Senate, 110th congress, 1st session. September 25, 2007. http://www.intelligence.senate.gov/sites/default/files/hearings/110849.pdf.
The [U.S.] National Security Archives, George Washington University, http://nsarchive.gwu.edu/NSAEBB/index.html.
Von Clausewitz, Carl. *On War.* Translated by Michael Howard and Peter Pare. Princeton, NJ: Princeton University Press, 2003.
The Wall Street Journal, United States, Daily Newspaper, English.
The Washington Post, United States, Daily Newspaper, English.
Weitz, Yechiam. "Discussion: Kasztner's Changing Image as a Reflection of the Public Image of the Holocaust." [Hebrew] *Cathedra* 69 (September 1993): 134–51.
Wikileaks Database. https://wikileaks.org.
Yediot Aharonot, Israel, Daily Newspaper, Hebrew.
Zur, Nadir. "The Awareness Test: The Second Lebanon War and the Exposing of the Meanings' Crisis within the IDF and the [Israeli] Society." [Hebrew] *Military and Strategy* 2, no. 2 (October 2010): 3–15.

Index

About the Author

Professor **Alexander Bligh**, PhD (Columbia University, 1981); chief scientist, Ministry of Science, Technology, and Space, Israel; formerly acting dean, Faculty of Social Sciences and Humanities, and director, Middle East Research Center, Ariel University; senior lecturer, Hebrew University of Jerusalem; president of *Strategic Objects*, an international strategic consulting firm dealing with risk analysis and civilian infrastructure projects. He served with the prime minister of Israel (1987–1992) during the last couple of years of his tenure as his advisor for Arab affairs. He devised within the framework of NATO workshops a nontechnological model of encountering terrorism.

Lightning Source UK Ltd.
Milton Keynes UK
UKHW01n0305160618
324228UK00007B/391/P

9 780739 194713